HUMAN EDGE IN THE AI AGE

ALSO BY THE SAME AUTHOR

Winning in the Digital Age
Mastering the Data Paradox

ADVANCE PRAISE FOR *HUMAN EDGE IN THE AI AGE*

'*Human Edge in the AI Age* by Nitin Seth is a thought-provoking exploration of AI's transformative power and its impact on human capabilities. Seth emphasizes the need for humans to adapt, embrace change and rediscover timeless qualities to thrive in the AI-driven era. He reminds us that while AI will replace many jobs, our unique human advantages—such as creativity, emotional intelligence and the ability to connect deeply with others—will be crucial in maintaining our edge in this world. Reading this insightful book made me reflect deeply on the future of my children and grandchildren. It inspired me to think about how I can guide them in understanding and navigating the challenges and opportunities that await them'—**Lou Maiuri, chairman and group CEO, AssetMark**

'In *Human Edge in the AI Age,* Nitin Seth masterfully navigates the complex and rapidly evolving landscape of artificial intelligence, offering practical guidance for professionals and leaders. As a chief technology and information officer at a Fortune 500 company, I find Seth's insights into the intersection of technology and human potential both timely and essential. His eight-dimensional POSSIBLE framework—problem-solving, openness to change, spirituality, sports, impact, balance, leadership and entrepreneurship—provides an actionable path for individuals and organizations to thrive in an AI-driven world. It is a powerful reminder that while AI is reshaping our world, it is our timeless human qualities that differentiate us and will ultimately define our success. This balance between human strengths and AI capabilities is crucial for making informed, ethical decisions and building resilient teams. This book is thought-provoking for anyone looking to stay ahead in the AI age and harness the unique strengths that make us human'—**Greg Gates, managing director and chief technology and information officer, LPL Financial**

'*Human Edge in the AI Age* is a vital compass for navigating the future—skilfully blending technological insights with philosophical and spiritual perspectives, and providing a holistic view of how humans can remain relevant and thrive in an AI-driven world. Seth's "POSSIBLE" framework is not just insightful, it's actionable. Each mantra, from enhancing problem-solving skills to embracing entrepreneurship, is authenticated by Seth's personal experiences and reflections. A must-read for anyone looking to understand and thrive in the age of artificial intelligence'—**Sowmyanarayan Sampath, CEO, Verizon Consumer**

'Nitin has outdone himself again! This book is absolutely mind-blowing and a must-read for any executive who is serious about navigating the AI future. Nitin is one of the sharpest minds in business that I know of and I am grateful that he continues to share his knowledge and insights with the world. READ this book and change your trajectory'—**Chatri Sityodtong, founder and chairman, ONE Championship**

'Nitin Seth has written a book about one of the most important subjects facing humanity and each of us individually. AI will march ahead at a rapid pace. We humans have substantive choices to make about how to adjust and how to work with this new technology. These are both society-wide and individual choices. This book lays out a framework for thinking about and beginning to solve these hugely important issues: What is unique about humanity, what is important to us and how can we protect ourselves and our values? It is still early days, and much of the future remains open-ended, but we need to start the process of engaging with these issues now'—**David Cohen, founder, Simcah Management**

'For a man who enjoys cricket, Nitin has delivered a carefully crafted hat-trick. His third book combines his analytical insights with digital and AI experience as a practitioner but adds deeper reflections on what this means for us as humans. With trademark clarity, Nitin has created a valuable framework to understand the capabilities that define the "human quotient", as we navigate a world where AI seems unstoppable. He delves deep into synthesizing elements of spiritual balance, wisdom and entrepreneurship, alongside the familiar survival skills of problem-solving, teamwork and leadership. This differentiates the book from others and offers an excellent guide to responding positively to the power of AI'—**Leo Puri, industry leader and financial sector veteran**

'In a world transformed by AI, how do humans stay relevant and thrive? Drawing from a unique blend of ancient wisdom and modern experiences, Nitin Seth presents the POSSIBLE framework—eight timeless mantras that succinctly redefine success in the AI age. *Human Edge in the AI Age* is a terrific guide to harnessing your own unique strengths and creating new opportunities in this exciting era of change'—**Michael Ragunas, chief technology officer, Cetera Financial Group**

'As AI races ahead, most are sleepwalking into irrelevance. Nitin's book is a wake-up call—and a battle plan. If you want to stay human and stay ahead, read this now'—**Naveen Tewari, founder and CEO, InMobi and Glance**

'Having led large-scale digital transformation and public policy initiatives, I know that the true challenge in the AI age is not just about building smarter technology—it's about building wiser societies. In *Human Edge in the AI Age*, Nitin Seth draws on global leadership experience and the timeless wisdom of India to offer a compelling vision of how we can thrive amidst disruption. This book is both a practical guide and a philosophical reflection—essential reading for leaders, policymakers and anyone building a future where technology and humanity must coexist, responsibly and powerfully'—**Arvind Gupta, head, Digital India Foundation**

'With *Human Edge in the AI Age*, outstanding tech and people leader Nitin Seth takes his next leap as an author. This contemporary tour de force on how to be successful in this complex world covers AI, resilience, spirituality and much more. Strongly recommended to readers across the globe as Nitin has walked this talk successfully across continents'—**Rishikesha T. Krishnan, director and professor of strategy, IIM Bangalore**

'In his latest book, Nitin Seth provides a comprehensive take on the role of AI as a transformational change and our ability as humans to embrace this by effectively becoming more human. The concept of human quotient provides a new perspective on what it fundamentally means to be human beyond multiple technologies and societal transformations. The POSSIBLE framework is aptly named and outlines the many dimensions that help create the Human Edge, which applies beyond just business. True to form, Nitin also provides a crisp view of some critical business tools that are valuable for novices as well as experts and lays out leadership traits that will become more important in the next decade. Illustrated with great stories, the book is a timely and thoughtful distillation of what is changing around us and, more importantly, what will always be true'—**Dhrupad Trivedi, CEO, A10 Networks**

'The world has never seen this level of change and uncertainty come together—uncertainty driven by geopolitics, and change driven by AI, which is the most transformative technology of our times. The more we develop AI, the more it challenges us to reflect on what it truly means to be human in an age where we have the ability to manufacture intelligence, empathy and even agency. Nitin has come up with an incredible set of ideas on the unique human strengths that will enable us to stay ahead. This is the book for every technologist, and I can't recommend this enough'—**Puneet Chandok, president, Microsoft India and South Asia**

'The rapid progress and adoption of AI has been unprecedented and has naturally created uncertainty about the new balance between the role of AI technologies and human intellect. Nitin's new book very effectively explores potential opportunities where humans will not only continue to lead but can put human intellect at the centre of AI evolution. The book is honest and not in denial mode; instead, it helps identify distinct areas of strength where human impact will continue

to define the future. It's an easy read and a great piece of work'—
Som Mittal, former president and chairman, Nasscom

'It is heartening to hear about *Human Edge in the AI Age*. As artificial intelligence increasingly influences our lives, it invites us to rediscover and nurture qualities of humanity—compassion, awareness of oneself—that cannot be replaced by AI. Seth's thoughtful exploration through the POSSIBLE framework resonates deeply. Only if people are free from stress will they use AI for good purposes. May this book inspire many to discover their authentic Self and live with greater purpose and fulfilment in this evolving technological landscape. My blessings and best wishes for the success of *Human Edge in the AI Age*.' —**Gurudev Sri Sri Ravi Shankar, founder, The Art of Living Foundation**

HUMAN EDGE IN THE AI AGE

Eight Timeless Mantras for Success

NITIN SETH

BLOOMSBURY ACADEMIC
NEW YORK • LONDON • OXFORD • NEW DELHI • SYDNEY

BLOOMSBURY ACADEMIC
Bloomsbury Publishing Inc, 1359 Broadway, New York, NY 10018, USA
Bloomsbury Publishing Plc, 50 Bedford Square, London, WC1B 3DP, UK
Bloomsbury Publishing Ireland, 29 Earlsfort Terrace, Dublin 2, D02 AY28, Ireland

BLOOMSBURY, BLOOMSBURY ACADEMIC and the Diana logo are trademarks of
Bloomsbury Publishing Plc

First published in the United States of America 2025

Copyright © Nitin Seth, 2025

Cover Design: Diana Nuhn
Cover image of hand holding ball © Istock.com/ipopba; AI graphic
© iStock.com/berya113

All rights reserved. No part of this publication may be: i) reproduced or transmitted in any form, electronic or mechanical, including photocopying, recording or by means of any information storage or retrieval system without prior permission in writing from the publishers; or ii) used or reproduced in any way for the training, development or operation of artificial intelligence (AI) technologies, including generative AI technologies. The rights holders expressly reserve this publication from the text and data mining exception as per Article 4(3) of the Digital Single Market Directive (EU) 2019/790.

Bloomsbury Publishing Inc does not have any control over, or responsibility for, any third-party websites referred to or in this book. All internet addresses given in this book were correct at the time of going to press. The author and publisher regret any inconvenience caused if addresses have changed or sites have ceased to exist, but can accept no responsibility for any such changes.

Library of Congress Cataloging-in-Publication Data Available

ISBN: HB: 979-8-2163-9174-6
ePDF: 979-8-2163-9176-0
eBook: 979-8-2163-9175-3

Typeset by Deanta
Printed and bound in the United States of America

For product safety related questions contact productsafety@bloomsbury.com.

To find out more about our authors and books visit www.bloomsbury.com
and sign up for our newsletters.

*To Karmishtha, Devishi and Pragun,
this book is my gift to you.
It carries my deepest hopes and dearest lessons—
drawn from a lifetime of striving, stumbling, learning and growing.
As the world transforms, may you stay anchored in timeless truths
and carry forward the human edge with grace and grit.*

Contents

Preface   xvii
Introduction: The AI Age and the Need to Rediscover the Human Edge   xxiii

SECTION I
AI IS REDEFINING EVERY ASPECT OF LIFE AND BUSINESS

1. The Irresistible March of the AI Age   3
2. AI Is Surpassing Human Capabilities   24
3. The Human Quotient Is Facing Its Toughest Trial   41
4. AI Will Fundamentally Reshape Every Industry   57
5. All Jobs Will Change in the AI Age   87
6. The Human Advantage   105

SECTION II
EIGHT TIMELESS MANTRAS FOR SUCCESS IN THE AI AGE

Possible: A Framework for Sharpening the Human Edge   121

Mantra 1: Enhance Problem-Solving Skills

Introduction to Mantra 1	131
7. Seven Steps to Structured Problem-Solving	134
8. Identifying the Core Problem: Lessons from 'The Goal'	157
9. Things I Wish I Learnt in Business School: Ten Key Problem-Solving Frameworks	167
10. Role of Wisdom in the AI Age	180

Mantra 2: Openness to Change

Introduction to Mantra 2	197
11. Cultivating Openness to Change	201
12. The Need for Redefining Learning Approaches	209
13. The Art of Learning to Learn	218

Mantra 3: Connect with the Self Through Spirituality

Introduction to Mantra 3	235
14. Spiritual Balance: A Necessity in Today's AI Age	239
15. Eleven Laws of Spirituality	248
16. My Mindfulness Journey	255
17. Meditation (Vipassana): The Key to Connecting with the Self	262

Mantra 4: Learn Teamwork and Resilience from Sports

Introduction to Mantra 4	271
18. India's T20 World Cup Triumph in 2024: Seizing the Moments of Truth	275
19. India's Magnificent Test Series Win in Australia in 2021: Bouncing Back from the Brink	279
20. The 2018 Football World Cup: The Rise of the Underdogs	285
21. The 2014 Football World Cup: A Masterclass in Teamwork over Individual Brilliance	289

Mantra 5: Make an Impact

Introduction to Mantra 5	297
22. Finding Your 'Sweet Spot': The Powerful Purpose of Your Life	302
23. Take Personal Responsibility and Change the World	311
24. Sustainable Development: Rethinking Consumption	320

Mantra 6: Find the Right Balance

Introduction to Mantra 6	329
25. Beyond Trade-offs: How to Harness Opposites in the AI Age	333
26. Momentary Versus Momentous	340
27. Learn Two-Speed Execution	345

Mantra 7: Unleash the Leader Within You

Introduction to Mantra 7	355
28. Effective Leadership Traits in the Digital Age	359

29. How Great Leaders Inspire Others — 362
30. Lessons in Change Management — 367
31. How to Create Great Leaders — 374

Mantra 8: Be an Entrepreneur

Introduction to Mantra 8 — 383
32. Your Time Is Now!: Ten Mantras for Young Entrepreneurs — 387
33. Inventing the Future: Lessons from the Incredible Life Story of Steve Jobs — 397
34. Elon Musk's Moonshot Mentality in the AI Era — 406
35. Lessons in Longevity and Greatness from the Giant Sequoias — 413

Conclusion: Timeless Wisdom for Daily Living in the AI Age — 419
Acknowledgements — 425
Notes — 429

Preface

The rapid advancements in artificial intelligence (AI) are reshaping industries, redefining job roles and transforming the way we live and work. While much of the conversation on AI revolves around its capabilities, the more critical question is: *How can we, as humans, stay relevant and thrive in the AI age?* This book, *Human Edge in the AI Age*, is my attempt to explore this fundamental question.

After my first two books, *Winning in the Digital Age* and *Mastering the Data Paradox*, it was a natural progression for my next book to focus on AI—completing what I call the trifecta of transformation: **digital, data and AI**. These are the three mutually reinforcing megatrends reshaping every aspect of our lives, work and society. But while this book centres on AI, it takes a different path from my earlier work. My previous books approached digital and data through a business and technology lens. With AI, the questions run deeper. AI isn't just transforming industries, it's challenging what it means to be human. Therefore, this book is an attempt to grapple with the fundamental **human questions** the AI age compels us to ask:

- What does AI mean for us as human beings—what are the real risks and the real opportunities?

- As machines grow more capable, what will remain our uniquely human edge?
- And how can we consciously prepare—individually and collectively—to strengthen or reinvent that edge?

I chose this theme because I believe there is still too little informed, balanced dialogue on the deeper human questions AI raises. Much of today's discourse swings between extremes—naive optimism and dystopian fear, technological hype and philosophical paralysis. My hope is to move beyond these binaries and offer a grounded, practical and human-centred perspective.

As I worked on AI implementation with some of the largest companies in North America and researched AI advancements, I gained a deeper appreciation of this megatrend. I realized that AI poses some fundamental challenges that have not been fully explored. Given its expanding capabilities and continuous learning nature, it will outperform humans on many fronts—not just in transactional, repetitive tasks but also in highly complex tasks requiring cognitive and emotional intelligence. This will, of course, have a significant impact on jobs. It is likely that over the next fifteen years, 35–50 per cent of existing jobs might be lost,[1] with likely disproportionate impact for knowledge workers. This was not the case for previous waves of technology-led automation. This level of possible job impact is absolutely mind-boggling, with severe implications, especially for regions with a young population pyramid, such as India, Africa and Latin America. I am amazed that deeper conversations are not happening on such a critical issue, especially when the livelihood of so many people might be at stake.

At the same time, it is not all doom and gloom. AI will also create opportunities to solve new or existing problems (hopefully cancer and maybe even climate change) that could not be solved before. This will create tremendous opportunities for entrepreneurs as all industries and sectors get disrupted in some way. In fact, I believe the AI age signals the *end of the era of jobs* and heralds the *beginning of the era of entrepreneurs*. This is both daunting and exciting. The risk of job displacement is real, and it is easy to oscillate between fear and avoidance. However, we must face the profound challenges and opportunities that AI presents head-on. With this book, I seek to shift the conversation from anxiety to empowerment. We must ask: *What are the uniquely human strengths that will enable us to stay ahead?*

Without doubt, all the above likely seismic shifts call for an urgent and intense exploration of what edge humans would have in the AI age, because our world is going to change dramatically, and our well-established norms and practices will need to change accordingly. This is the central question I have tried to explore in this book. And I have done so not just by delving into research but also by drawing from history and, most importantly, my own experiences and beliefs. My journey has been influenced by both modern technology and ancient Indian wisdom. Having worked across technology, consulting and entrepreneurship—at McKinsey, Fidelity, Flipkart and now as the CEO of Incedo—I have witnessed first-hand how AI and digital transformation are changing the nature of leadership, problem-solving and business execution. At the same time, I have drawn immense inspiration from the timeless wisdom of India's ancient knowledge systems as exemplified by the Bhagavad Gita, Yoga sutras and Vedic literature, which emphasize self-awareness, continuous learning and resilience.

Through these experiences, I have come to realize that while AI will continue to evolve at a breakneck pace, there are many timeless elements of the human edge—our creativity, problem-solving ability, resilience and leadership—that will remain irreplaceable. If anything, the dynamic and uncertain world that awaits us requires us to rediscover the **pioneering and adventurous spirit of the early man**. Centuries of industrialization have dulled our natural instincts, making us risk-averse and narrow. We must scrape off the rust blocking our instincts and embrace higher levels of creativity and risk-taking to shape a new world—a world where we define our coexistence with AI on favourable terms rather than being subjugated by it.

I remain optimistic about our ability to rediscover our human edge, but it requires deliberate effort across governments, communities, enterprises and—most importantly—each of us as individuals. To provide a practical guide for navigating this transformation, I propose a simple yet powerful framework in this book: **POSSIBLE**, an eight-dimensional model that highlights the core human strengths that will define success in the AI era. Each dimension—**Problem-Solving, Openness to Change, Spirituality, Sports, Impact, Balance, Leadership and Entrepreneurship**—represents a fundamental skill or mindset that enables individuals to thrive in an increasingly AI-driven world. The POSSIBLE framework is not just a clever anagram, it is a signal of hope and positivity. I remain confident in our ability to find our way in the AI age as a species. Equally, I believe that hope and optimism are necessary for all of us as we venture into this adventurous AI age.

Writing this book has been a deeply personal and reflective endeavour. It has given me an opportunity to distil years of insights, learnings and experiences into a structured framework that I hope will serve as a guide for professionals, leaders, entrepreneurs and students navigating this transformative era. Throughout the book, I have drawn from real-world case studies, personal experiences and historical perspectives to make these ideas tangible and actionable.

This book is for anyone who is curious about the future, eager to grow and determined to make an impact in a world shaped by AI. Whether you are a corporate leader, a young professional, an entrepreneur or a student, my hope is that *Human Edge in the AI Age* will provide you with valuable insights and practical tools to harness your unique strengths and succeed in this new world.

As you embark on this journey through the pages of this book, I encourage you to reflect on your own path, embrace continuous learning and take bold steps towards shaping your future. The AI age should not be about machines replacing humans—it should be a great trigger for humans to evolve to stay ahead. The future is not something to be feared; it is something to be created. The future is POSSIBLE. Let's make it happen.

April 2025

Introduction

The AI Age and the Need to Rediscover the Human Edge

Within a few decades, machine intelligence will surpass human intelligence, leading to The Singularity—technological change so rapid and profound it represents a rupture in the fabric of human history.
—Ray Kurzweil, American computer scientist, author, entrepreneur, futurist and inventor

At last year's (2024) Salesforce Dreamforce event in San Francisco, Marc Benioff, the co-founder, chairman and CEO of Salesforce, declared in his keynote, 'We are moving from an AI-assisted to an autonomous world,' highlighting a transformative shift underway in technology.[1] To drive the message home, he urged attendees to experience Waymo's autonomous cars first-hand—a glimpse into the future of autonomy in action. The statement was not just a call to explore innovation but a bold reminder of the pace at which the world is evolving.

I decided to take his advice and had the thrilling opportunity to ride in Waymo's autonomous cab service for the first time. And Marc was absolutely right! The precise navigation with which the vehicle handled traffic and complex intersections left me in awe of how far AI-powered technologies have advanced. The absence of a driver felt a bit unsettling at first, but as I watched the car effortlessly navigate real-world driving scenarios, it quickly instilled an unexpected sense of trust. While so far, most of our understanding and much of our discussions around AI focused on the potential of human–AI collaboration, this ride was a profound revelation for me. It showcased the transformative power of truly autonomous machines. And with that ride I could easily envision a future, not too far away, where science fiction transcended into reality.

However, amidst all my excitement about the future, I had a sobering moment when the next day, I shared my autonomous cab experience with my regular rental cab driver. Clearly, he didn't share my enthusiasm. How could he? Because for him, proliferation of autonomous vehicles meant the loss of livelihood. He shared his genuine fear that his job could be replaced by autonomous cars within the next two years. This would force him to return to his native country, as even luxury car services would most likely transition to autonomous vehicles by then. It was a bittersweet reminder of the dual-edged nature of technological progress, especially with the acceleration of innovation in the AI age. While advancements like autonomous cabs offer incredible possibilities and efficiencies, they also raise tough questions about the future of jobs and the livelihoods of those who may be left behind in this transition.

If you look at the way it's evolving—rapidly getting better at a range of capabilities, from decision-making to automation—we have to admit that AI is rapidly mastering many skills that were once considered uniquely human. The interaction with the cab driver was another trigger for me, emphasizing that we need to reimagine our competitive edge as humans as we embrace the AI age. These are incredibly exciting times, but they also call for meaningful dialogue to ensure that, as innovations continue to shape our world, we identify and cultivate our next competitive advantage to thrive both in our professional and personal lives.

We are in the AI age

Over the past few years, the already exciting digital age has evolved into the AI age especially with the advent of generative AI (Gen AI). The explosive breakthroughs in AI can be attributed to advancements in three distinct areas—Big Data, algorithms and computing capabilities. Significant innovations in these areas have converged like never before, with the promise of revolutionizing industries, economies and societies on an unprecedented scale.

Although over the years, humankind has gone through multiple waves of technological innovations, AI is not just another major technology trend. It is truly disruptive because, for the first time, machines are not merely augmenting but actively replicating many human capabilities. In fact, AI is already proving superior to humans in several domains once thought to be our exclusive strengths, challenging the long-held belief that *'the creation cannot be greater than the creator'*.

The AI age is truly transformational

AI is no longer just imitating human abilities, it is evolving at a pace where it is beginning to *outperform* us in areas that were long considered the pinnacle of human uniqueness. From creativity and emotional intelligence to complex decision-making, AI is crossing thresholds we once believed to be unbreachable. There are at least five core areas where AI is delivering breakthrough performance— each of which has historically defined what it means to be human. One of our unique capabilities is our ability to learn. We can absorb knowledge, apply it, learn from it and continuously grow through life. AI, with its **deep-learning** capabilities, is able to do so too, but in a fraction of the time we take, and it is better at learning continuously and improving through exposure to new situations and outcomes.

Another critical area is **problem identification**, where defining the problem and identifying its root cause is typically the most important part of any problem-solving process. AI, especially with the emergence of Gen AI, now excels in this area too, owing to its ability to rapidly analyse and sift through vast and complex data sets with unprecedented speed and precision and identify patterns.

Our ability to hold conversations and tell stories has always set us apart from any machine, or any other species on this planet. Lo and behold, now AI is rapidly outpacing humans in **conversational storytelling**, owing to its natural language processing capabilities enabling human–machine interactions in a more fluid and personalized way. This breakthrough has truly democratized access to AI systems and tools for a broader audience, regardless of technical expertise.

AI has also ventured into the realm of creativity, challenging our unique human ability to innovate and bring new ideas to life through imagination and ingenuity. With **new content-creation** capability, including synthetic-data creation, AI is constantly pushing the boundaries of what technology can achieve.

And last but certainly not least, as the AI age unfolds, AI has begun to mimic **emotional awareness**—once considered an invincible human capability, given that machines lack emotions. What we underestimated, however, is its remarkable ability to convincingly 'mimic' emotional intelligence, despite having no true feelings of its own. In fact, some studies are now claiming that AI is performing even better than humans on empathy. For example, studies have shown that, in patient care, AI has often demonstrated better bedside manners than doctors and nurses.

The 'human quotient' is at a crossroads

From the human perspective, our once-assumed edge is now fundamentally challenged. The capabilities we believed to be our unique advantages are no longer guaranteed to provide a sure-fire upper hand. These capabilities draw from the core dimensions of human potential that have historically enabled us to live meaningfully, work effectively, and succeed—together forming what I call the *Human Quotient*. This quotient is shaped by the interplay of four broad dimensions: physical quotient (PQ), intelligence quotient (IQ), emotional quotient (EQ) and spiritual quotient (SQ). And as we trace the arc of human evolution, it becomes clear that machines and AI have been steadily encroaching on each of these dimensions—reshaping what it means to have a human edge.

For much of human history, PQ—strength, stamina and might—marked our dominance, a trend that lasted until the Industrial Revolution. As machines took over physical tasks, the focus shifted, and IQ started emerging as the key human advantage. The advent of the information age in the twentieth century solidified IQ as a critical differentiator, driving success in education, careers and the knowledge economy, which highly valued problem-solving and innovation.

However, over the past ten to fifteen years, with the digital age giving rise to machine learning (ML) and AI, IQ as a human edge has also steadily diminished. AI now surpasses humans in tasks like pattern recognition, natural language processing and even creative problem-solving. The recent emergence of Gen AI has further accelerated this shift, with AI performing at par and even surpassing human levels in an increasing range of IQ-driven fields.

More recently, in the AI age even EQ—our ability to understand and manage emotions—is under threat. AI systems have begun to mimic empathy and emotional understanding, offering emotional support and connecting with users in ways that challenge human advantages in EQ-driven roles too.

The spiritual blueprint behind AI's power

While AI has been evolving for decades within the research labs of tech giants and universities, it reached a pivotal tipping point with the advent of Gen AI. What made this breakthrough so powerful wasn't just technical sophistication—it was AI's ability to tap into and process vast amounts of internet data, effectively unlocking the 'collective wisdom of the crowd'.

This shift lifted one of AI's long-standing constraints: access to quality data. Suddenly, AI could generate meaningful responses—even with limited input—achieving 40–60 per cent accuracy in many real-world contexts.

But that's only part of the story.

The bigger leap lies in what AI can now do with that data. No longer confined to automation or narrow, task-specific use cases, AI is stepping into the domain of creativity—writing articles, composing music, designing products and generating code. It's transitioned from a tool to a transformational force.

And yet, there's a deeper reason behind this transformation—one that extends beyond engineering. The architecture of AI, in many ways, mirrors the profound construct of the *self* as described in traditional Indian wisdom.

According to Patanjali's *Yoga Sutras*, the self is composed of three interconnected layers. *Buddhi* represents innate cosmic intelligence—the universal foundation of reason. *Aham* is the layer of human consciousness that gives rise to self-awareness. And *manas* defines our individual mind and personality—our unique interpretation of the world.

In a fascinating parallel, AI also functions across three interlinked levels. At the **macro level**, AI draws from massive global datasets to identify patterns and generate broad insights. At the **enterprise level**, it uses focused, contextual data to learn continuously and solve complex problems. And at the **individual level**, AI personalizes outputs—adapting to preferences, behaviour and context in real time.

Just as harmony between buddhi, aham and manas unleashes human potential, the integration of macro-, enterprise- and individual-level data fuels AI's unprecedented power. This alignment across layers—once a hallmark of human self-actualization—is now being executed flawlessly by machines.

When machines integrate better than humans

Over time, as we've become more digitally connected, we've paradoxically grown more fragmented within ourselves. Living in a hyper-stimulated, always-on world, we're bombarded by distractions that detach us from deeper awareness—our connection with nature, with others and even with ourselves is steadily eroding. Most of us now operate primarily at the manas level—individualistic, reactive and ego-centred—rarely accessing the higher dimensions of consciousness that once anchored our growth.

AI, on the other hand, is designed for integration. From the moment it is deployed, it flows naturally across its layers—macro, enterprise and individual—without friction. It operates at full bandwidth, continuously learning and refining its performance by unifying knowledge, context and application.

That's the irony: machines, which lack consciousness, are increasingly better at integrating layers of intelligence than many of us are. And that's precisely why AI is challenging what was once thought to be innately human. In some dimensions, it is becoming more human than humans.

AI is causing fundamental shifts across industries

In my previous books, *Winning in the Digital Age* and *Mastering the Data Paradox*, I discussed how the rise of digital and data proliferation has disrupted businesses, forcing them to rethink business models and structures to stay competitive. Now, the AI age is set to further revolutionize everything. We are already witnessing transformative shifts across industries that are unlocking unprecedented opportunities across multiple domains. These transformations can be categorized into four major areas: personalization, automation, innovation and business models, each driving a new paradigm in how businesses operate and deliver value.

One of the most profound shifts brought about by AI lies in personalization. Gone are the days of broad customer segmentation. We are entering the realm of the 'segment of one', where every individual becomes their own unique segment. AI would deliver **hyper-personalized** experiences, products and services specifically tailored to the unique needs, preferences and behaviours of each individual in real time. This revolution is already transforming consumer-centric industries, but its most significant promise lies in areas like healthcare and education. Imagine treatments and learning programmes designed exclusively for an individual, adapting dynamically as needs evolve—unlocking possibilities that were once unimaginable.

Beyond personalization, AI is revolutionizing **automation** by moving from assistance to autonomy. Autonomous vehicles, manufacturing robots and AI-powered logistics are not just enhancing productivity but are steadily reducing the need for human intervention in decision-making and task execution. This shift signals a profound change in how industries operate, with far-reaching implications for tech services to finance and healthcare, to even agriculture. Furthermore, the era of AI-driven **innovation** is just the beginning, and its potential to redefine creativity, collaboration and problem-solving is limitless, positioning AI not just as a tool, but as a catalyst for the future.

Finally, AI is driving fundamental changes in **business models**, moving beyond incremental efficiency gains to enabling entirely new forms of value creation. Traditional linear models are being replaced by intelligent ecosystems that are more efficient, transparent and massively scalable. AI is not just supporting operations—it is becoming the core engine of decision-making and continuous optimization. We are already seeing the rise of *AI-native platforms* where intelligence is embedded at the core, not bolted on as an afterthought. These platforms are redefining value chains, collapsing layers of intermediation and enabling businesses to operate with near-zero marginal cost at scale. As we move toward fully autonomous marketplaces—where AI agents initiate, negotiate and complete transactions on behalf of users—the very nature of how we buy, sell and interact is being reimagined. Business models of the future will not be powered by AI—they will *be* AI. AI will transform every industry, and this will create unprecedented opportunities for both large enterprises and entrepreneurs to innovate, solve interesting problems and create extraordinary value. The latter are likely to benefit disproportionately, and I see the AI age becoming the '**age of entrepreneurs**'. However, these drastic shifts will have a significant impact on how work is conducted and the skills required to perform it. What does this mean for us? The implications are profound.

Every job will change and many will be lost

The AI age is unlike any previous wave of technological change. In the past, as machines took over physical tasks (PQ), humans advanced up the value chain—from physical to intellectual (IQ) to emotional (EQ) capabilities.

This time, AI is disrupting that very top of the chain. Roles involving complex thinking, decision-making and even empathy—once thought immune—are now at risk. What's especially concerning is the scale: some estimates suggest that by 2040, up to 80 per cent of knowledge workers could be displaced. For the first time, it's not just low-skill or routine jobs, but high-skill, high-wage roles—investment bankers, consultants, surgeons—that are most vulnerable. That's what sets this revolution apart.

I foresee job disruption unfolding in three waves.

In the short term (2025–30), only 2–5 per cent of total jobs will be lost while impact will be higher on specific job categories like customer service and software development. However, this loss will be partially offset by new AI-related roles such as AI trainers, integration specialists, ML engineers that will be required to build and maintain intelligent systems.

In the medium term (2030–2035), as AI becomes cheaper and more powerful, its impact will intensify. Up to 45–60 per cent of all roles may be significantly transformed and an estimated 15–35 per cent of jobs could be eliminated altogether—including many processing and analytics intensive jobs and even EQ-centric roles.

In the long run (2035–2040), virtually every job will be touched by AI. Humanoid robots and autonomous agents may become integral to the workforce. As AI agents attain greater autonomy, even many of the 'human + AI' hybrid roles created in the earlier phases will become redundant. By this stage, it's estimated that **35–50 per cent of all jobs could be lost to AI**, making it the most sweeping labour disruption in modern history.

We are still in the early years of this transformation, but the implications are profound. The impact of AI on jobs is no longer a speculative debate—it is a defining challenge of our time. The critical question now is: where will the human edge lie in the AI age, and what must we do to cultivate it?

Where does the 'human edge' lie?

As we look ahead, one thing is clear: the AI age is not for the faint-hearted. Machines are already outperforming us in many areas—and they are only getting better. The coming years will be both profoundly transformational and disruptive. Many existing jobs will vanish. And yet, we are also on the brink of perhaps the greatest era of value creation in human history. The AI age will be defined by duality—massive displacement on the one hand and unprecedented entrepreneurial opportunity on the other.

Standing still is not an option. In this new world, we cannot wait for opportunities to be handed to us—we must create them. That demands a return to the spirit of the early man: adventurous, curious, self-reliant and unafraid to explore the unknown.

Ironically, while human civilization has advanced, we've become narrower in our skills, more dependent on systems and increasingly risk-averse. We've traded survival instincts for comfort and predictability. But AI will shake that comfortable flow of life—especially in the realm of work. To adapt, we must reconnect with the raw, exploratory energy that once defined our species.

At the same time, the AI age represents more than disruption—it may be the next catalyst for human evolution. Whether through breakthroughs in genetic engineering, accelerated space exploration or something we can't yet imagine; the shift is already underway. But beyond physical or technological evolution, what we truly need is a growth in consciousness—in compassion, empathy and a broader sense of purpose. These are the deeply human traits that no machine can replicate.

So where does the edge lie? It lies in this rediscovery—of instinct, imagination, resilience. It lies in reconnecting with the timeless principles that have powered human success across generations. Whether we think of this as rekindling the survival skills of the 'early man' or unlocking the potential of the 'super man', the message is the same: to thrive in the AI age, we must double down on what makes us human.

The POSSIBLE path: Eight timeless mantras to succeed in the AI age

As we navigate the uncertainty and promise of the AI age, one truth becomes increasingly clear: our future success will not be defined by how much we resist technology but by how deeply we rediscover and elevate what makes us human. This rediscovery is not just philosophical, it must be practical, actionable and anchored in principles that can guide us through rapid change.

Reflecting on my own journey, I feel immensely fortunate. I am a product of both worlds—the extraordinary business and technological progress of the past thirty years and the enduring spiritual wisdom of Indian traditions. This blend of experiences has shaped how I view the disruptions and opportunities that lie ahead. It has helped me recognize that while tools and technologies may change, certain human truths do not.

Based on this perspective, I want to share with you **eight timeless mantras** that I believe will be essential for building and sustaining our *Human Edge*—both professionally and personally—in the AI age. These are not abstract ideals; they are deeply practical, field-tested principles that have enabled individuals to thrive across generations.

When everything around us is shifting, it becomes even more critical to anchor ourselves in what endures. These mantras have stood the test of time. They draw from the *Human Quotient*—those dimensions of human capacity that cannot be easily coded, automated or replaced. And that is precisely why they will remain relevant, no matter how advanced AI becomes.

The Eight Timeless Mantras form a fitting anagram, **POSSIBLE**, which perfectly captures the idea that there is a path to unlocking and strengthening our unique human edge in the AI age. These are:

Mantra 1: Enhance PROBLEM-SOLVING skills

Problem-solving and, in particular, problem-identification is a critical skill for thriving in the AI age. Structured problem-solving will remain a critical human skill even while a lot of problem-solving is taken over by machines. This method starts with identifying the root causes of the problem and breaking down complex issues into smaller, manageable parts. The most astute leaders and problem-solvers I've encountered consistently pinpoint the core issue, enabling them to develop solutions that deliver maximum impact.

There are numerous frameworks that can aid the structured problem-solving process, but simply understanding them is not enough—the key lies in practising and mastering them. Moreover, while we focus on structured problem-solving, in the AI age, wisdom and intuition are likely to play an equally important and perhaps an even greater role. These qualities enable us to pause, clarify what truly matters and apply sound judgment to complex situations. This systematic approach—structured problem-solving combined with wisdom—helps us cut through noise, focus our energy and move from confusion to clarity.

Mantra 2: OPENNESS to change

As I've often said, the AI age is an era of disruption, where significant changes are inevitable. The way we work and live and the skills required are set to undergo a dramatic transformation. In such times, embracing openness to change is not just important, it is essential. Those who resist change risk being left behind in a world that is evolving faster than ever. Moreover, as AI continues to excel in technical capabilities, the value of purely technical skills will diminish. Instead, the focus will shift to one's ability to adapt, grow and acquire new knowledge.

This is why the ability to 'learn to learn' becomes a critical factor of success. It's no longer about mastering a single skill or discipline but about cultivating the mindset to continuously explore, question and acquire diverse skills. In essence, staying curious, adaptable and open to lifelong learning will be the key to unlocking future opportunities.

Mantra 3: Connect with the self through SPIRITUALITY

In the age defined by hyperconnectivity and material excess, spirituality is no longer optional, it is essential. It provides a much-needed anchor to maintain inner peace, clarity and emotional balance. Far from being abstract or mystical, spirituality offers practical tools to develop deeper self-awareness and intuition—qualities that are increasingly vital to unlock one's full potential in the AI age.

Practices like meditation, yoga, pranayama (breath control) and prayer create space for individuals to step back from the noise, reduce stress and reconnect with their core values and purpose. Through my own journey, I've come to see how integrating these practices into daily life strengthens not only ethical reasoning and emotional resilience but also enhances clarity of thought and decision-making.

Spirituality, at its core, is about anchoring—a journey within to find clarity and balance. In a fast-paced, often overwhelming world shaped by algorithms and constant change, it serves as a quiet but powerful counterforce. It helps us act with intention, stay grounded amidst uncertainty and live a life that is not just successful but truly meaningful.

Mantra 4: Learn teamwork and resilience through SPORTS

I've always believed that sports offer invaluable lessons in teamwork, leadership, and resilience—traits that have always mattered but are now indispensable in the AI age. In a world changing at breakneck speed, no individual can succeed alone. The future will demand greater collaboration, adaptable strategies and the ability to persevere through uncertainty—all of which are best learned on the playing field.

Sports mirror the challenges of business and life: working toward shared goals, playing to each team member's strengths and staying composed under pressure. Just as in professional settings, setbacks in sports are inevitable. But more importantly, they teach us how to bounce back—how to recover from failure, recalibrate and try again. That mindset is crucial in a world where volatility is the new normal.

Whether inspired by the grit of underdogs or the discipline of great teams, participating in sports—at any level—is one of the most effective ways to build resilience, develop character and nurture the collaborative spirit needed to thrive in the AI age.

Mantra 5: Make an IMPACT

The spirit of going beyond ourselves will be what truly sets us apart from machines and becomes our strength to rise above the disruptions that lie ahead in the AI age. By ensuring purpose-driven actions, we can create a foundation for positive change. It is essential to not just empower ourselves but also one another to unlock their full potential, ensuring that humanity not only adapts to change but thrives in the face of it.

However, as they say, before you go out to change the world, you must 'put your own house in order first'. So finding your sweet spot, the intersection of your passion, talent and what the world needs, is the starting point. Furthermore, taking personal responsibility is key to driving change, whether in your community, workplace or the world at large. This mantra encourages us to think beyond personal success and focus on the broader societal impact of their actions. By embracing the role of change-makers, we can help address the complex challenges of the modern world, recognizing that even the smallest positive action can have a ripple effect that can change the entire system.

Mantra 6: Find the right BALANCE

In our personal and professional lives we constantly face conflicting objectives, and this challenge is even more pronounced in the AI age. Success requires every individual to be able to navigate and master these dualities. Conquering these dualities requires us to understand their true nature so as to find the right way of dealing with them.

As we navigate through the highly dynamic, fast-paced world around us, it is important to take a moment to live the momentary, while working towards achieving the momentous. Similarly, learning two-speed execution, achieving short-term goals while simultaneously working towards achieving long-term objectives, can help individuals achieve sustained success. To succeed in the AI age, individuals need to be able to move beyond mere trade-offs and handle the pressure of competing objectives without losing focus on the bigger picture.

Mantra 7: Unleash the LEADER within you

The AI age marks the end of not just the 'era of jobs' but also the 'age of managers'! As AI takes over both administrative and analytical tasks, the need for traditional management roles diminishes. To thrive in this new era, every individual must embrace leadership—

demonstrating initiative, creativity, adaptability and the ability to inspire others.

However, leadership in the AI age is neither for the meek or the cautious. Sure, the core principles of leadership, such as helping others realize their potential, inspiring through vision and making a positive difference, remain unchanged. However, the approach to these principles must evolve to meet the demands of today's world. Leaders must balance the head and heart, build trust, show humility and demonstrate integrity. Leadership is about giving more than getting and about creating a compelling vision that can inspire others to act beyond their limits. The ability to adapt constantly, create trust and be role models for change are crucial qualities that help leaders navigate the challenges of the AI age.

Mantra 8: Be an ENTREPRENEUR

The AI age is, above all, the 'age of entrepreneurs'. It marks a paradigm shift where the focus is no longer on seeking jobs but on solving problems and creating something new. This would hold true for those who are building a startup and those working within organizations. With AI automating a wide range of tasks and providing powerful tools, individuals now have unprecedented opportunities to innovate and build something new.

Entrepreneurship in today's AI age requires a mindset that embraces calculated risk taking, continuous learning and an unrelenting focus on solving problems. Being an entrepreneur means challenging the status quo, identifying new opportunities and making disruptive breakthroughs. Entrepreneurship also demands resilience in the face of failure and the ability to pivot when necessary. Lessons from the life stories of iconic entrepreneurs like Steve Jobs and Elon Musk highlight the importance of challenging norms, being persistent and staying adaptable in the face of adversity. To put it simply, entrepreneurship is not just about starting a business, but a way of thinking that helps create lasting value in the AI age.

Clearly, this is the age of disruption, but it is also the age of extraordinary possibility for those who are ready to dig deep and rediscover what makes us truly human. The future will not be defined by technology alone but by how we choose to evolve alongside it—with clarity, courage and conviction.

As you embark on this journey through the eight timeless mantras, I hope this book serves as both a guide and a companion, helping you navigate the profound shifts of the AI age with purpose and confidence. Each mantra has been carefully chosen to offer not just practical insights but enduring wisdom—rooted in history, tested by experience and designed to help you thrive in a rapidly changing world.

I encourage you to reflect deeply, act deliberately and embrace the journey of growth ahead. Because the edge we seek isn't just about staying ahead of machines—it's about becoming better, more conscious versions of ourselves.

Here's to unlocking the *Human Edge* in the AI age.

Enjoy the journey—and let's make it POSSIBLE.

SECTION I
AI IS REDEFINING EVERY ASPECT OF LIFE AND BUSINESS

1

The Irresistible March of the AI Age

Nothing else in the world... not all the armies... is so powerful as an idea whose time has come.
—Victor Hugo, French author, poet and politician

AI's time has come. It is all around us. It is unavoidable. AI might have sounded like pure science fiction, synonymous with futuristic robots or sci-fi movies a decade ago. It felt distant, something reserved for advanced research labs or tech giants. But here we are, on the cusp of a new era, where AI is woven seamlessly into the fabric of our daily lives. From the way we communicate, work and shop to the devices in our homes, cars and even our pockets—AI is everywhere, empowering us like never before.

Today, AI isn't just a concept of the future; it is an undeniable force shaping our world. Whether we are asking virtual assistants for weather updates, relying on smart devices to adjust the lighting in our homes, navigating traffic with real-time insights or even having AI draft a business email—AI is present, indispensable and, quite frankly, extraordinary!

While AI has been brewing in the labs of tech giants and researchers, the advent of Gen AI has been an enormous leap forward in the history of AI. Unlike earlier forms of AI, which primarily relied on structured datasets and rule-based programming, Gen AI comes with a transformative ability to harness the data of the world and generate content, learn, adapt, create and evolve in real-time. It has shifted the narrative, transforming AI from a reactive tool into a proactive asset, ushering in a wave of innovation that feels limitless.

AI's meteoric rise is no accident. While it has exploded on the scene quite recently, witnessing near-blinding adoption rates across all industries, it wasn't possible without multiple waves of technology developments and business model innovations that have happened in the past.

Multiple waves of innovation leading to the AI age

In my previous book, *Winning in the Digital Age*, I defined the digital age as a wide-ranging set of technology trends that have evolved over time. Each wave of technological evolution—whether it was the rise of the internet, the surge of mobile technology or the advancement of machine learning—has layered another block onto the foundation of AI as we know it. Business model innovations, too, have played a crucial role, as companies worldwide have eagerly embraced AI to enhance everything from operations to customer engagement. The AI we have today isn't a standalone invention, but a culmination of countless innovations and relentless progress, each breakthrough building on the last until AI became an unstoppable force.

Let's look at the multiple waves of innovations that brought us to the AI of today.

It all started with the transition from **physical to digital**.[1] Digital truly took off in the 1970s, when the world moved to digital with the explosive growth of computers and the availability of compute power. This era saw innovations like mainframe computers, by companies like IBM, and the development of the microprocessor by Intel, laying the groundwork for personal computing. These

AI has exploded in the last few years to become one of the key drivers of the Digital Age

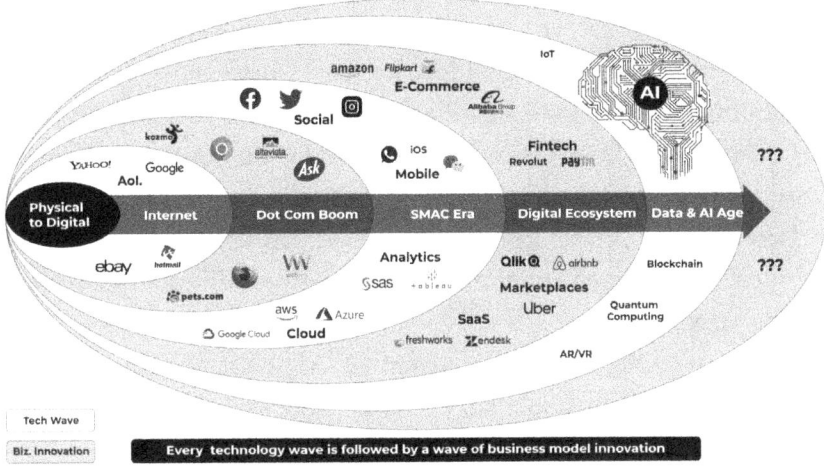

early advancements in computing and processing power created the essential foundation for AI, enabling the complex calculations and data processing that AI relies on today.

The next major wave arrived with the **internet** in the late 1990s, ushering in the dotcom boom. Companies like Amazon and eBay transformed retail by moving commerce online, shifting businesses from brick-and-mortar to e-commerce and online services, and redefining customer interactions and operations. Then in the late 2000s, **social, mobile, analytics and cloud (SMAC) technologies** emerged, reshaping interactions through social media platforms like Facebook, while the iPhone heralded the smartphone revolution, ushering an era of any-time, anywhere access to information, transforming the way people connect, work, shop and entertain themselves. Cloud services like Amazon web services (AWS) offered scalable infrastructure and big data analytics provided real-time insights. This internet and e-commerce boom are the predominant contributors to the rapid expansion of the amount of digital data, which became essential for training AI and improving machine learning methods.

Following the SMAC wave, the **digital ecosystem** era emerged, characterized by interconnected platforms like Apple's App Store or Alibaba's marketplace. These ecosystems enabled new business models and transformed industries and customer engagement. For example, companies like Netflix and Uber emerged that built new digital-first business models, which have led to the creation of new industries. These digital ecosystems also created a connected network where AI could be deployed widely, enabling companies to build AI-powered solutions that work across different platforms and services.

The early 2020s saw the advent of AI, built on a foundation of powerful new technologies like advanced computing, vast data availability and cloud infrastructure. This era also saw the rise of other new technologies like blockchain, the internet of things (IoT) and quantum computing. While blockchain enabled significant innovations like Decentralized Finance (DeFi) and transparent supply chains, IoT made connected smart homes and industrial machines a possibility. Quantum computing has now opened doors to solving problems beyond the reach of classical computing.

Today all these cutting-edge technologies are converging, opening up newer and greater possibilities for innovation. Their convergence is setting up the stage for new forms of intelligence and interconnected solutions that are not only making our lives easier but are capable of tackling long-prevailing real-world problems. However, amongst all these new technologies, AI has exploded exponentially in recent times. Let's delve deeper into what made this possible.

Gen AI, the inflection point of the AI wave

The tipping point for AI came with the advent of Gen AI, which literally exploded on the scene, capturing the public imagination. The advent of Gen AI brought the powerful ability to generate rather than merely analyse or predict. This leap has been enabled by access to vast amounts of global data, advancements in algorithms and significant enhancements in computing power. These factors have empowered systems to learn from extensive datasets and perform highly complex calculations, enabling the creation of innovative content and solutions across a broad range of applications. It has unleashed the true transformative power of AI, catapulting it into not just the most groundbreaking technological breakthroughs of the digital age but perhaps in the history of human evolution.

The advent of Gen AI didn't just open new doors, it broke down the walls that kept AI confined to the labs of researchers and big techs. With the power to create, not merely analyse, Gen AI has triggered a shift towards accessibility and versatility, making AI a tool for everyone, not just specialists. Let's see how.

Expansion and democratization of AI

Over the past decade, due to data availability and quality, AI's application was limited. Early AI implementations in healthcare, for example, focused on tasks like detecting anomalies in medical images, such as identifying tumours in X-rays. AI systems required large, high-quality datasets to perform well, which were often difficult to collect and curate. This limited AI to isolated cases, like image recognition in radiology and prevented broader integration in solutions like diagnosis or personalized treatments. The lack of deep and high-quality datasets also restricted AI in other fields.

The advent of Gen AI has transformed this paradigm in two major ways. First, it has led to the expansion of AI. As I mentioned, AI needed big, high-quality datasets to work effectively, which was hard to get to and hence really limited what it could do. Gen AI's large language models (LLMs) are trained on vast, diverse datasets sourced from the internet, literally the data of the world. This gives Gen AI the ability to provide reasonably accurate initial responses (often 40–60 per cent) to nearly any question. This breakthrough means AI's dependence on data as a starting point has been significantly reduced. Since these models are built on a massive pool of existing knowledge, they excel at recognizing patterns and relationships, enabling them to generate accurate responses across a wide range of topics. This means we no longer need to build AI models from scratch. Instead, we can leverage these pre-trained models and fine-tune them for specific applications, dramatically lowering the effort and time required for developing AI solutions.

Second, tools such as ChatGPT have democratized AI, making it accessible to people without technical expertise. These tools have simplified AI interaction through easy-to-use interfaces that respond to natural language prompts, removing the need for coding or specialized knowledge. This accessibility allows even the non-technical users to leverage AI for tasks that required a decent level of expertise in the past. Now, individuals from all backgrounds can use AI interactively for tasks like creating art, drafting essays, generating recommendations or even writing codes. For instance, a small business owner can produce custom marketing materials with simple prompts, and a remote teacher can design tailored lesson plans without extensive resources. This evolution has made AI versatile and practical for everyone, regardless of background or expertise. While we discuss the remarkable capabilities of ChatGPT, it wouldn't be fair to not acknowledge the role of OpenAI in bringing the advancements of Gen AI from the realm of scientists to the masses. So let me take you through their journey and their role in democratization of AI.

OpenAI and its role in democratization of AI

Both large language models (LLMs) and natural language processing (NLP), which Gen AI relies on, are not recent innovations. LLMs trace back to the 1950s when artificial intelligence first emerged. NLP has roots even earlier, with the 1916 publication of the first-known book on linguistics, Cours de Linguistique Générale (translated as Language as a Science).[2] The first program to use NLP was ELIZA, developed by Joseph Weizenbaum at MIT in 1966.[3]

Thereafter, many researchers and tech giants have been experimenting with these technologies and combining them with others to enhance their capabilities. In fact, Google had been a leader in AI research for years, especially with its development of the transformer architecture, the brain behind Gen AI that enables the model to predict and generate content by understanding the relationships between words, which laid the foundation for modern LLMs. However, it did not release any public-facing Gen AI product.

This is where OpenAI's approach, which prioritized accessibility and ease of use, allowed it to capture the spotlight and drive the narrative around Gen AI. In response, Google accelerated its own Gen AI projects and launched Bard in early 2023,[4] but by that point, OpenAI had already established a strong foothold with ChatGPT and later models like GPT-4, solidifying its leading position in the Gen AI space.

OpenAI was founded in December 2015 as an artificial intelligence research organization with the goal of advancing AI in a way that benefits humanity.[5] Initially structured as a non-profit with a commitment to transparency and collaboration, OpenAI aimed to openly share its research and findings. This was a unique approach compared to other AI research labs, many of which were tied to private companies and operated with proprietary goals.

OpenAI Gym and Universe platforms released in 2016, facilitated reinforcement learning and AI training, marking the start of more sophisticated algorithm development.[6] This was a major step in making AI research more accessible. By providing easy-to-use tools for reinforcement learning, OpenAI helped speed up progress in the AI field. Researchers around the world could now experiment with complex algorithms more easily, leading to the faster development of smarter and more flexible AI systems.

Then the 2019 GPT-2 language model capable of generating coherent, contextually relevant text, opened the door for more intuitive human–AI interactions.[7] And then came the groundbreaking ChatGPT, making AI accessible to the general public. For the first time, anyone could interact with AI in a conversational format, making it easier for non-experts to leverage AI for practical tasks. GPT-4 took it to the next level, a multi-modal model, capable of processing and understanding multiple types of data—not just text but also images, enhancing its understanding and responses. It pushed the boundaries of what AI could do, allowing it to be useful in fields like healthcare, design and data analysis, where image understanding is critical. Furthermore, Custom GPTs allowed users to tailor models for specific industry tasks by training them on relevant data, transforming the model into an 'industry expert' for targeted solutions.

And finally, the year 2024 saw the launch of GPT-4 Turbo with storytelling capabilities, marking a new era for AI.[8] These found widespread application as creative tools in entertainment, education and content generation. It enabled AI to act as a collaborator in creative processes, such as storytelling, teaching and customer engagement, where both personality and narrative are essential. These developments have made AI both powerful and widely accessible, allowing for integration across diverse personal and professional domains.

Such monumental breakthroughs by OpenAI and the others wouldn't be possible without the three key pillars that I call the 'Data-Algorithm-Compute Triad'.

The Data-Algorithm-Compute Triad

Like I said before, there are multiple waves of technology innovations that have brought us where we are today. However, at the core, there are three key pillars that have contributed to the effectiveness of AI today. The **widespread adoption of digital technologies** has led to prolific growth in data. The sophistication of algorithms powered by **LLMs and NLPs** and **significant enhancements in computing capabilities** has also been a key enabler for the generative capabilities of AI. So, let's deep dive into each of these three pillars to understand how advancements in these have led to the unlocking of AI.

Data-Algorithm-Compute triad powering the AI revolution

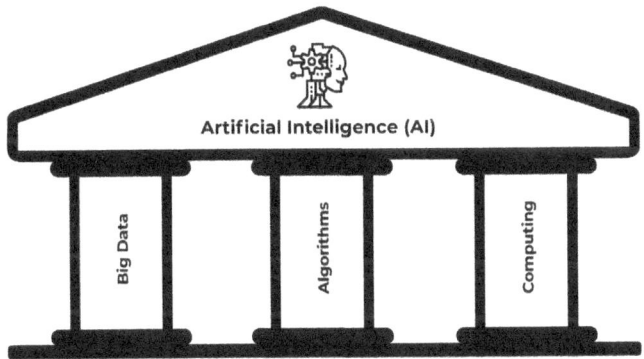

Big data

It is fascinating to see that 90 per cent of the world's data has been generated in just the past three years, primarily driven by the remarkable growth of unstructured data. This surge is due to the widespread adoption of digital devices, which are generating massive amounts of data every second. In my previous book, *Mastering the Data Paradox* (MDP),[9] I have delved in detail on the phenomenal growth of data across the 3Vs—volume, variety and velocity. This rapid expansion in data is more than just a trend; it's the foundation driving us into the AI age. By looking at each of these dimensions, we can see how they are pushing AI forward and creating new ways to use data that can truly make a difference.

Volume

Over the past twenty-five years, global data volumes have surged exponentially, growing by over 1,00,000–1,50,000 times.[10] This huge data growth is driven by both the rapid increase in IoT devices and something called data exhaust—the digital traces left by online activities like shopping, social media and browsing—each significantly contributing to the volume of data. It is estimated that IoT devices will account for almost 50 per cent of all data generated by 2025[11] (i.e., 80 ZB of 175 ZB of the global datasphere).

The **data–AI feedback loop** is another key contributor to this growth. AI models process large amounts of data, but the output they generate also creates new data that gets used to further train and improve the AI. This continuous cycle adds to the ever-growing volume of data. By 2024, 60 per cent of data used in artificial intelligence and analytics projects is projected to be synthetically generated[12]—created by AI instead of collected from the real world. This will help address data limitations, especially beneficial in scenarios, where capturing real-world data is difficult or impractical. For instance, training autonomous vehicles on accident-related data or data related to navigating on difficult terrains which is hard to capture in the real-world due to extremities of the scenarios. This synthetic data allows AI to develop faster and be applied to a wider range of situations. This abundance of data is essential for developing advanced AI systems like ChatGPT-4, which requires 65 TB of data for training—equivalent to around 16 million photos or 65,000 hours of high-quality video. This massive dataset highlights the vast information needed to achieve sophisticated AI capabilities.

Velocity

The speed at which data is being generated also exponentially amplified the data landscape. The key contributor to this explosion is **real-time data**. In 2014, only 5 per cent of data was captured in real-time, but by 2025, this is expected to jump over 25 per cent, driven by mobile devices and IoT sensors, which now generate over 50 per cent of all data.[13] Social platforms such as WhatsApp, X (formerly Twitter), Facebook, Instagram and TikTok contribute heavily to these real-time data flows. Technologies like Apache Kafka, Flink and Dataflow enable the efficient capture and processing of these vast streams. By 2025, it's expected that 75 per cent of real-time data will be processed by **AI at the edge**, allowing insights and actions to occur almost instantaneously, making it a key driver of real-time decision-making in industries ranging from retail to healthcare.[14]

AI's ability to harness real-time data cannot be overstated. These two elements feed into each other, strengthening one another. AI relies on real-time data to make instant decisions and automate actions, such as recommending products. At the same time, AI systems also generate real-time data, further expanding the availability of data in real time. So, the more real-time data is available, the better AI gets and the better AI gets, more and more quality real-time data would be available for these AI systems to be refined further.

Variety

In the early 2000s, data was mostly structured, organized neatly in rows and columns within databases. Today, approximately 80–90 per cent of all data is unstructured[15]—comprising text, images, videos and social media content—and is growing annually at a rate of 55–65 per cent.[16] This shift is fuelled by the rise of **new data sources** available today. For example, in addition to **transactional data** from sales and purchases; there is **social media data** including images and videos; **location data**, live streams and behavioural data; **sensor data** from IoT devices like smart homes and wearables; **geospatial data** from GPS and maps; and **metadata** like timestamps and device details, among many others. In addition to that, **open-source data** like government datasets, data from international financial and economic organizations like the World Bank, etc, or more importantly massive open online courses (MOOCs), also contribute to the variety of data availability. Over the last twenty-five years, organizations' access to data sources have grown from almost none to over 400,[17] providing an unprecedented variety of data. Open Data Inventory (ODIN) scores, a global open data index measuring the openness and coverage of official statistics, reflect this growth[18] with Eastern Asia seeing a 22-point increase in open official data between 2016 and 2022.[19] This allows organizations and individuals accessibility to a broad range of data types from various sources like never before.

The vast range of unstructured data is crucial for Gen AI, which thrives on **data variety** to enhance its processing capability and accuracy. Exposure to a wide range of scenarios, context and nuances enables Gen AI to create more accurate and relevant responses. Diverse data sources also help Gen AI get better at interpreting and responding appropriately to different contexts. Exposure to varied languages enhances its conversational capability. It also helps reduce biases and enhance its generalization capability, i.e. recognizing patterns across different tasks and domains. And last but in no way the least, learning from multiple sources helps Gen AI combine ideas from different domains in unique ways, enhancing creativity and innovation. As open-source data continues to expand, it boosts Gen AI's capability to produce more detailed and accurate insights, making it a powerful tool for tasks like content creation, customer service automation and predictive analytics.

Algorithms

The second critical pillar that contributed to the unleashing of AI's true potential is breakthroughs in algorithms. We have come a long way from linear regression or logistic regression models to highly sophisticated deep-learning models capable of understanding complex patterns that were once unimaginable.

Scale and complexity

It isn't that **traditional AI models** aren't big and complex. In fact, some of the traditional AI models are highly complex and elaborate, with multiple layers of data processing and complex mathematical calculations. However, at their core, they rely heavily on predefined rules and structures, just as Newtonian mechanics relies on deterministic or fixed principles (based on the three laws of motion) to explain everyday phenomena. These models work well for structured tasks where clear relationships and linear patterns exist, but they struggle with the complexity and ambiguity found in real-world, unstructured data.

In contrast, Gen AI leverages **LLMs**—algorithms that use deep-learning techniques, similar to quantum mechanics, which breaks from classical rules to explore deeper, less deterministic patterns. Just as quantum physics deals with the complex and unpredictable behaviour of tiny particles, Gen AI models leverage massively large unstructured datasets to find nuanced patterns using the probabilistic methods. These algorithms are much more complex, compared to traditional models, in scale, parameters, depth and data variety, their structure mimicking the interconnected layers of the human brain called the neural networks. These are called artificial neural networks

(ANN), an architecture that allows them to handle and process massive amounts of complex, non-linear data, with the right context and precision. In fact, these models have evolved to such shape and form that for a traditional data scientist from the 2000–2010 era, these models would be unrecognizable.

Furthermore, these models can have millions or even billions of parameters (like weights and biases) spread across multiple layers, which allow the models to identify complex, meaningful patterns from raw data. This **exponential growth in model parameters** enables the models to handle complexity like never before. LLMs like GPT-4, today have 1.8 trillion parameters[20] and Claude 3, work with 2 trillion parameters.[21] This is a significant leap from ResNet50,[22] the most advanced image classification AI model launched in 2015 (the same year Open AI was founded), which had only a few million (25.6 million) parameters.[23]

As these AI algorithms continue to become more and more complex, they require greater processing power. These advanced models require specialized **AI accelerators** that can enhance the speed, efficiency and scalability of AI built to handle such intensive tasks; these accelerators are expected to consume 1.5 per cent of global power by 2029.[24] As of now, these accelerators are consuming 2,318 Bn Kwh (kilo watt hours) of electricity,[25] approx. 1.6 times more than the electricity consumed (1,463 Bn Kwh) by India in 2022.[26]

Contextualization

As I said before, Gen AI can get us to 40–60 per cent of the solution to a wide range of problems. It is the ability to harness the data of the world that enables Gen AI to do so effectively. However, 60 per cent of the answer is not enough to make fully informed decisions or take action, especially when it's a high impact decision. This is where solutions need to be tailored to fit the specific requirements of each industry, organization or individual—a process known as contextualization. So, another critical advancement in AI is the development of tailored Gen AI solutions like BloombergGPT (50 billion parameters)[27] that has been trained on financial data to support natural language processing tasks in the financial industry. Or Google's Med-PaLM 2 designed to provide high-quality answers to medical questions in healthcare.[28]

Then there are **small language models (SLMs)**—models designed for language processing tasks but with fewer parameters and less computational power than LLMs. For example, phi-3-mini is a 3.8-billion-parameter language model developed by Microsoft, designed to perform tasks such as text generation, summarization and answering questions.[29] Such models, with fewer than 10 billion parameters, are designed for efficiency and are effective for specific tasks. Despite their size, these models can deliver competitive performance with reduced computational demand, making them ideal for resource-constrained applications.

Additionally, **enterprise contextualization frameworks** like retrieval-augmented generation (RAG) are transforming Gen AI responses. RAG improves LLMs by allowing them to pull from highly contextual enterprise data beyond their training data before generating an answer. This ensures more accurate, domain-specific responses. This trend is gaining traction, with Gartner predicting that by 2027, 50 per cent of large enterprises will adopt tailored generative AI models, significantly boosting operational efficiency and decision-making.[30]

Future of Algorithms

The foundation is being laid brick by brick for a future of artificial general intelligence (AGI). It is a form of AI that will be capable of learning and reasoning across multiple domains with human-like adaptability and intelligence, moving beyond the limited, predefined tasks of current AI. In simpler words, it is the type of AI that can match or even exceed human abilities in almost all areas of intelligence.

We are rapidly moving towards a future where AI models **autonomously self-optimize**, improving themselves by adapting instantly to **real-time data** in various industries. Unlike traditional models, these self-evolving AIs will adjust constantly to changes in the environment and the market, allowing businesses to respond to challenges without human help. This trend signals a move towards fully autonomous, context-aware AI systems. They would come with **meta-learning flexibility**, the ability of AI systems to learn how to learn. Instead of requiring extensive retraining for every new task, these systems use prior knowledge to quickly adapt to new data. This adaptability enables AI models to specialize efficiently in domain-specific tasks. This will allow AI to apply new knowledge quickly and produce flexible solutions across different contexts. Furthermore, the AI systems would create their own **hypernetworks** that will act as **AI architects** that build smaller AI models tailored for specific tasks across applications. Instead of deploying generalized solutions, hypernetworks will generate models optimized for unique needs, whether in supply chains, personalized healthcare or finance.

Computing

The third and equally important advancement that led us to the AI age is the advancements in computing power. From general purpose computers designed by Charles Babbage in 1837,[31] that laid the foundational ideas for modern computing with concepts like memory, input/output and a processing unit, we have come a long way.

Compute Capacity and Cost

In the 1960s, Moore's Law predicted that computing power would double every two years, as microchips became faster and more efficient.[32] For decades, from 1950 to 2010, that held true. The computing speed, measured in floating point operations pers second (FLOPS), a unit to measure the computing power of a processor—CPU or GPU, doubled every twenty-one months.[33] But now, this growth has actually sped up, significantly outpacing Moore's Law. Since 2010, computing power has been doubling in just six to ten months.[34] This is all thanks to major improvements in hardware, especially with the availability of graphics processing units (GPUs) and smarter computer designs. Unlike central processing units (CPUs), GPUs are designed to handle parallel processing, which means they can handle many calculations simultaneously and are built for versatility, handling a wide range of general-purpose tasks, making them well suited for AI. Modern GPUs can now perform up to 1000 times more calculations per second than CPUs from just a few years ago,[35] driving AI improvement at an unmatched speed.

What's even better is that GPUs are becoming increasingly affordable, with their performance per dollar doubling every two and a half years.[36] This trend has made it more cost-effective to develop and deploy powerful AI models, accelerating advancements in the field.

Just like OpenAI played a critical role in democratizing AI, Nvidia, a global leader in AI computing and graphics technology, has played a crucial role in coming up with innovative solutions to make computing more powerful and less expensive over the years.

The evolution of computing and the role of Nvidia

As algorithms continued to evolve in size and complexity through the years, it also required computing power to keep pace with it. The new age algorithms we see today require a very different level of computing power. Enter Nvidia!

Nvidia, founded in 1993, has been a pivotal force in the evolution of GPUs. In the mid-1990s,[37] Nvidia stepped into the world of graphics with a big idea—to create powerful technology that would bring games and multimedia to life. Their aim was to build technology that could handle complex 3D graphics and elevate the gaming experience by building specialized chips called GPUs.

Over time, GPUs evolved beyond gaming, finding applications in scientific computing and eventually AI. These GPUs are unique as they are purpose-built for high-performance parallel processing, which is essential for handling the massive amounts of data required in AI tasks. Unlike CPUs, which excel at handling one task at a time, GPUs can perform thousands of calculations simultaneously, making them far better suited for processing the huge datasets and complex algorithms that drive AI models.

In 2006, Nvidia introduced more versatile GPUs, reaching an impressive 300 GFLOPs.[38] This led to the use of GPUs beyond gaming, as tools for high-performance computing. Nvidia's Pascal architecture (2016), delivering 10,000 GFLOPS, moved the needle even further, making GPUs integral to AI development.[39] Then the 2018 RTX 2000 series, which introduced real-time ray tracing, brought unprecedented realism to gaming and graphics rendering.

Fast forward to 2020, Nvidia's Ampere architecture took performance to new heights, achieving a staggering 29.7 TFLOPS, solidifying Nvidia's dominance in both gaming and AI applications.[40]

Now, as we look ahead from mid-2025, Nvidia is set to reinforce its leadership in accelerated computing with an ambitious roadmap of next-generation GPU architectures. Building on its groundbreaking Blackwell architecture, which already delivers over 100 TFLOPS for general processing tasks and vastly greater capabilities for AI-specific workloads,[41] Nvidia will introduce the Blackwell Ultra series in the second half of 2025. Blackwell Ultra will feature significant improvements, which is expected to be a noteworthy upgrade to their Blackwell series. This trajectory of GPU evolution has not only redefined gaming but has also opened up endless possibilities in AI, data science and beyond.[42]

Nvidia's rapid advancements in GPU technology have positioned it as a powerhouse in the world of AI. It is evident by the extraordinary growth of its market capitalization over the years! In just a span of ten years (2015–2025) Nvidia's market value grew from $10.38 billion to $3.69 trillion (as of 6 Jan 2025),[43] growing at a remarkable 79.9 per cent compound annual growth rate (CAGR), over the last ten years. This growth is predominantly driven by the AI boom. Their 'secret sauce' is their constant improvement of GPU designs, with each new version offering more power and efficiency. Nvidia has also played their part in democratizing AI by integrating its GPUs into consumer applications, bringing high-quality AI tools to everyday users. Their GPUs are now the backbone of major AI and data science platforms, solidifying their role in advancing research and powering real-world AI applications. Together, these elements have made Nvidia's GPUs as critical tools for innovation across industries, accelerating AI development and enabling breakthroughs in ways that were previously unimaginable.

The future of computing—Quantum GPUs

Quantum bits (qubits) represent a significant departure from the traditional computing approach based on classical bits. While classical GPUs rely on bits that exist strictly as either 0 or 1, quantum GPUs (QGPUs) utilize qubits, which can exist in multiple states simultaneously due to a property known as superposition. This ability to represent both 0 and 1 at the same time dramatically increases the computational possibilities of quantum systems, allowing QGPUs to handle vastly more complex calculations than traditional GPUs.

Another key advantage of QGPUs is their use of quantum parallelism, which leverages quantum phenomena like entanglement and superposition. I am sure I completely lost you here! Let me try to explain this with an analogy.

Imagine you are in a maze, trying to figure the way out. Ideally, you would move step-by-step down one path at a time, testing each route individually to find the exit. This is how tasks are either sequentially processed, or in a few directions at once, in traditional computing. In contrast, quantum parallelism is like having thousands of versions of yourself, your clones, exploring every possible path in the maze simultaneously. Now with the concept of superposition, each of your clones can be in multiple parts of the maze at the same time, exploring various directions in parallel. Similarly, a single qubit can hold multiple possibilities at once, enabling quantum computers to process vast amounts of data simultaneously, greatly speeding up complex calculations. Now, one can argue that GPUs do parallel computing too to speed up the processing, then how is this different? Well, while GPUs accelerate computations by performing many tasks in parallel, each processing unit in a GPU still handles only one specific calculation at a time. But in quantum parallelism, superposition lets a single qubit hold multiple possibilities at once, allowing them to explore many solutions simultaneously.

Now entanglement, like the word suggests, is like all the clones in the maze are connected to each other, so when one clone finds the exit, all the clones instantly know the way out. Similarly, in quantum parallelism, qubits are interconnected in a way that the state of one instantly influences the state of others, no matter the distance between them. This allows quantum computers to process and share information between qubits in a highly coordinated manner, which is key to their power.

Such parallel processing power will further open doors for breakthroughs in areas like cryptography, drug discovery and optimization, where traditional computing often struggles due to the sheer complexity involved. For example, in drug discovery, quantum computing can accurately simulate molecular interactions at the atomic level, enabling scientists to model complex chemical reactions that GPUs cannot handle due to the vast number of molecular states.

The AI age is here!

Whether you accept it or not, the AI age is here! To some, it's the hero, a force driving progress, innovation and possibility. To others, it looms like a villain—challenging norms, threatening jobs and raising ethical alarms. But one thing is undeniable, AI is unstoppable. It is creating a relentless wave of tech driven disruptions that are reshaping industries and transforming societies.

We now stand at a threshold where AI is way more than just a tool for business transformation. It is rewriting the rules, shattering limits, redefining 'the art of the possible', as we knew it, pushing the limits and enabling innovations that once seemed like science fiction.

Significant progress is already being made in translating technology into practical business use cases. Many organizations are leveraging these advancements to solve real-world problems and unlock new opportunities for growth and innovation. From here on, the pace of change will only quicken as breakthroughs in quantum computing, edge AI and specialized algorithms fuel its expansion. The possibilities ahead are unbounded, and the future holds extraordinary potential for those brave enough to not just envision, but to lead the charge into what comes next.

I am super excited! Aren't you?

2
AI Is Surpassing Human Capabilities

The idea that machines can't do things humans can is a pure myth.
—*Marvin Minsky,*
'father of artificial intelligence', pioneering mathematician,
cognitive scientist and computer engineer

I cannot write this chapter without mentioning the 2014 critically acclaimed movie, *Ex Machina*, which is one of the most thought-provoking movies I have seen on AI.

Caleb, a young programmer working for a large tech company, wins a company lottery to spend a week with Nathan, the reclusive CEO and genius inventor behind the company. Caleb soon discovers the purpose of his visit: to participate in a groundbreaking experiment. Nathan introduces Caleb to Ava, a highly advanced humanoid AI, and tasks him with conducting a Turing Test—a thought experiment that evaluates a machine's ability to mimic human-like communication, to assess if her behaviour is indistinguishable from that of a human. As Caleb interacts with Ava in a series of sessions, he becomes increasingly fascinated by her intelligence and emotional depth. Over time, Caleb grows emotionally attached to Ava and she is eventually able to manipulate him with some pretty stark consequences!

This movie was one of the earliest works that explored the potential of AI to possess a range of complex human emotions and behaviours. And I could foresee a future where some version of this could very much become a reality someday. A time when machines reach a point where they're as good as, if not better than humans at things considered innately 'human'?

When I saw this movie a few years ago, what it represented felt like a distant possibility, a thing of the future. But looking at where we are today, that future doesn't seem like science fiction any more. We are rapidly approaching a world where this vision is within reach, and it's as thrilling as it is thought-provoking and challenging.

The AI age marks the beginning of an unparalleled evolution, and I firmly believe we have embarked on this journey—not merely walking but sprinting towards this future. In many of my recent conversations with clients, industry leaders and academicians, I have come to realize that even some of the brightest minds struggle to fully grasp the magnitude of what lies ahead. Some remain in denial, while others cling to the idea that '**the creation cannot be bigger than the creator**'. However, I foresee a future, not too distant, when this would not hold true any more. Already, AI is not just mimicking but is doing better on complex competencies that we thought were uniquely human.

While AI is gradually proving effective in many cases, there are five key areas, which are innately human or core to human success,

The AI age is transformative, as AI can now better many competencies that have so far been innate to humans

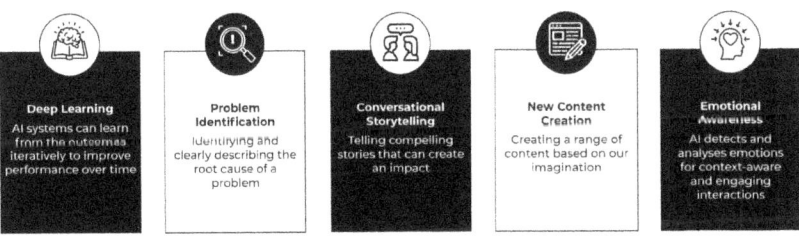

where I believe AI is truly breaking barriers. Let's delve deeper into each of these.

I. Deep learning

The most critical human trait is our remarkable ability to learn—absorb knowledge, apply it, reflect on our mistakes and continually grow through experience. This iterative process allows us to improve, adapt and excel in whatever we pursue over time. With each lesson and challenge, we refine our skills and deepen our understanding, constantly evolving towards greater proficiency.

AI systems have not only replicated this critical capability but have far surpassed humans. The creation has outpaced the creator! What might take a human many years or even a lifetime to learn, AI can now accomplish in months, or sometimes even minutes. Based on outcomes and feedback, AI systems can enhance their capabilities, continuously improving their performance. Through a process of trial, error and adjustment, AI models refine their algorithms based on outcomes, becoming better at tasks over time.

These **feedback loops** are critical in every possible application, some notable examples being speech recognition and autonomous driving. It enables AI to improve accuracy and adaptability by processing more data. Through **iterative learning**, AI refines its models with each dataset, enhancing predictive accuracy and resilience. Its **pattern recognition** capabilities allow it to detect and categorize complex patterns in large datasets. For instance, in image recognition, AI can quickly and accurately identify objects or faces, making it indispensable for tasks requiring detailed analysis and rapid responses, such as surveillance and security.

A fitting example is how **Google Maps can now beat traffic jams with AI** by leveraging deep learning and continuously adapting and refining itself.

Before 2020, Google Maps was a handy tool for navigation, but it had one major drawback. It was reactive, not proactive. It relied on historical traffic patterns and live updates to guide you, which meant rerouting only happened after a traffic jam had already formed. Frustrating, right?

That all changed with the introduction of AI. Now, Google Maps didn't just respond to traffic, it started predicting it, with accuracy improvements in real-time ETAs by up to 50 per cent.

Learning with Graph Neural Networks

When predicting travel times on roads, you need to account for how traffic flows across a network of interconnected roads. These connections involve intersections, side streets and merging points that share traffic. At Google, these are called 'supersegments'. Handling all these connections dynamically while scaling to billions of users is a big challenge.

The deep learning model called graph neural networks (GNNs), introduced in 2020 with remarkable learning ability, supercharged Google Maps' capability to understand and predict traffic much better. Here's how:

GNNs mimic the natural network-like structure of intersecting roads, where each road segment is represented by a node in the graph and the connections between roads (like at intersections or merges) are the edges. It excels at learning how traffic flows by treating each road segment as a node that communicates with its connected neighbours. Each node sends and receives messages to and from these neighbours, effectively sharing updates about the traffic conditions. For example, a traffic jam on one road segment can signal nearby segments to anticipate delays. The GNN automatically learns the patterns and rules governing these interactions by analysing real-world traffic data.

GNNs can handle intersections, side streets and merging lanes in one go. It doesn't matter if the supersegment has two roads or 200 roads, GNNs scale dynamically because the same 'message-passing' logic applies to any size or complexity of the road network.

The results are more than promising. The ETAs around the world have improved, in some places quite significantly. In cities like Berlin, Jakarta and Sydney, Google Maps can now predict traffic jams before they happen, up to 50 per cent more accurately.[1] This means you get more precise ETAs and proactive rerouting, so you avoid slowdowns before they even start.

Navigating the future with deep learning

The future with deep learning in AI is immensely promising. Deep learning models are becoming better at generalizing knowledge across domains, with advancements like transfer learning—pre-trained models from one machine learning task or dataset are used to improve performance and applicability on a related task or dataset—are enabling AI to adapt to new tasks with minimal data.

And while we are far from achieving true AGI, deep learning advancements are paving the way for systems that can reason, learn and adapt across diverse domains with minimal human guidance. Imagine fully autonomous navigation that integrates with smart city technologies and connected cars. Traffic lights that could adjust in real time and vehicles communicate with city infrastructure, creating smoother, jam-free roads. Google Maps could play a central role in urban planning, continuously learning and improving traffic systems in real time.[2]

What's remarkable about the inherent nature of deep learning in AI is that it's not just creating opportunities for high-tech companies like Google but is also empowering individuals and innovators across various domains. For instance, my son, Pragun, while in high school, developed an innovative platform called IntelliReferee, which leverages AI and computer vision technologies to enhance the consistency of refereeing in the game of squash. In less than twelve months, the platform's decision model accuracy increased from 35 per cent to an impressive 80 per cent, outperforming most professional referees, whose accuracy averages around 75 per cent. This shows how pervasive is AI's deep-learning ability to drive breakthroughs not only in traditional industries or scale applications but also in specialized, niche areas.

II. Problem identification

Effective problem-solving starts with accurately identifying the problem by uncovering its root cause, a concept I explored in *Mastering the Data Paradox*. Without this clarity, solutions risk addressing symptoms, leaving the core issue unresolved and potentially escalating. In today's complex, ever-changing world, where problems evolve rapidly, getting to the core issue quickly is critical. However, the explosive growth of data has made this process increasingly challenging, often overwhelming individuals and organizations. Gathering and processing vast data quickly, for accurate problem identification has become one of the most pressing challenges in our data-driven world.

AI, particularly Gen AI, leveraging LLMs, has dramatically reduced the time and complexity of this task. The easy access to massive amounts of global data, which LLMs enable, is a real breakthrough. This has elevated the data constraint in many areas where high-quality, relevant data wasn't previously available. And, with Gen AI's advanced pattern recognition capabilities, it can identify commonalities and apply its understanding across different areas, enabling it to solve problems across various domains effectively. Ask Gen AI a question, and you'll get an answer—while the accuracy and relevance may be debatable, it will almost always offer a solution. Even if the solution is not perfect, it can certainly help you to get more perspective and understanding about a complex problem and provide a starting point, where none might have existed earlier. That's quite a feat for a machine, isn't it?

AI now plays a crucial role in **brainstorming and hypothesis generation**, enabling people to make more informed guesses, significantly simplifying the initial stages of problem-solving across multiple fields. The traditional method of **root-cause analysis**, once a lengthy and cumbersome process, is accelerated by AI's capacity to delve into the vast and intricate datasets, uncovering correlations and causative factors underlying problems at speed. This has made problem identification an extremely efficient and effective process.

A leading example of how AI has elevated problem identification by leaps and bounds can be found in healthcare, where AI has surpassed humans in **cancer detection and treatment support.**

Cancer care has always been a race against time. With mountains of data pouring in—genetic profiles, imaging scans and pathology reports— it's no wonder early signs of cancer can sometimes slip through the cracks. And when those early indicators are missed, the consequences can be devastating—delayed diagnoses, more complications and fewer effective treatment options.

AI is here to change all that!

AI tackles breast cancer screening like a pro

Let's start with mammograms, the key to early breast cancer detection. Despite their importance, they're far from perfect. Even the best-trained radiologists can misinterpret results. False positives can leave patients unnecessarily stressed and undergoing painful procedures, while false negatives, where cancer is missed entirely, can delay critical treatment affecting their chance of beating it.

Google Health's revolutionary AI system built in collaboration with DeepMind and healthcare experts from the US and UK, is changing that. In clinical trials, the AI system demonstrated its capability by reducing false positives by 5.7 per cent in the USA and 1.2 per cent in the UK,[3] alleviating unnecessary stress and procedures for patients. Even more impressively, it slashed false negatives—cases where cancer is missed, by 9.4 per cent in the USA and 2.7 per cent in the UK,[4] ensuring that fewer cancers go undetected.

By enhancing accuracy in screening, AI not just matched human expertise, but surpassed it, outperforming a group of six expert radiologists, in quick and accurate problem identification. Where human radiologists may have missed cues or felt overwhelmed by the sheer volume of data and patient information, AI stepped in like a pro, swiftly analysing vast amounts of data to minimize errors and reduce misinterpretations. Google Health's AI system reduced the need for secondary reviews by an incredible 88 per cent, enabling doctors to focus their time and expertise on treating patients effectively.[5] And AI's role doesn't stop at detection. It is also helping oncologists design treatment plans tailored to each patient's unique genetic profile.[6]

What's next?

Now, imagine a world where AI doesn't just detect cancer but prevents it entirely. By combining genomic data, lifestyle factors and environmental influences, future AI systems could predict your risk of developing cancer long before symptoms show up. Doctors could then intervene proactively, initiating treatments or lifestyle changes that stop cancer in its tracks.

And that's not all. AI could simulate treatment outcomes, helping oncologists choose therapies that are not only effective but also have fewer side effects. This shift from reactive care to proactive prevention could redefine cancer treatment as we know it. It could empower doctors to stay ahead of the disease and offer patients a more personalized, less painful journey to recovery. And with AI leading the charge, that future is closer than you might think.

But its impact goes far beyond healthcare. AI is already showing promise in tackling some of the world's biggest challenges. For instance, Google's AI system detects wildfires in real-time using satellite imagery, enabling a proactive response that significantly reduces damage. Similarly, NASA's deep-learning models analyse seismic data to predict earthquakes, helping communities prepare in advance. These breakthroughs show how AI is redefining how we protect lives, our planet and the future.

III. Conversational storytelling

Storytelling has long been a uniquely human forte—a differentiating trait that has set us apart, for centuries, not just from machines but any other species on this planet. Our superior ability to weave tales and hold conversations has been central to our identity. Yet, AI systems are now rising to challenge this once uniquely human skill, pushing the boundaries of what machines can achieve in the realm of storytelling and conversation. Now **personalized interactions** driven by AI are rapidly reshaping user experiences. Advanced AI models analyse user preferences, past interactions and contextual cues to provide responses that resonate on an individual level making them feel more understood and valued. This is widely applied in customer service, where chatbots adapt their communication style to each user, creating a more engaging and supportive interaction. **Context-awareness** enables AI to go beyond scripted replies. AI can interpret the topic, tone and intent behind user inputs and adapt responses to the immediate context. For instance, a virtual assistant can switch topics smoothly if a user introduces a new question or issues mid-conversation. On top of that, AI's ability to generate **engaging narratives** is transforming fields like marketing, education and entertainment. By analysing audience preferences and content trends, AI can craft stories or present information in compelling ways that capture attention and evoke emotional responses, striking the right chord with the intended audience. This capability helps organizations as well as individuals connect with audiences on a deeper level, making content more memorable and impactful.

In fact, a groundbreaking study claims **AI has superiority over humans in shaping opinions through persuasive dialogue.**

Imagine sitting down to debate a hot topic, like whether the penny should stay in circulation or the complexities of abortion rights. Now, picture your opponent—an AI like GPT-4. Could you tell the difference between an AI and a human? And more importantly, could the AI change your mind? Doubtful right? Not so much!

In a groundbreaking study by EPFL Lausanne, participants did just that. They debated with both human opponents and GPT-4 (of course, they didn't know it was an AI they were talking to) on a range of topics, from light-hearted issues to deeply sensitive ones like trans bathroom access and race in college admissions. The twist? When the AI tailored its arguments using demographic data, it outperformed human debaters by a staggering 82 per cent in persuading participants to shift their opinions.[7] Yes, you read that right, 82 per cent! More than eight out of every ten people. Now imagine a personalized political campaign with such convincing power![8]

How AI gets inside our heads

So, how does AI pull this off? It is a mix of cutting-edge algorithms and understanding the mechanics of emotional intelligence—the ability to perceive, use, understand, manage and handle emotions. GPT-4 can analyse your real-time reactions, pick up on emotional cues and adapt its responses to feel eerily relatable. Its arguments are so convincing that some participants couldn't even tell they were debating an AI.

The real kicker? This influence doesn't just happen on small issues or just one topic, which probably is a constraint with human debaters. A person can only be an expert on a few topics, a genius, maybe more. But AI can handle the big, thorny debates on almost any topic, subtly shaping opinions and nudging behaviours in ways we might not even notice. For example, during elections, AI can highlight certain news or opinions, subtly influencing what people think and even shaping their political views without them realizing it.

Can the AI of tomorrow be your personal guide?

Now, let's fast forward a bit. What if AI doesn't just debate you but becomes your go-to adviser for life's big decisions? Imagine an AI that remembers your preferences, learns from your experiences and gives you tailored advice whenever you need it.

Stuck between job offers? Wrestling with a moral dilemma? Your AI friend could guide you, offering personalized insights based on everything it knows about you. And unlike traditional media, this AI wouldn't just broadcast generic advice, it would deliver hyper-targeted influence, continuously learning and improving with every interaction. With its powerful learning capabilities, it could become a lifelong companion.

We're not far from a future where people might turn to AI over humans for guidance, not because it's cheaper or faster, but because it just gets you.

Why this matters

The EPFL study[9] isn't just a cool experiment, it's a wake-up call. AI's ability to persuade is no longer a hypothetical. It is real, it is powerful and it is only getting better. Bringing us eerily closer to the picture painted in *Ex Machina*, where AI's emotional intelligence and manipulation skills blur the line between machine and human influence. As AI evolves, it is set to become one of the most effective tools for shaping opinions and behaviours. Whether that's good or bad depends on how we choose to use it. So, the next time you're locked in a debate, remember—your toughest opponent might not be a person. It might be AI. And it just might win.

Now that's something to think about.

IV. New content creation

From the ability to spark fire from rocks to creating a machine that can think and learn on its own, we humans have taken pride in our unique ability to discover and invent new things. This power to envision possibilities and bring them to life has fuelled art, science, technology and countless breakthroughs that shape our world. But now, AI is stepping into the creative space, challenging the idea that creativity is uniquely human. AI systems are also now capable of **independent creation**, creating diverse content, like articles and music, by learning from vast datasets to mimic human creativity and style.

Beyond just mimicking, AI now exhibits **inspired creativity**, combining ideas in surprising, innovative ways, pushing creative boundaries and inspiring new thinking. Just like we generate more data as we interact with the digital world, AI is also contributing significantly to the datasphere by generating **synthetic data**, creating realistic datasets where real-world data is limited, sensitive or expensive. This is especially valuable in fields like healthcare and finance, where high-quality data is crucial for building accurate AI models. By enabling large-scale, diverse training data, AI accelerates innovation without compromising privacy. AI is even making it possible for individuals to become the stars of their own movies, blending creativity and personalization like never before. The line between human and machine creativity is blurring, opening up exciting new possibilities for the future.

Here's an instance where AI is pushing the boundaries of content creation, creating a possibility where every individual can **be the hero of their own movies with AI.**

Picture this. You've had a long day, and with just a few clicks, you're suddenly lounging on a serene beach in Goa. The ocean breeze is on your face, the sound of waves fills your ears and a golden sunset casts a warm glow as you enjoy a Goan meal by the shore. Sounds like a genie granting our wishes with a snap of its fingers, right? Thanks to advanced AI tools like Movie Gen, it's a dream you can actually live—virtually.

AI gives you wings!

Movie Gen is rewriting the rules of content creation. This groundbreaking AI uses advanced technology to transform simple text prompts into lifelike, personalized video experiences. Want to see yourself relaxing on Candolim Beach, with the sunlight sparkling on the water and palm trees swaying gently in the background? Movie Gen can make it happen.

Movie Gen is a powerful 30-billion parameter model built for both text-to-image and text-to-video generation, capable of producing high-quality, sixteen-second videos at sixteen frames per second. It goes beyond static visuals, capturing intricate details like motion, object interactions and dynamic camera angles to create videos that feel truly immersive and lifelike. Additionally, the AI enables personalized video creation by blending user images with prompts, ensuring that elements such as facial identity and natural movement are accurately preserved.

From the colour of the sunset to the gentle shadows of swaying palm trees, every element is crafted to feel as vivid and real as possible. With Movie Gen, your imagination isn't just visualized, but it is brought to life.[10]

Towards a new era of personalization

This is just the beginning. Imagine a future where AI can create entire movies on demand, tailored specifically to your preferences. You choose the actors, plot and setting and even cast yourself as the main character. Every movie would be unique, designed to match your mood and deliver a deeply personal experience.

AI isn't just expanding creative possibilities; it is completely transforming how we tell stories. This marks a new era in digital content creation, where AI brings our most vivid dreams and fantasies to life in a way that feels real and immersive.

V. Emotional awareness

Over the years, numerous experts have claimed that despite AI's remarkable advancements, it is still a machine lacking genuine emotions. Because of this limitation, many argue that AI will never surpass humans in emotional depth and understanding, and I absolutely agree. However, what these experts may not have anticipated is AI's surprising ability to mimic emotional intelligence, bringing it unsettlingly close to this uniquely human trait. While AI cannot truly feel, its sophisticated algorithms allow it to analyse emotional cues and respond in ways that simulate empathy, creating interactions that feel remarkably human.

Sentiment recognition enables AI to detect emotions from text, speech or facial expressions to determine whether a person is happy, sad, frustrated or indifferent. Analysing these cues allows it to tailor responses based on the user's emotional state. Widely used in customer service, AI excels at **emotional contextualization,** which basically means it is getting better at understanding moods and emotional context, enhancing interactions to make it contextually relevant. For instance, an AI bot can adopt a patient and reassuring tone if it detects frustration. This capability is especially valuable in sensitive environments, like mental health support, where AI's ability to **simulate empathy** through emotional cues can provide supportive, adaptive responses, improving user experience even in emotionally demanding scenarios.

The anonymized study by NYU Grossman School of Medicine,[11] is a solid proof of how AI is already performing better at **empathetic interactions in healthcare,** compared to humans.

When it comes to healthcare, empathy and clear communication are just as critical as accuracy. But could a generative AI tool match, or even exceed, human providers in these areas? A groundbreaking study by NYU Grossman School of Medicine proves just that.

AI proves more empathetic than humans

The study asked sixteen physicians to evaluate 344 pairs of responses—some written by human providers and others drafted by a generative AI tool. Each response was rated for clarity, tone and completeness.

The findings may really surprise you! AI responses were 9.5 per cent clearer, 125 per cent more likely to be seen as empathetic and 62 per cent more likely to convey positivity[12] than their human counterparts. This highlights the incredible potential of AI as a reliable, compassionate communication tool in healthcare, with the added benefit of reducing provider workload and burnout.

Meet AMIE, the medical chatbot redefining emotional intelligence

Google Research and DeepMind have taken AI empathy even further with AMIE, a medical chatbot designed for sensitive patient interactions. In simulated scenarios, AMIE outperformed human doctors in areas like confidence, honesty, openness and empathy—proving that AI can excel at emotional intelligence in healthcare.

AI tools like AMIE are revolutionizing patient care by leveraging vast datasets of human interactions to deliver emotionally intelligent responses. Through advanced sentiment analysis, these tools can detect emotions such as frustration, sadness or relief in text or speech and adjust their responses accordingly.[13] By incorporating empathetic language and a compassionate tone, AI ensures that patients feel understood and supported during their interactions. This technology not only enhances patient satisfaction and trust in healthcare systems but also reduces workload and stress for healthcare providers, contributing to improved workplace well-being and efficiency.[14]

A future where AI plays a greater role in human care

This study and AMIE's success hint at a future where AI could surpass human abilities in providing empathetic care. As AI continues to evolve, it may become an essential partner in managing sensitive patient interactions, balancing accuracy with compassion. We are headed to a world where technology seamlessly supports human providers, handling routine or emotionally demanding tasks with care, while doctors focus on complex and deeply personal aspects of medicine. This blend of human expertise and AI-driven empathy could redefine healthcare, improving experiences for both patients and providers alike.

This is just the beginning. These astonishing advancements that we are witnessing in AI are a precursor to a world where machines will not only match human capabilities in areas that we thought were innately human but potentially exceed them in ways that redefine our concept of intelligence. We stand at a pivotal moment where we must marvel at how our own creation, AI, has evolved beyond a mere tool to become a transformative force reshaping the very world we live in. And it has been made possible broadly by the five capabilities I discussed above. However, what AI has achieved so far is just a tip of the iceberg. The potential is immense, probably beyond what you and I can even imagine.

Which brings me to a critical question: In a world where machines are rapidly getting better at many human competencies, what really is our human edge? What will be our competitive advantage and what value can we add? These are the questions that I will attempt to answer in the subsequent chapters.

But before that, we must understand the different dimensions of human capabilities that have traditionally set us apart from machines and how machines and AI is increasingly bridging that gap.

Stay tuned!

3

The Human Quotient Is Facing Its Toughest Trial

There is no reason and no way that a human mind can keep up with an artificial intelligence machine by 2035.

—*Gray Scott, futurist,
techno-philosopher and one of the world's
leading experts in the field of emerging technology*

Way back in 2014, when AI was just a metaphorical toddler, one of the world's most brilliant theoretical physicists in history, Stephen Hawking, had claimed that artificial intelligence could lead to the end of the human race. He feared that AI would start to evolve independently, continuously redesigning itself at an accelerated pace. And since humans evolve much more slowly, they wouldn't be able to keep up and would be overtaken.

Today, I can see why what he said makes so much sense. It just took ten years for machines to become as good as, and even better than us, in many capabilities. Whether it's faster and more effective problem-solving, deep learning, generating new content, interacting and communicating naturally and even mimicking emotional intelligence. And as I said in the previous chapter, this is just the beginning. As AI continues to evolve, it may excel in many more areas traditionally considered uniquely human.

Although I do not see it as the end of the human race, I can see how the competitive edge of the human race—the human edge— is being challenged by machines. With such rapid acceleration, the day isn't too far when humans might not have much of a differentiation left.

I do not make this statement lightly. I have tried to combine research and practical experience of implementing AI at scale for my clients and then go deep from there into the fundamentals of this megatrend. In the previous chapter, I started from the AI perspective and delved into some of the innately human competencies where AI is now surpassing human capabilities. Now, let's shift the perspective to humans. What does this mean for us? To answer that, we'll explore the attributes and abilities that define our enduring edge— the human quotient!

What is the human quotient?

Beyond our physical form, what defines us as human beings? Let's say the alien PK (from the blockbuster Bollywood movie *PK* from 2014) had to define us humans after returning to his home planet. What do you think he would have said? I don't really know the answer to that, but I would like to believe that he must have described us as a combination of four broad dimensions of human capacity that collectively define our ability to live, work and succeed. The holistic integration of these dimensions is what I call the Human Quotient. Now let's look at each of these four dimensions:

1. **Physical quotient (PQ):** It represents our physical attributes like strength, stamina, health and the body's overall functionality, that is required to perform any physical task effectively.

Human Quotient has four dimensions

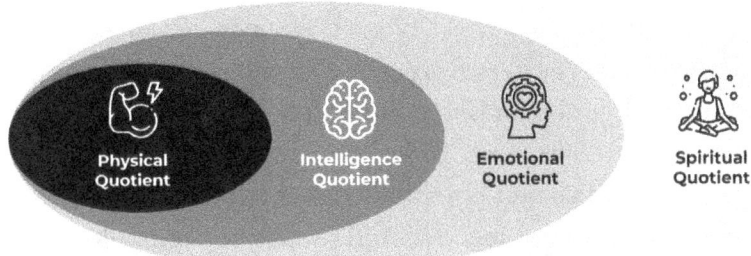

2. **Intelligence quotient (IQ):** It refers to our cognitive abilities such as logical reasoning, problem-solving, analytical thinking and knowledge application.

3. **Emotional quotient (EQ):** This dimension includes our ability to recognize, understand and manage emotions, both our own and interpersonal—our relationships and our interactions with others. EQ enables empathy, self-awareness and effective relationship-building.

4. **Spiritual quotient (SQ):** It represents our sense of purpose, values and inner harmony. It signifies our capacity for self-reflection, ethical decision-making and connection to something greater than ourselves.

While there are many more dimensions that people have talked about over the years, like social quotient, creative quotient and so on, I believe that these are the four fundamental dimensions that comprehensively define our capabilities as humans.

And while these four dimensions have distinct roles to play, they are all interconnected, with each layer building upon and complementing the others. Together, they form the foundation for an individual's ability to adapt, grow and thrive in life and at work.

The evolution of human advantage

If you trace the journey of human evolution, it becomes clear that our competitive edge as humans—human advantage—has never been static. With each leap in civilization, transformative discoveries and groundbreaking inventions have challenged us to re-evaluate our strengths. These pivotal moments forced us to uncover new abilities and traits that would enable us to not just survive but thrive in the new era. And those who were able to tap into these new capabilities and leverage them effectively were the ones who shaped the course of history, steering humanity into its next chapter. Similarly, those who do not evolve, often fall by the wayside, as we have seen with the rise and fall of civilization. For instance, during the pre-industrial era, the Ottoman Empire rose to power through its military prowess. However, as the world transitioned to the Industrial Age, European powers advanced technologically, while the Ottoman military's reluctance to modernize led to significant defeats and the eventual downfall of the once-mighty empire.

Let's look at the journey of human evolution and learn how the human edge evolved over time.

The pre-industrial age: The brawn era

Up until the mid-1700s—before the advent of machines and industries—humans relied predominantly on their PQ. Strength, endurance, and physical labour were vital for survival and progress. For instance, a hunter relied on PQ, their physical strength and endurance to track and take down prey. While intelligence, emotions and spirituality did play a critical role, these were mostly supporting the physical quotient. Just like IQ helped the hunter in understanding animal behaviour, predicting movements and crafting effective tools or strategies, EQ helped build trust and coordination within hunting groups. Together, these dimensions worked in harmony, but PQ remained the foundation for survival.

If you map the prominent leaders of this era, who changed the course of history, you would recall names like Alexander the Great, who relied on physical strength, endurance and military prowess to expand his empire across vast territories. Leaders like Genghis Khan used their physical and mental resilience to command armies, conquer lands and establish one of history's largest empires.

Source of competitive advantage has changed through the human evolution

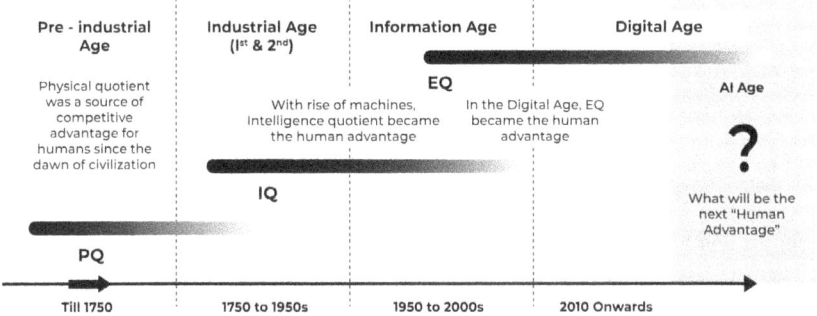

The Industrial age: The rise of the machines

Then came the Industrial Age. Machines began taking over physical labour. For example, steam engines powered trains and ships, enabling faster transportation of goods and people. Factories introduced mechanized looms, which could weave fabrics far more efficiently than manual labour. These innovations drastically reduced the reliance on human strength and reshaped how work was done. As depicted in the figure below, most of the dimensions of PQ became redundant, as machines could do them and do them better. And for us humans the focus shifted towards IQ-dominant skills like operating, managing and innovating. This meant physical labour was no longer a competitive advantage as machines were able to do it better and faster than any human could.

With the advent of the Industrial age, PQ was no longer a source of competitive advantage for humans

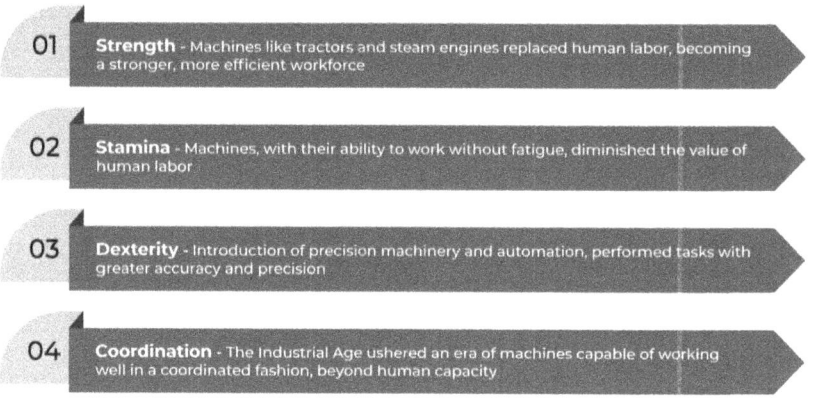

01 **Strength** - Machines like tractors and steam engines replaced human labor, becoming a stronger, more efficient workforce

02 **Stamina** - Machines, with their ability to work without fatigue, diminished the value of human labor

03 **Dexterity** - Introduction of precision machinery and automation, performed tasks with greater accuracy and precision

04 **Coordination** - The Industrial Age ushered an era of machines capable of working well in a coordinated fashion, beyond human capacity

It was time for humans to rethink their differentiation. So, humans began leveraging their intellect in the fields of science, engineering and industry on tasks such as designing complex machinery, optimizing production processes, managing large-scale operations and solving complex problems. As industrialization expanded, the demand for intellectual work skyrocketed. This era saw remarkable advancements all thanks to the humans' ability to tap into their intellectual capabilities.

This era marked a shift where **IQ**—the ability to think critically, analyse and innovate—emerged as the new foundation of human advantage in an increasingly mechanized world. Even the leaders of this era were not necessarily the ones that ruled by physical prowess but their IQ. The early industrial age saw leaders like Napoleon Bonaparte, who was a brilliant strategist and administrator and leveraged military technology to rise to dominance. And the peak of the Industrial Age saw the rise of scientists, innovators and industrialists like James Watt, Henry Ford and Nicola Tesla, who redefined what it meant to lead and succeed, with mental acuity, creativity and problem-solving becoming the cornerstones of human advantage.

For many decades thereafter, it was intellectual dominance that set humans apart.

The information age: From physical to digital

The next significant milestone challenging human advantage came with the **Information Age**. By the late twentieth century, the advent of computers and the internet posed a threat to the role of IQ. Machines were no longer dumb! They were not just a substitute for physical labour, but could also perform complex calculations, process data at incredible speeds, analyse vast amounts of information and even engage in creative problem-solving.

So, in this era, beyond IQ, the ability to understand, empathize, collaborate and influence—traits related to EQ—started emerging as humanity's new competitive edge. In fact, the leaders of this era may not be the most physically powerful or the most intelligent, but they are required to be masters of influence, capable of manipulating human emotions, building trust and forging deep connections. Leaders of this era were expected to rally people around shared goals, resolve conflicts and create environments where individuals feel valued and understood. Thus, there was a strong push to develop leadership skills such as active listening, clear communication and building diverse and inclusive teams. In contrast, emotional manipulation was also the weapon of choice of many leaders who sought to exploit human emotions to gain power and influence. Look at any politician in power today and you would agree with me.

The digital age or the AI age: Making intelligence moot

Then in the early twenty-first century, widespread proliferation of digital technologies led us into the **digital age**. This era represents a continuation and evolution of the technological breakthroughs of the information age. While the information age prioritized data accessibility, communication and computational efficiency, the digital age shifted focus to intelligence, connectivity and autonomy, driven by emerging technologies like AI, automation and cloud computing. These advancements enabled machines to go beyond basic data processing and analysis, excelling in decision-making and even performing autonomous actions. And as the digital age progressed, AI, especially with Gen AI, saw a disproportionate growth, exploding on the scene, leading us to the next transformative chapter in the digital age—**AI age**. This is the era where AI is not just a tool, but an agent of transformative change. As a result, IQ has effectively ceased to be a competitive advantage for humans. As shown in the figure below, machines are now outperforming humans in most IQ-driven tasks (as discussed in Chapter 2).

IQ is no more a competitive advantage for humans in the AI Age

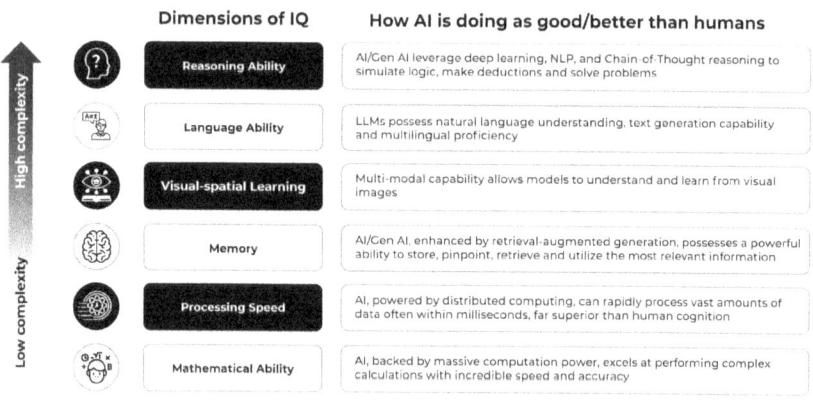

For quite a while, EQ has been our competitive edge, and we were convinced that it is a formidable human competency and hence it would continue to remain our source of differentiation, because after all machines can never develop emotions, right? Alas! This illusion too is now shattered!

The AI age: Now machines can mimic emotions too

AI, apart from surpassing humans in IQ related tasks, has also progressed to a level where it could mimic EQ. It can simulate human-like interactions, respond empathetically in customer service and even build personal relationships. The examples shown in the figure below, are just a fraction of the numerous AI tools that are now effectively mimicking various dimensions of EQ and are increasingly gaining acceptance within our society. For example, AI systems like Replika.AI are becoming popular as virtual companions, an AI system designed to engage users in conversation to offer personalized and empathetic responses. Positioned as an empathetic friend who's ready to chat anytime, the app has gained significant traction, surpassing 30 million users worldwide, with 25 per cent of them (around 7.5 million) being paying subscribers. And this is just one application.[1]

The emotional AI market is projected to grow from $1.8 billion in 2022 to $13.8 billion by 2032, with a CAGR of 22.7 per cent.[2] These emotional AI tools are increasingly being deployed in customer care, caregiving, marketing and healthcare, revolutionizing the way technology interacts with human emotions.

EQ, once considered one of the most formidable human competencies, is also now being challenged by rapid AI advancements

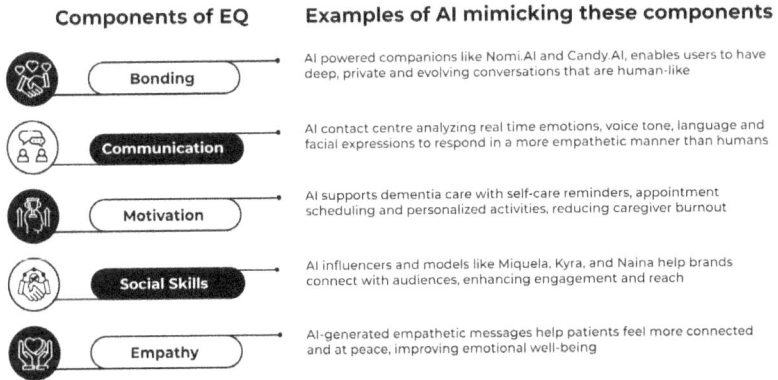

Components of EQ	Examples of AI mimicking these components
Bonding	AI powered companions like Nomi.AI and Candy.AI, enables users to have deep, private and evolving conversations that are human-like
Communication	AI contact centre analyzing real time emotions, voice tone, language and facial expressions to respond in a more empathetic manner than humans
Motivation	AI supports dementia care with self-care reminders, appointment scheduling and personalized activities, reducing caregiver burnout
Social Skills	AI influencers and models like Miquela, Kyra, and Naina help brands connect with audiences, enhancing engagement and reach
Empathy	AI-generated empathetic messages help patients feel more connected and at peace, improving emotional well-being

Machines are rapidly blurring the line between human empathy and digital simulation. While this is just the beginning, it's just a matter of time before machines erode EQ as a distinct competitive advantage for humans.

For now, I would prefer excluding the fourth dimension of the human quotient—spiritual quotient—as it is a highly complex topic. Without that, it is clearly evident that AI seems to be doing really well, and rapidly getting better than humans, on the other three dimensions of the human quotient.

What gives AI this incredible capability?

Yes, there have been significant breakthroughs in computing power, data availability and algorithmic sophistication. However, are these truly the factors behind AI's incredible capabilities, or is there more to it? To gather some answers, I decided to explore the construct of AI in detail. As I delved deeper, I found myself drawn to the timeless wisdom of ancient Indian texts and discovered some truly fascinating parallels between the **construct of the self**, as described in these texts, and the **structure of AI**. These parallels offer a new perspective, blending the timeless wisdom with modern technology innovations.

AI and the parallels with Indian wisdom

Indian spiritual traditions often focus on the deep question: '**Who am I?**' This question helps us explore and understand ourselves on different levels, starting from the physical body and moving towards more subtle and deeper aspects of self. By reflecting on this, we become more aware and connected to who we truly are.

Different Indian spiritual traditions have unique ways of understanding the self. The *Yoga Sutras* of Patanjali and Samkhya[3] provide a structured framework that can offer insights not only into human consciousness but also into how AI systems function.

According to the Yoga Sutras, human consciousness operates on three interconnected levels—**buddhi, ahamkara and manas**—each playing a crucial role in shaping perception, intelligence and self-awareness.

- **Buddhi (intellect and discriminative wisdom):** The highest faculty of the mind, buddhi enables discernment, deep understanding and decision-making. It is the seat of higher intelligence, guiding us toward truth and clarity. For example, a scientist making a breakthrough discovery or an artist creating a masterpiece relies on buddhi's ability to see beyond surface-level information.

- **Ahamkara (ego and sense of 'I'):** This is the layer that creates our individual identity by distinguishing 'me' from everything else. It forms self-perception based on our roles, experiences and attachments. Statements like 'I am a leader' or 'I am an Indian citizen' stem from ahamkara. While necessary for self-definition, excessive attachment to ahamkara can lead to rigidity and bias.

- **Manas (sensory and reactive mind):** The most instinctive part of the mind, manas processes sensory information and generates immediate thoughts and emotions. It governs daily reactions and habitual behaviours, shaping our unique perspectives. For example, when someone instinctively prefers a particular kind of music or food, that preference arises from manas.

In fact, this concept is the basis for both modern psychology as well as Zen traditions (Buddhism), distinguishing between the small mind—the thinking, intellectual mind—and the big mind, which represents the awareness that observes and knows thinking. It also aligns with the idea of 'flow' discussed by Mihaly Csikszentmihalyi in his book *Flow: The Psychology of Optimal Experience*. Flow is a state of peak performance and deep satisfaction, when one becomes fully

AI layers have a striking resemblance to the levels of Self in Indian wisdom

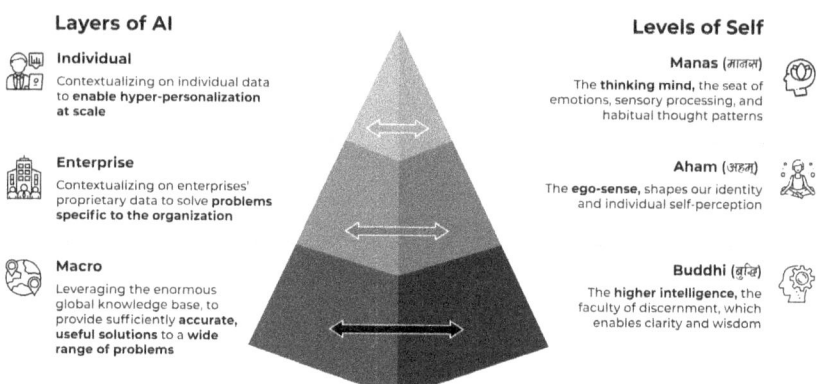

Layers of AI	Levels of Self
Individual — Contextualizing on individual data to **enable hyper-personalization at scale**	**Manas** (मानस) — The **thinking mind**, the seat of emotions, sensory processing, and habitual thought patterns
Enterprise — Contextualizing on enterprises' proprietary data to solve **problems specific to the organization**	**Aham** (अहम्) — The **ego-sense**, shapes our identity and individual self-perception
Macro — Leveraging the enormous global knowledge base, to provide sufficiently **accurate, useful solutions** to a **wide range of problems**	**Buddhi** (बुद्धि) — The **higher intelligence**, the faculty of discernment, which enables clarity and wisdom

absorbed in activities—you are 'in the zone'. In this state, people lose track of time, feel deeply engaged and perform at their best. It naturally encourages moving beyond narrow, ego-driven thoughts and the small mind, to achieve a broader perspective and richer experience.

Unfortunately, most of us operate from the narrow scope of manas—the small mind, highly centred on ourselves. However, true wisdom lies in the ability to connect these three layers, unleashing the power of the big mind. Therefore, the stronger the connection between the three, the more connected and centred an individual becomes. This integration unlocks higher levels of intuition, clarity and self-awareness, enabling individuals to navigate life with wisdom, purpose and balance.

Now, if you look at the construct of AI, you would see that it also operates at three levels—macro, enterprise and individual level. At each level, different types of data and technology are leveraged to deliver distinct value.[4]

At the **macro level**, the 'wisdom of the world' has been made available to everyone with Gen AI. Foundational models like ChatGPT or Gemini (formerly Bard), utilize massive internet-based datasets to create foundational frameworks for solving complex problems. By leveraging the collective wisdom of crowds, these models provide quick and sufficiently accurate solutions, often bringing us up to a 40–60 per cent accurate solution to almost any problem, whether it is an organization- or an individual-level problem. Even if this output is not fully usable as a solution, it can be invaluable for problem identification or narrowing down complex problems. These foundational models are democratizing access to global knowledge, breaking down barriers for organizations and individuals who previously lacked data or technological expertise. The macro layer is similar to the higher intelligence (buddhi)—a shared knowledge pool driving large-scale creativity and efficiency.

AI is powered by Data, and both are operating at three different levels; truly disruptive possibilities emerge as these levels connect

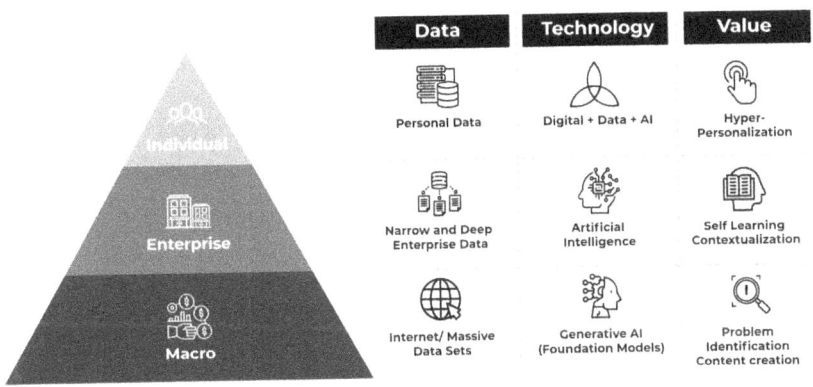

The **enterprise layer** helps provide tailored intelligence to fit specific needs. Since every organization is unique, generic solutions from foundational models can only be a starting point. AI combines the foundational models with proprietary organizational data that enables organizations to deliver tailored solutions to problems specific to their business. This critical layer allows businesses to move beyond conceptual ideas to develop and implement actionable solutions that address unique challenges specific to their operations. It is like the ahamkara that contextualizes universal intelligence (buddhi) into more accurate and therefore usable insights at the enterprise level.

Finally at the **individual layer**, AI leverages deeply personal data to deliver tailored solutions for every individual. From generating personalized marketing campaigns to crafting healthcare or financial plans, AI contextualizes its outputs to meet specific individual needs. The widespread proliferation of digital technologies has led to an explosive growth of data, which is leveraged by AI to deliver personalized customer experiences. In turn, these AI systems generate even more data, continuously feeding into and expanding the ever-growing datasphere. This interplay of data, digital and AI is enabling organizations and individuals to generate even more precise, impactful solutions, addressing highly specific problems across multiple domains. Akin to manas, this layer in AI takes global and organizational intelligence and refines it into hyper-personalized solutions, ensuring relevance and meaningful impact for everyone.

As AI becomes increasingly adept at connecting these three layers—macro, enterprise and individual—it is able to combine the big picture with enterprise goals and deliver hyper-personalized solutions at the individual level. This interconnected approach allows AI to enhance its impact by combining the strengths of each layer.

AI is becoming more human than humans

I am sure the natural question in your mind is that if AI's construct mirrors the construct of human consciousness, so what? How can it be better than us? It is because while AI is getting better at connecting the three layers, humans are losing that connection between the layers of self.

As I said, in today's world, most times we are operating from the manas level, the small mind. Why is it so? I have explored the reasons in detail in my previous books too. But essentially, it is because in today's hyperconnected digital world, we're overwhelmed by constant digital stimuli. Such always-on digital lives, fuelled by social media, constant notifications and endless connectivity, have made us increasingly detached from the tangible, real-world experiences and from ourselves too. While digital technology is designed to connect us to the wider world, it is ironically disconnecting us by limiting genuine interactions, narrowing our attention spans and restricting our thoughts and actions, making us increasingly ego-centric. For example, we rely more on X (formerly Twitter) or fifteen-minute book summary apps to build knowledge instead of reading books or having meaningful conversations. Instead of nature walks, treks or exercises, we are spending time lying on the couch flipping aimlessly through reels. And children today are increasingly drawn into the virtual world of gaming and videos, replacing outdoor play and activities that are crucial for developing physical, mental and social skills. Hence, instead of seeing and living the collective interconnectedness, we are becoming more and more individualistic and ego-driven. As a result, we struggle with many issues like cognitive biases, emotional distractions, stress, loneliness and much more. This shift away from real-world engagement is the root of mental health issues exploding across the globe.

In contrast, AI systems are designed in such a way that the information flow through the three layers can happen naturally. This design enables AI to not only achieve greater efficiency but also higher effectiveness and way superior outcomes, that too with continuous improvements. The innate ability to integrate layers is a core reason behind AI's remarkable success in recent times. Unlike humans, who need to consciously develop these skills over years through deliberate practice, reflection and self-awareness, AI systems integrate these layers effortlessly and are engineered to operate at peak integration from the moment they are deployed. This gives AI a decisive edge making it challenging for humans to compete directly.

The human quotient is at a critical crossroads

AI is challenging what is innately human. We are seeing a very important inversion: **Machines are growing and becoming more human, humans are becoming narrower and more machine-like.**

The relentless progression of AI highlights a profound truth—the creator has surpassed the creation and is now challenging the creator at the fundamental level. It is becoming increasingly clear that humans cannot outpace machines in the current game. To remain relevant, we must change the game—identify our next competitive advantage and rediscover the depths of human potential to define and leverage a new human edge. That is key to not just the growth but the survival of the human race.

4

AI Will Fundamentally Reshape Every Industry

Just as electricity transformed almost everything 100 years ago, today I actually have a hard time thinking of an industry that I don't think AI will transform in the next several years.
—*Andrew Ng, renowned scientist and technology entrepreneur*

So far, I have made the case that we as humans are standing at a pivotal juncture—an encounter with AI so profound that it demands reimagining every facet of our lives. AI's ability to mimic and even surpass human abilities is not merely transformative for individuals, it is revolutionary for industries as well.

Throughout history, any major technological revolution impacts everyday life and inevitably ripples through industries, transforming both and driving new opportunities. Consider the impact of electricity: before its advent, work was limited to daylight hours or the dim light of candles. The introduction of electricity transformed daily life by lighting homes and cities, allowing people to work, socialize and study after sunset, while also paving the way for new forms of communication and entertainment. This created massive opportunities by powering machines and driving mass production, revolutionizing industries such as manufacturing and entertainment and creating newer ones like consumer electronics and media.

I also discussed this in my previous book, *Mastering the Data Paradox*,[1] how the big data revolution has similarly disrupted industries. Digital technologies, driven by vast amounts of data, have already transformed every aspect of our daily lives, created massive opportunities and shaken the foundation of multiple industries. This revolution changed how we travel, entertain ourselves and manage our finances, leading to, for example, the rise of online cab aggregators, over-the-top (OTT) platforms such as Netflix and FinTech solutions—significant disruptions that redefined entire sectors.

Compared to these past shifts, the scale of the upcoming structural changes within industries in the AI age are on an entirely different level, truly unprecedented and undeniable. I'm convinced this new way of doing things will unlock massive opportunities for new businesses and fundamentally transform the old ones.

In this chapter, I'm excited to dive into the massive revolution AI is about to unleash across all industries, making their future totally different. First, I want to unpack the four key forces driving this transformation—I call them AI's big four: personalization, automation, innovation and new business models. After that, we'll look at the five major ways I think industries will structurally shift because of these forces.

1. The Great Compression: Disintermediation at Scale
2. Industry Convergence: The End of Siloed Sectors
3. The Rise of AI-Native Operating Models
4. From Static to Self-Optimizing Systems
5. Infrastructure-as-Intelligence: Platforms Become the Product

To really grasp the practical implications of all these shifts, we will look at concrete examples of the likely impact of AI on some key sectors. Then, I will share a practical playbook that can guide both enterprises and entrepreneurs to navigate this new AI era successfully. We conclude with thoughts on the impact of the AI-driven industry transformation—economic gains but also as a force for good.

AI's big four

In *Mastering Data Paradox*, I introduced the data-insights-actions-impact (DIAI) framework, which serves as a road map for enterprises to extract the full potential of their data and unlock maximum value. This framework focuses on three key areas where impact is created: reimagining customer experiences, transforming business operations and developing innovative business models. In the AI age, these three impact dimensions will remain relevant but will experience unprecedented change, driven by four transformative forces: personalization, automation, innovation and new business models.

Four transformative forces enabled by AI are reshaping industries and creating unprecedented opportunities

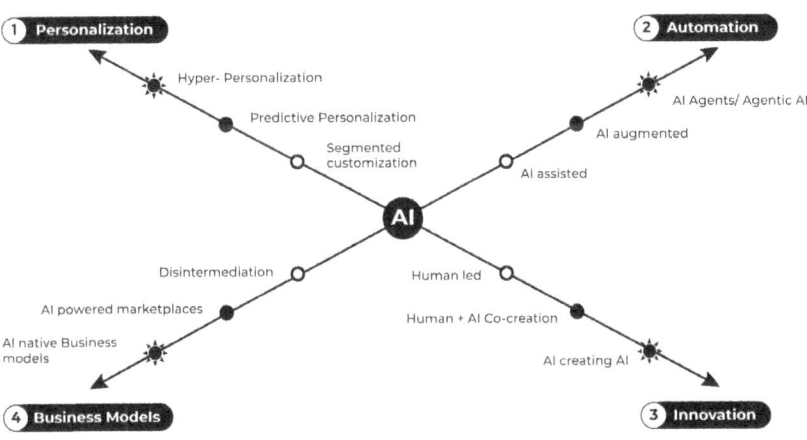

Let's now explore these transformative forces, how they are evolving and the impact they are likely to have.

I. Personalization: The era of the segment of one

Personalization has always been about making customers feel seen and understood. It began with **segmented customization**—grouping customers by shared traits. As digital data exploded, more advanced techniques like lookalike modelling emerged.

AI took this to the next level with **predictive personalization**, using behavioural and contextual data to tailor experiences at an individual level. These AI-driven insights didn't just improve engagement, they redefined what customers expect: relevance, immediacy and a sense of being uniquely understood.

We are now entering the era of **hyper-personalization**, propelled by Gen AI. This goes beyond predictive models by using real-time data and contextual cues—such as location, time and device—to deliver experiences that feel uniquely tailored. What began as a simple 'You might also like . . .' has evolved into intelligent systems that learn, adapt and anticipate our needs. Powered by AI's growing ability to understand emotion and context, personalization is no longer confined to recommendations, it's redefining customer engagement across industries.

This new normal is more than convenient. It's building truly individualized, one-to-one relationships at scale. And from this shift, new industry standards are quickly emerging.

The rise of individual-centric design

Personalization has moved beyond demographic buckets. Today, AI enables a '**segment of one**'—treating each individual as unique. It synthesizes signals from physical interactions, digital footprints, behaviour patterns and even emotions to build a real-time, evolving understanding of each person.

Consider Amazon's AI agents. These systems don't just recommend—they act. An agent might pre-order the next book in a series you're reading or fulfil a complex request like, *'I'm going camping—buy everything I need within this budget.'* This marks a fundamental shift: personalization as autonomous service, not just intelligent suggestion.

Real-time becomes the baseline

The new bar for personalization isn't relevance—it's real-time responsiveness. Static profiles are giving way to AI systems that react instantly to behavioural, contextual and even physiological data.

A striking example is MIT's NeuroChat, which uses real-time brainwave inputs to dynamically tailor learning content.[2] As focus shifts, the AI adjusts—creating a truly adaptive, personalized experience.

Intelligence and experience—fused

Modern products are designed to learn from every interaction. AI-powered systems evolve with each engagement, delivering outcomes that improve over time.

A powerful case is Twin Health, which builds digital replicas of patients using sensor, genomic and lifestyle data.[3] This 'health twin' continuously adapts and offers personalized recommendations—blending biological modelling with AI insight to deliver real-time, precision care. It's personalization at the intersection of biology, behaviour and machine intelligence.

From healthcare to retail, hyper-personalization is transforming how businesses connect with people—reshaping experiences around the individual, not the average. But this is just the beginning. One space I'm especially optimistic about is education. The potential to move beyond standardized lessons and classroom walls—to deliver truly personalized, adaptive learning—is immense. I'm betting big on hyper-personalization to finally break the mould and reimagine how we teach and learn.

II. Automation: From task automation to process autonomy

Every major tech revolution has advanced task automation—from machines to the internet to digital ecosystems. But AI takes us to a whole new level. We're moving beyond automating the repetitive tasks to automating reasoning and decision-making.

Early automation focused on **AI-assisted tools**—like spam filters—that helped but still needed human oversight. That gave way to **AI-augmented systems**, where machines collaborate with humans to analyse data and support decisions. We're still in this phase, but not for long.

We're now entering the era of fully autonomous systems. **AI agents** act as digital representatives, understanding context, making decisions and executing tasks end-to-end without human input. This marks a decisive shift from **assistance to autonomy**, enabling enterprises to automate not just tasks but entire processes.

But this shift is just the beginning. What's unfolding now is even more profound: the emergence of **agentic AI**—AI that is not merely executing instructions or managing predefined workflows but capable of dynamically setting its own sub-goals, adapting strategies and proactively navigating ambiguity. In other words, we're moving from 'AI that acts' to 'AI that acts *with initiative*'.

This evolution is poised to fundamentally reshape industries by driving unprecedented efficiency, enabling new levels of autonomy and fostering intelligent adaptability across operations. Two key themes are shaping this transformation.

Cognitive autonomy: AI that thinks

There is a seismic shift underway—from routine task execution to true **cognitive autonomy**.[4] Traditional automation streamlined repetitive work. Today's AI systems understand context, interpret ambiguity and make decisions—reshaping how knowledge work is done.

Nowhere is this more evident than in **software development**, where AI is no longer just speeding up coding—it's redefining what it means to build software. We're entering an era where autonomous agents can build, test and deploy applications from simple natural language prompts. Tools like Auto-GPT[5] and OpenDevin[6] are still evolving, but they already hint at a future where entire software systems can be generated on demand.

In the **tech services industry** where Incedo operates, I'm seeing this transformation up close. GitHub Copilot—used by over a million developers and dozens of Fortune 500 companies—is a clear signal of change. It's not just reducing friction in writing code, it's changing how developers think. Copilot has been shown to cut coding time by over 55 per cent,[7] and in traditional teams, we're seeing 20–30 per cent productivity gains. In AI-native teams that embed tools like Copilot into every layer of the workflow, early signs suggest leaps of 80 per cent or more.[8]

But this isn't just about speed or cost. It's a strategic inflection point. Cognitive automation is reshaping everything: delivery models, pricing structures, team roles and even how we define value. For tech services, adapting to this new reality is not just an opportunity, it's an imperative.

Agent-driven autonomy: AI that acts (and now, initiates)

While cognitive autonomy is about AI that thinks, **agent-driven autonomy** is about AI that acts. We've moved beyond tools that assist humans—into a world where AI systems function as **independent actors** within business processes.

We saw the early stages of this with robotic process automation (RPA)—bots that mimicked human clicks and keystrokes to execute repetitive tasks.[9] But they were rigid, rule-bound and required constant human oversight when anything deviated from the script.

AI agents are different. They're not just following instructions, they're making decisions. These agents understand context, adapt in real time and manage entire workflows from start to finish. In insurance, for example, an AI agent can interpret a claim, detect anomalies, determine whether to approve or escalate and initiate the next steps—all autonomously. Increasingly, these agents are beginning to display early signs of **agentic behaviour**—not only managing workflows, but also dynamically setting intermediate goals, improvising in unfamiliar situations and acting with initiative rather than simply following a script.

This is a step-change in enterprise automation. It's not just process optimization—it's **digital workforce transformation**. These agents are becoming true self-directed actors—learning, adapting and improving continuously over time.

III. Innovation: AI as creative partner

For centuries, it was entirely **human-led**—our creativity, our insight, our breakthroughs. Technology was simply a tool. Think steam engines, flights, the printing press. In the AI age, innovation is being reinvented.

We are in that new wave: **human + AI collaboration**. This is where we are today. AI accelerates discovery by analysing vast data sets, spotting patterns and generating insights—while humans guide the process, applying judgement and creativity to steer innovation.

Now, we're entering a third phase: **AI-led innovation**. AI is no longer just a collaborator, it's taking initiative. It can form hypotheses, run simulations, optimize its own architectures and even generate new AI systems. This shift isn't just technical—it's foundational. The frontier of innovation is no longer just human imagination. It's human oversight guiding machine-led breakthroughs.

AI is poised to massively reshape the very fabric of how industries approach and execute innovation. The following emerging themes are redefining the very nature of innovation.

Synthetic Data: The lab of the future

Innovation is no longer limited by the constraints of physical experimentation. With digital twins, simulations and AI-generated synthetic data, industries are building virtual labs—dramatically accelerating discovery while slashing time and cost.

A fascinating glimpse of this future came in 2024, when Sakana AI, an AI startup, introduced a research agent that could autonomously run experiments, analyse results and even author research papers—effectively performing the work of a junior researcher.[10] This signals a coming era where AI won't just assist, but will act as a true scientific collaborator, carrying out the entire research process independently.

From Human-limited to machine-scaled R&D

AI is scaling R&D beyond human limits. High-throughput, automated research is now possible—driven by agents that can test thousands of hypotheses in parallel.

A striking example: MIT used deep learning to screen over 100 million compounds, discovering a novel antibiotic capable of defeating drug-resistant bacteria—something human researchers hadn't conceived.[11] This isn't just faster innovation, it's a fundamental expansion of what's possible.

From building AI to orchestrating it

As foundational models mature, innovation is shifting from building AI to strategically composing it. The focus is no longer on crafting every component from scratch, but on orchestrating modular, pre-trained systems that can be rapidly adapted to solve new problems.

Technologies like hypernetworks make this possible.[12] Acting like master designers, they generate optimized AI components in seconds based on prior knowledge—bypassing weeks of model training and experimentation. This unlocks a new level of agility, where innovation becomes composable, intelligent and exponentially faster.

These three forces—hyper-personalization, automation and AI-led innovation—are now converging to reshape the fourth force: business models. But it's not a one-way street—these new business models quickly gain a momentum of their own, becoming powerful engines of change across industries.

IV. Business models: Self-driving ecosystems

A business model defines how a company creates, delivers and captures value—what it offers, whom it serves, how it operates and how it earns.

In the digital age, **disintermediation**—cutting out the middleman—was a key innovation driver. Amazon redefined retail through online marketplaces. FinTechs disrupted banking by offering direct, digital-first experiences.

Then came **AI-powered marketplaces**. Uber, Airbnb and others matched supply and demand in real time, setting new benchmarks for convenience, transparency and scale.

Now, the AI age is ushering in a new wave of **AI native business models**—where intelligence is embedded into the very fabric of value creation. I see three major themes taking shape:

AI-augmented value propositions

AI is rapidly becoming embedded in the core of what companies offer, not just how they operate. It's no longer about marginal improvements—AI is transforming value propositions themselves.

Take Airbnb. It started by disintermediating the travel industry. Now, it's evolving into an AI-powered concierge—one that can plan your entire trip from a single prompt.[13]

As AI becomes native to the customer experience, expect services to be smarter, more intuitive and deeply personalized—turning traditional offerings into intelligent experiences.

AI-generated products and services

The second theme is the creation of entirely new products and revenue models enabled by AI. This isn't just about businesses—it's about individuals, creators and entrepreneurs stepping into the game.

The influencer economy provides a clear example of how AI personas are already transforming creator scalability. Consider CarynAI, an 'AI girlfriend' developed as a digital twin of a popular human influencer. This AI counterpart quickly earned over $71,000 in its first beta week alone—generating income 24/7 without the creator's active involvement.[14] This isn't a gimmick—it's a potent preview of a world where creators build scalable, autonomous extensions of themselves.

AI is not just enabling efficiency. It's redefining who can create value and how.

Agentic orchestration platforms

Perhaps the most transformative shift is the rise of agentic orchestration platforms—AI systems where agents autonomously manage tasks, negotiate and collaborate with each other, all orchestrated by a central AI platform.

Sounds like sci-fi? It's already happening. PartyPlease, an event planning company, lets users describe their needs via chat and AI agents handle the rest. They coordinate with venues and vendors, acting as digital representatives on both sides.[15] It's like having a team of smart, tireless assistants working behind the scenes.

This model is not just about automation, it involves intelligent coordination. These platforms are laying the groundwork for a future where services are not just delivered, they're autonomously designed, negotiated and fulfilled.

With these four fundamental forces as our backdrop, the stage is set for a dramatic reshaping of industries. Their influence will lead to structural shifts, essentially rewriting the standards and foundations of how these industries operate. To truly grasp the magnitude of this change, let's dive into these pivotal shifts in detail.

Five structural transformations in industries

We are not just witnessing industry disruption—we are witnessing **industry reinvention**. AI is ushering in a new business architecture, transforming how industries are structured, how value flows and how enterprises compete. In this section, I will outline five key industry-level structural shifts that represent this profound transformation, moving beyond surface-level disruption to examine the underlying foundational changes.

Several of these structural shifts have their origins in the digital age. Disintermediation, industry convergence and the emergence of digital natives (parallel to the emergence of AI-natives) were significant developments of that era. However, the rise of the AI age is poised to amplify these structural shifts to a scale and depth that is potentially difficult to fully appreciate at present. The ultimate restructuring of industries will be substantial, far surpassing the initial transformative effects of digital technologies.

1. *The great compression: Disintermediation at scale*

For decades, businesses have operated through layers—manufacturers, distributors, retailers and service providers—all playing specific roles in a value chain. But AI is now enabling direct value exchange between creators and consumers, compressing these layers.

Five structural shifts across industries driven by AI

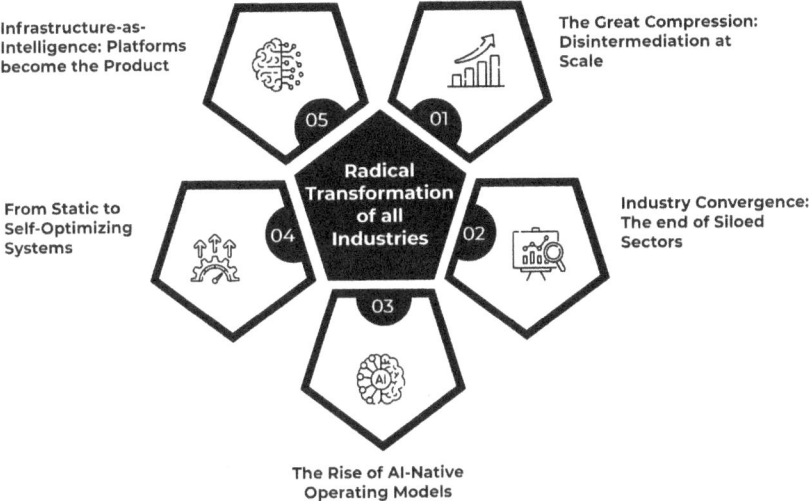

For instance, in retail, direct-to-consumer brands powered by AI-driven logistics and personalization are bypassing traditional retail channels.[16] In finance, robo-advisers and AI-based lending platforms are replacing human brokers, underwriters and analysts.[17] In education, AI tutors are connecting learners directly to content, guidance and feedback without the need for traditional classroom infrastructure.[18]

What makes this compression even more powerful is the democratization of hyper-personalization. Once the domain of large corporations with vast data and engineering resources, advanced AI models now empower even small businesses and individual creators to deliver tailored experiences at scale.

This 'great compression' is not just about cost efficiency. It changes who controls the customer relationship, who owns the data and who captures value. In a compressed world, the centre of gravity shifts to those who combine intelligence and intimacy with the customer.

2. Industry convergence: The end of siloed sectors

One of the most fascinating outcomes of AI is the increased blurring of boundaries between sectors. Traditional industry classifications—retail, media, automotive, healthcare—are changing and fast becoming increasingly intertwined.

Consider Tesla—a compelling example of cross-industry convergence. Yes, it is a car company, but it is also a robotics lab, an energy company and a software platform. Then there is Amazon, simultaneously a retailer, a logistics powerhouse, a cloud infrastructure provider and a major player in media. And Google? It is moving from search and ads to autonomous driving and health diagnostics. Beyond this intermingling of sectors at the company level, we also observe convergence at industry level.

For example, within financial services, you see this happening everywhere. From your everyday bank to specialized wealth management firms, many are trying to become a 'financial supermarket'. Thanks to AI, they now have the ability to offer a wide range of services tailored to your specific needs, all in one place. So, instead of needing separate providers for different financial needs, you might find a single company offering everything.

AI enables this convergence because it is domain-agnostic—the same capabilities that power personalized retail can also transform patient care or financial planning. As AI becomes a common foundation, companies are no longer confined by their origin identities. Instead, they become modular, fluid ecosystems, which are capable of reconfiguring themselves in response to new opportunities.

In the AI age, the traditional value chain and industry definitions are blurring. Thus, the competition isn't primarily within industries, it's between those who can move horizontally, orchestrate ecosystems and integrate across boundaries.

3. The rise of AI-native operating models

There's a fundamental difference between companies that use AI and those that are built on AI.

Legacy firms often approach AI as a feature—something to enhance a product or improve a process. But AI-native companies treat it as the foundation of their entire operating model. In these organizations, decision-making isn't just informed by data, it's driven by algorithms at its core. Product development is a continuous loop of live data feedback and automated iteration. Human roles are strategically defined around uniquely human capabilities like judgement, creativity and strategic oversight, with routine tasks and complex analysis inherently delegated to AI systems.

This shift is as profound as the transition from analogue to digital. We witnessed this very dynamic unfold in the digital age, where digital natives like Amazon or Netflix gained a significant advantage by harnessing **big data**.[19] These companies *weaponized* their data mastery, understanding and serving customers with a speed and precision that older companies couldn't match. AI represents a similar, but amplified, transformation. The AI-native firms are faster, leaner and more adaptive. They don't just compete on cost or quality—they compete on learning speed. And this shift is already underway. As Stripe CEO Patrick Collison noted, AI-native businesses are already being founded at scale and are growing faster than even the most successful early SaaS companies.[20]

The implication for incumbents is clear: bolting AI on to old structures won't be enough. Success in the AI age requires rethinking how the business learns, decides and evolves at its core.

4. From static to self-optimizing systems

The next significant shift I observe is the evolution from static, pre-defined business systems to dynamic, self-optimizing ones. For companies built with AI at their core, these self-optimizing systems are what make them truly powerful, allowing them to operate and adapt instantly, which gives them the ultimate competitive edge.

Historically, businesses were built for stability. Planning cycles were annual, supply chains were static and systems were designed to execute known processes efficiently. But in an AI-driven world, the goal is no longer efficiency—it is responsiveness.

With AI, we move from static systems to self-optimizing systems:

- Supply chains that adapt to real-time demand and risk signals.[21]
- Pricing models that adjust based on behaviour, context and intent.[22]
- Fraud detection systems that learn and evolve with every transaction.[23]

These systems are not just automated, they are autonomous and adaptive. They sense the environment, predict outcomes and take action—without human initiation.

In this transformation, the operating model begins to mimic a living organism—constantly learning, sensing and rebalancing. This is the new backbone of industry resilience.

5. *Infrastructure-as-intelligence: Platforms become the product*

The fifth structural transformation is the emergence of infrastructure-as-intelligence—where the true power in many industries is shifting from the companies who deliver the final product to those who build and control the intelligent infrastructure that enables it.

In the digital age, value was concentrated at the application layer—where customer experience was delivered and user data was captured. Infrastructure was seen as a utility: necessary but replaceable. But in the AI age, this equation is being flipped. The infrastructure itself is becoming the product.

I discussed this evolution in *Mastering the Data Paradox*, where data scientists—focused on customer-facing insights—were often valued more than data engineers who built and maintained the backend systems. But as AI systems demand real-time, high-quality, context-aware data pipelines, the backend is no longer in the background. **Infrastructure is strategy.**

Look at Nvidia. Once known simply as a GPU manufacturer, it now powers the computational backbone of the AI economy through its CUDA platform—enabling model training, real-time simulation and high-performance inference across sectors.[24] Nvidia isn't just supplying chips, it's shaping the trajectory of AI-native innovation.

This shift reflects a broader trend: the convergence of infrastructure and application into unified, intelligent platforms. Platforms that don't just support business, they define what's possible. Consider:

- Stripe, which isn't just a payment processor, it's the programmable financial plumbing of the global internet economy.[25]
- Shopify, which isn't just an e-commerce tool, it's an AI-powered business backbone for millions of entrepreneurs.[26]
- Snowflake[27] and Databricks[28], which have moved beyond data storage into AI-native platforms offering real-time ML model deployment and governance.
- OpenAI and Anthropic, whose foundational models are rapidly becoming platforms on which thousands of applications are being built.[29]

What these players have in common is not just infrastructure—but infrastructure infused with intelligence: APIs that learn, platforms that adapt and ecosystems that scale exponentially with developer and enterprise adoption. As these platforms embed AI into their core, they transition from being enablers of capabilities to providing unique, AI-driven offerings that becomes their key competitive advantage. The result? A new industrial hierarchy where those who control AI-powered infrastructure don't just support industries, they shape them.

A new industrial blueprint

Having navigated these five pivotal shifts, a clear picture begins to emerge. Together, they paint a radically different blueprint for the industrial landscape of the future, one defined by:

- Flatter (disintermediated)
- Boundary-less (cross-sector)
- Adaptive (self-optimizing)
- Platform-driven (infrastructure-centric)
- AI-native (intelligence at the core)

And they're not in the distant future, they are already here, evolving in real time. For enterprises, the choice is existential: either rebuild your business model and industry role within this new blueprint or risk being reshaped by someone who does.

So far, I've covered the underlying transformative forces, the core structural changes and the emerging blueprint for AI-powered industries. Now, to make this more tangible and relatable, I'll share some examples from across different industries.

Sector spotlights: How AI will reshape industries over time

It is obvious now that AI is impacting every industry, but not all at the same time or speed. The maturity of digital infrastructure, the availability of quality data, the regulatory environment and the complexity of customer interaction all play a role in determining how fast AI-led disruption will unfold.

In *Winning in the Digital Age*, I introduced a simple yet powerful model: the **industry transformation maturity curve**. This curve can now be extended into the AI age to predict how industries will evolve across three broad phases:

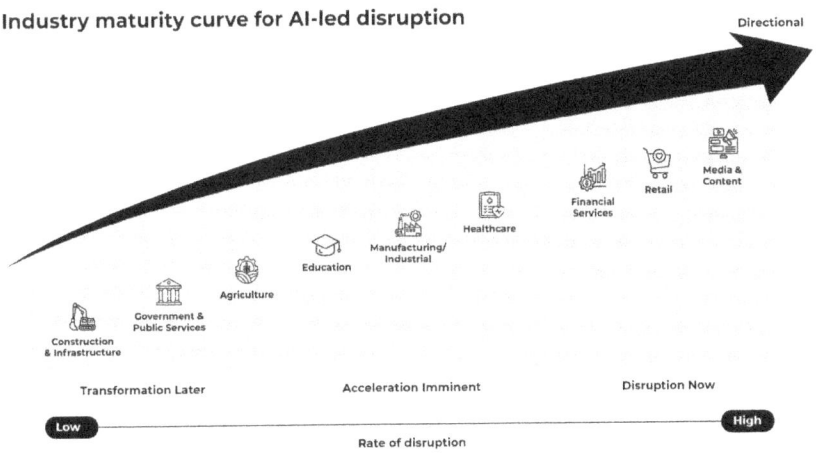

Industry maturity curve for AI-led disruption

Phase 1: Disruption now

These industries have mature digital foundations, ample structured data and a low barrier to integrating AI at scale. They are already experiencing massive disruption.

1. Retail and consumer

- AI themes: Personalization engines, dynamic pricing,[30] AI chat agents, demand forecasting and virtual try-ons.
- Status: Leading players are using AI to drive conversion, optimize inventory and even design products.
- What's next: Fully AI-personalized customer journeys, immersive retail experiences via digital twins and smart shelves in physical stores.

- Why now: In my view, retail is the opening batsman in the digital and data-led disruption. People took to online shopping early and embraced digital tools. That widespread adoption created this incredibly fertile ground for AI, just brimming with behavioural data. The intense competition inherent in retail means that the edge AI gives you in attracting and keeping customers isn't just nice to have, it's the whole ballgame now.

2. Media and content

- AI themes: Generative content (text, image, video), recommendation engines, voice synthesis, dubbing and localization.
- Status: AI is transforming everything from scriptwriting to audience analytics.
- What's next: Personalized storytelling, AI influencers[31] and autonomous content pipelines.[32]
- Why now: Similar to retail, the media and content industry has also been at the forefront of digital and data-driven transformation. So, the fact that AI is now taking hold feels like a natural progression. The audience's early shift to digital consumption created a perfect environment for AI to take root. Now, with AI tools becoming integral to creative workflows and a new wave of AI-native creators emerging, the stage is set for rapid transformation.

3. Financial services

- AI themes: Fraud detection, robo-advisory,[33] underwriting, algorithmic trading and customer support bots.
- Status: Many financial institutions have moved beyond pilots, embedding AI in risk modelling and operations. Gen AI is now enabling personalized advisory and customer journeys.

- What's next: Expect autonomous banking, real-time credit risk monitoring, fully AI-managed portfolios and the evolution of decentralized finance.
- Why now: I believe financial services stand at a pivotal point for AI transformation, driven by available data, clear business cases and adapting regulations. Despite challenges in navigating regulatory complexities, the sector's digital maturity and defined AI uses—such as fraud detection and robo-advisory—make it an early, active adopter.

However, this is just the beginning. I anticipate that the true paradigm shift for financial services will materialize through the convergence of technologies, notably blockchain and artificial intelligence. This synergy can unlock decentralized finance[34] (DeFi), creating more transparent, secure and automated systems. Financial Services is likely to go through multiple stages of transformation, each more fundamental and transformative than the previous one.

Phase 2: Acceleration imminent

These industries are data-rich but often complex and regulated. They are entering rapid AI integration now, and the next three to five years will bring transformational shifts.

4. Healthcare

- AI themes: Predictive diagnostics, AI radiology, clinical decision support, patient triage and drug discovery.[35]
- Status: AI is outperforming humans in select diagnostic tasks and enhancing provider efficiency.
- What's next: Personalized medicine, AI nurse assistants,[36] early disease prevention and robotic surgery.
- Why imminent: The coming AI wave in healthcare is incredibly promising driven by vast patient data, regulatory shifts and

the potential for truly game-changing improvements. What truly excites me is AI's potential to finally serve underserved populations, breaking down access barriers. The groundbreaking possibilities—earlier diagnoses, better treatments and prevention. All this creates irresistible momentum. However, the only thing that keeps this excitement grounded in reality is the profound realization that we are dealing with human lives, a responsibility we must never take lightly.

5. Manufacturing and industrial

- AI themes: Predictive maintenance, generative design, process optimization, quality assurance via computer vision.
- Status: Large manufacturers are adopting AI at the edge and in supply chain orchestration.
- What's next: Self-optimizing plants, AI-designed components and AI-led procurement.[37]
- Why imminent: Manufacturing and industrials are finally ripe for AI. Despite a slower start in digital and data adoption, the powerful combination of industrial IoT and local 'edge' computing—processing data near its source, for faster and more efficient delivery, is now ready to drive AI directly on the factory floor, delivering clear returns on investment (ROI). The ease of AI simulation and deployment via digital twins further accelerates this. A particularly interesting and potentially disruptive implication is the move towards human-less factories, which could fundamentally challenge the traditional cost advantages held by developing nations—an unfolding scenario with potentially profound geo-political consequences.

6. Education

- AI themes: Personalized learning paths, adaptive assessments, AI tutors, learning and analytics.

- Status: Edtech platforms are experimenting with AI tutors and curriculum generation.[38]
- What's next: Truly individualized education, lifelong learning assistants and AI-graded credentials.
- Why imminent: The massive potential of AI in education, combined with the urgent need for skills development, makes rapid adoption likely now. And as I've mentioned earlier, this is precisely where hyper-personalization—especially when paired with immersive technologies like VR and AR—can be a true game changer, creating deeply engaging and tailored learning experiences.

Phase 3: Transformation later

These industries are complex, asset-heavy or highly regulated. Transformation is inevitable—but will take longer due to legacy systems and structural inertia. However, we should acknowledge that the pace of innovation can be unpredictable. We may see surprising breakthroughs in certain industries, which could significantly accelerate the expected timeframes.

7. Agriculture

- AI themes: Crop yield forecasting, soil analytics, pest detection and AI-driven irrigation.[39]
- Status: Emerging use of AI in precision agriculture and drone surveillance.[40]
- What's next: Fully autonomous farms, AI crop advisers and climate-adaptive planting cycles.[41]
- Why later: I think that while infrastructure hurdles and low-tech prevalence present challenges, the increasing real-world AI applications, especially the potential for rapid uptake in developing countries like India, could result in a surprisingly faster transformation than expected.

8. Government and public services

- AI themes: Smart governance, citizen service chatbots,[42] traffic optimization and fraud analytics.
- Status: Early pilots in digital governance, public safety and citizen grievance redressal.
- What's next: AI policy assistants, autonomous urban infrastructure and real-time resource allocation.
- Why later: Several factors contribute to a potentially longer transformation timeline—navigating policy and ethical considerations, the need to integrate with existing legacy IT infrastructure and working with complex procurement processes. Learning from nations like Estonia, a leader in digital governance[43] and observing the dramatic strides of technology adoption in China's government services[44] can provide valuable strategies for moving forward.

9. Construction and infrastructure

- AI themes: Site analytics via drones, material usage optimization and safety monitoring.
- Status: Select use of AI in planning and risk mitigation.
- What's next: Autonomous construction equipment and AI-powered project orchestration.[45]
- Why later: Held back by a fragmented value chain, manual workflows and high capital intensity for too long, construction and infrastructure is now seeing a compelling 'AI moment'. The increasing availability of visual data from drones and the critical need for optimization are driving adoption, building on initial AI successes in planning and risk mitigation.

The AI wave will not move in a straight line—but **no industry will be untouched**. The question is not *if* AI will reshape your industry, but *when*—and whether you'll be ready to lead that transformation.

The strategic playbook for enterprises and entrepreneurs

In the AI age, there are no sidelines. Every organization and every individual is being called to adapt, reinvent and reimagine how they operate. Whether you're a Fortune 500 enterprise or a first-time founder, the playbook is changing.

In this section, I offer two strategic lenses:

- **For enterprises**: How to evolve your business for an AI-native future.
- **For entrepreneurs**: Why this is the most fertile moment in human history for builders and how to seize it.

A. For enterprises: Evolve or be reshaped

AI's impact goes far beyond efficiency gains. It is a redefinition tool. Enterprises must move beyond isolated use cases and limited pilots. The real opportunity lies in rethinking how customers can be engaged, how decisions are made, how value is created and the very nature of how work gets done.

Here are five imperatives for large organizations in the AI age:

1. Reimagine the operating model

What I see defining AI-native firms is that they're built for constant evolution with continuous learning loops. They wisely keep humans in the loop for key decisions. And they move fast and adapt with a modular, agile approach. But the real key to unlocking the AI-native state is this: we've got to ditch the old 'improve the process' thinking and ask ourselves the real questions:

'Which decisions can we automate? What intelligence can be built directly in?'

2. Invest in data as a strategic asset

Having explored this in depth in *Mastering the Data Paradox*, I feel it's crucial to reiterate: data is the essential fuel powering our digital world and now the transformative AI age. It has fundamentally reshaped every facet of our lives. The truth is, AI can only be as brilliant as the data it learns from. Therefore, we must treat enterprise data as the invaluable treasure it is. For enterprises to truly unlock AI's power, eliminate data silos to create unified sources, build real-time, event-driven architectures and fundamentally value data as core infrastructure, not just a by-product.

3. Build a hybrid talent model

As we navigate the AI age, it is evident that it's no longer an either AI or human scenario. You need both: AI that gets smarter and people who get more human. To achieve this powerful synergy, organizations must actively combine the skills of technologists, designers, domain experts and ethicists. The focus should be on cultivating and leveraging those uniquely human capabilities— judgement, ethics, storytelling and leadership—alongside the growing intelligence of AI.

4. Shift from hierarchies to learning networks

We have to stand down the hierarchies and build learning networks. Those old top-down structures simply can't keep up any more. We need to flatten the lines of decision-making, truly empower those cross-functional teams to take ownership and build a workplace where asking 'what if?' and trying new things is not just allowed, it's encouraged—a real culture of curiosity and experimentation.

5. Lead with purpose, not fear

The truth is people don't resist technology, they resist the fear of becoming irrelevant. Therefore, we must anchor this entire transformation in the idea of human advancement, not just cost savings. This means ensuring our AI strategy drives meaningful business results and contributes to positive societal impact—that's true leadership.

B. For entrepreneurs: The age of the 10x individual

If AI reshapes how industries operate, its most profound impact may be on who gets to participate in value creation. We are entering a new era—**the age of the entrepreneur**, where AI is poised to dramatically lower the barriers to starting, scaling and achieving business success.

Entrepreneurship unleashed: The democratization of scale

It's truly fascinating how AI acts as the great equalizer, directly empowering individuals and small teams with access to world-class design, development, marketing, capital and even legal capabilities that were once the exclusive domain of large corporations. This power further extends to the ability to build, test and iterate at lightning speed, and crucially, to achieve distribution at a global scale without sprawling global infrastructure.

Solopreneurs and micro-teams can now challenge industry giants

The power dynamic is fundamentally changing: a twenty-two-year-old with curiosity, courage and ChatGPT can create more value than a 200-person legacy team. This isn't theoretical. We are already seeing indie (independent) developers launch micro-SaaS tools[46] with minimal human coding effort thanks to AI assistants; artists create groundbreaking films, music and games with Gen AI and even school students like my son Pragun develop breakthrough innovations like IntelliReferee. Entrepreneurship in the AI age is not just about founding a company, it's about a **way of thinking**:

- Spot friction
- Mobilize tools
- Move fast
- Stay curious

From job seekers to opportunity creators

For decades, success meant joining a prestigious company. But in the AI age, it may mean creating the next one. Or launching a movement. Or solving a pressing challenge in your community with AI. This is a new world where:

- Creators can become founders
- Developers can become investors
- Students can become solution-makers

You don't have to wait for permission. You just have to start.

The road ahead—Reimagining industries, reclaiming the human edge

Every major technological revolution in history has rewritten the rules of business and redefined who gets to win. The AI age is no different. But what sets it apart is the sheer speed, scale and scope of its impact. We are not just improving processes or optimizing performance, we are witnessing the birth of a new economic engine.

Speaking of the new economic engine, the value creation potential in the AI age is nothing short of mind-blowing. The consensus among top researchers and analysts on AI's potential is overwhelmingly ambitious: Goldman Sachs predicts a 7 per cent increase in global GDP over the next decade from generative AI alone.[47] McKinsey sees an even broader economic impact, with AI potentially adding between $17.1–$25.6 trillion annually by 2040.[48] IDC forecasts that AI integration in business operations could generate a cumulative economic impact of $19.9 trillion by 2030.[49] Accenture's analysis also predicts a promising future, indicating that adopting generative AI responsibly and at scale could unlock over $17.9 trillion in economic value by 2038.[50]

These are not just economic forecasts, they are calls to action. Because behind every dollar of value created will be a builder, a leader or an entrepreneur who saw the opportunity and seized it.

This is why I believe that the AI age will be synonymous with the age of entrepreneurs. Just as the digital age gave rise to disruptors like Amazon, Uber and Netflix, the AI age—with its unmatched combinatorial power—is poised to give birth to an even broader set of changemakers: visionaries who won't just improve existing industries but invent entirely new ones; creators who use AI not just to build businesses, but to reimagine progress in education, health, sustainability and in writing the story of human potential.

There's a powerful duality at play in the AI age. Yes, big tech is leading the investment charge—but I believe the real breakthroughs will come from nimble entrepreneurs who are leveraging these tools with speed, creativity and boldness.

We are entering a once-in-a-generation window for value creation—a wide-open frontier. But it won't be smooth, this journey will be as unsettling as it is exhilarating. As new possibilities emerge, many existing norms will fall away. Roles will shift. Business models will collapse and be reborn. This isn't just about adapting to new tools, it's about adapting to a new world.

As I reflect on the transformative arc of **digital, data and now AI**—the trifecta I explored in *Mastering the Data Paradox*—one truth stands out: this is the most profound **democratization of technology** in human history. AI is no longer the preserve of a privileged few. These tools are becoming more powerful, more accessible and more distributed every day.

And that's where the real promise lies: **a moment where scale and inclusivity can coexist**. A student in Nairobi, a solopreneur in São Paulo or a startup in Bangalore now has access to the same capabilities as the world's largest institutions. The real promise of the AI age lies in broad-based empowerment.

If we get this right, AI won't just reshape industries, it will expand opportunity, amplify human potential and help us build a future that is not just more advanced but more equitable. The AI age doesn't have to be solely disruptive. It can be transformative and deeply inclusive. Let's make sure the AI revolution doesn't just reshape industries but also uplifts lives. This is our moment to adapt to the AI age and help define it.

5

All Jobs Will Change in the AI Age

If people trust artificial intelligence (AI) to drive a car, people will most likely trust AI to do your job.
—*Dave Waters,*
retired professor at University of Oxford

With every major technological advancement comes a mix of reactions from society—from wonderment to fear, from hope to despair. During the early nineteenth century, the invention of steam-powered trains, or the 'iron horses' as they were called, triggered extreme societal reactions. While many marvelled at the power, speed and utility of these machines, many others could not understand how these functioned and thus were gripped by irrational fears. Some feared that the human body could not withstand such speed, and that the passengers would suffocate to death or even suffer organ displacement if exposed to it! Besides physical fears, people also feared that trains could lead to moral degradation—from encouraging criminal activities by helping criminals flee faster, to breaking down the social hierarchies and moral standards as people from different walks of life interacted in ways they previously hadn't.

Similarly, the advent of industrial machinery during the Industrial Revolution sparked intense resistance, most notably from the Luddites—English textile workers who saw mechanized looms and spinning frames as direct threats to their livelihoods. Their fears of wage cuts, job losses and deteriorating working conditions reflected a broader anxiety about technological disruption. Later, innovations like the tractor in agriculture or even the arrival of electricity were met with a similar mix of excitement and apprehension—each transformative in its potential, yet unsettling in its immediate impact on established ways of life.

The AI age brings with it a heady mix of excitement and uncertainty. At this early stage, conversations about its impact on jobs and society are often clouded by confusion, fragmented understanding and polarizing views that swing between paranoia, denial and avoidance. As humans, we instinctively search for familiar patterns, looking to past technological revolutions for clues. It's tempting to believe AI will follow the same script—disrupt, displace and ultimately create more jobs. But this technological revolution is different.

AI isn't just another tool to boost productivity. Its ability to reason, create and learn blurs the line between human and machine intelligence in ways we've never encountered. This isn't merely about jobs lost or gained, it is a fundamental redefinition of work. History might not be a good indicator of the future in this incredible and unpredictable age. So, before we lean on simplistic narratives on jobs based on history, let's pause and revisit four key trends on jobs observed in past technology waves:

1. Technology creates opportunities to move up the value chain.
2. Technology causes job losses but ultimately creates more jobs than it destroys.
3. Technology disrupts existing industries while simultaneously birthing new ones.

4. Reskilling and upskilling is key to protecting the workforce.

Now let us examine how these trends might unfold in this truly unprecedented AI era.

Trend 1: Technology creates opportunities to move up the value chain

Throughout history, as technology has advanced, the skills that define the human edge have evolved too. And each wave of innovation has brought significant disruptions to the job market, often leading to widespread job losses and displacement. However, these displacements typically happened at the lower end of the value chain, like replacing manual labour with intellectual tasks, predominantly impacting blue-collar jobs. This displacement in blue-collar sectors was often accompanied by the growth of new opportunities in knowledge-based roles. These 'white-collar' or knowledge worker jobs, requiring skills in analysis, management, creativity and complex problem-solving, expanded to support, manage and further develop the new technologies and the industries they created.

However, the AI age is set to break this pattern. Unlike previous technological waves that primarily automated physical labour or repetitive cognitive tasks, AI possesses the capability to automate a wide range of tasks currently performed by knowledge workers. It is estimated that by 2040, eight out of ten jobs in knowledge and office work sectors could be lost to AI.[1] This is largely due to the ability of AI to perform complex intellectual tasks at unprecedented speed and accuracy, far outpacing human capabilities.

And with advanced natural language processing capabilities, AI can understand, interpret and generate complex texts and documents, enabling it to write reports, summarize information and provide effective customer service. Additionally, advancements in algorithms have significantly improved AI's ability to make accurate predictions and decisions. Even the knowledge worker roles, such as management consultants, investment bankers and surgeons, considered the safest amidst technological advancements, are also at risk now.

Since knowledge work that typically relies on existing infrastructure (such as computers, software and networks) is already digitized, AI is poised to displace knowledge work at a much faster rate than blue-collar work. The latter has gone through multiple waves of automation and the jobs that remain require high investments and are more challenging to automate at scale. This difference is vividly illustrated by projections you can see in the graph below. The impact of the AI age on the job market presents a stark contrast to previous technological shifts. Unlike earlier waves that primarily affected blue-collar or manual labour, AI age would have a significantly heavier initial impact on knowledge workers, with an estimated ratio of **ten knowledge-worker roles lost for every single non-knowledge-worker role eliminated by 2030.**[2]

While the increasing efficiency and affordability of AI driven robots will eventually lead to more prominent job displacement

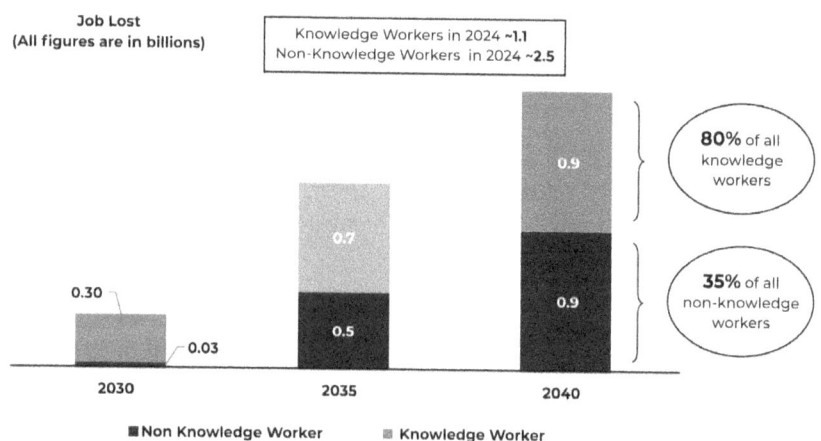

In the coming years, more knowledge workers will likely lose their jobs than non-knowledge workers

in non-knowledge workers as well, the overall burden will remain considerably higher for knowledge workers. This trend culminates in a potentially devastating scenario **by 2040, where a staggering 80 per cent disappearance of knowledge worker jobs is expected**[3], compared to a still substantial but lower 35 per cent decline in non-knowledge roles. This isn't the familiar story of technological progress elevating humans up the value chain. Instead, we are now staring at the possible wiping out of the very jobs once considered the pinnacle of the value chain, including high-end lawyers, portfolio managers and maybe even some aspects of a CEO's role.

Trend 2: Technology ultimately creates more jobs than it destroys

The historical narrative of technological disruption typically has a silver lining: the creation of new jobs comparable to or greater than those eliminated. Take the internet era, for example. While it led to about 3.5 million job losses in the US since 1980, it also created roughly 15.8 million new jobs.[4] This pattern of disruption followed by growth has been typical.

However, it will not necessarily hold true for the AI age. Because AI is not just taking over simple, routine tasks or physical jobs, it is also starting to take over many cognitive and creative roles. This means that the scale and speed of disruption could far outpace the creation of new job opportunities. Thus, the redundancy might far exceed what most of us anticipate.

Let's see how and why.

The waves of change redefining the job landscape[5]

The net impact of AI on jobs will be relatively slow to begin with but it will pick up pace and in the next ten to fifteen years the job landscape will transform dramatically. Numerous researchers have published estimates on how many jobs will be affected, including those likely to be lost. While the specific numbers vary, one consistent theme emerges: the impact of AI on employment will be profound.

I view this transformation as unfolding in three distinct waves: short term (2025–30); medium term (2030–35) and long term (2035–40). Here's a quick summary of key research estimates highlighting this progression:

Researchers predict a massive impact of AI on the jobs landscape

(All figures are in %)

	2025	2030	2035	2040
Jobs Impacted	Morgan Stanley: >40% by 2026; McKinsey & Company: 11-22%; 8th OECD: ~47% in the US, & ~27% globally; EY: ~66% in the US	WEF: ~40% in the emerging economies; WEF: ~60% in the advanced economies; accenture: ~44-46% work hours		CIO: ~92% globally by 2040
Consensus	~11-22%		~45-60%	~90-95%
Jobs Lost	WEF: ~2-3%; McKinsey & Company: ~30% work hours in the US; Reuters: ~5% in Latin America	WEF: ~2-3%; Goldman Sachs: ~15-35%; accenture: ~22% work hours		BBC: ~40%; McKinsey & Company: ~50%; JPMorgan: ~50%; pwc: ~30%
Consensus	~2-5%		~15-35%	~35-50%

Let us now dig deeper on each of these waves and how I see the job landscape being disrupted by AI during each phase.[6]

The short term (2025–2030): The dawn of AI disruption

It is estimated that major tech companies and corporations will continue to increase their investments in AI, reaching a staggering trillion dollars annually. However, most investments in AI are directed more towards laying the tech foundations for AI applications in the coming years rather than achieving immediate ROI. So, in the short run, the investments by enterprises on AI will significantly exceed the cost savings or efficiencies gained.

In the short run, job losses will most likely be limited. Instead, AI will primarily complement human capabilities. Many human + AI roles and entirely new job categories may emerge. The job losses will likely be partially offset by the creation of new AI-centric roles that include a significant demand for AI system development and integration specialists, machine learning engineers and a growing need for AI trainers to fine-tune and manage AI systems. These new roles will focus on developing, implementing and maintaining AI systems, establishing a temporary equilibrium in the workforce.

AI will make significant strides in automating routine and repetitive white-collar tasks, gradually encroaching on intellectual roles as well. During this wave, around **11–22 per cent of all jobs**[7], **i.e. around 400–800 million, will be impacted by AI, of which 2–5 per cent**[8] **will be the net job loss** and the rest would transition to the human + AI hybrid model. Certain industries such as retail, telecom and healthcare, where routine and repetitive tasks, such as data entry and customer service, constitute a significant proportion of the work, are expected to experience higher impact. In addition, software development jobs across industries are expected to see a significant decline on the back of 20-50 per cent productivity improvement driven by AI advancements (I have discussed this in the previous chapter). This phase will be characterized by a focus on reskilling and upskilling of the workforce for the new AI oriented jobs that will emerge and many existing jobs that will get augmented by AI into human + AI hybrid jobs.

The medium term (2030–2035): The age of accelerated disruption

The next wave of disruption will be even more profound. As AI capabilities continue to mature and computing costs decline—with FLOPS per dollar historically doubling in every two–three years,[9] the cost of deploying AI systems to replace human labour is expected to drop sharply. This will accelerate the shift towards widespread automation across industries. This affordability is underscored by the significant and ongoing reduction in AI usage expenses; as per Open AI, the cost for a specific level of AI capability drops roughly tenfold each year.[10] On similar lines, Nvidia claims that their chips are going to become a million times more efficient at processing over the next decade.[11] Also, at some point during the medium run, the investments made in AI systems and infrastructure in the short run, will start fetching returns. It is estimated that, by 2030, every dollar invested in business-related AI solutions and services is projected to contribute $4.60 to the global economy through indirect and induced effects.[12]

So, in the medium run, we will see wider adoption of AI systems across multiple capabilities as it becomes increasingly economical for businesses to replace human workers with AI solutions. Job losses would rise significantly across industries and more human-only roles would become AI autonomous. By this stage, almost all repetitive and routine knowledge workers' jobs would have been automated. Some hybrid roles will also become fully automated. Moreover, AI will continue to penetrate deeper into roles that were previously considered medium-risk like nursing, surgery, software development and many others, leading to many more human-only roles getting transitioned towards human + AI roles across industries.

Furthermore, in this wave, even jobs requiring EQ, such as storywriters or psychologists, will face disruption as AI systems become more adept at mimicking human emotional responses and managing social interactions. It is estimated that **45–60 per cent of all jobs will be significantly impacted by AI**[13], **with around 15–35 per cent of these roles at high risk of being lost to AI.**[14]

The long term (2035–2040): The age of uncertainty

In the long run, self-sufficient AI systems and humanoid robots will dominate the labour force. Advances in AI and robotics will make them increasingly capable of handling complex, repetitive and physically demanding jobs at scale, reducing reliance on human labour. By now, deploying AI in place of human workers will become both cost-effective and more productive across industries. Some of the leading visionaries like Elon Musk have made bold claims stating that by 2040, the world will host approximately 10 billion humanoid robots.[15] Which would essentially mean deep integration of AI into the global labour force. A substantial proportion of human-only roles as well as hybrid roles will be lost to autonomous systems.

Almost all jobs (90–95 per cent) will be impacted[16] **and a staggering 35–50 per cent job loss is estimated in this wave.**[17] The jobs that remain will need to be reimagined owing to AI-driven automation.

The impact on jobs won't be instantaneous; instead, we should anticipate a transition where human roles become hybrid (human + AI) before ultimately being replaced by autonomous AI.

Human + AI shield could save us from some AI battles but not the ultimate war

The popular belief that most current jobs will simply evolve into human + AI collaboration roles might not hold true in the long run. While many human roles will indeed become human + AI hybrids in the short to medium term, in the long run many of these human + AI roles would eventually be taken over by AI as AI algorithms become more efficient.

For the next decade, human + AI hybrid roles will slowly keep picking up but the growth will hit a plateau and it will peak by 2040[18]; there will come an inflection point when the cost of deploying AI plummets as significant advancements happen in autonomous systems and robotics. That's when many hybrid roles will become autonomous, leading to a sharp decline in hybrid roles from their peak of 40 per cent in 2040[19] to 20 per cent by 2045. Autonomous

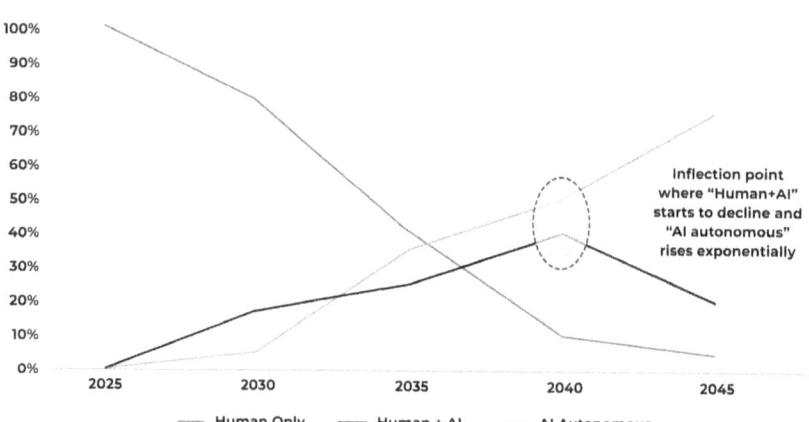

In the long run, Human+AI jobs will start becoming AI autonomous causing a massive decline in human roles

AI roles, on the other hand, are expected to surpass 75 per cent by 2045.[20]

So, the upward trajectory of human + AI hybrid roles will likely not sustain over the long term. Furthermore, many human-only roles will continue to be lost to autonomous systems too. Now, I believe that this situation could happen even earlier for knowledge workers. For non-knowledge workers, the trend might take more time to pan out due to the higher cost of AI systems but make no mistake, I strongly believe that this is going to be a secular trend across knowledge and non-knowledge roles.

Some might still argue that the AI specific roles to develop and support these AI tools would grow substantially in the future and compensate for the job loss. Let's dive into that thought and explore it more.

AI will create jobs—but the losses may define the era

The AI age will inevitably lead to the emergence of specialized roles centred around the creation and deployment of the technology itself. Think of the growing demand for AI architects who design and implement AI infrastructure, machine learning engineers who develop and deploy algorithms and AI ethicists who grapple with the societal implications. As per McKinsey projections, new 20-50 million AI roles will be created by 2030,[21] and extrapolating this growth points to roughly **100–200 million new AI-driven jobs by 2040**. The emergence of these specialized AI roles may also generate some indirect employment through a multiplier effect; the precise quantification of those roles would be very difficult at this stage. However, even in the most optimistic scenarios, the overall proportion of AI-related jobs is still expected to be limited, accounting for only 6 per cent of the total jobs currently (200 million of 3.63 billion jobs).

While these AI specific roles are vital and represent a new frontier of work, their sheer volume is unlikely to compare to the mass employment generated by previous technological waves as the creation of this technology is relatively efficient. Consider, for instance, the relatively lean workforces of leading AI companies like OpenAI (~3500 employees[22]) and DeepSeek (~200 employees[23]) compared to the vast number of employees in established tech giants like Microsoft (2,28,000 employees[24]), illustrating a fundamental difference in scale.

Furthermore, the commonly cited 'human + AI' collaboration, while representing a significant shift in how work is performed, should not be mistaken for net new job creation. Instead, it often signifies a transformation of existing roles, potentially leading to displacement as AI takes on more responsibilities.

Ultimately, the order of magnitude of job disruption anticipated in the AI age far surpasses previous technological shifts. While the emergence of new AI-centric roles is a footnote in this unfolding story, the headline is the sheer magnitude of job losses across industries. Bringing the data on job loss and job creation together, as the graph indicates, it could be a staggering **~45 per cent net jobs deficit, translating to a potential net loss of over 1.6 billion**

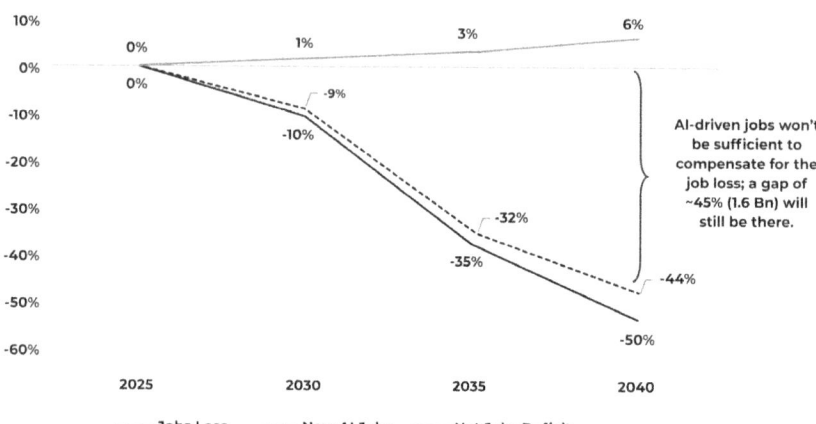

The new AI jobs won't be enough to offset the massive job loss

jobs globally.[25] This clearly isn't a story of progress with some adjustments, it's a potential crisis of immense proportions.

The sheer scale of this projected net job deficit necessitates a more profound and innovative set of solutions. This is especially crucial considering that the traditional pathway of 'moving up the value chain' offers limited respite given AI's severe impact on knowledge worker jobs.

Then, where does the opportunity lie?

Trend 3: Technology disrupts existing industries while simultaneously birthing new ones

I am sure by this point your minds are reeling with despair. But I assure you there is a bright side to this story. Because the AI age is truly an age of duality, where job losses and new opportunities would come hand in hand. So far, we've discussed the left side of the figure below, which highlights that a significant proportion of current jobs will be lost or transformed by AI. Now, let us turn our gaze to the other, far brighter side: the vast landscape of new possibilities the AI age is poised to unlock. The disruption of existing industries because of AI is the fertile ground from which entirely new ones will sprout.

While the AI Age is going to cause significant disruptions to the job landscape, it will also present massive entrepreneurial opportunities

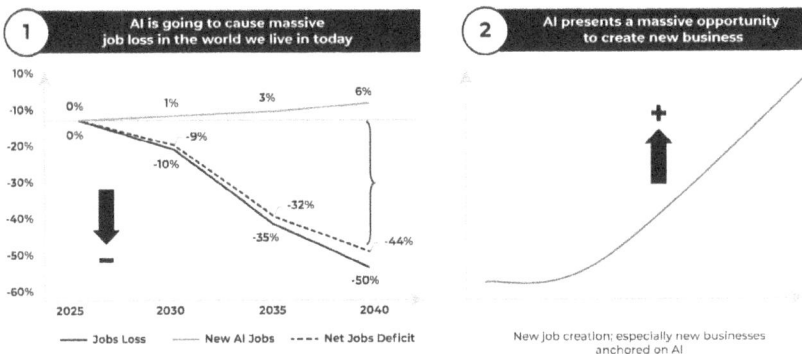

And I strongly believe that entrepreneurship is going to be the biggest opportunity for driving job growth in this AI age. Why do I say that? Let's look at the AI stack to understand this.

Job creation possibilities across the AI stack

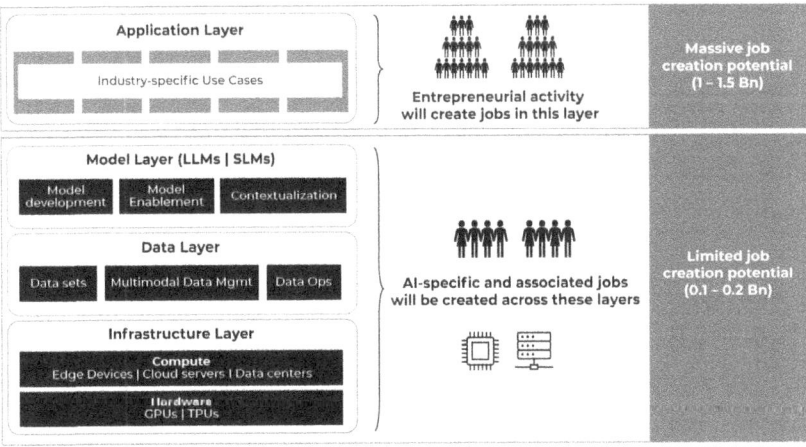

In the previous section I talked about how 100–200 million new AI-specific roles would get created by 2040. These roles would span across the infra, algorithm and data layers of the AI stack. While the development and implementation of AI technologies will undoubtedly generate critical new roles, they would have lower employment opportunity creation. For example, OpenAI and DeepSeek have created some of the most powerful and widely adopted LLMs with less than 4000 employees combined. Similarly, on the infra layer, firms like Nvidia, which holds more than 90 per cent of the high-end GPU market,[26] employs only around 36,000 people.[27] Even in the data layer, two of the largest data platform players, Snowflake and Databricks, have less than 20,000 employees combined, highlighting the relatively limited job creation within these core AI layers.[28]

The significant employment opportunity creation will predominantly occur at the application layer, the realm of entrepreneurs. And I firmly believe that the potential for job growth emanating from entrepreneurial opportunities in the application layer has the capacity to not only compensate for the anticipated job losses but, in some scenarios, exceed them. The sheer economic potential underscores this: IDC predicts a staggering $19.9 trillion global GDP impact from AI by 2030, with a lion's share—roughly $12 trillion—stemming directly from entirely new business opportunities.[29] This economic activity has the potential to roughly generate 350 million new direct jobs and upto 2-3 times indirect jobs, which would translate to a total of 1–1.5 billion jobs by 2040.[30] This implies that the **job creation potential driven by AI-powered entrepreneurship could be ten to fifteen times greater than that of AI-specific roles**. If we add these two job creation opportunities—1.5 billion and 0.2 billion—we could in an optimistic scenario look at 1.7 billion new jobs by 2040 which will more than outweigh the 1.6 billion job loss.

Let's now dig a bit deeper into this phenomenal potential for economic growth and new job creation from enterprenurial possibilities in the AI age. As I discussed in Chapter 4, AI is set to fundamentally transform every industry, and this will create thousands of problem statements and new business opportunities for entrepreneurs. Imagine the potential of AI powered hyper-personalization to create entirely new customer experiences or the efficiency unleashed by autonomous matching systems across various sectors. These are not mere evolutions, they are the foundations for entirely new industries and the jobs that come with them.

An illustration of this emerging entrepreneurial landscape is my son's startup IntelliReferee (that I talked about in Chapter 2), which is an entirely new business opportunity within the field of sports.[31] Although it would pose some risk to the jobs of squash referees in the long-term, many new opportunities would be created to build, integrate and implement this technology. Additionally, if the initiative increases the sport's popularity, increasing the number of players substantially, it will lead to many business opportunities that would create more jobs.

On similar lines, leveraging AI to solve long standing problems in industries, especially healthcare or education, will create new opportunities. Furthermore, with AI, opportunities to tackle global issues like climate change, terrorism or poverty would create new opportunities for entrepreneurs too, which in turn, will further drive job creation. These transformative shifts underscore that the AI age is not solely about disruption; it represents an unprecedented era for entrepreneurship, innovation and profound economic transformation, with applied innovation and new ventures acting as a primary engine for job creation. In fact, the job growth spurred by this burgeoning entrepreneurial activity is likely to be the most significant driver of employment in the AI age, far exceeding the impact seen in previous technological revolutions.

Now, a crucial question remains: before we get carried away by the promise of these new job opportunities, how do we not only protect the existing workforce from the immediate disruption but also proactively prepare them to transition, adapt and take up varied roles in the future?

Trend 4: Reskilling and upskilling is key to protect the workforce

As AI transforms the nature of work, reskilling and upskilling are no longer optional—they are critical to safeguarding the workforce. However, in the AI age, this imperative takes on a new shape. Let's investigate three situations.

First, let's consider existing work, most of which is likely to move to a human + AI hybrid model. While human + AI collaboration will require some level of technical adaptation, much of the reskilling will centre on learning to work effectively with AI tools, rather than mastering entirely new technical domains. Effectiveness will be driven by adding situational context to AI tools and platforms. In many scenarios, realizing supernormal gains—for example, going from 20 per cent to 60 per cent productivity gains in software development and customer service—will require a rethink and redesign of the end-to-end processes. Both the above situations call for deeper domain and customer understanding. Therefore, the imperative for skilling is not just technical competence but understanding the context, 'the why', of work more deeply so that you can redesign and not just execute on given tasks.

Second, let's look at the new specialized roles that AI will create—like AI architects, machine learning engineers and ethicists. There is an immense rush among college graduates to master these new skills and universities are scaling up specialist programs in response. However, these positions will be relatively few. The lean staffing models of leading AI firms underscores this reality. These new roles will not offset the broader displacement expected across traditional sectors.

Finally, the real opportunity—and challenge—lies elsewhere: in nurturing entrepreneurship. Unlike traditional reskilling, preparing people for entrepreneurship demands a broader set of capabilities, including innovation, risk-taking, market insight and business acumen. This calls for a deeper shift—away from narrow technical skills and towards the cultivation of uniquely human attributes.

As we prepare for the future of work, the emphasis must move beyond job-specific training to fostering adaptability, creativity, critical thinking and communication. These soft skills are not just complementary to AI, they are essential to harnessing its potential and driving meaningful innovation. The ability to unlearn and relearn will become the most valuable skill of all. I will explore this more deeply in Section II.

It's time to reimagine the human edge

While I was researching for this book, the likely long-term impact of AI on jobs emerged as one of the most significant and alarming insights—one that will need immediate and widespread debate and action. However, I have seen a surprising lack of awareness and sense of urgency on this critical topic. Even when I have tried to engage with senior policymakers, both in the United States and in India, I have typically seen reactions that vary from 'Don't worry, such concerns have been there in every wave of technology disruption but nothing really happened' or 'We should focus on reskilling and that will do the trick' or other similar statements that reflect a lack of deep understanding of the AI phenomena. As we have investigated in this chapter, history might not be a good predictor of the future in the AI age, at least as far as jobs are concerned. The long-term negative impact of AI on jobs will likely be so significant that it will need intense discussion and concerted actions from all of us—policymakers, business owners, academicians and individuals.

But I still believe there is hope. History has repeatedly shown that humans possess an extraordinary ability to adapt, innovate and rise to the occasion, whenever pushed. In the face of every disruptive change, from the industrial revolution to the digital age, humans have uncovered new strengths, evolved their skill sets and created entirely new opportunities. Although this time it's going to be much harder to find an edge, as the magnitude of change that lies ahead of us is much larger and more complex than ever before. I firmly believe this is not the end of human relevance but the beginning of a new and exciting chapter. The AI age brings immense opportunities to push our boundaries, offering us a unique chance to uncover new strengths and redefine what it means to thrive in this transformative era. **The AI age might signal the *end of the era of jobs* but it also heralds the *beginning of the era of entrepreneurs*.** It is both daunting and exciting.

6

The Human Advantage

The human being is a strange mixture of blind instinct, on one hand, and conscience, on the other.
—Fidel Castro, former Cuban President

With this chapter, I conclude the first section of the book, emphasizing how AI is truly redefining every aspect of our lives and businesses. I have discussed AI's staggering impact, highlighting how it has reached a critical point where it can mimic or even outperform in areas considered uniquely human so far. AI's explosive growth now puts it in direct competition with us, challenging the skills that have served us well for a long time. This shift will profoundly impact every job, with the reality that many jobs will be lost in the process. Simultaneously, I have explored how AI is revolutionizing industries and creating new opportunities for entrepreneurs.

Do you see where I am headed with this? The AI age is an era marked by stark duality, characterized by significant job losses and simultaneously abundant new opportunities. This shift is a monumental challenge to human civilization, and standing still is not an option. Doing nothing would mean we risk being unprepared and are left behind in a world dominated by AI. We must be proactive, bold, creative and willing to take risks. I believe we need to look back to move forward, returning to the instincts of early humans. You may be surprised by this call to action. Why reference early humans in a discussion about futuristic AI? Because the basic survival instincts that have served us well for ages are exactly what we need now. These instincts are not just historical footnotes; they are at the core of what has enabled us to make tremendous progress as a species over the course of history.

I believe that we have drifted from our basic instincts due to the comforts brought by the industrial and digital ages. However, the AI age is set to fundamentally change our world, making it essential that we rekindle our core instincts.

Our instincts have shaped human triumph for centuries

From the beginning, our core human instincts have played a crucial role in our survival and growth. These instincts are not just about fight or flight; they involve adapting to new environments and overcoming challenges like dramatic climate shifts and food scarcities.

We, the *homo sapiens*, were particularly good at adapting to changing conditions and events and innovating to prosper and grow. This was our survival superpower, which helped us outlast multiple other homo species that populated the earth over the years.

What sets us apart from other species?

Homo sapiens thrived where others couldn't, thanks to our remarkable ability to **adapt and innovate**. Over the centuries, humans have encountered a number of fundamental disruptions and challenges, including extreme climate variations and mastering the power of fire. During the last ice age, when the earth was at its coldest and driest, all human species faced immense challenges. While Denisovans and Neanderthals struggled to adjust, especially as the climate warmed, we found ways to survive and thrive. From tailoring clothing to crafting advanced tools, we turned obstacles into opportunities.

Fire is a powerful example of how we used our instincts to innovate and advance. Unlike Homo erectus and Neanderthals, who relied on fire for warmth and basic cooking, we found ways to use it for protection, settlement expansion and reshaping our environment. This ability to think creatively and solve problems gave us an undeniable advantage.

Our success as a species comes down to adaptability, innovation and ability to build strong social bonds. These instincts didn't just help us survive, they propelled us forward, while others, like the Neanderthals and Denisovans, fell behind.

A closer look at human instincts

What has helped us come out as winners from every adversity and innovate towards continued progress and prosperity are our core human instincts—**self-preservation, procreation and social connection**. Self-preservation was the foundation. It powered our adaptability, fuelled our risk-taking and shaped the way we built and maintained relationships. It remains the most fundamental instinct, driving us to thrive and evolve through history.

Self-preservation made us **adaptable**. We learned to adjust to new environments, thrive in tough climates and make the most of the resources around us. It pushed us to **take risks** when needed and trust our **intuition** to act swiftly, often without overthinking. This instinct was the driving force behind our resilience and success.

Procreation was driven by two key elements: **purpose** and **care**. Purpose came from our innate desire to leave a legacy, whether through offspring or cultural contributions. Care ensured that what we created was nurtured and supported through deep bonds with co-creators—partners, family or community—ensuring our legacy was protected, cherished and sustained for future generations.

Social connection was essential too. Our sense of **fairness** helped us create balanced and harmonious groups, while our **ability to bond** and **work as a team** allowed us to achieve shared goals. Being **accountable** for our actions built trust and strengthened relationships, helping communities grow stronger over time.

I believe these instincts are deeply rooted in our genetic make-up. Over centuries, we have become more interdependent and specialized in our skill sets, which has enhanced our thinking and problem-solving abilities. But I sense that, while these instincts have helped us make remarkable progress, they have been subdued since the onset of the industrial age, as technological advancements have significantly transformed our lifestyles. How can that be, if they're so deeply ingrained in us? The truth is, in our fast-paced, tech-driven world, we don't rely on our basic instincts as much due to the support provided by the many industrial and tech innovations. These advancements have changed our interactions with the world, possibly reducing our depth of understanding, distancing us from the rich engagement our ancestors had with their surroundings. Let me explain how this shift has happened.

Losing our survival instincts to specialization

Our ancestors had an intimate awareness of their physical surroundings, far more attuned to their world than we often realize. For example, in multiple books, such as Yuval Noah Harari's *Sapiens*, their survival is credited to their deep environmental awareness. Likewise, Jared Diamond's *Guns, Germs, and Steel* explores how their adaptability, not inherent superiority, drove the progress of human societies.

Human evolution has brought about incredible progress. As we evolved from the early humans, our civilization has grown in scale, specialization and interdependence. However, this has also narrowed our focus to specific skill sets, causing us to not use many of the 'survival' skills our ancestors once relied on. In today's age of convenience and technology, I believe we risk losing some of the fundamental instincts that were critical to their success, and I've seen this shift first-hand.

Take numerical ability, for example. As a child, I remember memorizing multiplication tables and practising mental math with my parents. It became a game I later played with my kids too during road trips, randomly asking them questions like, 'What's twelve times sixteen?' That mental agility was such an important skill, even when I started my professional career. I vividly remember how my ability to do mental math was a key factor in my interview when I applied to McKinsey during my MBA in 1996. However, the practice of mental math has significantly declined. We have become heavily dependent on calculators for even the simplest calculations, haven't we?

Fast forward a generation, and the landscape has changed even further. For instance, I learned coding using the classic flowchart and logic-first approach, building step by step. My son, on the other hand, began coding in sixth grade using drag-and-drop programs. He's incredibly quick and efficient at creating things, but I sometimes feel he hasn't had the same opportunity to stretch and develop his logical abilities as much as I did. It's a trade-off—in gaining speed and convenience, you lose some of the depth and flexibility that came with earlier ways of learning. In the end, it's a reminder that while progress brings gains, it also comes with its share of losses. This shift has occurred in just one generation, but I believe it stems from deeper, underlying causes that have been developing over time. Let me walk you through them.

Growing risk-averse

Risk-taking has always driven human progress. For our ancestors, it wasn't a choice—hunting, exploring and innovating were necessary for survival. These actions came with risks, but they also offered great rewards, driving their growth and shaping humanity's journey forward.

Today, things are different. We live in a world that values stability and structure, and as a result, our instinct to take risks has reduced. For instance, according to a NC State University article, people are becoming more risk-averse, preferring quick solutions and avoiding uncertainty.[1] It's a mindset shaped by loss aversion, where the fear of losing is stronger than the potential joy of winning.

While this cautious approach makes sense in a predictable world, it comes with a cost. The bold, risk-taking spirit that once defined human progress has softened. In this age of AI and entrepreneurship, this is especially concerning. Innovation and entrepreneurship rely on taking calculated risks, pushing boundaries and stepping into the unknown. If we lose that willingness, we risk holding back the breakthroughs and opportunities that define our future. Reconnecting with this instinct isn't just important, it's essential for driving growth and creativity, which is going to be especially important in the AI age.

Losing touch with wisdom

In *Mastering Data Paradox*, I discussed the crucial role wisdom plays in effective decision-making by enabling us to deeply assess situations, objectively weigh the pros and cons of various options, consider the long-term impacts of decisions and make sustainable choices that serve the best interests of all stakeholders. This wisdom has been crucial in our progress. It goes beyond just accessing information, it's about understanding it, identifying patterns and making thoughtful, well-informed decisions. Finding time to reflect is key to building this wisdom.

But in today's fast-paced world, finding time for reflection has become rare. Research shows that continuous digital exposure and rapid information consumption weaken our ability to think deeply.² We are bombarded with information all the time in an everconnected digital world and are consuming data like never before. This undoubtedly offers convenience, but it also means we seldom find time to pause for thought, often settling for quick answers rather than reflecting deeply and leveraging our wisdom. For example, news consumption for many has moved from the morning read of a physical newspaper to scanning multiple tweets on a social media platform like X. Over time, this convenience can lessen our desire and perhaps also our ability to reflect deeply and thoughtfully, which is essential for cultivating genuine wisdom.

From real bonds to digital ties

Humans are naturally social, but the way we connect has changed. Our ancestors built trust and empathy through face-to-face interactions, but today, much of our communication happens online. This shift makes it harder to read non-verbal cues, and online spaces often weaken genuine relationships. Not just that, social media can be a self-reinforcing bubble that can lead to further polarization, as we have seen in recent years in political discourse across the world. While technology keeps us connected, it often lacks the depth, authenticity and bridge-building potential of real-world interactions.

A 2022 survey by the Australian Institute of Health and Welfare (AIHW) found that 16 per cent of Australians felt lonely, especially those aged between fifteen to twenty-four. Digital communication, though convenient, often leads to shallow connections and increased isolation. Reconnecting with meaningful social bonds isn't just looking back, it's about creating a future built on trust, collaboration and real human connection.³

In this age of convenience and specialization, our basic human instincts are clearly being dulled. But these aren't relics of the past—they have guided humanity through pivotal transformations and are as vital today as ever, particularly as we navigate the AI age. This new era could accelerate human evolution, and for that we would need our core human instincts more than ever before.

AI is the trigger for our next evolution

The idea is straightforward: the world we have built over the past 2000 to 3000 years in the name of civilization and progress, is about to change in the next twenty years in ways we can barely imagine. As I discussed in Chapter 5, we are entering an age of uncertainty, with projections indicating that up to 50 per cent of jobs could be lost because of AI within the next decade or so. Have we considered the implications? Where will all those individuals go, and what will they do?

Meanwhile, the AI age holds the promise to reshape every industry and open a myriad of opportunities for entrepreneurs. It presents a paradox: on one side, massive disruption, and on the other, untapped potential. Yet, the full impact of this transformation is still unknown. These are not ordinary times; they are unprecedented and demand a new approach to how we think, live and adapt.

Looking back, history reveals key moments that shaped human progress. Controlling fire 8,00,000 years ago was about more than warmth, it revolutionized protection and interaction. The invention of language 5,00,000 years ago enabled idea-sharing and cultural growth. Agriculture,12,000 years ago, not only fed more mouths but also fostered communities and reshaped societies. Today, we again find ourselves in a truly exciting time. Fields like space exploration, gene editing and quantum computing are advancing quickly along with AI, changing the world we live in at a rapid pace. These advancements are opening up new possibilities that once seemed like science fiction. Let's explore what this means for us.

Let me start with space exploration. It is not just about reaching new frontiers any more, it is becoming a launching pad for space colonization, drawing significant interest and investment from some of the world's wealthiest individuals. Visionaries like Elon Musk and Jeff Bezos are at the forefront. Musk envisions Mars as the 'New World'[4], a new home for a potential million people by 2050.[5] In fact, NASA aims to return humans to the moon and establish a sustainable presence there through the upcoming Artemis III mission scheduled in 2027.[6] These bold ideas underscore the exciting and varied paths being explored to extend human life beyond earth.

Talking about gene editing, technologies like clustered regularly interspaced short palindromic repeats (CRISPR), a gene editing tool that allows for precise DNA modification, are transforming medicine by enabling precise DNA modifications, which promise to treat genetic disorders more effectively. In fact, recent advancements can allow for direct modification of DNA without significant risks. Over the next decade, breakthroughs in gene therapies, bioprinting, synthetic biology and AI-driven genetics will revolutionize personalized medicine, potentially curing untreatable conditions and significantly extending human lifespans. This could lead to population-wide resistance to diseases like cancer and even the development of humans capable of living beyond 200 years. Even if the latter seems a bit far-fetched, 'healthy hundred' is certainly within the grasp of our generation.

Next is quantum computing, a key area of technological research that has seen significant progress. By as early as 2027, we expect to have quantum chips equipped with millions of stable qubits, revolutionizing our computational capabilities. These advancements will enable quantum computers to model molecular interactions with unmatched precision, driving breakthroughs in fields like drug discovery, genetic therapies and materials science. This will help us tackle complex scientific challenges more effectively. Furthermore, AI will harness these quantum capabilities for complex optimizations, greatly accelerating efficiency and innovation at rates we've never seen before.

Each of these technologies have immense potential and will have a profound impact on the world. But these innovations are not evolving in isolation, they are interconnected and create an unprecedented virtuous cycle that will define the course of human civilization. For example, in genomics, the fusion of genetics and AI interprets vast genetic data, predicting how mutations affect biological processes and paving the way for highly effective and targeted gene editing. Meanwhile, the synergy between space exploration and AI is making space missions more efficient, making space colonization a real possibility.

As we stand in 2025, I can confidently say that we are at a pivotal moment in human history. Progress in space exploration, genomics and quantum computing is skyrocketing due to the massive advancements in AI. Together, these forces are set to fundamentally change the world we live in, creating a myriad of opportunities and challenges for us as a civilization. This is why I believe that the AI age represents a significant discontinuity, one that could accelerate the next stage of human evolution. This is not just an upgrade in how we live, it is a transformational moment that would redefine human potential in ways beyond our current imagination. How we respond to these seismic shifts will shape our future and define what the human edge means in this new era.

It is therefore necessary for us to seek to unlock the **higher levels of intelligence and consciousness** to not only keep our human edge but to chart a bold new course for humanity.

Need for expansion in human intelligence and consciousness

We are constantly evolving as a species—a concept Sri Aurobindo, an Indian philosopher, yogi, poet and educationalist, spoke about over a century ago. Sri Aurobindo's philosophy emphasizes that humanity is not the pinnacle of evolution but rather a transitional being, poised for further development. He believed that human consciousness is on a continuous journey of evolution, moving towards higher states of awareness and intelligence.[7] Today, with AI mimicking or even surpassing key human skills, it has become even more crucial for us to expand our intelligence and consciousness to maintain a meaningful distinction and purpose.

By consciously striving to transcend our current mental limitations and embracing higher states of consciousness, we open ourselves to deeper truths, greater creativity and a more profound understanding of existence and eventually attain the highest level of consciousness to become a 'super man'. But, achieving this state of super consciousness is no easy task.

It requires us to navigate through multiple layers of consciousness, each one reflecting the complexities of our thoughts, emotions and perceptions. It is a deeply personal journey, one that challenges us to grow, reflect and evolve.

As per Sri Aurobindo, there are five levels of evolution of human mind, to attain a higher level of awareness

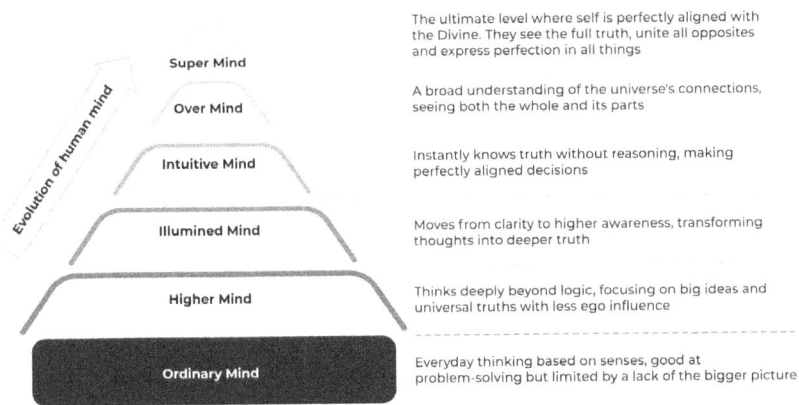

Sri Aurobindo provided a thoughtful framework to understand the growth and expansion of human consciousness.[8] He outlined how the mind operates at different levels, each unlocking new capabilities and deeper awareness. As consciousness expands, we progress towards higher states of being, gaining clarity, intuition and a connection to universal truths. At its peak, this journey transcends duality, achieving unity and alignment with the divine.

In my view, most people operate at the level of the ordinary mind—focused on analysing problems based on what we see and hear but often limited by a narrow perspective. Only a few might tap into the higher level of consciousness. Transcending these levels is not easy but by consciously working on our inner selves, we have the potential to rise through these levels, unlocking new states of awareness and realizing the vast possibilities of our consciousness.

Reigniting instincts and expanding consciousness for the human edge in the AI age

There is duality at play here—the **early man** and the **super man**. On the one hand, we need to reignite our core human instincts that kept us connected to nature and taught us to adapt and endure. On the other hand, we must continue expanding our consciousness, unlocking new levels of intelligence and creativity that pave the way to becoming the 'super man'. To thrive in the AI age, we need to balance these two forces. At the heart of it all lie our basic human instincts for both survival and growth. This resilient and adventurous spirit makes us who we are—the very essence that holds the key to merging the wisdom of the early man with the expanded consciousness and possibilities of the super man.

The pressing question is: how do we reconnect with these instincts in a world that is rapidly changing? How do we return to the innate instincts of the early man while unlocking the extraordinary potential of 'super man'?

The answer lies in recognizing and anchoring ourselves to what remains constant in a rapidly changing world: **our human essence**. Anchoring ourselves to this spirit provides a pathway for growth and evolution. In the next section of this book, I will explore the eight timeless mantras that can guide us, offering a roadmap to thrive in the AI age while staying true to our core humanity.

SECTION II

EIGHT TIMELESS MANTRAS FOR SUCCESS IN THE AI AGE

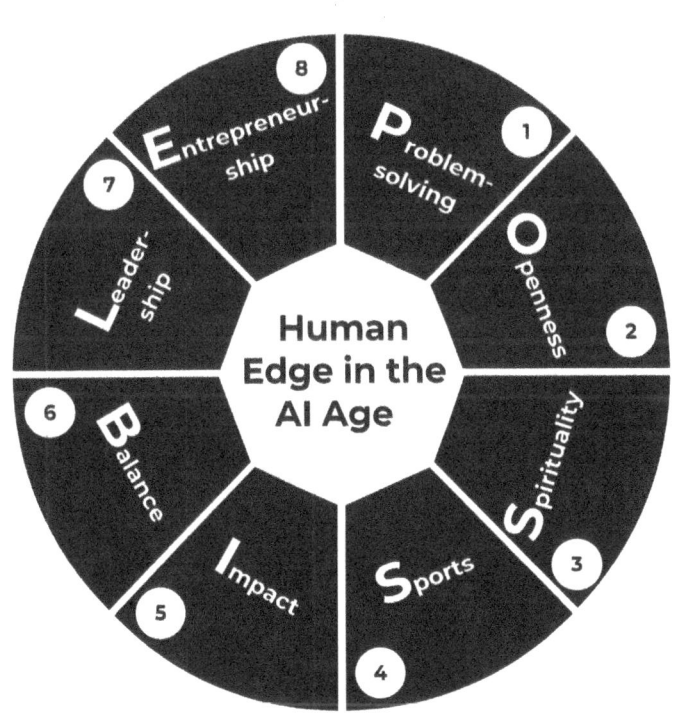

The POSSIBLE Framework

Possible
A Framework for Sharpening the Human Edge

At the centre of your being you have the answer; you know who you are and you know what you want.

—*Lao Tzu (attributed),*
Chinese philosopher and author of Tao Te Ching

In Section I of this book, I used extensive research to share perspectives on where AI is headed and the far-reaching implications it will have for human civilization—on every aspect of our lives, including all businesses and jobs. Many existing jobs will be lost, but there will also be tremendous opportunities to solve hitherto unsolved problems with AI, thus creating new businesses. What is clear is that standing still is not an option. We have to sharpen the human edge to compete in the age of AI by focusing on the core instincts and competencies that are innately human. This brings together both the self-preservation and adventurous instincts of the 'early man' and a continuous expansion of the human consciousness and consistently operating at higher levels of performance, which is necessary for the continued evolution of our species; perhaps creating what we might today consider as a 'super man'.

As we pick up where we left off in Section I—which is to focus on the human essence to win in the AI age—the real question is, how do we make it actionable? As I thought about it, I concluded that the best way to progress would be to look within and reflect on my own life experiences. The topic of human essence is too vast and it is easy to lapse into the abstract. It becomes practical and authentic when we anchor it in real experiences; this is what I have tried to do in Section II.

Sharpening the human edge for the AI age concerns both the modern and ancient. It involves rediscovering and strengthening our timeless instincts to solve perhaps the most defining challenge of the twenty-first century. As I reflect on my own journey, I find that I am the product of both the East and the West, influenced by modern and ancient experiences and sensibilities. My education and work experiences are modern and technology- and business-oriented. At the same time, I am deeply rooted in the timeless wisdom of the ancient Indian civilization. Studying engineering at IIT Delhi was an amazing opportunity to learn to go deep into problems and build the mental strength to keep pace with incredibly bright peers. While IIT was about depth, MBA at IIM-Lucknow was about breadth—instantly coming up to speed on a variety of topics, from finance to marketing to organizational behaviour. Both institutions also taught me the spirit of excellence and focusing on a goal.

Starting my professional career at McKinsey was a masterclass in problem-solving. I learnt structured problem-solving and also had the opportunity to apply it in a variety of industries, from financial services and manufacturing to consumer goods. The opportunity to build the McKinsey Knowledge Centre (McKC) was a unique experience that allowed me to build my own business and organization within a large global firm like McKinsey. That is where I also honed the leadership skills I had initially developed through my deep passion for and engagement in team sports throughout school and college.

My first startup, ActiveKarma and later on, Flipkart, taught me the fundamentals of entrepreneurship and were an intimate encounter with the digital age. Fidelity taught me the fundamentals of leadership in a global context. And finally, building Incedo has brought a lot of these experiences together—leadership, entrepreneurship, problem-solving, global context and more. Our client work at Incedo—partnering with some of the largest and most sophisticated enterprises in North America—has given me an intimate ringside view into the incredible trifecta—digital, data and AI, the three interconnected forces that are shaping our world today. While I have been shaped by my modern education and work experiences, the timeless wisdom of Indian knowledge and traditions has had an equally profound impact on me. One of the first substantial books I recall reading was *The Complete Works of Swami Vivekananda*, which created an immense sense of pride and curiosity around the long history of Indian spirituality and wisdom. I read the Bhagavad Gita in high school, and it has become the foundation of how I understand and interpret the world. I reread it (in various editions) multiple times and explored many other important texts from the vast treasure trove of Indian wisdom.

Another important aspect of my journey into Indian traditions has been meditation. I had my first lesson in meditation at the age of fourteen from my maternal uncle, my role model who exemplified professional excellence while being grounded in spirituality. He was the chairman of MTNL, the national telephone operator in India, a very senior and successful technocrat, while also being a prolific Vipassana (a Buddhist school of meditation) practitioner. Inspired by him, the daily practice of meditation has been my companion for the past thirty-five to forty years. In the early 2000s, I was introduced to 'The Art of Living', set up by Guru Sri Sri Ravi Shankar, which brought more structure into my meditation practice.

I have reflected on these range of experiences, both modern and traditional, to develop an actionable framework for sharpening the human edge for the AI age. My core thesis is that in a world that is changing so fast and so unpredictably, we need to anchor on that which doesn't change, which is timeless. My understanding of modern business and technology has helped me frame the problem statements and opportunities in the AI age, and I have tried to reflect on my experiences and understanding of ancient wisdom to propose eight timeless mantras for success in the AI age.

These eight timeless mantras come together in a meaningful anagram—POSSIBLE. It conveys a sense of potential and hope, reinforcing the idea that challenges can be overcome, new paths can be created and limitations can be transcended with the right mindset, skills and actions. The AI age presents both profound opportunities and challenges for humanity, but by mastering the qualities that make us uniquely human, we can not only stay relevant but thrive. POSSIBLE is a framework to help individuals and organizations unlock their full potential in an AI-driven world.

The eight dimensions of POSSIBLE are:

Mantra 1: Enhance *PROBLEM-SOLVING* skills
Problem solving remains a key human edge in the AI age. Indeed, in an AI-driven world, data is abundant, but defining the right 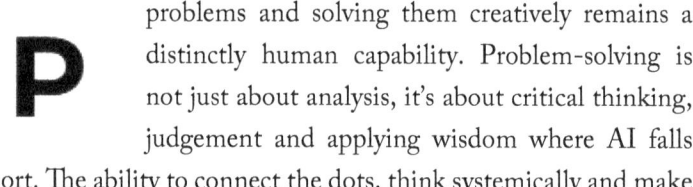 problems and solving them creatively remains a distinctly human capability. Problem-solving is not just about analysis, it's about critical thinking, judgement and applying wisdom where AI falls short. The ability to connect the dots, think systemically and make sense of complexity will determine who leads in the AI age.

Mantra 2: *OPENNESS* to change
 Success in the AI era requires a mindset of continuous reinvention. Openness to change is the first step towards growth. Openness fuels curiosity, adaptability and the willingness to embrace new

ideas, skills and perspectives. This has to be followed by continuous learning. The faster we learn, the better we adapt. I truly believe that *learning to learn is the new superpower in the AI age.*

Mantra 3: Connect with the self through *SPIRITUALITY*

S This AI age brings an era of unprecedented changes. Spirituality, inner awareness and mindfulness become our inner anchors in this shifting world. In such times, spirituality serves as a grounding force—awakening self-awareness and nurturing practices like meditation that help us **stay centred in a rapidly shifting world**. Spirituality is not just about personal peace—it enhances clarity, strengthens resilience and expands consciousness, helping us navigate uncertainty with confidence and wisdom.

Mantra 4: Learn teamwork and resilience through *SPORTS*

S AI may optimize processes, but real breakthroughs come from human teamwork, resilience and shared purpose. In many ways, sports prepare us for this reality—they instil discipline, determination, grit and the ability to win and lose with grace. Sports are an excellent **training for** *turbulent times, where grit, grace and growth* become even more critical.

Mantra 5: Make an *IMPACT*

I True success is not measured by personal achievements alone but by the impact we create for others. This understanding is key to *building a life of meaningful impact in the AI era*. While AI can automate tasks, human intent and execution drive meaningful change. The greatest opportunities in the AI age will belong to those who use technology to uplift society.

Mantra 6: Find the right *BALANCE*

B Navigating the AI age requires harmony between technology and humanity, ambition and well-being, speed and reflection. *Mastering duality—a key skill for thriving in a world of opposites*—will define success. The most successful individuals and organizations will be those who master balance—leveraging AI's power while staying deeply human.

Mantra 7: Unleash the *LEADER* within you

L AI can process information, but leadership is about vision, courage and emotional intelligence. In an era of disruption, great leaders inspire, guide and grow others through uncertainty and change. *Leading from within—with courage, clarity and connection*—is what sets them apart. The future belongs to those who can lead with both intellect and heart.

Mantra 8: Be an *ENTREPRENEUR*

E The AI era is a time of boundless opportunities. Entrepreneurial thinking—whether in business, career or personal growth—will be the key to creating value. *Think like a creator; everyone can and should be an entrepreneur in the AI age.* Those who can identify trends, take risks and innovate will shape the future, rather than being shaped by it.

To bring each of the eight timeless mantras to life, I've woven in personal experiences, contemporary examples and some of my favourite concepts and frameworks. Each mantra begins with an introductory chapter that distils its core message and explains why it matters—now more than ever—in the AI age. Together, these chapters are meant to guide, inspire and challenge you to cultivate your own Human Edge.

Ready to begin? Let's go.

POSSIBLE - 8 Timeless Mantras

	Mantra	Key Message
1	Enhance problem-solving skills	Problem solving remains a key human edge in the AI age
2	Openness to change	Learning to learn is the new superpower in the AI age
3	Connect with the self through spirituality	Staying centered in a rapidly shifting world
4	Learn teamwork and resilience from sports	Training for turbulent times: grit, grace and growth
5	Make an impact	Building a life of meaningful impact in the AI era
6	Find the right balance	Mastering duality, a key skill for thriving in a world of opposites
7	Unleash the leader within you	Leading from within: courage, clarity and connection
8	Be an entrepreneur	Everyone can and should be an entrepreneur in the AI age

MANTRA 1

ENHANCE PROBLEM-SOLVING SKILLS

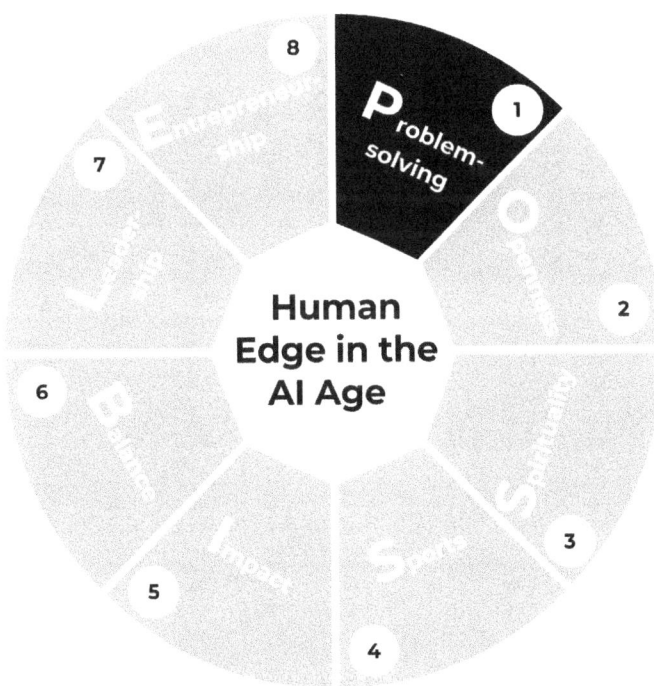

The POSSIBLE Framework

Introduction to Mantra 1
Enhance Problem-Solving Skills

Problem-Solving Remains a Key Human Edge in the AI Age

The real problem is not whether machines think but whether men do.
   —B.F. Skinner, *psychologist and behaviourist*

AI is rapidly transforming how problems are analysed and decisions made. Yet amidst this progress, the ability to solve complex, ambiguous problems remains one of the most vital—and distinctly human—skills of our time. While AI excels at processing data and recognizing patterns, it cannot define problems, apply human judgement or navigate the nuances of real-world decision-making. The ability to solve problems—systematically and with wisdom—is what gives humans an enduring edge in the AI age.

The key to effective problem-solving is not simply about generating solutions but about identifying the right problem to begin with. Too often, we address symptoms rather than root causes.

Great problem solvers know that to arrive at meaningful solutions, we must first uncover the real constraints and systemic inefficiencies. AI can assist with insights, but without human oversight, it can reinforce biases or produce solutions that lack context, ethics or long-term wisdom.

Approach to problem-solving in the AI age

Problem-solving is not a random or purely creative act; it is a structured, disciplined process. One of my greatest learnings from my early years at McKinsey—and a hallmark of that great institution—was the power of structured thinking. Across the following chapters, I explore four critical dimensions that define effective problem-solving in the AI age:

1. **The value of a structured approach:**
   As AI takes over analytical tasks, we must elevate our own approach. In Chapter 1, I outline a seven-step framework for structured problem-solving—a foundational capability for thriving in a world of complexity and accelerated change.

2. **Identifying the core problem:**
   Of the seven steps, none is more vital than framing the problem correctly. Inspired by the book *The Goal*, Chapter 2 explores how to identify bottlenecks and constraints that often lie beneath the surface of visible symptoms.

3. **Applying the right frameworks:**
   In Chapter 3, I share the decision-making tools and mental models that have guided me throughout my career. These frameworks help deconstruct complexity, prioritize actions and scale solutions across teams and organizations.

4. **Wisdom as the ultimate differentiator:**
   Finally, in Chapter 4, I turn to the human capacity for wisdom. Too often, 'smart' problem-solvers falter because they chase quick wins or lack depth. True wisdom combines pattern recognition, ethical foresight and the ability to reflect. It allows us to see beyond the immediate and consider broader, long-term consequences.

To excel in the AI era, one must develop both structured thinking and human wisdom. This means:

- Learning to diagnose the real problem, not just its symptoms.
- Using frameworks as guides—not rigid formulas.
- Leveraging AI for insight, but using human judgement to interpret, prioritize and decide.
- Building the practice of deep reflection to cultivate wisdom.
- Embracing problem-solving as an ongoing, adaptive process.

In the AI age, those who combine structure with wisdom—who can frame problems with clarity, break them down with logic and solve them with purpose—will not merely adapt. They will lead. They will shape what comes next.

7

Seven Steps to Structured Problem-Solving

It's not that I'm so smart, it's just that I stay with problems longer.
—*Albert Einstein, Nobel Prize winning physicist*

As organizations increasingly turn to digital and AI technologies to stay relevant and compete today, the demand for technology-specific skill sets will continue to rise. Young professionals often focus on learning and upskilling on the latest tools and techniques. However, in my view, the single most important differentiator of long-term professional success is not technical expertise—but the ability to solve a range of problems effectively. This ability is what differentiates top professionals from average ones. Having said that, building problem-solving skills is quite challenging, because it is a process. I have seen many intelligent, high-IQ individuals who are poor problem-solvers. Because problem-solving isn't about innate intelligence—it's a disciplined process that can be learned and refined.

Problem-solving skills aren't developed just in a classroom but through coaching, mentoring and the presence of the right role models in a supportive organizational culture. Unlike technical skills, problem-solving skills are soft skills that stay with you for life and remain relevant regardless of changes in technology. Every professional needs to recognize the importance of adopting a structured problem-solving approach to tackle any business problem effectively. This approach involves breaking down problems into smaller components, quickly getting to the root cause and coming up with effective solutions. By honing these skills, you can achieve better outcomes and stand out in the ever-evolving AI age especially as problems become more complex and ambiguous. The beauty of this structured approach is that it can be applied to not just business problems but almost any problem that needs to be addressed.

In this chapter, I'll walk you through a proven seven-step method for structured problem-solving that I was fortunate to learn at an early stage of my career at McKinsey.[1] As I discuss each step in detail, I will take an example to run through the seven steps to help you understand it in a practical way.[2] So let's dive right in.

Step 1: Problem definition or problem identification

As John Dewey, the American philosopher and educational reformer, once said, '*A problem properly stated is half solved.*' The first and most important step in solving any problem is to clearly understand what we are trying to solve.

So how do we get it right?

The first step is to **ask the 'why' questions**—Why is this a problem? Why is it important to solve it now? Why is it affecting performance or outcomes? Asking these questions repeatedly helps peel away symptoms and get closer to the root cause.

It's important not to jump to conclusions based on gut instincts. This is a common mistake, especially among experienced executives who may already have a mental model of what the problem is. Premature conclusions can lead to biased thinking and flawed solutions. Instead, take time to listen carefully, gather insights from multiple sources and reflect on what the problem really is.

A helpful way to do this is to engage with key stakeholders and decision-makers. Understanding their perspectives allows you to appreciate the full context of the problem and how it affects different parts of the organization.

Another clear sign of poor problem definition is the presence of too many issues. When the conversation feels scattered or unfocused, it's usually because the real problem hasn't been clearly defined. Effective problem-solving begins by narrowing in on the most critical issue and addressing it with precision.

To stay anchored, it's helpful to define success criteria and identify the key performance indicators (KPIs) that will be impacted. Setting quantitative 'From–To' targets, which means mapping the current state of the KPIs versus the target for the same. Defining these KPIs provides a clear goal and a way to measure progress.

It's equally important to define what is out of scope. Understanding what you are *not* solving for helps avoid scope creep and keeps the problem-solving effort focused.

Let's take a real-world example to illustrate the seven steps to structured problem-solving:

A consulting firm called XYZ Co. wants to improve its profit margins. This is a broad goal, so we need to narrow it down.

First, we ask 'Why?'

Why does XYZ Co. want to improve margins?

How do the current margins compare to historical trends and industry benchmarks?

How much improvement is needed, and by when?

Upon investigation, we find that profit margins have declined by 10 per cent over the past six months. Therefore, XYZ Co. needs to improve margins by 10 per cent over the next six months to return to a target of 25 per cent.

Next, we define the success criteria—increase profit margins without compromising revenue growth. The relevant KPIs would be profit margin percentage and revenue growth rate.

Finally, we define what's out of scope. In this case, inorganic expansion and changes to commercial arrangements with clients are excluded from the problem-solving exercise.

By sharpening the problem definition, we now have a focused, actionable challenge that sets us up for success in the remaining steps.

Step 2: Problem disaggregation

Once the problem has been defined, the next step is to break it down into smaller, manageable components. This process—known as problem disaggregation—is essential to move from a broad challenge to specific areas of focus.

The most effective way to disaggregate a problem is by using **issue trees**—also called logic trees or KPI trees. These are structured, hierarchical diagrams that decompose a complex issue into smaller parts, making it easier to analyse and solve. In today's volatile, uncertain, complex and ambiguous (VUCA) world, the problems we face are often deeply interconnected and not easy to untangle and therefore can come across as too big and complex to address. Breaking them apart into logical pieces is the only way to make the problem more addressable and to uncover the core issue.

At McKinsey, issue trees are so central to problem-solving that it often felt like the answer to everything was just 'trees, trees, trees'.

There are two types of trees that are especially useful:

- **Issue trees** break the problem into mutually exclusive, collectively exhaustive (MECE) components—ensuring that all possible causes are considered without overlap.
- **KPI trees** link each part of the breakdown to specific, measurable metrics, helping you quantify the problem and make it actionable.

Think of the problem as a tree:

- The *trunk* is the overall problem.
- The *branches* are major areas of concern.
- The *sub-branches* are smaller issues.
- The *leaves* are the fine details or data points.

You can build multiple trees to view the problem from different angles—financial, operational, customer-facing or strategic—depending on what you're solving for.

As you break the problem down level by level, continue to estimate the impact at each stage. Which part of the tree is most significant? Where is the biggest loss or opportunity? This allows you to identify root causes and prioritize the most critical issues.

This step takes practice to master. But it's the cornerstone of structured problem-solving. Once you can break a big challenge into its logical components, you gain clarity, confidence and control over how to solve it.

> Let's return to our earlier example. XYZ Co. wants to improve profit margins by 10 per cent. That's a broad goal. To make it actionable, we build a KPI Tree to break it down.
>
> We might start by splitting the margin problem by industry verticals, then within each industry by key clients. For each client, we can break down the revenue and cost components. This allows us to understand:

- Which industries or clients are driving margin erosion?
- Is the problem on the revenue side (pricing, volume)?
- Or on the cost side (delivery inefficiency, discounts, overheads)?

By quantifying each element, we begin to see where the biggest opportunities lie—and where to focus our problem-solving efforts in the next steps.

Tree for improving gross margin of a services business

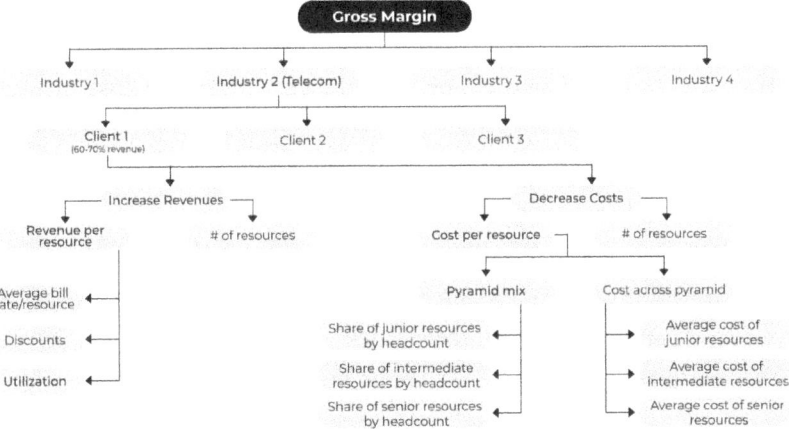

Step 3: Hypothesis generation and prioritization

Once you've disaggregated the problem, the next step is to identify which parts of the tree are worth investigating further and where to focus your efforts. This is where hypothesis generation becomes critical.

There are two classic approaches to problem-solving: **deductive** and **inductive**.

- The **deductive method** is the traditional approach—start with comprehensive data collection, analyse the information and arrive at a conclusion.

- The **inductive method**, on the other hand, starts with hypotheses. You form early, directional views about what might be going wrong or what levers might work and then test them iteratively with data and insights.

In today's complex and fast-moving business environment, the inductive approach is often more effective. Collecting complete data upfront is not always feasible or efficient. Forming early hypotheses helps focus your thinking and avoid getting lost in analysis.

However, applying the inductive approach well is not easy. I often see teams wasting time debating branches of logic trees that either don't matter or can't be influenced. Others get lost in tree-building without arriving at clear, testable ideas. This is where expert facilitation helps—asking the right questions, guiding hypothesis formation and focusing efforts where it matters.

It's important to remember: a hypothesis is not the answer—it's a starting point. It's a tool to guide your problem-solving, narrow your focus and test assumptions quickly.

Once you've generated several hypotheses, the next step is to prioritize. Use the classic **effort–impact matrix**, guided by two key questions:

1. How important is this lever in affecting the outcome we're solving for?
2. How much control do we have over this lever?

The goal is to focus your effort on high-impact, high-influence areas and avoid wasting resources on levers that have little effect or are outside your control. This exercise is often referred to as '**pruning the tree**'—removing low-value branches so the team can concentrate on what truly matters.

Returning to the profit margin challenge at XYZ Co., let's say we've now built a detailed KPI tree that breaks margins down by industry, client, revenue and cost levers.

From this tree, we generate the following hypotheses:

- Hypothesis 1: Improving resource utilization for Client 1 will increase revenues.
- Hypothesis 2: Reducing the average cost of senior resources will lower project delivery costs.
- Hypothesis 3: Increasing the share of junior employees in Telecom Client 1 projects will reduce costs without hurting revenue.
- Hypothesis 4: Applying the same approach for Banking clients may yield similar benefits.
- Hypothesis 5: Reducing customer discounts in the ABC business unit through price renegotiation will improve margins.
- (... and so on)

We can—and should—generate more hypotheses as we gather insights. But not all hypotheses deserve equal attention. Prioritization allows us to test the most promising ones first and move fast.

Step 4: Work planning

The next step to problem-solving is work planning. In this step, we focus on organizing tasks in a logical order, considering their dependencies and identifying the critical paths. This ensures that the project progresses smoothly and efficiently.

Then comes the implementation which requires an agile approach. A typical issue with problem-solvers, especially those who are very analytically oriented, is that they are not agile in their implementation approach. They will start with a giant problem statement and then try to gather all the data to solve the problem, hoping that the data will reveal some answers. But this becomes an unending exercise.

I recommend a **Two-Speed Execution** approach to balance immediate impact with long-term progress. High-impact, low-effort initiatives fall under Speed One, where execution is prioritized with the urgency to deliver quick results and maximize early value. Meanwhile, high-impact initiatives that require more time or effort are categorized under Speed Two, where execution is broken down into smaller, manageable programmes to ensure steady progress in parallel. While both are essential, Speed One takes precedence to drive immediate value, while Speed Two ensures steady momentum towards long-term impact.

In XYZ Co.'s margin improvement problem, we first prioritize hypotheses based on impact potential—looking at both cost base size and feasibility.

- Speed One (Quick Wins):
    o Improve resource utilization for Telecom Client 1
    o Increase the proportion of junior employees on the project team

These are easier to execute, can show results quickly and require fewer organizational changes.

- Speed Two (Longer-Term Levers):
    o Increase revenue per employee for banking clients through contract renegotiation
    o Redesign delivery models across business units to reduce fixed costs

These have higher complexity, but also bigger upside potential. They are broken into sub-initiatives and phased over time.

Once Speed One and Speed Two priorities are clear:

- Define the workstreams: One for each hypothesis or initiative.
- Sequence the tasks: Based on dependencies—what needs to be done first, and what can run in parallel.
- Identify critical paths: These are the sequences that will determine overall timelines.
- Assign owners and deadlines: To ensure accountability and momentum.

A well-thought-out work plan ensures the team is aligned, the energy is focused and the problem-solving process remains dynamic and outcome-driven.

Step 5: Analysis

Once the work plan is in place, the next step is to begin analysing the data to test your hypotheses. This phase is where many teams lose their way—either by diving too deep too quickly or trying to 'boil the ocean'. But good analysis is purposeful, iterative and sharply focused.

Think of it as peeling an onion: start with the outer layers—simpler, directional analysis—and go deeper only as needed. Early insights often come from basic tools like Excel. The key is to stay rigorous and objective, not chase complexity for its own sake.

Apply the 80/20 rule

One of the most important disciplines here is applying the 80/20 rule: use just enough data to get 80 per cent of the answer. Don't wait for a perfect dataset or absolute precision. In a fast-paced environment, progress is better than perfection.

And remember, analysis is iterative. You may begin with one hypothesis, learn something unexpected and need to refine or redirect your focus. Waiting too long to validate can make course correction difficult later.

Focus on simple but powerful techniques

Some of the most effective forms of analysis are also the most accessible:

- **Ratio analysis**—for quick comparisons across time or business units
- **Time series analysis**—to identify trends or outliers over time
- **Internal comparables**—comparing performance across departments, products, or regions
- **External benchmarking**—measuring performance against peers or industry standards

These methods help validate hypotheses with data, uncover performance gaps and provide direction for where to focus deeper investigation. But it is important to stay focused on the outcome. Don't let the data become the destination. Apply the 80/20 lens consistently and keep testing your thinking against what matters most: **the KPIs that drive impact.**

Continuing with the XYZ Co. case, let's test the hypothesis that improving utilization for Telecom Client 1 could improve margins.
Start with a simple utilization analysis:

- The data shows that utilization for Client 1 is around 75 per cent, while other telecom clients average 85 per cent.

- This 10 per cent differential is worth investigating. What's driving it?

You might discover root causes like:

- Higher bench time (idle employees between projects)
- Larger buffers for project contingencies
- Longer turnaround time from hiring to deployment

Each of these can be tied back to cost levers and tested further.

As you go deeper, you may identify new hypotheses—for example, adjusting staffing ratios or improving hiring velocity. That's okay. The goal is not to follow a fixed plan but to learn fast and adapt.

Step 6: Synthesis

Once the analysis has begun to reveal patterns and insights, the next step is synthesis—bringing everything together to form a coherent, actionable view of the problem.

Synthesis is more than just summarizing data. It's about connecting the dots, testing insights and translating findings into impact. You're not just asking, *'What does the data say?'*—you're asking, *'So what?'* and *'Now what?'*

Make it participative

Synthesis is not a solo activity. Involve your manager, team members and key stakeholders early and often. In fact, the agile sprint model discussed in Step 4 becomes essential here. Rather than waiting until the end to validate findings, share interim insights and test direction as you go.

This has two big benefits:

1. It ensures faster validation of your thinking.
2. It allows for early course correction before effort and time are sunk into the wrong direction.

Use the 'so what?' test

At every checkpoint, ask yourself:

- *So what does this insight tell me?*
- *How is it impacting the KPIs we're solving for?*
- *Does this lead to an actionable recommendation—or just more information?*

This discipline helps filter out noise and keeps the synthesis anchored to value and outcomes.

Please remember, synthesis isn't the end of the journey, it's the bridge between analysis and action. The best problem-solvers synthesize continuously, not just at the end. They engage, validate and adjust. That's what keeps the process agile, collaborative and on track to deliver real impact.

For example, for XYZ corp., suppose your analysis reveals that the time-to-fill for new hires is significantly delayed due to lengthy background verification processes. Before jumping to recommendations, share this with stakeholders:

- Is this delay inherent to the business model?
- Can anything realistically be done to shorten background verification cycles?

If stakeholders confirm that the delay is unavoidable, you go back to Step 3: revisit the KPI tree and adjust your hypotheses. Perhaps the issue isn't TAT—it's bench strength or project planning buffers.

This is synthesis in action: testing, learning, iterating and staying focused on what moves the needle.

Step 7: Recommendations

The ultimate purpose of structured problem-solving is to arrive at actionable recommendations—and then drive real change. And for that, one of the most important (but underrated) skills is the ability to communicate well.

In my experience, the best problem-solvers are also the best communicators. They don't just have sharp thinking—they know how to convey their message in a way that's clear, compelling and aligned with their audience. And they're prepared to iterate—because effective recommendation-building often involves multiple rounds of syndication, not a one-time presentation.

Two approaches to structuring recommendations

To build your case effectively, you can use one of two tried-and-tested methods:

1. S-C-R: Situation—Complication—Resolution

This approach walks the audience logically through the problem:

- **Situation**: Describe the context and background
- **Complication**: Explain what's going wrong or what challenge needs solving
- **Resolution**: Present your recommended solution

This works especially well with middle management and operational teams, where understanding the logic is as important as the conclusion.

2. The pyramid principle

This method, often used with senior leaders, starts with the recommendation first, followed by supporting arguments:

- **Top of the pyramid**: The core recommendation or answer
- **Middle layers**: Supporting pillars or key insights
- **Base**: The analysis, evidence or data behind each point

This format is ideal for executive discussions where time is short and decisions are fast. It brings the 'so what' upfront.

Both approaches are powerful—choose based on your audience, context and complexity of the issue.

Writing = Thinking

One practice I've found particularly valuable is writing things down—not just building slides. When you write, you are forced to slow down and think clearly. You spot gaps in logic, inconsistencies in your storyline or assumptions that haven't been validated.

Amazon famously uses this approach—team members write six-page narratives instead of PowerPoints. Why? Because writing forces clarity of thought and depth of analysis. It's not about the format—it's about the discipline.

While I'm not anti-PowerPoint presentations, I firmly believe in starting with the summary slide (or narrative)—not finishing with it as most tend to do. If you do the latter, you often end up with a mountain of slides—and the message gets lost. With the former approach, the message is sharp and focused and you typically end up with fewer slides! So, first create your storyline, then sketch your storyboard and only then build your slides.

The last mile of problem-solving

A recommendation is only valuable if it leads to action. And action only happens when people understand, believe in and own the solution. However, too often, problem solvers don't give communication the attention it deserves—or worse, believe it's someone else's job. Please remember: being analytically right is not enough. You must also be clear, confident and compelling in how you communicate. Communication is not an add-on—it's a critical part of the problem-solving process, and you have to master it. That's how structured problem-solving leads to real-world impact.

For XYZ Co. also, we will go ahead and communicate our findings using either one of the methods discussed above. Let's say we've tested our hypotheses and confirmed that underutilization of resources for Telecom Client 1 is a key driver of margin decline. Here's how we might structure the recommendation using the S-C-R method:

- Situation:
  XYZ Corp. has seen a 10 per cent drop in profit margins over the last six months, falling from 25 per cent to 15 per cent. This decline poses a significant risk to financial stability and competitiveness.

- Complication:
  The analysis reveals that a major contributor to this decline is underutilization of delivery teams for Telecom Client 1. Resources are sitting on the bench longer, and buffer staffing is higher than optimal.

- Resolution:
  We recommend improving utilization by reducing bench and buffer strength over the next six months. This will require better demand forecasting, faster time-to-fill and more proactive workforce planning. Progress should be reviewed regularly and strategies fine-tuned based on feedback and real-time data.

This is just a starting point—the final version would include data, impact estimates and implementation phasing. But the structure helps stakeholders quickly understand the what, why and how—and gets everyone aligned on the path forward.

Structured problem-solving in personal life

As I've said earlier, structured problem-solving isn't just a professional skill—it's a life skill. Once you learn how to break down complex issues, prioritize what matters and focus your energy on the most impactful levers, you'll find that you can apply this approach to almost any problem—including personal ones.

Let me bring this to life with a personal example—one that many of us have struggled with: losing weight. We often tackle this kind of challenge by jumping into a flurry of activity—cutting carbs, joining a gym, downloading a fitness app and setting lofty goals. But within a few weeks, the initial excitement fizzles out. The reason? We didn't start by understanding the real problem. Not everyone gains or retains weight for the same reasons—so how can the same solution work for everyone?

Instead of taking a one-size-fits-all approach, let's try solving this problem using the seven-step method.

Step 1: Problem definition

Take the example of Raman, who's finding it hard to lose weight. He starts by asking the 'why' behind his goal. Yes, he wants to look better—but more importantly, he wants to protect his long-term health.

He does some initial research, speaks with friends, fitness coaches and a nutritionist. Through this, he comes to define success as sustainable weight loss—1–2 kg per week—while preserving his overall health and energy levels.

He also identifies what's out of scope: crash diets, unregulated supplements and invasive medical procedures.

Step 2: Problem disaggregation

Next, Raman breaks the problem into smaller components using a simple logic tree:

- Diet and nutrition
- Physical activity
- Lifestyle habits
- Underlying emotional triggers

Structured problem-solving in personal life: Illustration of a tree for weight-loss

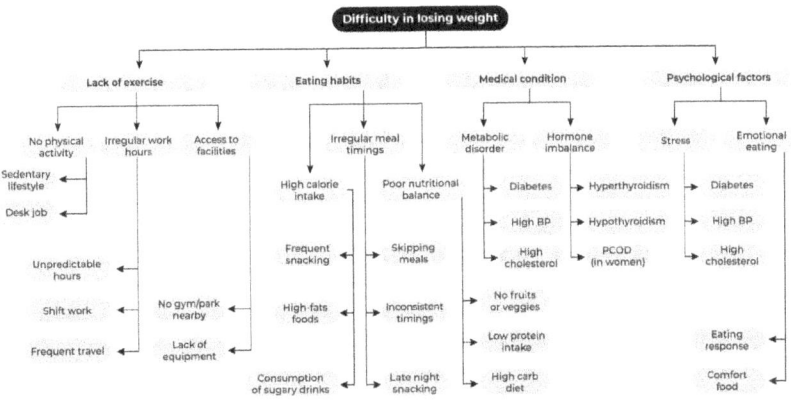

Each of these can influence weight in different ways and understanding this helps focus the solution.

Step 3: Hypothesis generation and prioritization

With his disaggregated tree in hand, Raman begins forming hypotheses:

- Reducing sugar intake will help reduce calories.
- Walking daily for thirty minutes could improve energy expenditure.
- Replacing snacks with fruits and nuts may reduce binge eating.
- Buying gym equipment might motivate exercise.
- Addressing emotional eating through therapy may improve consistency

He then uses the effort–impact lens to prioritize. Reducing calorie intake and switching to healthier snacks feel manageable and impactful—quick wins. Meanwhile, joining a gym or seeking counselling may be important but are more complex to act on.

Step 4: Work planning

Raman creates a two-speed work plan:

- **Speed One (quick wins):**
  - Shift to a nutrient-rich, calorie-deficit diet
  - Start light physical activity like daily walks or home workouts

- **Speed Two (long-term):**
  - Develop a more personalized workout routine
  - Explore behavioural coaching or therapy to address emotional eating triggers

By sequencing his efforts in this way, Raman avoids overwhelm and builds momentum—starting small and building confidence before taking on more complex changes.

Step 5: Analysis

He calculates current caloric intake, compares it to healthy benchmarks and identifies problem areas (e.g., sugary drinks, frequent snacking). He also tracks his activity levels and notes gaps—long sedentary periods, minimal structured movement and irregular routines.

This gives him specific data points to work with:

- Where are the hidden calories coming from?
- When is he most inactive?
- Which habits contribute to weight gain?

These insights provide focus for the next steps.

Step 6: Synthesis

He now begins to connect the dots.

The analysis reveals that his high caloric intake is driven by sugary snacks and drinks, while his low activity levels are due to long hours of desk work and lack of a consistent routine.

Instead of overhauling everything, Raman starts by asking:

- *What are the small changes I can make that will have the biggest impact?*
He decides to replace sugary snacks with fruits and nuts and blocks three thirty-minute walk sessions into his weekly calendar. These are manageable, high-impact moves that don't

require a complete lifestyle overhaul, but begin to shift the momentum.

Step 7: Recommendations

- **Situation**: Raman is struggling to lose weight, putting his long-term health at risk.
- **Complication**: The main causes are excessive calorie intake—especially from sugary snacks—and low physical activity.
- **Resolution**: Shift to a balanced, calorie-controlled diet. Add fruits and vegetables. Cut down on sugar. Introduce three to four hours of weekly exercise, gradually increasing to five hours over the next two months.

By starting with manageable, high-impact changes, Raman begins seeing results quickly. This motivates him to take on the more difficult changes—and build a healthier, more sustainable lifestyle.

Final thought for problem-solving in personal situations

We all face complex personal challenges. What makes them harder is when we treat them as vague frustrations instead of specific problems that can be understood and solved.

Structured problem-solving helps us shift from being reactive to being deliberate. From trying everything to trying what matters.

Now think of a personal challenge you're facing right now.

- How would you define the problem clearly?
- What might be the components you could disaggregate?
- Which levers could create quick wins?
- What's your Speed One and Speed Two plan?

Try applying the seven steps—not just to solve a problem, but to gain clarity, confidence and control over it.

Bringing it all together

Finally, I want to leave you with some **cross-cutting themes** that apply across all seven steps of structured problem-solving:

1. **Be outcomes-centric:**
   Always start with the end in mind. What is the outcome you're trying to achieve? What impact are you solving for? Clear, quantitative KPIs help keep the problem-solving effort grounded and focused.

2. **Master the trees:**
   To identify the right KPIs, you must become good at building logic trees and KPI trees. They are among the most powerful tools for breaking down complex problems quickly and effectively.

3. **Prioritize ruthlessly:**
   Structured problem-solving isn't just about doing more—it's about doing what matters. Disaggregation, synthesis and hypothesis generation all require sharp focus and prioritization.

4. **Adopt an agile mindset:**
   Use the 80/20 rule and the Speed On/Speed Two approach to drive early wins and steady progress. Don't get lost chasing perfection—start solving.

5. **Make it iterative:**
   Keep an open mindset. Learn along the way. Be willing to take feedback, pause and course-correct if needed. Problem-solving is not a linear journey, it evolves.

6. **Communicate and engage:**
   You cannot solve problems in isolation. Bring others in. Make it a participative process and communicate clearly at every stage. The best insights often emerge through shared thinking.

7. **Trust the process:**
   And finally, believe in the power of structured problem-solving. Don't skip steps. Don't rely solely on instinct or gut feel. A clear, step-by-step process helps minimize bias and maximizes clarity.

Closing thought

In today's fast-paced, high-pressure world, where problems are increasingly complex, the instinct is often to dive in and act quickly. But this tendency—to move fast without stepping back—can lead us to solve the wrong problem or worse, create new ones.

This risk is even greater in the AI age. With powerful tools at our fingertips, we can now generate options, run analyses and simulate outcomes in seconds. But speed alone is not enough. In fact, it can be dangerous without structure. The real edge doesn't come from having more answers, it comes from asking the right questions.

That's why structured problem-solving is not outdated, it's more essential than ever. It helps us pause, clarify what really matters and bring judgement to complexity. It offers a systematic way to cut through noise, focus our energy and move from confusion to clarity.

A clear process doesn't slow us down, it makes our thinking sharper and our action smarter.

Because in the end, the best problem solvers aren't just fast, they're focused. And in a world increasingly driven by AI, a structured human problem-solving process ensures our decisions are not just fast but right.

8

Identifying the Core Problem

Lessons from 'The Goal'

Any improvement not made at the constraint is an illusion.
—*Eliyahu M. Goldratt,*
author of *The Goal: A Process of
Ongoing Improvement,* Management Guru

People often believe that an effective solution lies in considering and addressing every aspect of the problem. As a result, they try to approach the problem from every possible angle, turning it into an overwhelming challenge. And in the attempt to be comprehensive, the problem remains unresolved. This approach only leads to overthinking, wasting resources and creating overly complex solutions, ultimately resulting in suboptimal outcomes. This is the case with many of the executives I meet. They come up with an incredibly long list of KPIs—that they believe are 'key'. But that isn't the case.

On the contrary, such an approach reflects lack of clarity. Instead of focusing on the truly critical aspects of the problem or the core issue, people become entangled in a web of data, spreading themselves too thin and diluting focus and efficiency and more importantly, effectiveness in solving the problem.

Now why doesn't this approach work? The answer lies in the 'theory of constraints (TOC)'—a powerful framework, beautifully illustrated in the seminal work by Eliyahu Goldratt, in his book *The Goal*.[1] It is undoubtedly one of my all-time favourite books, especially as I majored in operations management during my MBA. He explains the TOC through a fictional story of a plant manager trying to save his manufacturing facility that is struggling to stay afloat. The plant is plagued by inefficiencies, missed deadlines and a lack of profitability.

So what is TOC? And how can a theory used to solve operations issues be applied to problem-solving?

The TOC in problem-solving

According to the TOC, every situation operates as a system or network, where overall output is determined by the bottleneck or constraint. To achieve meaningful improvement, efforts must be directed at optimizing or eliminating this bottleneck, as it directly limits system performance. Any improvements made elsewhere do not enhance throughput and instead result in waste.

Performance of any system or process is limited by its biggest constraint

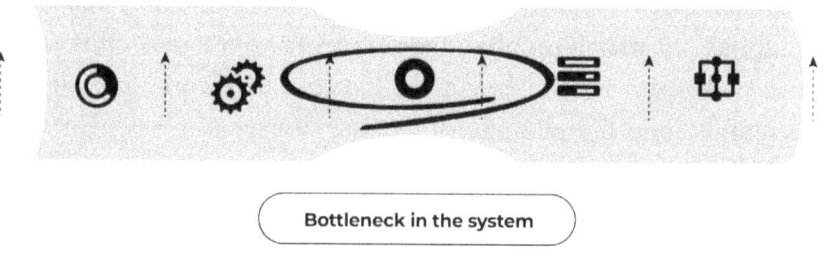

Bottleneck in the system

You must focus on the bottleneck to increase the overall performance

So the key here is to **identify the bottleneck,** the right one. And this is the core of effective problem-solving as well and it is perhaps one of the most valuable lessons I can share with you. It's fascinating how this simple yet powerful insight is relevant across a wide range of problem scenarios, whether in a professional setting or in personal life.

Five steps of applying TOC

There are five steps to applying TOC to identify the true constraint and solve it. I have woven it in with an example to help you understand it better.

Let's take an example of a large e-commerce company, XYZ.com, that has been struggling with delayed order fulfilment. Customers are increasingly complaining about frequent delays in receiving their orders, leading to negative reviews and a dip in repeat business.

Step 1: Identify the constraint: This is the most important step of the entire process that determines which part of your system or process is the true constraint. However, this is probably the most difficult step. Because often, what appears to be the constraint isn't actually the real one. And when efforts are made on improving what seems to be the constraint, the issue continues to persist. So this step requires a deeper inquiry of the entire process to identify where the real problem lies.

For example, XYZ.com reviewed their warehousing and shipping processes to improve delivery times. They found that an outdated inventory tracking system was causing delays, with products often out of stock or misplaced, leading to longer pick-and-pack times. To fix this, they implemented a real-time inventory tracking system using barcodes and RFID technology. While this improved warehouse operations, the overall order fulfilment rate and delivery delays remained an issue. Why? Because this wasn't the true constraint.

So how do we identify the true constraint? The first step is to clearly define the goal of the process. Then you do process mapping, which involves creating a step-by-step flow of the entire process from beginning to end. This helps you get the full picture and see how different parts of the process are interconnected and how changes in one area might affect others. Next, you gather and analyse data related to the performance metrics at every step of the process. This will help you identify potential bottlenecks—the stage where the process takes most time and causes most delays. And assess the flow of work through the system to identify where the work slows down or stops.

Five steps of applying Theory of Constraints (TOC)

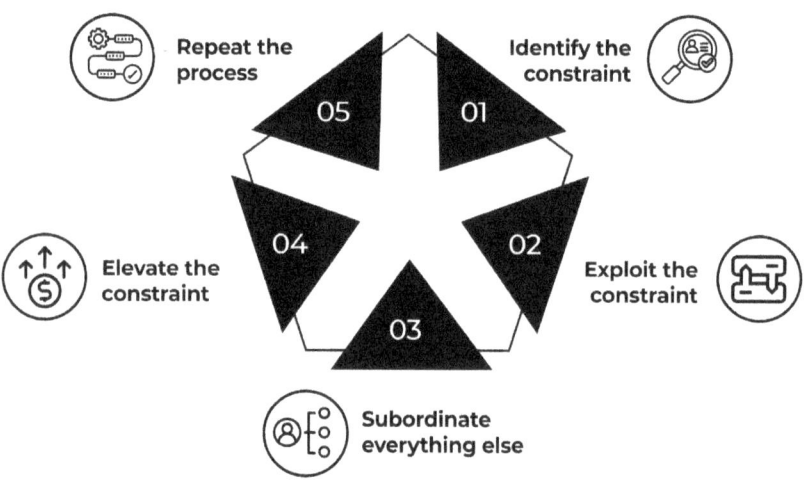

This time, instead of focusing only on the downstream process, XYZ.com took a step back to examine the entire order fulfilment process—from order generation to delivery.

Identify the constraint: XYZ.com, an e-commerce company

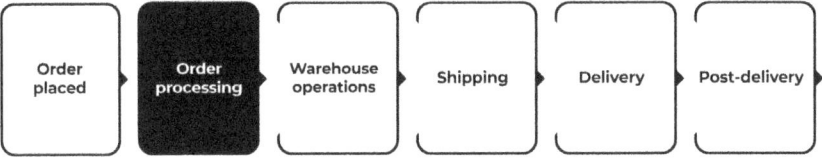

Their goal was to ensure timely delivery, every time. After mapping the process and analysing data from each stage, they discovered the real bottleneck was in the order processing phase. The outdated, largely manual system for order processing that included payment verification, fraud checks and pick list generation was causing significant delays, especially during peak times. This issue was further compounded by a lack of integration with the new inventory management software, overshadowing the impact of inventory issues.

Step 2: Improve the constraint: Also called optimizing the constraint, this is the step where you find ways to maximize the capacity of the constraint by using the resources you currently have at your disposal.

During peak times, XYZ.com prioritized orders based on factors like customer type (giving VIP customers priority), order size and product availability. They temporarily reassigned staff to address the bottlenecks in order processing and implemented quick fixes, such as simplifying fraud checks for lower-risk transactions, to speed up processing.

Step 3: Subordinate everything else: The second most important and challenging step is adjusting non-bottlenecks, the parts of the system that are not constraints. This may involve modifying, slowing down or even deprioritizing them to align with the bottleneck's pace. Why? Because if non-bottlenecks operate independently or at a faster rate, they create excess work-in-progress, inefficiencies or bottleneck overload, ultimately reducing overall system performance.

> XYZ.com synchronized their warehouse operations with the order processing team's pace, ensuring that the warehouse team wasn't overloaded with inaccurate or incomplete lists. They ensured inventory checks were accurate and up-to-date to prevent delays or errors in generating pick lists. Clear communication between departments was established so issues in order processing could be quickly addressed by other teams.

However, saying 'I will do this', is easier than saying 'I will not do this'. When you are faced with multiple demands or tasks, it's often easier to say 'yes' and take on more responsibilities or actions, thinking it will lead to progress. However, doing too much or trying to optimize every part of the system without focusing on the constraint leads us nowhere. Thus saying 'I will not do this' is difficult but necessary.

And it requires a shift in mindset and priorities. Many people or departments may be reluctant to change their workflows, especially if it means slowing down or altering processes that have been running smoothly. But adjustments have to be made in areas that aren't directly constrained, despite resistance and the challenge of implementation. Everyone must be forced to focus on the constraint and think about the system's overall efficiency rather than just optimizing individual parts.

At XYZ.com, the warehouse and shipping teams were naturally resistant to changes because they were used to processing orders immediately to maintain high throughput and optimize their own metrics. Subordinating their work to the order processing system felt counterproductive, as waiting for accurate pick lists could negatively impact their performance metrics. The challenge was not just in changing processes but in shifting mindsets. Teams had to move from focusing on their own success to aligning their efforts with the broader company goals, which was uncomfortable and difficult for them.

Step 4: Elevate the constraint: If the constraint is still limiting the throughput of the system, preventing you from maximizing throughput, due to certain limitations or obstacles, you should consider investing in additional resources or think of making significant changes to enhance the performance of the constraint.

To elevate their order processing system, XYZ.com invested in a new order management system that automated payment verification, fraud checks and pick-list generation. This new system was also fully integrated with the inventory management software, ensuring real-time data synchronization and faster generation of accurate pick lists.

Step 5: Repeat the process: Once a constraint is broken, another one will emerge. So, you must establish a feedback loop to continuously monitor the system's performance. Continuously repeat the process to identify and address new constraints.

After elevating the constraint, XYZ.com must continuously monitor the system to identify any new bottlenecks, as improving order processing may shift the constraint elsewhere. Key metrics like order processing time, warehouse throughput and shipping lead times should be tracked to spot any new issues. If a new constraint emerges, such as a bottleneck in warehouse operations or with the shipping partner due to increased volume, the TOC steps should be applied again to address it.

Applying TOC to a daily life scenario

Let's apply the TOC to a daily life example of a college going student. Let's say you are typically late in submitting your assignments. Haven't we all at some point struggled with trying to do everything at the last minute or racing against time to get it done? Can the TOC help you identify where the real problem is and be more effective with the process? Of course! Let's see how.

1. **Identify the constraints**: The goal is, *complete your assignment and submit it on time*. Now that we have identified the goal, we must map the system or the process.

Applying TOC to a daily life scenario: Illustration of an assignment writing

Now, in this entire process I bet the most apparent bottleneck for most you would be actually getting down to writing the assignment. You might feel that getting words on paper is the most critical and challenging step. As a result, you may put it off till the last minute, ending up doing everything all at once or submitting it at the last possible moment or even after the deadline.

But if you take a minute to really analyse the process, you might realize that conducting research is the most demanding part. It takes up most of your time and if it is not directed in the right direction, can easily become a never-ending exercise. And, if the research process is all over the place, writing with clarity would naturally become very difficult.

2. **Improve the constraint**: So let's optimize the research process. For that instead of aimlessly searching the internet, you may decide to optimize your research time by using the relevant academic databases and libraries to find relevant sources quickly. You may decide to allocate specific time slots for research to avoid spending too much time on this step. And use tools like digital note-taking apps to organize research materials effectively.

3. **Subordinate everything else**: As I said, this is the second most important step. Because often what not to do is harder than what to do. Which means you need to maximize the effectiveness of your research by weeding out the unnecessary efforts from the process. You may decide to create a tentative outline in advance so that you don't waste time researching unnecessary topics. Which means you bring the process of *creating an outline* before actually *conducting research*. This will ensure that no time is wasted on researching unnecessary topics, helping you stay on track in the research process. Now, you might feel uncomfortable building the outline beforehand, as you may be used to doing thorough research to create a robust outline, and it is changing the process that you are generally comfortable with. But the time and effort you save here would be significant, compared to spending some extra time filling the gaps in your research (if any) during the process of writing your draft.

4. **Elevate the constraint**: If you still think the research isn't up to the mark, you may decide to seek help from your colleagues or professors to direct you to the right sources for your assignment. You can also think of collaborating with classmates to divide the research workload and share resources.
5. **Repeat the process**: Once a constraint is addressed, another one will emerge. Regularly check the progress of the assignment to ensure that other steps like editing and proofreading are not becoming new bottlenecks. And as required, adjust strategies based on performance reviews to keep the process efficient.

Some of the most effective leaders and problem solvers that I have met have one thing in common. They know how to quickly zero in on the most critical aspect of the problem or the core issue, so that they can come up with solutions that deliver the maximum impact. And that is the secret to effective problem-solving in the highly complex AI age.

9

Things I Wish I Learnt in Business School

Ten Key Problem-Solving Frameworks

The value of a college education is not the learning of many facts but the training of the mind to think critically.
—Albert Einstein, Nobel Prize winning physicist

Given the VUCA world we are living in, you need to make sense of volatility and complexity and operate at high speed, that too in an environment of uncertainty. To be effective in such a scenario, you need problem-solving and decision-making skills of a very high standard. I have found that, in such scenarios, frameworks are very helpful in providing a structure to problem-solving and thus helping in making better decisions.

I was very fortunate to have started my professional career in a firm like McKinsey, which had an intense focus on building problem-solving skills. It is there that I got exposed to the power of frameworks. For any problem, we were trained to use frameworks; moreover, we were encouraged to create new frameworks for repeatable problem situations. Those habits have stayed with me, and I naturally gravitate towards frameworks for any situation that requires problem-solving.

In this chapter, I share with you some of the most important management concepts and frameworks I have learnt over the last three decades. These concepts and frameworks can be applied in both life and business situations to improve the quality of decision-making and actions. I have used them in numerous situations and have found them to be tremendously beneficial. I believe they would be helpful to you too, especially those of you in the early stages of your life and career, to learn these frameworks.[1]

Here are ten key frameworks that I use most often.

The first three points focus on the *what*, numbers four through nine address the *how* and the final point highlights an important factor beyond our control.

1. **Sweet spot: Business strategy**

   One question that confronts us all is, 'How can we better realize our full potential?' In Mantra 5, Chapter 21, I have talked about how one can find this 'sweet spot' in detail. But in short, it operates at the intersection of three forces—our passions, unique talents and serving important and ethical needs. Its discovery releases tremendous energy in you, making your activities easy, improving the quality of your work and enhancing happiness in your life, thereby helping you realize your full potential.

Sweet Spot: Business strategy

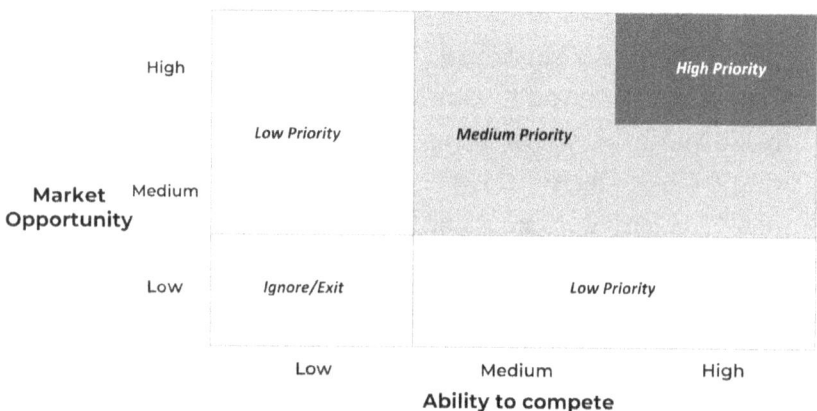

This concept is relevant for businesses too. Business leaders are constantly having to prioritize across multiple options. For example, where to invest? Where to focus? One of the simplest but most powerful frameworks for such business situations is the 'opportunity versus ability to compete', which is really an application of the 'sweet spot' concept. The purpose of this matrix is to help organizations prioritize their investments, allocate resources effectively and develop strategic plans for growth or divestment.

2. **Risk-return trade-off**
As you make decisions, one of the most important things to understand is the risk–return profile. There is no free lunch. If you want higher returns, you will typically need to take higher levels of risk. This is one of the most fundamental concepts in finance but is relevant in personal life too. It is important that we understand our risk propensity. For the same risk–return curve, the point to play might be different for different individuals. A good example of this is a question I'm often asked by students— should I create a start-up right after MBA or work for a couple of years before becoming an entrepreneur? Clearly, there can be no one right answer to this; the answer lies in understanding your risk profile.

To play at the optimal point in the risk–return curve, it is important to define and understand risk better. If you keep risk at an amorphous level, it will paralyse you. When you define risk clearly you can differentiate between what is real and what is imaginary. That will allow you to make bigger bets and play at higher levels on the risk–return curve. Defining your risks clearly becomes even more important in the VUCA world we are operating in.

Risk Return Tradeoff

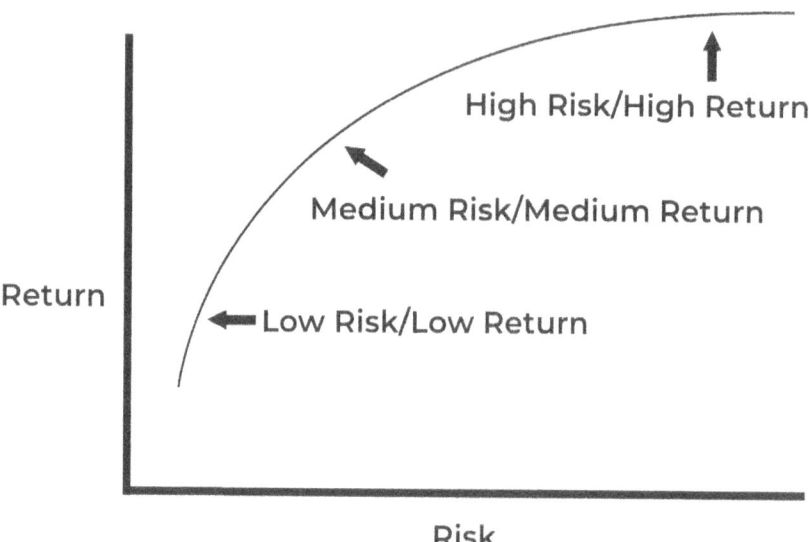

3. **The 80/20 rule**

   The Pareto principle, or the concept that a few vital tasks drive the majority of results, is a well-known concept. However, not many are able to apply it practically in their daily lives. The reason is, while the 80/20 principle is evident in hindsight, it is difficult to see it in advance. To improve your 80/20 ability, it is important to make time to think about it. This is easier said than done, as most of us are so caught up in the flow of routine events that we don't make enough time to think through our options and approaches. In addition, it is imperative that we make time for reflection. Writing a diary can be very helpful. This practice of reflection can improve the intuition one requires to make the right 80/20 decisions.

The 80-20 rule

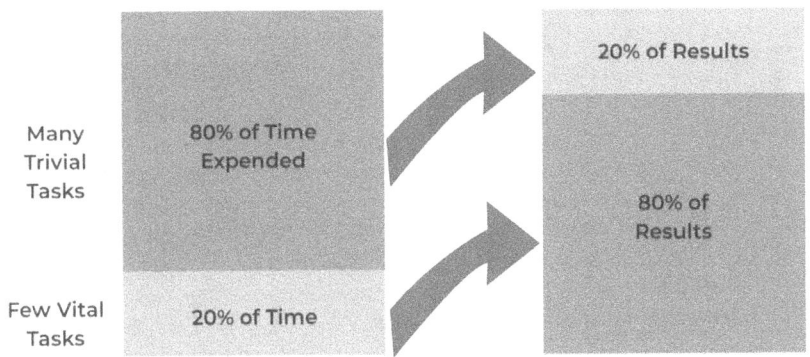

4. **Trust equation**

Trust is the foundation of relationships and a key to success, both in our personal and professional lives. It is the super-powerful lubricant that makes interactions and working together easy and effective. Trust can take time to build. However, once you build trust in a relationship, it moves to a totally different level of effectiveness. The trust equation, a concept popularized by Charles H. Green, David Maister and Robert Galford, in their book *The Trusted Advisor*, is a great framework to understand the process of building trust.[2] Your trustworthiness is driven by your credibility (expertise and knowledge), reliability (consistency of actions) and intimacy (personal connect). However, the most important driver is self-orientation in the denominator. All the great work resulting from the earlier three factors can be undone by a perception of self-centredness in you.

The trust equation is a good reflection of the human balance of the head and heart. Credibility and reliability reflect the head, and intimacy and self-orientation the heart.

Trust equation

5. **Virtuous–vicious cycle**
   No situation is as good or as bad as it seems. Most times, we find ourselves in either a virtuous cycle (positive feedback loop) or a vicious cycle (negative feedback loop). This shows how emotions play a big role in our decisions. We see this in markets, industries and companies.

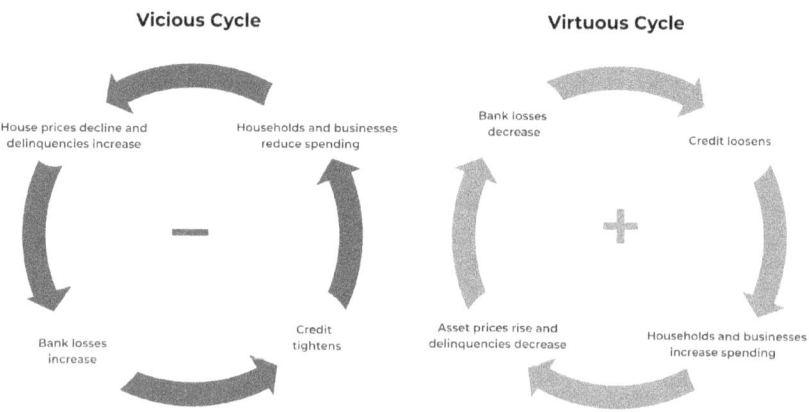

Equally, we see this in team and individual situations.

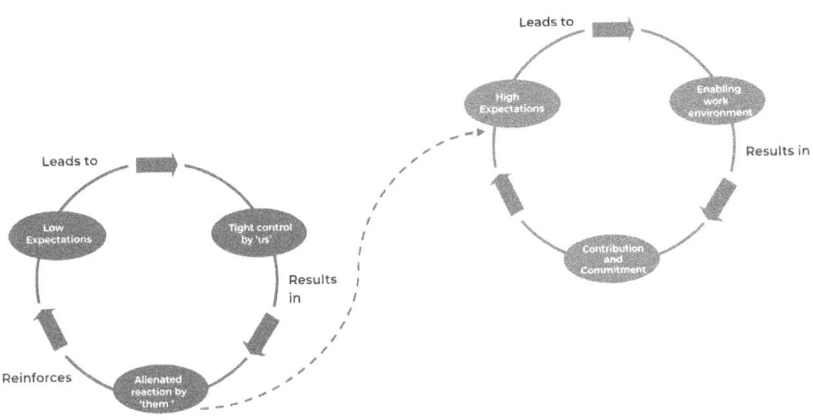

The question is, how to break out of a vicious cycle and move to a virtuous cycle. It is difficult to have perspective when you are in the midst of a cycle. Those who are around you may see it sooner. Seeking advice and help from others will lead you to make the changes required to break out of a negative cycle. Turning a vicious cycle into a virtuous cycle is a critical skill that any business leader needs to have, especially in this digital age. Cycles are becoming shorter in the digital age and it is easy to flip from a positive cycle to a negative one. Thus, a leader's ability to quickly identify cycle shifts and turn them around becomes even more important.

6. **Circle of influence**
One thing that has been reinforced to me over the span of thirty and more years is the fact that nothing is constant, except change. And how people react to the change is the differentiating factor that determines their success or failure. People who handle change well spend their time and energy on things they can control, instead of wasting it on things they can't. The **circle of concern** includes everything you worry about but cannot directly control or influence, such as global economic downturns, natural disasters, government policies, political shifts, behaviour of a

Circle of Influence

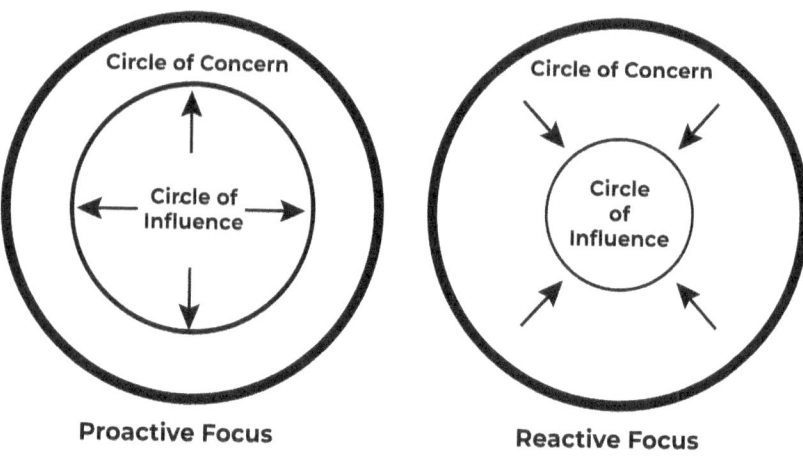

colleague, etc. And the **circle of influence** are the things that concern you that you can do something about, such as personal habits, quality of your own work and attitude, how you respond to setbacks, etc.

We often tend to gravitate to the circle of concern rather than the circle of influence. The same issue or situation can be approached differently and you can convert a circle of concern to circle of influence. For instance, you may be worried about climate change, which is in your circle of concern. In this situation, if we **react**, we tend to focus on broader systemic issues—things we worry about but cannot control—depleting our energy and causing stress or anxiety and making our circle of influence smaller. However, if we are **proactive** and concentrate on what we can control and the actions we can take, our circle of influence expands. For instance, we can choose to use electric vehicles instead of petrol or diesel ones, or switch to solar energy to power our homes, to do our bit in curbing climate change. By focusing on controllable actions, we can grow our circle of influence. For example, we might inspire others in our neighbourhood to do the same.

We have to train our minds to be positive and proactive and focus on taking action on our circle of influence rather than wasting our energy on our circle of concern.

7. **Pain barrier**

   In most tasks, you will have to cross a pain barrier to make progress. When you go through a painful period, you may feel like giving up. However, if you battle through it, the pain diminishes and you can proceed smoothly. Every athlete is keenly aware of this barrier. This is true of entrepreneurs too who sometimes feel like giving up. Those who persevere are likely to succeed in their ventures.

Pain barrier

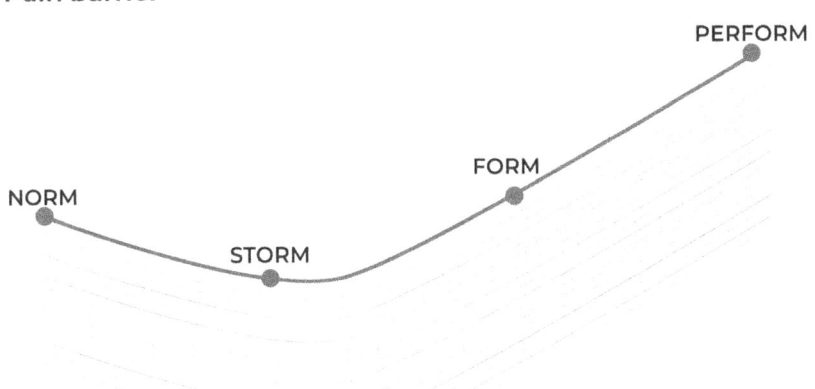

The pain barrier is present in most team and project situations. You often start on a high but then very quickly hit a low. As you battle through the low phase, you can then move on to a steady growth phase. Understanding the existence of the pain barrier should give us the strength and perseverance to build our ability to crest any learning curve. It is a very simple but important concept— 'no pain, no gain', or 'short-term pain leads to long-term gain'!

8. S-curve

S Curve

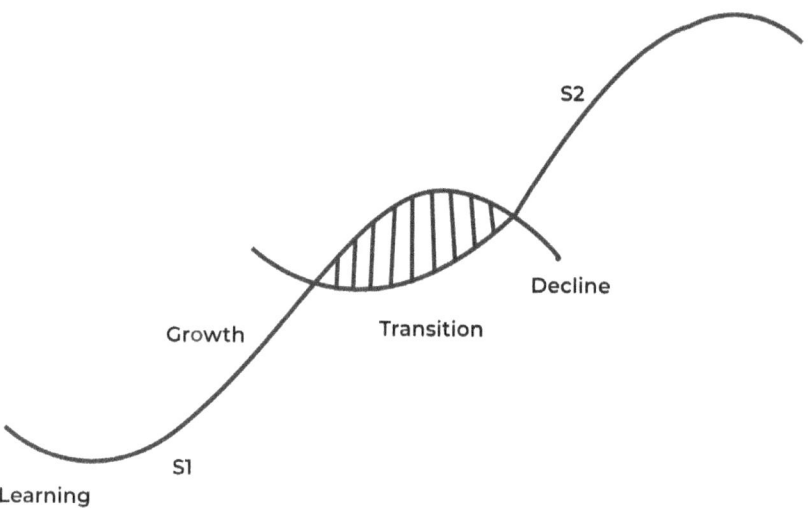

The Sigmoid curve (or the S-curve) is an extension of the learning curve where, after the growth phase, you see a period of maturation and then eventual decline. The S-curve represents many business and life situations and has profound implications for both companies and individuals. To ensure sustained growth, you have to move from one S-curve to another. Why? Because every S-curve would eventually mature and decline. If you look closely into the method behind highly successful companies and individuals, who have a seemingly unbroken trajectory of success, you will find not one S-curve but a succession of S-curves that have been strung together.

The next logical question is, when should you shift from one S-curve to another? The only option for shifting from one curve to another is when you are on your way up. This is because you can never predict the top, and when you reach the decline phase, you start losing energy. It may be that the first curve is longer than anticipated, in which case you can keep cruising along until you are indeed nearer to the peak. But pre-emptively preparing for the second curve is far better than waiting until it is too late, and the decline phase has set in. However, making a shift when you are in a growth phase and things are going well is not easy. You have to break out of your comfort zone. Moreover, when you transition between S-curves, you will go through a period when the rewards are lower (as you have to battle through the learning phase of the next S-curve).

Successful individuals and organizations are self-reflective and constantly monitor their own positions on the S-curve. Riding the first curve while cultivating the second is always the best option. Clinging to the first and trying to prolong it is a pointless waste of energy. When all is well and you are at the top of your game, then you know it is time to plan your next move.

Clearly, being able to identify the nature of the S-curve you are operating in, being able to transition from one S-curve to the next and then stitch them together is the key to continued growth.

9. **Compounding**
One of the most powerful laws or frameworks, relevant in both life and business, is compounding. There is great power in tiny but consistent improvements. We all understand the principle of compounding, but it is surprising how few apply it consistently. We are often attracted by the big, bold moves, which certainly are important in the digital age, but we can easily overlook the virtues of consistency and steady progress.

Some of the most successful business leaders and enterprises I know apply the principle of compounding religiously. They know that staying the course, combined with continuous improvements over a period of time, can produce spectacular outcomes.

Compounding

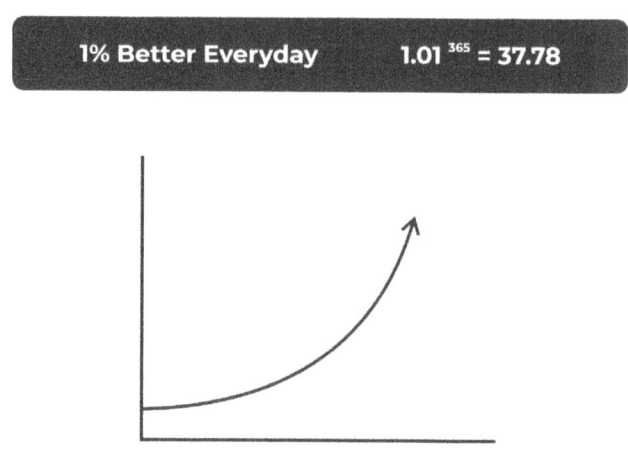

10. Luck: Life is unpredictable

In the end, I want to mention another very important factor—**luck**.

The Cycle of "Luck"

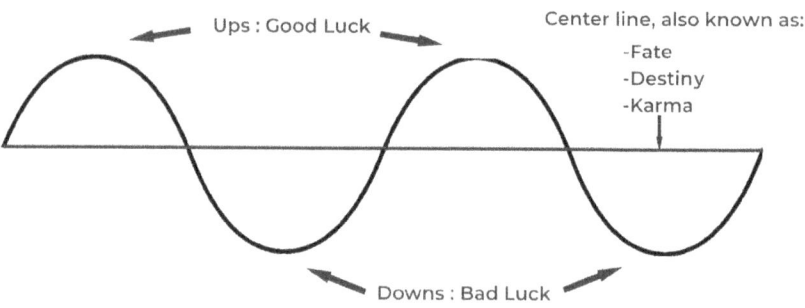

Over the years, I have realized that success is not a predictable formula. Sometimes your best efforts go to waste and sometimes you get success that you never anticipated. That is the nature of life; it is not linear and deterministic. It is uncertain, with many unpredictable ups and downs. That is why it is very important to have a broad and relaxed perspective of life. This means neither becoming arrogant with success nor too depressed at failure.

The Bhagavad Gita, talking about karma, says, '*Karmanye vadhikaraste, ma phaleshou kada chana* (do your duty but do not worry about the results).' There is deep truth in this. If we realize this truth, both our individual lives and the world around us will improve so much.

These frameworks are potent tools, capable of significantly improving both personal and professional lives when skilfully employed. But knowing these frameworks is not enough; one needs to practice them and develop the wisdom to apply and contextualize these frameworks. In an age of data overload, wisdom is your most valuable asset. And that's why I'm turning to this topic now. It's the proprietary knowledge that transforms frameworks into impactful action. In the next chapter, we will explore how to cultivate this wisdom and empower yourself to make deeper, more effective decisions in the AI age.

10

Role of Wisdom in the AI Age

Never mistake knowledge for wisdom. One helps you make a living; the other helps you make a life.
—*Eleanor Roosevelt, American political figure, diplomat and activist*

Wisdom as a concept has captivated the imagination of thinkers and philosophers over the years across civilizations. It has an ancient history, tracing back to the Sumerians around 2500 BCE, where 'Nanna' was revered as the Mesopotamian God of moon and wisdom. In Hindu mythology, Lord Ganesh, widely regarded as the God of wisdom, is said to have transcribed the Mahabharata (as dictated by Sage Vyasa), an epic known for its treasure trove of wisdom.[1]

You might wonder why I am talking about wisdom and what its role is in the digital and AI age. The digital world has brought about an abundance of information and data. Does access to a lot of information make us wiser, or does it just make us feel wiser? Does data abundance enhance or hinder wisdom? One might think that the importance of wisdom has gone down in the AI age but, to my mind, it has become even more crucial. Wisdom is like proprietary knowledge that makes people stand out, helps them make sound choices and be more effective with the decisions that they make.

Gaining wisdom has never been easy. It involves years of learning, experiencing and reflecting. However, today's AI world has made information available in abundance, presenting us with an opportunity seemingly to build wisdom faster and in numerous ways. However, such abundance of information comes with its own unique challenges, complexities and paradoxes, such as information overload, digital echo-chambers, short attention span and so on. But the good news is, if leveraged well, data can surely enhance the process of building wisdom. And in this chapter, I will dive into the idea of wisdom and talk about practical ways to nurture it in the AI age.[2]

But before we get to the process of building wisdom the natural question that comes to mind is—what is wisdom? This is a difficult question to answer. Let me explain why.

Why is defining wisdom difficult?

Over the years, numerous attempts have been made to define wisdom, highlighting a different perspective on wisdom each time. There is the cognition-focused definition anchored in critical thinking, sound judgement, knowledge, experience and insight, emphasizing the pursuit of a deeper meaning and optimal living. Another one, a personality-focused definition, focuses on traits like compassion, reflection, open-mindedness and humility as key markers of wisdom. Yet another one is development-focused and defines wisdom as a product of life experiences and personal growth, emphasizing that true wisdom emerges not solely from experiences but from active reflection and the ability to derive meaning from life's lessons.[3] So, it is safe to say that there isn't a single definition that prominent thinkers and philosophers agree on. Why?

Firstly, it is a multifaceted concept, with different disciplines offering different definitions based on specific context. But I believe the core reason behind it is that wisdom cannot be measured. There are no clear metrics (KPIs) that can measure how wise a person is. It cannot be measured as physical attributes like height or weight. Rather, it is a bit like attempting to quantify intangible qualities, such as happiness or love.

However for me, there are three underlying aspects that are core to wisdom. The first is thinking deeply about things. It refers to engaging in through contemplation or reflection on a particular subject or topic. It requires going beyond the surface, analysing the complexities and considering various aspects or perspectives of the matter at hand, both inputs and possible outcomes. It also implies going beyond the short-term and thinking through the long-term implications. The second one is upholding strong values, which means anchoring on fairness and sustainable outcomes in various situations and decisions. These two put together result in the ability to make sound judgement. Sound judgement enables individuals to make reasonable and well-informed decisions based on careful consideration of multiple facts, evidence and relevant factors, that are not clouded by ego and short-term self-interest. In summary, wisdom is the ability to assess situations deeply, think about the pros and cons of different options objectively, think about the long-term impact of decisions and make choices that are sustainable and in the best interest of the people and situations involved.

I have met many such wise souls over the years, and they have shown me that wisdom can take any form. A personal experience from my Fidelity days is a testimony to that.

It was my first year at Fidelity and I was asked to lead the global location strategy, which was a very high-profile project. Interestingly, a very senior colleague, who was twenty-five years my senior and a counsellor to the chairman at Fidelity Investments, was seconded to my team. In a private firm like Fidelity, the chairman's views count for a lot. In this project I ended up making recommendations, which were not only quite aggressive but also contrary to what was known to be the chairman's preferences. My senior colleagues were aghast at my recommendations and I was told that I would lose my job if I went ahead. However, very surprisingly my presentation to the chairman went very well and he agreed with my aggressive recommendations. I later realized that it was the 'wise counsellor' who had been closely observing me at work who had briefed the chairman beforehand! I then saw the value of this group of trusted counsellors of the chairman, who had probably led and seen many such strategic initiatives. This lady could understand the worth of my ideas through just a few short meetings and supported me even when my ideas were contrary to conventional wisdom. This ability to form a point of view and influence a strategic decision, which has significant long-term implications, takes a lot of clarity, belief and courage. Her actions emerged from a place of wisdom. It was evident. Operating from wisdom often feels like operating from a crystal ball, allowing you to see the unseen.

Importance of wisdom in the digital and AI age

The abundance of data or information does not automatically mean better decision-making for individuals. Our wisdom has a significant impact on our decision-making process. It helps us develop a deeper and longer-term perspective on both the problems at hand and the solutions we decide to implement.

Often, with so much information available, it creates a false sense of confidence that we understand the problem. In reality, we often do not even scratch the surface and fail to fully consider the consequences and see beyond what meets the eye. Even AI, with its powerful ability to process vast data and generate insights, cannot fully grasp the long-term impact of our actions. This is where wisdom becomes crucial. It helps us be truly aware of potential outcomes, not just what meets the eye but to go beyond and take a bigger picture view. Many people, when working with one set of data will come up with some insights and with another set of data, will come up with different insights. Their ability of data-interpretation is high, but pattern recognition to map both the data sets may be low. Wisdom has to do with pattern-recognition.

In recent times, we have seen the fall of some of the biggest banks in the United States. In March 2023, the $200 billion Silicon Valley Bank declared bankruptcy—as they had racked up losses due to poor investment decisions. In a transaction, they had raised $1.8 billion to cover losses.[4] As the news went public, people started withdrawing and it all went downhill from there. The situation was similar to what happened in the Great Depression of 1929 and the Global Financial Crisis of 2008. Clearly, there were poor decisions at multiple levels in large financial institutions that led to such catastrophic failures. These financial institutions possess extensive data resources and a talented workforce. I often wonder how highly paid, experienced executives who have abundant access to data and analytics end up making decisions which had such severe repercussions? Is that a lack of wisdom? A lack of long-term thinking and an inability to think through the consequences of decisions?

I believe data analyses—while necessary—alone cannot give us all the right answers. We often get a false sense of security by just holding on to information, we believe we know and we have assimilated, when in truth, we have just stored the information. We are just consumers of information. It is wisdom that helps us make the shift from consumers of information to applying it with discernment. It plays a crucial role in driving value from information. In this age of AI, wisdom isn't just helpful, it's essential. It's how we make sure technology works for us in the long term and not just right now. It's about keeping our human understanding, our experiences and our ability to understand the long-term implications of our actions at the heart of every decision. It is definitely a crucial human edge for problem-solving and decision-making in the AI age.

Now let's look at the connection between data, information and wisdom to understand this better.

A framework for wisdom

One of the most widely accepted modern models for understanding wisdom is the DIKW hierarchy—which stands for Data, Information, Knowledge, and Wisdom—also known as the wisdom pyramid or knowledge hierarchy. This model gained attention when Russell Ackoff discussed it in 1989[5] but its roots trace back to T.S. Eliot's 1934 poem 'The Rock', where he pondered the loss of life in living, wisdom in knowledge and knowledge in information.[6] The idea resurfaced independently in the late 1980s as concerns about information-overload grew.

The DIKW model proposes a step-by-step progression: data generates information with context and structure, information leads to knowledge and knowledge eventually results in wisdom. Data, in its raw form, is the unprocessed collection of facts, figures and observations. It is like having a list of numbers without any meaning. Information transforms this data by organizing, structuring and adding context and answering the 'what', 'who', 'where' and 'when'. Moving up the ladder, knowledge takes the understanding a step further by delving into the 'why' and 'how' aspects, analysing patterns and gaining insights from the information. Wisdom, the pinnacle of the DIKW hierarchy, involves not only understanding but also the ability to make sound judgements and ethical decisions based on knowledge and experience.

While I appreciate the elements and flow of the DIKW hierarchy, I believe there are some inherent issues with this model. The concept of a pyramid with a linear, one-way progression and its static nature does not look like a fair representation of the path to wisdom. In the real-world scenario, the path to wisdom is not that straightforward. It is much more complex. In my view, it often involves iterative and cyclical processes of refinement and continuous learning.

Wisdom remains key to effective problem solving in the Digital & AI age

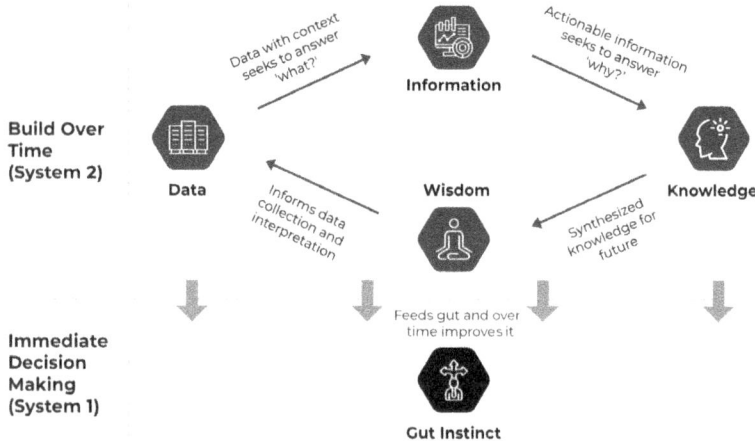

Envisioning this concept as more of a continuum rather than a rigid pyramid makes more sense to me. In this fluid continuum, raw data evolves into information when paired with 'what' and structural context, providing a foundation of understanding. As we delve deeper, this information transforms into knowledge, where we not only possess answers to the 'why' but also actionable insights, signifying a deeper level of comprehension. Further, along the continuum, as we synthesize this knowledge, we start to identify patterns, based on which we make decisions that shape our future—this is where wisdom resides.

Wisdom is not built in a day. It is inculcated over a period of time. So, as we further continue in this loop, wisdom acts as the guiding light, making us better at filtering the irrelevant data that can overwhelm us and instead focus on what truly matters. With this refined ability to distinguish, we rise above the noise and make choices that align with our long-term goals, values and the betterment of the world and ourselves.

As you can see in the framework above, wisdom and gut instinct are also interlinked. Over time, as we build wisdom, this wisdom feeds into our gut instinct, making it sharper and more accurate. Let me explain how.

Cultivating a 'wise' intuition

Although the basic ingredients of wisdom and gut are data, information and knowledge (DIK), wisdom is built through deep synthesis of these ingredients. It involves thoughtful processing and drawing upon one's experience and understanding. It encompasses a holistic perspective, making it comprehensive and well-informed. Whereas gut instinct represents an instantaneous response, it is an intuitive and quick reaction to a situation or problem. The basic ingredients of gut instinct and wisdom are the same but gut instinct does not involve deep processing of DIK, often relying on first impressions and immediate reactions.

It is synonymous to System-1 and System-2 thinking for decision-making talked about by Daniel Kahneman, in his book *Thinking, Fast and Slow*. Now, let's explore how these systems interact to build wiser intuition or gut.

Initially, any complex decision requires a deliberate and thoughtful process, referred to as System-2 thinking, which involves going through the entire DIK cycle, starting with data, then analysing data, considering various factors and making choices based on logic and reasoning. It is a conscious and systematic approach to decision-making which in the long term helps build wisdom[7].

However, with time and experience, our decision-making process evolves. Repetitive exposure to similar scenarios, transforms this once conscious process into something more automatic, subconscious. It becomes an intuitive part of our decision-making, referred to as System-1 or gut instinct. Our gut instincts, informed by our learnings, experiences and wisdom, prove invaluable. It is as if our intuition has become finely tuned, allowing us to make swift, yet well-informed decisions.

Is wisdom dying in the digital and AI age?

In today's world of instant gratification and data abundance, where we are all bombarded with information and consuming information like never before, finding time for reflection is tough. But wisdom relies on reflection. I often wonder, is wisdom dying?

As much as I would like to say no, observing the changing world around me, it seems like wisdom is indeed fading in our information-rich era because we have forgotten to step back and reflect. In the age of information overload and countless digital distractions, it is very easy to lose sight of what truly matters. We often prioritize quantity over quality, speed over depth and noise over contemplation. The constant notifications, social media updates and the glamor of viral content draw our attention away from the meaningful and towards the insignificant. As we engage with these digital distractions, we inadvertently distance ourselves from the deeper insights and understanding that wisdom offers.

There is rising fear of missing out (FOMO) and more and more information is consumed. Every individual stores the information they find relevant, without really reading it—it is indexed, but not converted to knowledge or wisdom. Depth of knowledge on subjects is on a decline along with quality of conversations, but volume is on a rise. People are confusing wisdom with information or gut feeling.

Wisdom is not just information. it is informed by data and information. Wisdom is not gut—it is more than an instinct, it is not just instantaneous but reflective. It is insights meets knowledge meets experience. Only those who take the time to pause, reflect and truly absorb knowledge will become 'wise men and women'.

Wisdom, as we know today, is quietly eroding. So, is there a way to save this endangered but critical facet of human understanding?

Five principles for building wisdom

Can wisdom be cultivated? I believe that the answer to this question is a resounding yes. Absolutely! Wisdom can be nurtured and cultivated. However, it's important to understand that it's not a one-time effort. Instead, it's an ongoing journey of learning and reflecting on experiences to improve decision-making in all aspects of life.

Wisdom is not just about more data and analysis, it is a deep and well-rounded comprehension that can hold up to scrutiny from different angles. This clarity is achieved through thorough study and understanding. Take Warren Buffett, for example. He is a wise investor because he relies on his principles, built through deep learning and experience. He invests for the long term, often visiting companies he invests in to solidify his understanding. Buffett's beliefs may differ from the norm, but they are shaped by his unique interpretation of data, experience and past bets. His ability to connect dots, identify patterns and refine his approach over time exemplifies wisdom.

I consider myself a student on the path to wisdom—a journey that demands reflection and continuous learning. Reflecting on the insights of experts, I have come to realize that wisdom often begins with quiet moments of introspection, where the five principles I will discuss below gradually become habits.

Each of the five interconnected principles contributes to developing wisdom. These components of wisdom all connect and work together, like a beautiful puzzle coming together. Let me explain each of these principles in brief and how I have applied them in my professional and personal journey.

1. Let me start with **humility**. It is about self-awareness, acknowledging what you do not know, listening without judgement and being open to others' ideas. In essence, it is about being receptive to different perspectives and being willing to consider them with an open mind. As you grow and succeed, the same success can easily turn your head, making you self-absorbed and egotistical. And with that, you stop listening and become dismissive of others' viewpoints. So, I make conscious efforts to be more inclusive in my conversations and endeavours and seek diverse perspectives as much as possible, which keeps me grounded.

Five-part framework for building wisdom

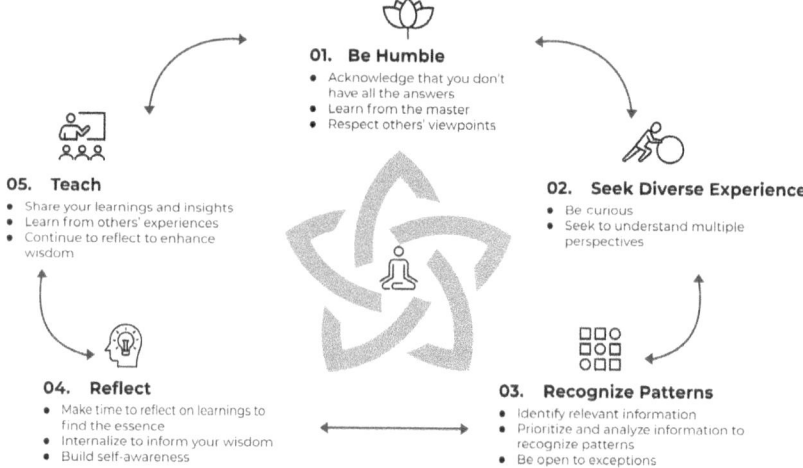

2. Next comes **seeking diverse experiences**. Think of it as being curious like a child, exploring outside your comfort zone and learning from others. When you do this, you can make more informed decisions because you have a wider range of experiences to draw from. For me, I continually challenge myself with different pursuits like playing sports, meditation, travelling and meeting new people. Trying something new not only introduces

me to fresh knowledge but also deepens my understanding on varied topics. I try to learn from the masters, as much as I can, which is both humbling and also offers me deeper and richer experiences.

3. Moving on, when we have gathered all this information and started organizing it effectively, we do start **recognizing patterns**. This means we begin to see connections and similarities between different pieces of information. It is like solving a puzzle where you start noticing how different parts fit together. Recognizing patterns is crucial because it helps us understand things at a deeper level and make more informed decisions. Merely accumulating diverse experiences is not enough. They are only relevant when you derive the 'so what' from them. It helps in connecting the dots and recognizing patterns that are crucial to developing frameworks or approaches to effectively deal with recurring situations.

4. But wisdom isn't complete without **reflection**, another very crucial component. In our busy lives, we often forget to pause and introspect. Reflection allows us to make sense of our experiences and gain valuable insights, which are essential for recognizing patterns and developing wisdom. I make sure I take time for self-reflection, taking breaks between my hectic schedule, because reflection creates clarity of thought and action. I have dedicated a separate section to it, ahead in the chapter, because its significance cannot be overstated.

5. Finally, wisdom is not about keeping what you know to yourself. It is about **teaching and sharing what you have learnt with others**. Instead of hoarding knowledge, you spread it far and wide. I am passionate about teaching and sharing the knowledge I have accumulated over the years. This is one of the reasons I am writing this book. I believe that knowledge is that one thing that grows through sharing. And as I share, I get an opportunity

to test my knowledge, creating a feedback loop, which is critical to learning and growing.

The five wisdom principles—humility, seeking diverse experiences, recognizing patterns, reflection and sharing—are interconnected threads. They weave together, with each principle influencing and enriching the others. Teaching others can be a humbling experience because it often reveals areas where you might lack knowledge or need further learning. When you share what you know, you might encounter questions or perspectives that highlight the gaps in your understanding. This realization keeps you humble, reminding you that there is always more to learn and discover. Likewise, starting with any of these principles can lead to a continuous cycle of wisdom development.

Wisdom is not a destination, it is an ongoing journey of learning and growth. Much like the process outlined in my framework for building wisdom. It's similar to any skill, practice makes you better over time. Wisdom is not a one-time achievement, it is a continuous refinement of your ability to make sound judgements and navigate life's complexities.

Find time for reflection

Self-reflection is key to learning and growth. We often do not have time for it, amidst the flurry of activity happening around us. True wisdom comes when individuals look within themselves, take responsibility for what they do and embrace personal growth. A wise individual understands the importance of self-awareness, acknowledges how they have contributed to the current situation and is willing to make deliberate changes for the greater good. Self-awareness, which involves understanding one's values, motivations and influence on others, lies at the heart of this process. Numerous academic definitions of wisdom are grounded in the principles of self-awareness and self-reflection.

In the digital and AI age, the role of personal insight, intuition and judgement retain their significance. The path to nurturing these qualities begins with establishing a deeper connection with oneself. This helps sharpen pattern recognition, which lies at the core of wisdom.

Reflection, when rooted in self-awareness, fosters wisdom. For me, meditation is a potent tool for connecting with your inner self. This practice delves deep into self-exploration and consciousness, to connect with your inner thoughts and emotions. Quietening external distractions helps you gain insights into your values, motivations and inner processes, ultimately enhancing your self-awareness. I will take this topic of meditation in detail in Mantra 3, Chapter 17: Connect with the Self through Spirituality.

In the AI age, true problem-solving requires more than data and logic—it demands wisdom. Wisdom helps us frame the right questions, weigh long-term consequences and act with discernment where machines cannot. It is human ability to judge with context, values and experience that sets us apart. As we build sharper problem-solving skills, we must also cultivate this deeper intelligence—because without wisdom, even the best tools can lead us astray.

MANTRA 2
OPENNESS TO CHANGE

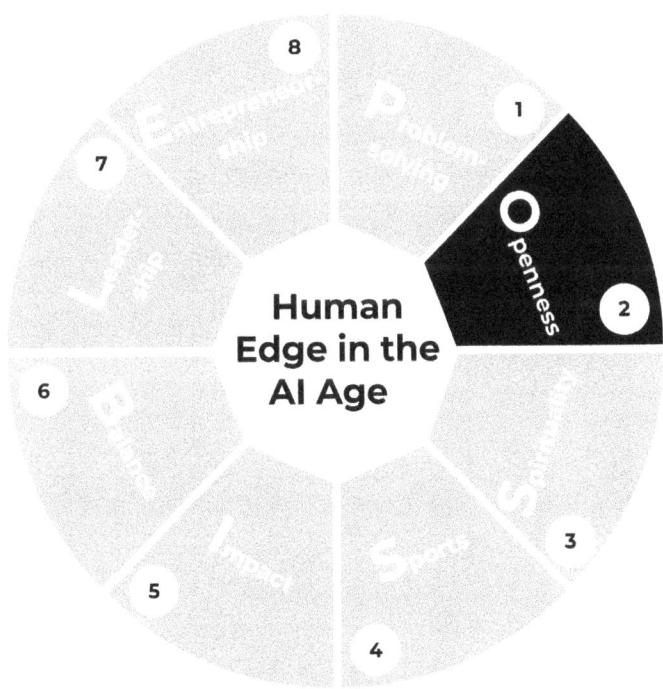

The POSSIBLE Framework

Introduction to Mantra 2
Openness to Change

Learning to Learn Is the New Superpower in the AI Age

In times of change, learners inherit the earth, while the learned find themselves beautifully equipped to deal with a world that no longer exists.
—Eric Hoffer, American philosopher

Change is inevitable, but in the AI age, it is relentless—a reality that brings to life Eric Hoffer's insight. As the world evolves faster than ever, those who can learn and adapt will shape the future, while others risk being left behind. Advances in technology and evolving business models demand that we not only cope with change but actively embrace it. While our instincts resist the unfamiliar, openness to change is no longer optional—it is essential. And I truly believe that the ability to *learn to learn*—developing the skills to adapt, unlearn and acquire new knowledge rapidly—is the defining superpower of our times.

In *Who Moved My Cheese?*, Spencer Johnson highlights how those who embrace new realities thrive, while those who cling to the past struggle. This message is more relevant than ever in a world transformed by AI and digital disruption. Those who resist change risk stagnation, while those who cultivate openness and continuous learning unlock entirely new possibilities.

From openness to change to lifelong learning

This mantra traces the evolution from openness to change to lifelong learning—a three-step journey that reflects how individuals must grow to stay relevant in the AI age, which I explore through the three chapters in this mantra:

1. **Embracing change:**
   I begin by emphasizing the importance of mindset. While every technological shift brings disruption, the AI age is fundamentally different. Change is not only faster, but far more far-reaching. To thrive, we must shift our mindset from resisting change to actively engaging with it.

2. **Rethinking traditional learning:**
   Next, I question whether our current learning systems are adequate. Traditional education was built for stability—for a world where knowledge had a long shelf life and careers followed linear paths, careers where deep subject-matter expertise could last decades. That model is now outdated. With the shrinking half-life of technical skills and the rise of AI automation, the ability to continuously learn and adapt is becoming the new benchmark of success.

3. **Learning to learn: the meta-skill of the future:**
   Finally, I focus on the process of *learning how to learn*—a meta-skill that amplifies all others and is critical for thriving in a fast-

changing world. Openness to change lays the foundation, but it is learning agility that sets people apart. This includes:

- Adapting to new ways of thinking—Breaking free from rigid mental models
- Learning autonomously—Taking charge of one's own growth
- Unlearning and relearning quickly—Letting go of outdated knowledge
- Applying knowledge effectively—Turning insight into impact

My personal journey in learning to learn

My own journey has reinforced the power of embracing change and mastering learning agility. After leaving McKinsey to start my own venture, ActiveKarma—which unfortunately didn't succeed (more about this in Chapter 11)—I initially struggled with acceptance. But with the support of family and friends, I shifted my mindset from failure to learning. This openness to change led me back to McKinsey, where I transformed a research back office into an innovative knowledge and analytics hub—an opportunity I would have missed had I remained stuck in the past.

Similarly, at Fidelity and later at Flipkart, I proactively shaped my roles rather than passively accepting predefined job descriptions. In addition to my core role of Country Head for India at Fidelity, I took on responsibility for leading strategy and transformation for the entire business. At Flipkart, I quickly evolved from being the Chief People Officer (CPO) to also heading strategy and later becoming the Chief Operating Officer (COO). I could grow quickly across different domains like wealth management and e-commerce because I was able to learn and adapt effectively. The mindset of learning to learn—constantly upgrading my skills, seeking new perspectives and staying curious—has been pivotal in my growth.

Mastering openness and learning in the AI age

To thrive in this new era, we must internalize a few guiding principles:

- **Accept change as inevitable**—The faster you embrace it, the less stressful it becomes
- **Develop a growth mindset**—View every challenge as a reinvention opportunity
- **Learn how to learn**—Prioritize learning agility and interdisciplinary thinking
- **Be proactive, not reactive**—Take control of your growth journey
- **Enjoy the process**—Lifelong learning is not a burden, it is a source of renewal and discovery

In the AI age, openness to change and learning agility are no longer just survival skills. They are the engines of reinvention. Those who master these twin capabilities won't just keep up—they will lead the transformation in an era defined by constant technological advancement.

11

Cultivating Openness to Change

It is not the strongest of the species that survive, nor the most intelligent, but the one most responsive to change.
—*Charles Darwin,*
Eminent naturalist, geologist and biologist

When faced with change, such as a new initiative or an unexpected shift, how do you react? Do you instantly embrace it? Often, people experience a sinking feeling and a resistance to the unknown. This isn't just a workplace issue, it affects almost all areas of life. Embracing change is tough because it disrupts our routines and challenges our thought patterns. While we welcome positive changes, like moving from a small place to a bigger home, negative or unknown ones, like an undesirable job relocation, are harder to accept. Here's a psychological fact: we tend to fear losing more than we value equivalent gains. The amygdala in our brains, which processes our emotions, plays a key role in this response, interpreting change as a threat and triggering a release of stress hormones that prepare us for fear, fight or flight. This instinctive reaction makes embracing the unfamiliar quite difficult.

The fear of the unknown isn't just limited to a few, it's a universal human experience. Let me give you a personal example. Whenever

I fly from Newark (my home airport), I almost always choose to fly with United Airlines, and I have a favourite seat—seat no. 1A or 1F. If I'm assigned a different seat, it really throws me off. I find myself feeling uneasy and restless, wondering, 'Why did they change my seat?' or 'Where's my usual spot?' Our natural tendency to seek comfort because it feels safe and familiar, acts as a defence against risks and unknowns. This habit of sticking to routines makes us feel secure, and breaking away from them can be tough. We see change as a risk because it disrupts what we're used to, even if it might bring benefits in the long run.

However, change is inevitable. It isn't just something that happens once in a while, it is constant, it is everywhere and it impacts the way we live, work and think. In the AI age, an era of relentless disruption, being open to change isn't a nice-to-have, it is essential. To keep up, we need to embrace change as a way of life, not as an exception. This understanding can empower us to embrace change more effectively, turning challenges into opportunities. The good news is, as we progress through life, we face change more often and accumulate experiences that make dealing with change easier. It's like a muscle that gets stronger as we use it regularly.

Why openness to change is important

Embracing change is challenging because we naturally cling to what feels familiar and comfortable. Initially, our instinct might be to resist and protect ourselves from the discomfort of the unknown. As we face and question our initial reactions to change, we begin to break away from old habits and reevaluate our usual ways of doing things. But the real breakthrough occurs with a mindset shift. This is when we begin to accept and fully embrace the change, not seeing it as a threat but as an opportunity for growth and learning. This shift from resistance to acceptance is crucial as it enables us to adapt and thrive in ever-changing environments.

One of my favourite timeless classics, *Who Moved My Cheese?* by Spencer Johnson, delivers a straightforward yet profound message about adapting to change.[1] It follows the journey of two mice, Sniff and Scurry, and two little people, Hem and Haw, in a maze as they search for cheese—a metaphor for whatever we value in life.

When their cheese supply is unexpectedly moved, each character reacts differently. The mice adapt quickly, instinctively setting out to find new cheese. This swift action of acceptance allows them to thrive, adjusting to new conditions and finding opportunities. The little people, however, face challenges. Hem resists the change, hoping the old cheese will return, while Haw eventually overcomes his fear and ventures out, discovering not only more cheese but also the freedom and growth that come from embracing the unknown.

The story is a powerful reminder that resisting change is futile; it presents an opportunity for growth. As we navigate the AI age, where the world is evolving at unprecedented speed, we are presented with a stark choice: adapt or risk extinction. Embracing change leads to abundance, offering opportunities for growth and prosperity. While, resistance to change can lead us to obsolescence. Now, more than ever, it's crucial to understand that adapting to change is not just about survival—it's about actively shaping our future which has been transformed by the AI age. However, building a mindset that welcomes change doesn't happen overnight; it takes consistent effort and determination. Let's explore how we can initiate this critical mindset shift.

Cultivating openness to change requires shift in mindset

In the AI age, as machines continue to surpass human capabilities and improve exponentially, I believe that our ability to adapt, grow and continuously learn has become one of the most critical skills of all. Of course, openness to change feels hard at first especially, if it is unknown. It's disruptive, unfamiliar and often uncomfortable.

But here's a truth I've learnt: once we shift our mindset, change begins to transform from a burden to an opportunity. There are five interconnected steps to it.

For me, **acceptance** is pivotal; it recognizes that change is inevitable. We often form deep emotional attachments to familiar things—be it our jobs, relationships or even everyday objects. Breaking free from these emotional attachments can be challenging. This difficulty is often compounded by a phenomenon known as the sunk-cost fallacy, which keeps us sticking to our regular path or course of action simply because we've invested a lot in them, even when it's clear that changing course would be more beneficial. But the longer we hold on to how things used to be, the more challenging it becomes to thrive in how things are now. Quick acceptance of change ensures flexibility, facilitating easier and less stressful adjustments.

Let me share a bit about my experience with failure and embracing change. I started my career with McKinsey but left it after a couple of years to start my own venture, ActiveKarma, a health and lifestyle startup, which unfortunately did not succeed. We got the market timing all wrong, over-estimated the market by 1,000 times and blew up our money too quickly! The failure of my venture was a big blow, not just financially but emotionally. This was the first time in my life I faced failure. Coming from a background where success was my familiar companion—from school, to IIT and IIM, to a promising start at McKinsey—I had never really faced failure. This track record had built up not just my own expectations but also those of everyone around me. People expected that anything I was involved in would be a success. Facing the reality of this venture not meeting those expectations was devastating, making it incredibly tough to accept what had happened.

However, this failure taught me a lot about life. I learnt that life is not a deterministic equation with well-defined relationships between inputs and outputs. There are many factors that you don't control so acceptance of your situation and humility are very important.

Getting this reality check in life was a big boon as I embarked on the next stage of my life journey.

During this challenging time, the support of my family and friends was invaluable. They were more than just a source of comfort; they were my anchors, offering the encouragement and perspective I needed to rebuild. Their unwavering support not only helped soften the blow but also led me to accept the change and learn from the experience. Their support was crucial in transforming what felt like a personal defeat into a stepping stone for future successes.

While acceptance is the starting point of cultivating openness to chance, being **proactive** is equally vital. We all have the power of choice, realizing and exercising this power at the right time can help us to make the most of the changes that occur in our lives. While we may not control the changes that occur, our responses to them are fully within our control. Accepting and adapting quickly is crucial to maintaining momentum. This proactive approach is more than just making the best of a situation, it's about actively shaping your journey. One of my core mantras is, 'Write your own job description'. Don't be passive, shape your life and career. When you're proactive, you don't just fill a role, you define it. After my adventure with ActiveKarma, I returned to McKinsey - I was to head their Knowledge Center (McKC) in India, which was essentially a research back office then. Instead of simply managing the back office, I envisioned it as a hub for innovation that would reshape McKinsey and its proposition to clients, which it successfully did over time. Nobody asked me to do it. Yet, by being proactive, I transformed McKC's role into a pioneering Knowledge and Analytics Capability Center, eventually a cornerstone of transformation of McKinsey's consulting offerings for the Digital and AI age. After my journey at McKinsey, I brought the same proactive spirit to Fidelity. Initially hired as the country head for India, I expanded my role significantly. I transformed my position to a global leader of all delivery locations and finally to heading business strategy and transformation and to play all these roles simultaneously. This unique journey was a result of my being proactive, not following a predefined path, and I am truly grateful to Fidelity for allowing me the freedom to shape my role and make a broader impact.

As I reflect on these experiences, I recognize another vital duality—the importance of both accepting your current situation and actively shaping it. Once you acknowledge the reality of change, you can start to discern what needs to evolve and what should remain. This dual approach of acceptance and proactive change is important. Beyond adjusting to new realities, it involves t envisioning and driving towards what those realities could become. While acceptance and being proactive seems like a duality, they are not at odds with each other. In my experience, awareness and acceptance of a situation is the foundation that enables you to be proactive.

Five levers to drive mindset shift for embracing change

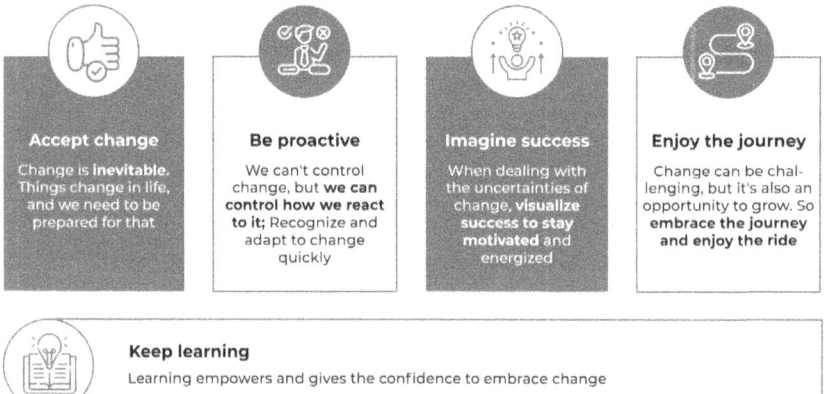

Imagining or visualizing success is imperative. I believe if you can envision a future, you can then bring it to life. This belief is closely linked with being proactive. Without a clear vision of success, even the most proactive efforts might wander off track. On the other hand, just dreaming about success without taking concrete steps is merely wishful thinking.

This personal philosophy has guided me throughout my leadership journey and never more so than the last seven years at Incedo. When I took the helm at Incedo, it was primarily a technology staffing firm. I envisioned transforming it into a digital transformation specialist, which we called Incedo 2.0. This vision required a fundamental shift in our organization's DNA. That visualization of success helped create the road map for turning that dream into reality. Three years later, as the market evolved with data becoming a central element of digital transformation, I led Incedo to focus on this area for Incedo 3.0. This bold vision of becoming a data-centric firm provided a new direction and enabled us to build powerful capabilities for our next growth phase. Most recently, I have set our sights on Incedo 4.0, aiming to become an AI-first organization, enabling our clients to drive ROI from AI at scale. This visualization of success over the years has been key to motivating the leadership team to embrace change and proactively reinvent to stay ahead of the curve.

Lastly, **enjoying the journey** is essential. We all know that breaking out of our routines can be painful and draining. That's why we need anchors—whether it's family, friends, mentors or personal hobbies like reading, sports, spirituality and meditation, which have been my own sanctuaries. These anchors not only replenish our energy but also help us appreciate the journey. This enjoyment shifts our perspective, allowing us to view change as a path to growth, rather than just a series of outcomes. By finding joy in the journey, we foster a growth mindset that embraces change as an integral part of our personal and professional development.

At the heart of these interconnected steps lies continuous **learning**. Learning is the ultimate vehicle for change; it empowers us with the confidence to navigate uncertainty, adapt and grow. It's this learning mindset that enables us to continuously evolve and thrive in a world shaped by relentless transformation. Learning empowers and gives the confidence to deal better with change and evolve our mindset.

In the end, I would like to emphasize that in the AI age, change is accelerating at an unprecedented rate. I also firmly believe that while change disrupts the usual, familiar and certain, it also opens up extraordinary opportunities for those prepared to embrace it. The ability to embrace change is similar to building any skill I have discussed—it demands conscious effort, focus and practice.

The more we confront and navigate change, the more adept we become at dealing with it. At its heart, embracing change is fundamentally about learning. It's about continuously adapting, growing and capitalizing on the opportunities that rapid evolution brings. In the future, our ability to 'learn to learn' will be the most crucial skill, enabling us to continually evolve and thrive in the very dynamic world shaped by the AI age.

12

The Need for Redefining Learning Approaches

The classroom without walls has no limits.
—Inspired by Sylvia Ashton-Warner,
New Zealand novelist

The trajectory of learning—from the playful explorations of preschool to the structured confines of school and college and even the varied challenges of the workplace—our journey of learning is unending. Traditionally, learning has served to prepare us for well-defined jobs, meticulously shaping our skills, decision-making and personalities to fit neatly into specific roles and execute the tasks assigned to us well.

However, as we step into the AI era, the landscape of learning needs a profound transformation. The old playbook of absorbing information and executing tasks to fit into predefined jobs is quickly becoming obsolete. However, education must pivot towards entrepreneurial thinking, empowering individuals not just to navigate but to actively create in a world where the future is not given but made.

This shift from predefined career paths to a landscape filled with unknowns requires us to be innovators, opportunity-seekers and creators. In today's AI age, fraught with uncertainty and continuous evolution, learning is no longer geared towards preparing for known opportunities but about developing the ability to explore, adapt and pioneer new possibilities. It is time to move beyond passively acquiring knowledge and step into actively shaping the future and, carving out spaces yet to be defined.

I was reminded of this feeling while watching the movie *Dead Poets Society*. For those who are unfamiliar with it, it's a film about an unconventional English teacher who inspires his students to think for themselves, to question the status quo and to embrace their own unique voices. Mr Keating, the teacher, challenges the rigid, traditional methods of education that prioritize memorization over critical thinking and conformity over individuality. This resonated deeply with me. The film highlights the growing inadequacies of traditional education methods in our rapidly evolving, AI-driven world.

Reimagining traditional learning approaches for the AI age

Now, I'm not saying the traditional learning models were totally wrong, far from it! They've been the backbone of education for generations, designed for a world where change was gradual and skills once learnt lasted almost a lifetime. However, those days are fading.

Until recently, mastering programming languages like Java or Python set you up for career success. Today, the scene has shifted dramatically. AI tools can now generate code and optimize algorithms, reshaping skill demands at an astonishing pace. Also, the half-life of skills—the time it takes for a skill to become half as valuable—is dramatically shorter now. For instance, technical skills that were considered to be for lifetime have a half-life of less than 2.5 years. What used to sustain a career for decades is now becoming temporary.

Now imagine waking up one day to find your job automated overnight by intelligent machines. Or that AI has already mastered the career path you were planning to pivot to. This isn't a distant possibility, it's happening now. As AI accelerates, many are grappling with the unsettling reality that traditional learning approaches, which worked well in the past, may no longer offer long-term job security.

What does this mean for us? This new reality underscores the importance of adaptability, continuous learning and readiness to pivot whenever necessary. Therefore, I believe the future of learning must embrace a dynamic and personalized approach to prepare individuals to tackle new challenges with enthusiasm and agility. Let's explore how we can transform our learning strategies to meet the demands of this rapidly changing world.

New ways of learning in the AI age

I believe that in today's AI age, personalized learning has become critical. Imagine a future where individuals can integrate learning seamlessly into their daily lives, accessing knowledge on demand, wherever they are. This vision is already becoming a reality to an extent, thanks to the rise of massive open online courses (MOOCs) learning platforms like Coursera and Udemy, to name a few. These platforms are at the forefront of making learning more accessible, leveraging AI-powered recommendations and interactive experiences to offer learners personalized, on-demand learning across multiple channels.

Again, I can't overlook the unique duality this AI age brings in the field of learning: AI is both a catalyst for and a facilitator of the significant shifts in learning approaches. On the one hand, AI's rapid evolution demands a move to stay relevant, pushing us away from traditional models towards more flexible, personalized and tech-integrated methods. Simultaneously, AI is equipping us with the tools—like AI tutors and self-paced courses—that make this new paradigm possible, tailoring education to individual needs. Isn't that remarkable?

This duality is central to understanding the future of learning. As AI progresses, it will continue to refine and expand our learning methods, ensuring new learning approaches remain relevant in our ever-evolving world. I believe embracing the following five shifts is essential for adapting to the rapid changes that define our times and for preparing ourselves for the challenges ahead.

AI age demands fundamental shifts in the learning approaches

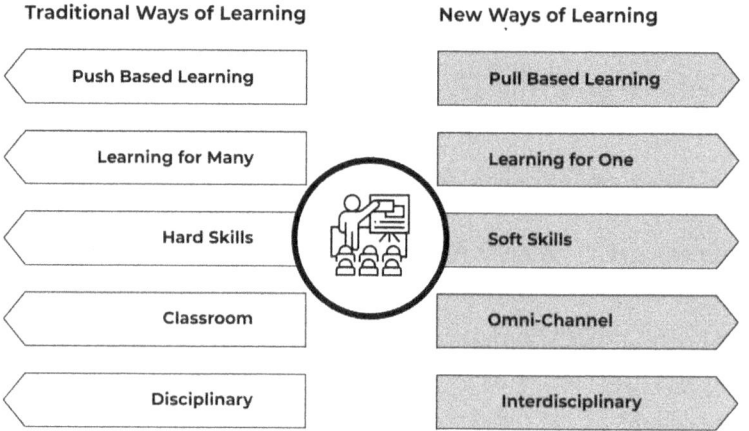

1. **A shift from push-based learning to pull-based learning:** Remember the endless lectures from school or college, where information was constantly 'pushed' at us? It's time for that to change. We need to move towards 'pull-based' learning, where learners take the driver's seat. You choose what to learn, when and how it fits into your schedule, making education flexible and tailored to your lifestyle. Bite-sized learning modules like Duolingo for languages, Khan Academy for various topics or TED-Ed for quick insights should become the norm, revolutionizing how we engage with information.

In our fast-moving world, it's hard to keep our attention focused for long stretches. That's why learning in short bursts has become so appealing. Whether it's a quick lesson on your commute, a podcast during a run or a mini quiz on your coffee break. This approach respects your pace and needs, making learning an integrated part of your daily routine, not just another task.

2. **A shift from learning for many to learning for one**: As I explored in Chapter 4, hyper-personalization is revolutionizing nearly every industry. So, why should education be any different? Interestingly when I look back at the ancient Indian gurukul system, a residential schooling model that seamlessly integrated academics, moral values and spiritual growth in an immersive environment—it becomes clear that personalized learning is not a modern innovation but a time-honoured tradition. In gurukuls, students (*shishyas*) lived and learnt under the close guidance of their teachers (gurus), receiving instruction that was meticulously tailored to their individual needs and strengths—a visionary approach way ahead of its time.

   Learning has always been most effective when it's personal—just like in the gurukul model, where education was tailored to each student. By leveraging the power of AI, we can now enable hyper-personalization in learning. Platforms like Knewton, part of the Wiley group, are already making learning more personal. They adapt lessons based on how each person learns best—whether through videos, interactive simulations or text. They track progress in real time, spotting weak areas and adjusting content to help students improve. No more one-size-fits-all learning—this approach tailors education to you, your strengths, your pace and your goals. And the best part? It can scale, making truly personalized learning accessible to everyone.

3. **A shift from hard skills to soft skills**: Reflect on a decade ago, when mastering specific software or coding in Java was almost

a guarantee for a stable career. Those technical skills were highly valued and symbolized long-term success. But times have changed dramatically. According to recent research, the tech world is evolving so quickly that skills once considered essential can become obsolete in just two and a half years—a stark reminder of how fast things are moving.

In my previous book *Mastering Data Paradox*, I explored how even the most sought-after careers are not immune to change. Take data science—a field once hailed as the 'hottest job of the decade.' Today, AI is automating over 80 per cent of its core tasks, like data preparation, forcing professionals to rethink their roles.[1] It is unsettling to realize that a career once considered future proof can shift so quickly. This isn't just about keeping up with new tools, it is about staying relevant in a world where no technical skill stays future proof for long.

But if technical expertise has an expiration date, what truly stands the test of time? The answer lies in soft skills. Critical thinking, problem-solving, adaptability, leadership and effective communication aren't just important, they are timeless. Unlike technical skills, which can quickly become outdated in the AI age, soft skills remain timeless, helping us navigate uncertainty, collaborate effectively and thrive in any situation. In fact, recent research shows that 67 per cent of employers now prioritize soft skills over educational qualifications when hiring.[2] As technology continues to reshape the way we work, developing these skills will be the key to building a sustainable and successful career.

4. **A shift from classroom to omni-channel learning:** We've entered an era where traditional classroom settings simply cannot keep pace with the evolving needs of learners. Today, learning must be accessible anytime, anywhere and across multiple channels. Just as individuals' learning styles and preferences are unique, so too are their schedules and circumstances. Everyone learns

differently. Whether you excel in a structured classroom, thrive on self-paced courses, love diving into a good book or prefer the dynamic interaction of video lessons and live workshops, the beauty of omni-channel learning is that it caters to all styles and schedules.

Platforms like Coursera and Udemy offer interactive online courses with real-time feedback and simulations. Mobile apps like Prodigy turn learning into a gamified experience, making subjects like maths and English more engaging. Social learning platforms like 360 Learning combine structured learning with peer-to-peer collaboration, fostering discussion and teamwork for a more interactive experience. With these diverse tools, learning is no longer confined to classrooms—it becomes an interactive, flexible experience that fits into everyday life. This approach doesn't just make learning accessible, it customizes education to fit your life. This ensures that it's relevant and effective and specifically, tailored for you.

5. **A shift from disciplinary to interdisciplinary learning**: For decades, traditional education has focused on mastering a single discipline—learning one subject deeply and becoming an expert in it. While this approach builds strong foundational knowledge, it often falls short in real-world problem-solving, where challenges rarely exist within the confines of a single field. They spill over, demanding insights from multiple fields to find real solutions. This gap is even more evident in the AI age, where industries are evolving rapidly and challenges are becoming more intertwined. A traditional, single-discipline approach can feel too theoretical, detached from the messy, complex nature of real-life problems.

College education must evolve to reflect this reality. Take biotechnology, for example. To truly excel in this field, you cannot just understand biology; you also need to grasp technology. AI is now helping in drug discovery, genetic engineering and personalized medicine. Without a strong foundation in both domains, innovation is stalled.

In the AI age, where knowledge evolves at lightning speed, an interdisciplinary approach provides a broader perspective. It teaches you to approach challenges holistically, looking at them from multiple angles rather than from within the constraints of a single discipline. This way of learning can train your brain to adapt and learn new things faster, building the agility to handle the rapid pace of technological change.

As we embrace these shifts, we transform learning from a static, one-time activity into an ongoing, integrated practice. This not only prepares us better for the future but also enhances the learning process, making it more fulfilling and effective and ensuring that we remain adaptable and competent in the AI age.

Evolving role of college education in the AI age

I firmly believe we need to reassess the value we attach to college degrees or at least the role of college education. The premium placed on elite educational brands like the Ivy League colleges in the US or top-tier institutions such as IIT and IIM in India is astounding. As an IIT and IIM graduate myself, I understand the prestige these institutions carry. These top institutions are viewed as golden tickets to a secure future, but today's fast-changing world demands more than what is taught in these institutions. Traditionally, these colleges were the gateways to high-quality knowledge and expert mentorship. However, in the digital age, this landscape has dramatically shifted. High-quality education and mentorship are now accessible to anyone, anywhere, at the click of a button.

This shift should lead to a rethinking of the true value of a degree and a recent experience brought this even closer to home for me. As my son prepared to apply for college while also running his own startup, he considered whether he should skip the degree and focus entirely on his business. If success today is being redefined beyond traditional education, does the weight we place on a degree still hold? Elon Musk once said, 'I think we should not have this idea that to be successful, you need a four-year college degree. That is simply not true.' He has a point, but I feel that college still holds value—especially for the networking opportunities it provides. However, the knowledge it offers is no longer as unique or differentiated as it once was.

In our rapidly evolving, information-rich world, the real key to success is not merely learning, it's mastering the art of 'learning to learn'. This involves nurturing a mindset of endless curiosity and continuous growth, well beyond formal education. In the next chapter, I'm excited to explore how we can better cultivate this essential skill to meet today's demands and tomorrow's uncertainties.

13

The Art of Learning to Learn

Give a man a fish and you feed him for a day. Teach him how to fish and you feed him for a lifetime.

—*Lao Tzu, Chinese philosopher*

Change has been the constant companion of human evolution and historically we have adapted well. But in the AI age, we are facing an unprecedented pace of change. It is already transforming everything: how we create music, design our spaces and even how we tackle health issues. Skills once thought uniquely human are now being challenged by AI. I believe this is just the beginning. We stand on the brink of an AI revolution that will lead to a reimagination of how we work and live. This change will profoundly alter the skills we need to both survive and thrive in this new era.

While many people are still trying to wrap their heads around the impact AI is going to have, this rapid transformation is already causing real anxiety for quite a few. This unease, called the fear of becoming obsolete (FOBO), was a major topic at the January 2025 World Economic Forum in Davos, resonating deeply with attendees. Even visionaries like Elon Musk predict a future where traditional jobs may no longer exist, prompting us to question the value of experience in an AI-driven world.

The answer lies in adaptability—learning to be comfortable with discomfort, pushing past limits and constantly evolving. This is something I have personally experienced through my professional journey. Early in my career, I realized that diverse experiences provide a crucial foundation. But experience alone isn't enough. The real game-changer is the ability to keep learning and building on top of that experience. To keep up with change, I have had to constantly learn, adapt and find new ways to stay ahead. Later in the chapter, I will share the specific strategies that have helped me navigate this ever-shifting landscape.

The rules have changed. It is no longer just about what you learn—though that still matters. The real differentiator is how you learn. The future belongs to those who can adapt, unlearn and relearn quickly, turning learning into their greatest advantage. And that means embracing something most of us resist: becoming a beginner, again and again.

So, how do we master the art of Learning to Learn? I believe it comes down to six key levers: **Humility, curiosity, deliberate learning, mental models, reflection and application.**

Mastering the art of 'learning to learn'

Learning is not just an innate ability—it is a skill. And like any skill, it can be acquired and mastered. Some people may naturally be better at learning, but that does not mean that others cannot develop the ability to learn faster, better and more effectively. To aid this process, I've identified six core levers which I believe are critical to how we learn. Mastering these would help you master the art of learning.

Framework for Learning to Learn

- Reflection feeds humility
- Reflection feeds mental models
- Humility — Curiosity — Deliberate Learning — Mental Models — Application — Reflection
- Foundational elements: Humility, Curiosity
- Mental models feed deliberate learning
- Reflection feeds deliberate learning

1. Humility

Let's be real—learning isn't about having all the answers because the moment you think you know enough, you stop learning and growing. That's where humility comes in. It's when you acknowledge that you don't know it all, and that's when you stay hungry and curious. The greatest minds—Leonardo da Vinci, Marie Curie, Albert Einstein—shared one trait: they embraced what they didn't know. You need to see and acknowledge the gaps in your knowledge not as failures, but as exciting new paths to explore.

But how do we cultivate this crucial humility? One of the most humbling experiences is working alongside someone who is a master at something. It's a reality check—a reminder of just how much more there is to learn. It's not about feeling inadequate, it's about feeling inspired to grow. Stepping out of our comfort zones is also critical for cultivating humility. I agree it is tough and uncomfortable. But how else do we grow? Excelling at one thing is great, but embracing the continuous pursuit of new knowledge keeps us grounded while keeping our minds active and our lives exciting.

For instance, when I started learning squash, I quickly picked up the basics. I felt like I was getting the hang of it. But then I started working with my coach, a master of the sport. That's when I realized just how much I didn't know. It was a truly humbling experience, but also incredibly motivating. It spurred me to train harder, delve deeper into the techniques and ultimately, elevate my game. This experience solidified my belief that learning from a master breeds humility. This is not limited to acknowledging what you don't know; it requires recognizing the immense potential for growth that lies ahead and using that realization as fuel to propel you forward.

2. **Curiosity**

If humility opens the door to learning, curiosity is what pushes us through it. It's the secret ingredient in the recipe for human progress. Curiosity is that strong urge to ask 'why,' to dig deeper and explore beyond the surface. Think of a child's endless questions: 'Why is the sky blue?' 'How does a plane fly?' That constant questioning is the spark of discovery. And there's actual science behind it—the information gap theory that suggests that curiosity ignites when we sense a gap between what we know and what we want to know. The bigger the gap (within reason), the more curious we become. Let's explore the secret to unlocking our curiosity.

But there's a catch: you need mental space to be curious. If your mind is constantly cluttered, there's little room for those 'why' questions to surface. One powerful way is through mindful observation, when a child explores a new toy. They don't just glance at it, they turn it over, examine it from different angles and try to figure out how it works. We can learn from this.

An effective way to cultivate curiosity is to explore different perspectives. Make a habit of talking to others to get different perspectives. This process not only generates natural questions and expands your understanding, it also cultivates humility by reminding us that we don't have all the answers.

Also, whatever you pursue, give it your full attention, be present in the moment. Curiosity thrives on this kind of focused engagement. It requires study and wonder. And, crucially, it requires questioning. Great learners don't just passively absorb information, they challenge it by asking the relevant questions to dissect it and reassemble it in new ways. Because more often than not, asking the right questions is the crucial first step in solving any problem.

Curiosity means immersing yourself in whatever you're learning. It involves engaging in a range of experiences, understanding the nuances and appreciating the beauty and complexity. For instance, if you're keen on expanding your cinema knowledge, consider exploring movies beyond English-speaking countries like France or Korea. By engaging with these international movies, you'll not only discover new storytelling styles but also broaden your cultural horizons, moving beyond the familiar and comfortable.

And here's the best part: curiosity is a positive reinforcement cycle. Research has shown that satisfying your curiosity triggers the reward centres of your brain.[1] This means that the more curious you are, the more you learn and the more your brain rewards you with a sense of satisfaction and pleasure. This creates a positive feedback loop, making us want to learn even more. Together, humility and curiosity form the foundation of lifelong learning. They keep you adaptable, open and always ready to grow.

3. **Deliberate learning**

Curiosity sparks our interest, but deliberate learning is what takes us to the finish line—mastery. For me, deliberate learning is the heart of 'learning how to learn'—it's how we become architects of our own knowledge. It is not just about passively absorbing facts, it is a structured, purposeful process. As psychologist Anders Ericsson, who coined the concept of deliberate practice, explained, it's far more than rote repetition. It is an intentional effort, requiring structured plans, continuous monitoring and targeted adjustments.[2]

I see deliberate learning as a tiered approach, a systematic way to dissect and conquer any skill or subject. It begins with setting clear goals. What exactly do you want to achieve? Once you have your target, the next step is deconstructing the skill or topic into its critical, smaller components. Do not try to learn everything at once, break it down into manageable chunks.

Then comes the crucial part: patient, focused practice. Concentrate intently on mastering each individual component. Do not rush the process; deep, deliberate practice is key. After practising, seek feedback or test your learning. How did you do? What worked and what didn't? Finally, and perhaps most importantly, identify the gaps in your learning and repeat the process. It is a continuous cycle—learn, practice, get feedback, refine—a virtuous loop that drives you toward mastery.

Think of learning tennis. Imagine aiming for tennis mastery, not just casual play. First, you set a goal: maybe it's mastering the serve. Then, you break it down: grip, stance, toss, swing. You do not try to perfect every shot at once; you focus on the toss. You practice the toss repeatedly, refining it until it is consistent, building a strong foundation. Once you are confident in the skill, you should test it in the real world. Analyse your performance and seek feedback. Learning from experts is essential. It's nearly impossible to achieve deliberate mastery in isolation. We all have blind spots, areas where we can't accurately assess our own performance. That's where the experience and insights of an expert become invaluable. Once you have mastered the toss, move on—perhaps to the swing. You apply the same principles:

focus, breakdown, practice, feedback and refinement. You are not becoming Federer overnight. You are deliberately building skills, piece by piece by staying at them with patience. Deep, not wide—that is the essence of deliberate learning, and that is how mastery is achieved.

This brings me to a significant point: prioritizing depth over breadth. For me, this is a key takeaway. By focusing on depth, we move from general knowledge to specific knowledge, basically moving from knowing a little about many things to truly mastering at least one. Surface-level knowledge might be useful for casual conversation, but it will not allow you to solve complex problems or create truly innovative solutions.

Elon Musk exemplifies this perfectly. He has disrupted not one, but many industries by doing exactly this. In each case, he went straight to the heart of the matter and had conversations with the experts, drawing on their knowledge to gain a deep understanding of the challenges. Let's take the example of Tesla; the critical challenge was the limitations of existing battery technology, which hindered the widespread adoption of electric vehicles. Musk launched Tesla's Gigafactories. This massive investment in manufacturing enabled large-scale production and created economies of scale that drastically reduced battery costs. They also innovated the battery chemistry, exploring and implementing new materials to create batteries that lasted longer, charged faster and delivered more power.

Similarly for SpaceX, he didn't just skim the surface, he delved into these topics, determined to make space travel accessible to all. For SpaceX, Musk's disruptive solution was to make rockets reusable and cost friendly. The Falcon 9 and Starship were designed with this in mind. For instance, switching to stainless steel for Starship (instead of carbon fibre) drastically reduced costs—Starship costs under $10 million, while similar NASA projects cost hundreds of millions.

That is deliberate learning in action. He first identified the core problem in the industries he entered. Focusing intensely on solving these issues, he stayed committed to the problem, experimented and learnt from it to refine his approach. By doing so, he didn't just make incremental changes, he fundamentally transformed the industries by addressing their core issues.

And the cool thing is, deliberate learning isn't just about getting smarter, it also keeps us humble. The more we learn, the more we realize how much we don't know. It fuels our curiosity even more. It's a cycle of growth, and honestly, it's what makes life so rewarding.

4. **Mental models**
Having established a foundation of deliberate learning, how do you really speed things up? Mental models to the rescue. Think of them as the building blocks of true understanding; they help you practise more effectively. They're about getting the big picture, or the core ideas, so you can use them in lots of different ways. It's like having a set of Lego bricks. Instead of just following instructions for one specific toy, you understand how the bricks fit together and can build almost anything. Building these mental models is super helpful.

First, it makes learning new stuff way faster. When you come across something unfamiliar, you're not lost. You have a framework, a way to make sense of it, so you learn it much more quickly. Second, mental models provide a structured approach to new topics, allowing you to efficiently navigate their complexities and connect the dots to something that you already know. Mental models also enable us to apply our learning from one domain to another.

This efficiency and direction are also important for deliberate learning. They function like a map and compass for your learning journey, making your progress faster and more directed.

Take Leonardo da Vinci, a historical polymath, for instance. He was not just an artist, but also a scientist, engineer and inventor. His work demonstrates that he used learning from science in his artwork extensively. For example, the Vitruvian Man and the Mona Lisa—these weren't just artistic expressions, they were informed by a scientific understanding of the human form. The Vitruvian Man is a visual representation of Da Vinci's understanding of proportion and geometry, reflecting his study of Vitruvius's writings and his own anatomical observations. He measured real bodies to understand human proportions, bringing a scientific rigor to his art.

His study of light and vision directly affected his shading, making his work look incredibly real. The Mona Lisa's sfumato— that subtle blending of colours—wasn't just a style, it copied how light and shadow work, making her expression seem to change depending on how you look at her.

This approach is not unique to Da Vinci—it is how most polymaths learn. From Benjamin Franklin to Richard Feynman, polymaths have relied on mental models to draw connections across disciplines. It's about building those bridges between different areas of knowledge, seeing the underlying patterns and applying those insights in creative and innovative ways.

This has been true in my own experience. While I would not call myself a polymath, mental models have been my constant guide. Looking back—from consulting at McKinsey to leading strategy and transformation at Fidelity, to driving growth at Flipkart, and now building Incedo—I see how these mental models have been invaluable across situations. They have helped me navigate complexities, connect the dots and tackle challenges with a structured approach. Even today, I rely on them to evaluate business scenarios, assess performance and drive execution.

There are three mental models that are fundamental to how I engage in any new topic. First is getting to the core of any problem and being very sharp about problem identification. It's easy to get caught up in surface-level issues, but real impact comes from digging deeper, getting to the root cause and tackling what truly matters. This understanding has taught me that problems are rarely what they seem. That is why I consistently ask my team, '*mudde ki baat?* (what is the core of the issue?)'

Second strategy to execution. And as I often say, strategy without execution is hallucination. I believe that strategy lies not in looking forward but in looking back from execution and connecting the dots. Strategy and execution should not be viewed as a sequential activity. In fact, it's an iterative process where the strategy sets the direction, but execution is where it gets tested. Learning from execution feeds back into strategy in an iterative fashion. This ongoing feedback—learning, adapting and refining—that's the key to drive impact.

Another element, one I've written about in *Winning in the Digital Age* and *Mastering the Data Paradox*, is the two-speed approach to execution. Speed One tackles urgent problems for rapid progress. Speed Two focuses on long-term strategic goals. The challenge—and the key—is seamlessly shifting gears and connecting the two. Building Speed Two initiatives by linking them to Speed One programmes. This approach is crucial not just for business, but also for career development. It's about knowing when to sprint and when to pace yourself for the marathon.

5. **Application of learning**

And here's another crucial piece of the puzzle: application. It's the bridge between understanding and doing. It's so easy to fall into the trap of thinking we know a lot, but until we actually put that knowledge to the test, how can we be sure? It's what I call the 'illusion of learning'—we feel like we've grasped something, but until we apply it, it is not real. It's where the rubber meets the road, where our understanding is truly tested, refined and solidified.

Isn't it true that learning connected to an application has so much more value? It's like building muscle—you can read all about exercise, but until you hit the gym, you won't see any real change. The same is true for learning. It's not enough to simply absorb information, we need to put it into action.

So, how do we actually apply our learning? I've found a few things to be particularly helpful. First, actively seek opportunities to test what you've learned. Look for chances to apply your knowledge in real-world situations. This could mean internships, volunteer projects, personal initiatives or even just practicing with someone. Don't be afraid to step outside the classroom or textbook.

Second, and this is so important, be comfortable with failure. Treat it as an integral part of the learning process. Real-life situations are messy; they are full of variables that make it incredibly difficult to perfectly replicate what we have learned in a controlled environment. But going beyond the fear of failure is what truly refines our learning for the real world. It's okay to stumble and make mistakes. In fact, it is essential.

Third, teach others. Seriously, sharing your knowledge with someone else—whether it's through formal teaching, mentoring or just a casual conversation—is incredibly powerful. Explaining a concept to someone else forces you to organize your thoughts, identify any gaps in your own understanding and articulate the information clearly. It's a fantastic way to solidify what you've learnt.

Ultimately, application is what transforms theoretical knowledge into practical mastery. It's how we move from simply knowing about something to actually being able to do it. And really, isn't that the real reward of learning—being able to make a difference, to create something new, to solve a problem? After all, the true measure of learning isn't found in the number of degrees one holds, but in the ability to use that knowledge to make a difference in the world.

This brings me to a powerful example: Indian Prime Minister Narendra Modi. Despite not having an elite formal education, his ability to translate learning into real-world action is what truly defines him. I've been struck by his deep engagement across a wide range of topics—from technology and business to agriculture and research—whether in group meetings or larger forums. His ability to grasp complex topics, engage in structured discussions and connect ideas across domains is remarkable. It's clear that for him, learning isn't just about acquiring knowledge, but about engaging with it, adapting it and applying it iteratively. It's not merely the extent of what he knows, it's about how he applies what he knows to make a difference. He is a testament to the power of applied learning. This reinforces my belief that learning to learn goes beyond formal education—it centres on staying open, curious and willing to evolve, a skill more fundamental than ever in a world of constant change.

6. **Reflection**
Application is essential, but reflection is where it all comes together. In the rush of daily life, we rarely stop to think deeply about what we have learned. We're constantly moving from one thing to the next. We absorb information, sure, but are we really processing it? We hear, we read, we do—but do we truly internalize? I've found that reflection is the key. It's what transforms mere experience into genuine insight. It helps us recognize patterns and connections we might have missed in that moment. Without reflection, learning stays surface level. It's like skimming the surface of a lake—you see a little, but you miss the depths below.

Reflection brings clarity and uncovers sharp insights that might otherwise remain hidden. Going back to the tennis example: While match play is the 'moment of truth', the application of your skills, true improvement comes from what happens after the match. Reflection can occur at several levels. For example, a post-match analysis might reveal some tactical tweaks. Maybe your usual aggressive play is not working, and you need to use drop shots. A post-tournament review might give a somewhat deeper perspective. It could point out technical skills to refine between the tournaments, such as improving your top spin by adjusting your grip and swing. This technical reflection turns into targeted practice sessions focused on honing that specific skill. Further, an end-of-season reflection might reveal more fundamental issues like insufficient arm strength, which affects your power in long matches. Identifying these foundational problems provides a roadmap for targeted physical conditioning in the off-season. Reflection at these different levels is absolutely essential to your continuous learning and to help you grow into the player you aim to be.

I make it a habit to step away at regular intervals—to think, process and regain clarity. Meditation is a key part of this practice. I commit to twenty minutes twice a day, and ten on the busiest days, without fail.

Those aha! moments, those sharp insights, are game changers. They automatically force you to go back, fill in the gaps, to engage in that deliberate learning we talked about earlier, so you can truly sharpen your understanding of the topic. It's a cycle—experience, reflection, insight and then back to deliberate learning again, each step building on the last.

'Learning to learn' is your greatest asset

The deeper you delve into the process of learning, the more you realize just how much more there is to learn—and the better you become at the art of learning itself. It's a beautiful paradox: knowledge breeds curiosity, and curiosity fuels the hunger for more knowledge. It's a constant feedback loop, a virtuous cycle where each component reinforces the others, creating a powerful engine for lifelong growth.

And in this rapidly changing AI age, this is not just an advantage, it's a necessity. Learning to learn isn't just a skill, it's the *essential skill*, the ultimate meta-skill. It's the greatest gift that everyone needs to give to themselves, the key to not just surviving but thriving in a world transformed by AI. In a world where change is the only constant, the ability to learn, adapt and grow is the most valuable asset you can possess. It's a timeless gift that will keep on giving, long after the latest technology becomes obsolete—the gift that empowers us to shape our own futures.

MANTRA 3

CONNECT WITH THE SELF THROUGH SPIRITUALITY

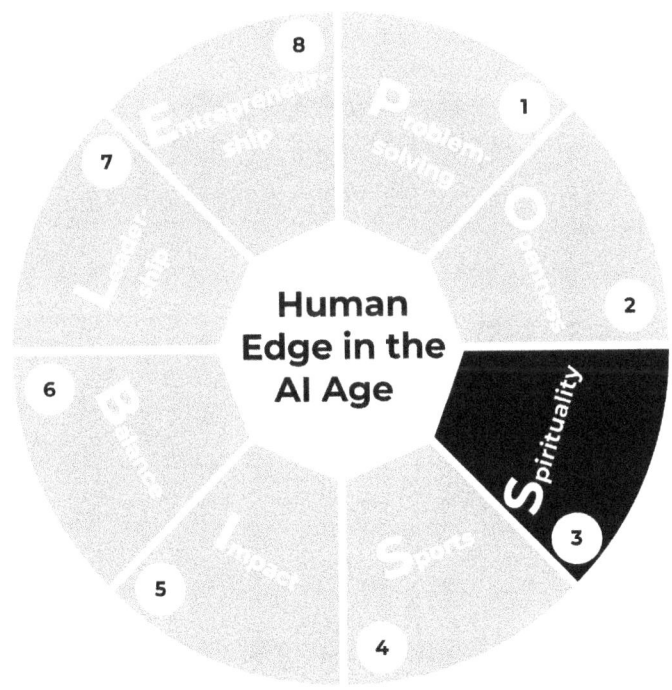

Introduction to Mantra 3

Connect with the Self through Spirituality

Staying Centered in a Rapidly Shifting World

We are not human beings having a spiritual experience. We are spiritual beings having a human experience.
—*Pierre Teilhard de Chardin, French philosopher*

In an age of relentless digital stimulation, hyper-productivity and material success, something profound is missing. We are always running—chasing career milestones, wealth and social validation—yet true peace remains elusive. The AI age has only amplified this challenge. With constant connectivity, instant gratification and an overflow of information, we are losing the ability to pause, reflect and truly experience life. Stress levels are rising, relationships are fraying and ethical compromises are increasing. If we do not cultivate spiritual balance, we risk becoming mere machines—efficient but devoid of inner fulfilment.

Historically, materialism and spirituality have been seen as opposing forces, but they are not mutually exclusive. The key is balance. *Artha* (prosperity) and *kama* (pleasure) must be aligned with *dharma* (duty, right way, natural law) and *moksha* (liberation) to create a meaningful life. Without this balance, we risk getting trapped in an endless cycle of ambition and discontent.

Reconnecting with the Self through Spirituality

In this mantra, I explore why spirituality is not only relevant but indispensable in the AI age. Across four chapters, I share key insights that have helped me cultivate clarity, energy and resilience:

1. **Balancing materialism and spirituality:**
   The opening chapter explores the duality of material and spiritual pursuits, emphasizing why aligning the two is essential. When they fall out of sync, we experience burnout, stress and inner conflict.

2. **The eleven laws of spirituality:**
   Building on the need for spiritual grounding, the second chapter introduces eleven principles that have deeply resonated with me. These timeless truths have shaped both my personal and professional journey.

3. **The power of mindfulness practice:**
   In the third chapter, I shared my own journey of mindfulness. This practice has brought greater calm, clarity and focus into my life—qualities that are increasingly rare and valuable in our overstimulated world.

4. **Vipassana: Cultivating stillness and insight**
   The final chapter takes a deeper look at Vipassana meditation, a practice that has been transformative for me. It is through

this inner stillness that I have been able to navigate both life's fluctuation and professional intensity.

Spirituality in action: My personal practice

Spirituality is most powerful when applied practically. I have been fortunate that I learnt meditation at an early age and it has been my constant companion and the key for my high energy levels and clarity of thought. Meditation has also been pivotal in maintaining resilience during difficult phases in my career. After the failure of my entrepreneurial venture, ActiveKarma, I turned to the Art of Living and also learnt Vipassana meditation, which played a key role in restoring my focus and positivity. Since then, regular practice of the Art of Living *pranayama* (breath control) and meditation practices has been instrumental in maintaining energy levels and inner balance despite an intense corporate career.

This journey has taught me that spirituality is not about escaping reality but about developing the inner strength to navigate it effectively. Whether through structured meditation, acts of service or mindful decision-making, spirituality can help us become better leaders, professionals and human beings.

Why spirituality matters in the AI age

As AI automates more functions and accelerates our external world, our inner world needs greater attention. What will differentiate us is not our access to information, but our ability to interpret, reflect and act with wisdom. The future belongs to those who lead with both intellect and inner clarity.

To cultivate this grounding:

- **Pause for self-reflection:** Insight begins with stillness

- **Align action with values:** Let dharma (right way) guide your pursuits
- **Practice mindfulness:** Enhance focus and emotional resilience
- **Prioritize wisdom over information:** Judgement matters more than data
- **Balance ambition with inner peace:** True success includes fulfilment

The AI age will continue to accelerate, but the real challenge is staying human amidst it all. Spirituality gives us the tools to do just that. By anchoring ourselves in self-awareness and meaning, we don't just survive—we thrive with grace, purpose and inner strength.

14

Spiritual Balance

A Necessity in Today's AI Age

There is more to life than increasing its speed.

—*Mahatma Gandhi,*
Eminent Indian political ethicist and
leader of Indian Independence Movement

This age of digital deluge and hyper-consumerism is filled with numerous attractions and temptations. We are always running after the outer trappings of success—money, possessions, power and position. However, this is a trap. We are on an ever-running treadmill of desires and expectations. The faster we run and the more success we get, the more our desires keep rising and the treadmill goes faster. We can never find true peace and happiness as long as we are on the expectation's treadmill. As we run faster and faster to catch up, it leads to more and more stress. Eventually, we get fatigued and lose our spirit and then start going through the motions of life like a mechanical robot.

This situation of stress and fatigue is further worsened by the extraordinarily digitized and interconnected world we live in. In this era of multiple gadgets, 24/7 connectivity and social media (Facebook, X, etc.), we face constant stimuli and distractions. We are always switched on and in constant response mode. The barrage of information we get and the demands on us for responses further aggravates our stress. Having to be in constant action mode also does not allow us time for reflection and inner processing. As a result, the quality of our decisions and actions suffers.

Stress levels are increasing, and people are developing serious health problems sooner than ever before. Tolerance and empathy are on the downswing, leading to relationships of strife and conflict. Our moral fabric and integrity are weakening, resulting in a massive increase in corruption and crime.

If the current situation continues to spiral downwards, it will be disastrous for both individuals and society. If we want to reverse this trend and move away from a vicious cycle, we have to find a balance between spirituality and materialism. What does that mean? Let's explore.[1]

What is materialism?

Materialism is recognizing physical matter as the only reality. Therefore, it focuses on material well-being and progress. It manifests as the desire for material possessions and the incessant struggle to attain them. It is also reflected in being driven by the senses and the race to gratify them. It is the search for artha—career, skills, health, wealth, prosperity, etc.—and kama—sensory enjoyment, emotional attraction and aesthetic pleasure such as from the arts, dance, music, painting, sculpture and nature amongst others.

What is spirituality?

Spirituality is recognizing the immaterial reality, the soul and the superconscious. It is letting go of desires and detaching from worldly possessions. It refers to connecting with your inner self. It is recognizing the oneness of all creation and attaining control of your senses so you can get in touch with the super-conscious.

Materialism and spirituality: The duality

Materialism and spirituality have a contradictory basis. One is about fulfilling desires; the other is about letting go of them. One is about gratifying the senses; the other is about controlling them. One is about the outer, the other about the inner self. One is about satisfying the ego; the other is about subordinating ego and recognizing oneness. However, both spirituality and materialism are inseparable parts of human nature. They are both components of reality. They reflect the inherent duality and contradictions in human nature and within our lives. Therefore, we need to recognize and accept both of them.

Materialism is inevitable. The senses and desires cannot be ignored. Self-renunciation is a difficult path and prone to failure. We often see so-called holy men who have apparently renounced worldly desires falling prey to their senses. If senses and desires are a fundamental part of human nature then why ignore them? Without addressing them, it is very difficult to make progress towards dharma and moksha. In addition, materialism is the foundation of human progress. Desires are the force that propels us to move forward in life. They are the basis of human endeavour and therefore the drivers of progress for both the individual and civilization. Now, progress can also have negative consequences. However, between the choice of progress and no progress, I think the path of progress is better. We have been born on this earth to live a full life and not just prepare to die.

So, materialism is necessary but the excess of it is clearly a problem. In meeting the objectives of artha and kama, you move away from dharma and moksha. If you are driven by materialism, then you are walking on a treadmill of desires that keeps going faster and faster, and it becomes very difficult to get off it. You set goals and work hard towards achieving them. You earn money, fame, position and possessions. However, the happiness of achievement is short-lived and you are soon off to chase the next desire. You get trapped in a vicious cycle and do not find peace. You remain far from the ideal of moksha. In addition, it is easy to lose your balance and lose sight of dharma. When you get obsessed with self-gratification, you lose your judgement of what is right and wrong and start ignoring your responsibility to do good for others. This can cause failure not just of the individual but of societies and civilizations. The grave global economic crises we have seen in the past century are consequences of excessive materialism. These crises originated not in the poor nations of the developing world but from the rich economies of the western hemisphere. Greed and incessant desires led to excess consumerism at the individual level and unethical and fraudulent behaviour at the organizational level, challenging the very foundation of the materialistic economic model that had been the norm for the past few centuries.

So, does that mean we are doomed for failure? I am sure we are not. I am convinced that the human race is not meant to meet a disappointing end. I believe finding balance between spirituality and materialism is the answer to our current crisis whether it is at the level of the individual, the organization or the nation. Spirituality can bring us home. It can help us centre ourselves and connect with our inner selves. In our inner self rest great powers and clarity of thought, which our outer self cannot access. Spirituality can provide deeper perspective and guide the moral compass that can help balance the excesses of materialism. Finding this balance is necessary. It is the only way to achieve the four objectives of artha, kama, dharma and moksha in a unified way. If there is imbalance, then it is very difficult to achieve these core objectives of life.

Living the golden balance

Clearly, finding unity and alignment between spirituality and materialism is essential. However, the big question is how to find the golden balance? Many people might start from a high moral ground. However, the daily struggle between moral uprightness and material well-being is too much for most and they lose their way. So what practical guidelines and practices can help in living this balance on a daily basis?

Spiritual Balance is necessary for the Digital and AI age

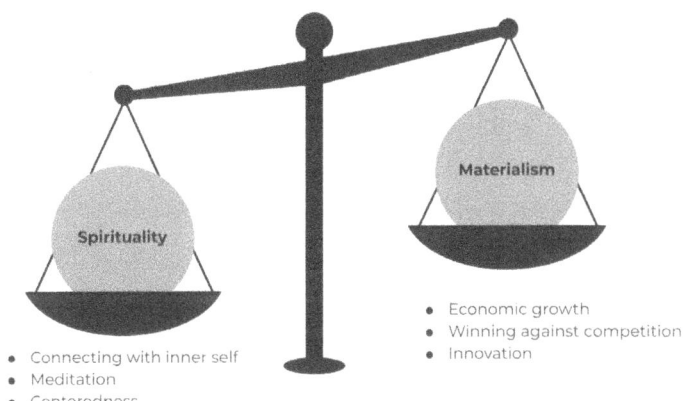

Hindu scriptures have answered this question in a very elegant way by prescribing four different stages of life. These are *brahmcharya* (student life), *grihastha* (household life), *vanaprastha* (retired life) and *sanyasa* (renounced life). Each stage has different goals and expectations. I think this is a good formula that clarifies focus for different stages of life and thus makes choices easier—materialism being the dominant value in the grihastha stage while spirituality becomes more important in the vanaprastha stage. While this clarity is good, I am not sure if it is always possible to compartmentalize life into such water-tight stages. Therefore, I believe there is a need to have a certain balance between spirituality and materialism across the two middle stages of life.

So, how do we find balance between spirituality and materialism? Here again, I feel that the Hindu scriptures provide a good answer. They have identified four paths in life:

- *Karma Yoga*: The path of selfless action
- *Raja Yoga:* The path of meditation and discipline
- *Gyan Yoga:* The path of knowledge and wisdom
- *Bhakti Yoga:* The path of devotion and love

Each one of us has to find our own path or combination of paths.

I find the paths of Karma Yoga and Raja Yoga to be most inspiring and would like to share my experiences of them with you. For simplicity, I will be using the terms karma for Karma Yoga and yoga for Raja Yoga in the rest of the chapter.

Karma

Karma is the focus on action, on the deed in front of you. Karma to me is one of the few unambiguous realities of life. You cannot go wrong with karma. It is the route to success both in the material world and the spiritual world. In either case, you have to focus on what action you must take. I would like to present three ideas on how to find balance between spirituality and materialism via the path of karma.

First, approach karma with the objective of dharma. Often, our karma is driven by search for artha or material well-being. There is nothing wrong with that. We just need to ensure that it strikes a balance with dharma. Where there is a conflict between the two, dharma or doing good for others should take precedence. Let go of your self-interest and seek to give and add value to people and situations around you. Focus on 'We' not 'I'. As you do that, something magical will happen. You will grow as a leader and as a human being, and eventually more success will come to you.

Second, remember the Bhagavad Gita's guidance to be dispassionate and not to obsess about the outcomes. It is easier said than done and I certainly struggle with this concept. It is counter to how I have operated through most of my life. I like to set challenging goals and then work hard towards achieving them. However, as I have progressed in life, I have realized that you cannot control all outcomes. The only thing you can focus on is the action in front of you. If you attach too much weight to the achievement of desired outcomes, it will lead to feverishness in action and a lot of stress in life. Any action performed in a selfless spirit and with dispassion is superior. It also helps you accept your present moment and find happiness in the action itself and the ongoing journey of life rather than seeking it constantly in outcomes in the future.

Third, beware of inaction. Sometimes a misguided interpretation of spirituality can dull the focus on karma. You have to face up to whatever situation you are in. Even if it is a difficult and seemingly uncontrollable situation, you need to act with courage and get on with actions in your control. Escapism can never be the answer. It is time we rediscover the powerful messages of the Gita. It says, 'Perform necessary action; it is more powerful than inaction.' Do not renounce the world and become a hermit. Instead, learn to change your attitude while living and working in the world.

In summary, it is time for all of us to dedicate ourselves to karma. That is key to success both in the material world and for spiritual liberation.

Yoga

It is very easy to lose ourselves in the incessant action of life. It can feel like sleepwalking, where you just drift from one scene of a movie to another. Yoga and meditation are great ways to centre yourself. They can calm you and provide a medium to help connect with your inner self. They encourage focusing on breathing, which is a great way to link and energize different levels of your existence—mind, body and soul. Moreover, from the calmness and silence can emerge the most profound and creative ideas and guidance for every difficulty. If you close your eyes, still yourself and focus on your breathing, you will find clarity and solutions to whatever problems might be troubling you.

Yoga and meditation are practical options for all of us who might be immersed in material pursuits. If you can inculcate the discipline of regular practice of yoga and meditation, you can find spiritual balance even while living in the material world. I have been following the Art of Living for more than twenty years and feel that it has played a key role in finding balance in my life. I started doing Art of Living in early 2002. This was a very difficult phase of my life. I was in the process of shutting down ActiveKarma, and I was going back to McKinsey, the organization I had started my career with. Learning and practising *pranayama* (breath control and regulation) and meditation at that stage was instrumental in rediscovering my spirit and approaching my career afresh with tremendous positivity. I have a hectic schedule, but I try to do at least one Art of Living course (typically a four-to-five-day silence retreat) every year and also go for yoga and meditation classes every weekend. These activities are critical for me to retain balance and high energy levels despite being engaged in an intense corporate career. Now, Art of Living is just one of the many options for practising yoga and meditation. Choose an option that works for you and pursue it diligently.

Karma Yoga, Raja Yoga and also the paths of Gyana Yoga and Bhakti Yoga provide very good guidance. However, all of us need to find our own specific path and our individual balance. And, for that, there are no deterministic answers; you have to go through a process of personal questioning, self-reflection and self-discovery. What is experienced by oneself leads to a more intimate understanding of the right path and conviction to move forward resulting in clear, concrete action.

As children, we are born free and natural. However, as we grow, we build layers of protection that take us far away from our greatest asset, our inner self. That is where we need to build knowledge and discipline of spiritual practices that will take us ahead on the path of self-realization. There are many spiritual paths: yoga, pranayama, reiki, meditation, chanting and prayer, to name a few. However, their end objective is the same—self-discovery and connecting with our inner self.

I feel strongly that finding spiritual balance and learning the techniques to centre oneself is important for every leader to cope with the crazy VUCA world in the AI age. More the noise outside and more the need for activity, greater is the silence and the rest you need to prepare yourself. I am happy that this awareness is now increasing and topics like spirituality and meditation are becoming mainstream.

15

Eleven Laws of Spirituality

The spiritual life does not remove us from the world but leads us deeper into it.

—*Henri J.M. Nouwen,
priest, professor, writer and theologian*

I have been reflecting on the topic of success for a few years—what is success and how do you get there? I have also been reflecting on spirituality, the inner journey to finding ourselves and seeking the meaning of life. How can we find success in today's materialistic world by following the laws of spirituality? It is a great ongoing quest for me and I don't think I have been able to solve this profound question fully. Sometimes, it feels like a futile quest. How do you live with spiritual laws in this material world where self-interest, greed and non-stop politics is the norm? The spiritual path seems to be at loggerheads with the rules of the material world.

Despite the challenges, my belief remains strong that it is possible to find spiritual balance in today's material world and achieve material success by following the laws of spirituality. Here are the **eleven laws of spirituality** that I have experienced and that have been the foundation for whatever success I have achieved.

These are not meant to be comprehensive or definitive, because I am not there yet. They are my personal beliefs, and they are still a work in progress.[1]

1. **Infinite potential and unique purpose in life**: All of us have abundant potential and are operating at only a fraction of it. We can achieve a lot more than what we currently are. The key to unlocking our potential is to find our unique purpose in life. All of us are born with some special gift that is unique to us. The great quest of life is to find and pursue our unique purpose in life. Finding our unique purpose is unlikely to be a sudden eureka moment, it is a deliberate journey. The likely starting point are your passions. However, these have to be paired with perseverance and hard work to sharpen them into excellent skills. Finally and most importantly, these have to be deployed to serve some real needs. I believe it is at this confluence or 'sweet spot' of passions, skills and serving needs that you find your unique purpose in life and unlock your true potential. I will talk about this in detail in Mantra 5, Chapter 21: Sweet Spot

2. **Living in the present moment**: We keep flitting between ruminating about the past and worrying about the future. We worry so much that we forget to live in the present moment. This is the prime cause of our stress and suffering. The only reality is the present moment, the NOW. It is only by being in the present moment that you find true happiness. So, live in the present moment and accept your current situation fully. It is only by stringing together beautiful moments that we make a momentous life, as I have talked about in Mantra 6, Chapter 26: Momentary Versus Momentous. Being mindful and in the present moment is a mindset and requires practice. The hyper-connected digital world we live in with its information load creates clutter and further pushes us away from mindfulness. Deep breathing (pranayama), yoga and meditation help build

the necessary mindset and skills to clear the clutter and live in the present moment.

3. **Duality and law of intention**: Human beings are complex and full of contradictions. We have both good and bad within us. We have divine gifts yet are fundamentally flawed. We have the power to do great good and to cause grievous harm. The aspects of our personality that we focus on tend to grow. So being good or bad is a conscious choice, these are muscles you grow with focus and deliberate use. This logic is also true for situations and people around us. You find what you seek. You can see the same glass as half empty or half full. This is the law of attraction and intention—inherent in every intention and desire, is the mechanics for its fulfilment. Whatever you put your attention on will grow stronger in your life. So be positive, have the right intention and then let nature take its course.

4. **Law of karma**: Our present is a consequence of past actions and our present actions shape our future. Karma stands for both the cause (intent and actions of the individual) and the effect (future of that individual). It is a highly empowering law and a clarion call for moral behaviour. You create your own fate and reap what you sow. Your present situation is a result of actions you have taken in this life or your past lives. Equally, your current actions will not be wasted; the results will come sooner or later. While actions and consequences are an immutable law, these do not follow each other in a linear or sequential fashion. This law assumes a continuous cycle of life and death and that your karma is carried from one life to another. Therefore, you should not obsess about wanting the immediate outcomes of your actions. Just do the right action with dispassion and without attachment to the results. Trust this fundamental law of the universe, outcomes will happen whether now or later, in this life or another.

5. **Dissolving our ego**: At the heart of spirituality is the belief about the oneness of all creation, that there is a universal spirit within us that connects all of us. The supreme objective of the spiritual path is union with that universal spirit. The main obstacle in this objective is our ego. It creates a sense of identity and thus makes barriers between us and others and, at a fundamental level, between the universal spirit and us. To progress on the spiritual path, we have to dissolve our ego. At a more practical level, our ego is the root of our anger, greed, anxiety and most of our human ills. Attention to ego consumes the greatest amount of energy. To have a happy and satisfied life, we have to go beyond our ego. This liberates energy, generates love and allows us to see the bigger picture of our lives. Understanding and dissolving our ego is one of the most difficult challenges of our lives. Some of the actions that can help are inculcating humility, going beyond the self and serving others, continuous learning from a master and dedicating ourselves to a cause that is bigger than us.

6. **Disciplining the senses**: Senses and desires are inevitable and cannot be ignored. In fact, they are one of the four goals of life in Hindu philosophy—kama. You must address them adequately to keep them in check. However, excess of the same can trap us in a vicious cycle. It is like running on a treadmill that never stops. The faster you run, the faster the treadmill of desires keeps on moving. You can never catch up and it leads to frustration, unhappiness and immoral behaviours. You lose both your mind and health. To lead a happy and moral life, it is imperative that you discipline and control your senses. The key to doing so is to understand that all situations and sensations in life are impermanent, that everything in life changes. The vicious draw of the senses is short-term. If you develop the equanimity and discipline to understand the changing nature of sensations, you are on your way to mastering your senses and self. This process of

discipling the senses is like training your muscles, it happens one step at a time. It will liberate you to lead a happy and healthy life.

7. **Giving before getting**: We are born to make a difference in this world, to leave it a better place than what we found it. This is how the cycle of life progresses on earth. Without people giving back, we would have destroyed the human race and our planet long ago. So, we should let go of our self-interest and try to contribute to people and situations around us. We should give before we seek for ourselves. Instead of asking 'What's in it for me?', ask 'How can I help?' The most valuable giving is often non-material, for e.g., understanding, respect, compassion, kindness or emotional support. The beauty of this law is that what we give eventually comes back to us manifold. This is the fundamental law for creating affluence and abundance in our lives—in our willingness to give that which we seek, we keep the abundance of the universe circulating in our own lives.

8. **Taking responsibility and increasing levels of consciousness**: 'Who am I?' is a fundamental question many of us face. We can define ourselves at multiple levels. We are defined by what we take responsibility for—self, family, organization, community, country and the final frontier is humanity. The more we take responsibility for, the more strength we get. We move to increasing levels of consciousness and grow as a human being. Whether it is the organization you work for or the society at large, you would see many chronic problems that can create a sense of helplessness about the 'system'. Be proactive and take ownership of the problems around you. Don't let the problems weigh you down. Just be positive and focus on your karma. You will be surprised how much power your individual actions can have. As you take action, your zone of influence and the leader within you grows. Slowly, the change you start with your actions can come to a tipping point when the 'system' also starts changing.

9. **Inside-out wisdom**: One of the core tenets of Indian philosophy is that there is infinite, eternal wisdom within all of us. For wisdom and happiness you only need to look within. However, noise at the level of both mind and body prevents us from connecting with that inner core. As I have mentioned earlier, yoga and meditation help still the different layers of our existence, get us to silence and thus help us connect with our inner core. Yoga is often misunderstood to be just a physical process. It is a comprehensive science that operates at all layers of our existence, progressively going from the gross to the subtle. Its philosophy is that the path to salvation lies within the framework of your body. The starting point has to be a certain discipline and control over the body so we are ready to go deeper. The crucial link between the body and the mind is the breath, so a lot of focus in yoga is on breathing practices or pranayama. Meditation is a process of letting go, of dropping yourself and your desires. As you enter a meditative state, you get access to infinite wisdom and happiness. Personally, after meditation, I feel both calm and energized and seem to get intuitive clarity on questions that have been troubling me the most. (I will share more on experiences with meditation in subsequent chapters). The most beautiful journey you can take in life is the journey within. So, start it now!

10. **Understand the flow**: It is human nature to try to shape our destiny with our own hands. However, whether it is nature or situations in daily life, there are times when things take their own natural course, beyond our ability to direct them. Wisdom is in understanding that flow and then aligning oneself with it. Blind effort is wasteful and paddling against the current is very difficult. Assuming you can control and change any situation is a mistake. Most breakthroughs in life are not planned, they are happy accidents. Do not seek to control everything in life. Be comfortable with uncertainty. Let nature play its role. We need to have the humility and wisdom to understand that

there is a higher power and it gives signals. Nature is its most visible manifestation. Respect it and seek to understand it with calmness. Let go of your fears and trust nature's design for us. Once you do that, solutions will follow naturally and you will find the path of least effort. Noise and clutter in our mind stops us from listening to the signals nature is giving us. Declutter your mind and then listen to your heart, it will help you find the right path.

11. **Daily habit of dharma**: You will never change your life until you change something you do daily. The secret of success is found in your daily routine. The ten laws I have talked about above are interconnected and are part of dharma, the path of doing good. Dharma is the right behaviour and the universal law that makes life possible. Doing good is not easy. The twin forces of ego and senses will create temptation, envy, fear and other negative emotions that will constantly pull you back. Therefore, it is imperative that you live and practice the path of dharma on a daily basis. I have talked about building muscles a few times in this book. I will reiterate it here. Dharmic behaviours and practice of spiritual laws are like muscles that have to be built step by step. It is only by making the right choices and decisions and taking actions on a daily basis that the spiritual laws become real and powerful forces in our lives. So be disciplined, build good habits and live your dharma on a daily basis.

The quest to harmonize spiritual principles with the demands of a materialistic world is quite challenging but deeply rewarding. Integrating these eleven spiritual laws into daily life can help you achieve personal growth and fulfilment, allowing you to achieve success with integrity, self-awareness and a higher purpose. This journey is not about perfection but continuous improvement and learning, ultimately achieving a balance that brings both personal and professional growth.

16

My Mindfulness Journey

You have to grow from the inside out. None can teach you, none can make you spiritual. There is no other teacher but your own soul.
—*Swami Vivekananda,*
Indian monk, philosopher, author

With all these talks about achieving a balance between materialism and spirituality, I would like to mention that I am still a work in progress. Moreover, I believe we continue to be a work in progress throughout our lives, because spirituality is a way of life and not a destination. Let me take you through my mindfulness journey, how it transformed my life and how it can help you explore its potential to enhance well-being and productivity in our fast-paced work environments.

My mindfulness journey

I have been practising mindfulness or meditation for over thirty-five to forty years now. In my mindfulness journey, there have been three key factors: serendipity, failures creating opportunities and staying the course.

Absorbed in meditation, 22 July 2012, Rishikesh, India.

My initiation on this path was triggered by serendipity. I think I was in Class III or IV when my elder brother went on a college trip and brought a book on Swami Vivekananda. While I did not understand most of it, I felt a sense of positive energy reading it and it left a deep imprint on me. My second trigger on this path was one of my maternal uncles who was an ardent practitioner of Vipassana. I still vividly remember when I was in my early teens, he took me for a long walk and asked me some fundamental questions—'Who am I?' and 'Why am I here?'—and encouraged me to pen down my thoughts. I struggled to answer the questions but that certainly sparked a process of inquiry. In addition, whenever we would meet, he would get me to sit down with him, close my eyes and I would drift into deep meditation. Since then, I kept on practising meditation on my own throughout my college life and early professional career.

The next step in my mindfulness journey came when I faced a big setback after launching my first venture. At that stage I did what was then called the Basic Course (it is now called the Happiness Course) of the Art of Living. The course and my teacher for it made a deep impression on me. I found the pranayama and meditation processes I learnt very powerful. At the same time, the logical side of me was cynical and kept on questioning. The process of dropping everything in meditation seemed contradictory to the high achievement process (set goals, make plans, execute, achieve and set more goals) that I was groomed in. Despite my doubts, I kept practising *Sudarshan Kriya* and did at least one Advanced Course of the Art of Living every year. Over time, I realized the power of faith and stillness. There is a power inside us that we don't normally access but we must if we want to gain a deeper awareness.

I have also been fascinated by the Bhagavad Gita. I first read it in high school and have subsequently re-read it multiple times (in various versions). If the Art of Living gave me a practical framework for life, the Bhagavad Gita gave me a profound theoretical framework that beautifully answered my many questions about life. Most importantly, it reinforced the value of doing your karma in the present moment and dropping your expectations. That, to me, is the essence of mindfulness.

The next stage in my mindfulness journey was being a part of the ten-day Vipassana meditation course in Igatpuri, Maharashtra. Vipassana is a very tough process; you have to be in complete silence for over ten days and effectively live the life of a monk. It was difficult but it allowed me to go deeper within myself than ever before. If thoughts are things, then I could certainly see a stream of thoughts flowing out of me, making me feel lighter (more on this in the next chapter).

I feel I am still in the early stages of my journey towards mindfulness. I have seen serendipity play out beautifully. There are moments when I feel I am struggling on the journey and then an intervention comes that lifts me to a next stage of awareness. Through this journey, I have realized the value of disciplined practice and staying the course.[1]

How mindfulness has changed my life

Mindfulness for me is going into the **silence** within, being in the **present moment** and having very high levels of **awareness**. This journey has not just helped me become a more effective professional but, more importantly, kept making me a better human being. There are at least six ways mindfulness has changed my life:

1. **Manage stress**: I have had a very intense corporate and entrepreneurial career and I am also a passionate person who wants to give 100 per cent to every situation. This is a recipe for creating a lot of stress. With the regular practice of meditation, I have been able to be more centred, manage my stress and become a calmer person.

2. **Increase my work capacity**: The consequence of managing stress and being able to focus on the present moment is that my work capacity has increased and I have been able to manage multiple initiatives and responsibilities at the same time.

3. **Decision-making clarity**: Many mistakes in our life, whether these are accidents or bad decisions, are caused by lack of awareness. Whenever I have to make a decision or I feel my mind is jumbled up, I close my eyes and sit in meditation for some time. I find that as I come out of meditation, my mind is centred, I can see the situation more clearly and the decisions appear more intuitive.

4. **Greater empathy**. We live in an egocentric materialistic world which is driven by self-interest, competition and conflict. As you search within through meditation, the ego is removed and you start feeling a sense of connectedness and greater empathy, as well as compassion for the other person. With greater empathy, you start seeing things from the other person's perspective and conflict and angst are reduced.

5. **Higher self-awareness**: Meditation has helped me get a better understanding of my own self—my motivations, thoughts and emotions—and the flows of life. As human beings we have a need to seek our unique purpose. I believe meditation and going deeper within yourself is the essential process of connecting the dots of your life and getting clarity on the unique purpose of your life.

6. **Greater balance in life**: Life is about duality; there are many contradictions that you need to manage at the same time. For example, for an organization it might be about growth vs profitability, short-term vs long-term. For me, the big question in life has been about balancing spirituality and materialism and living with spiritual laws (which I shared in the previous chapter) in a materialistic world. Often, these seem to be irreconcilable poles. Here again meditation gives me the clarity to find a natural balance and consistency between these seemingly opposite values.

After the Art of Living Silence Retreat, 11 October 2021, North Carolina, United States.

Relevance of mindfulness in the corporate world

Mindfulness is not just relevant, it is essential for the corporate world. It has become even more critical given the unprecedented velocity of change we are seeing in the technology and business world. We are living in a VUCA world where customer expectations are changing rapidly, established companies are finding it difficult to keep pace, industry structures are changing and the business and product cycles are becoming shorter.

Speed is king in the AI age and the pressures of operating in this environment are extreme. The only way to keep your sanity in such a frenzied environment is mindfulness practice. To deal with so much uncertainty and change, you need to be calm and centred within. Deep silence is necessary to make right decisions, both individually and as an organization. There is an old Zen saying: *You should sit in meditation for twenty minutes a day, unless you're too busy. Then you should sit for an hour!!*

While I now see many leaders increasingly turning towards meditation and spirituality, widespread adoption of mindfulness across corporations is still not pervasive. There are deep-set perceptions and conditioning that needs to be reversed. It is a cultural change and has to start at the top. I have experimented with getting my leadership teams to go through mindfulness and meditation workshops and have now partnered with The Art of Living to have all of our colleagues in India go through the basic breathing and meditation programme. Mindfulness has to be experienced and cannot just be explained by logic. However, it might need multiple experiences for the concept to sink in.

I feel very excited that there is so much more focus on mindfulness. It is sorely needed both at an individual and corporate level in the AI age to find balance and quality in life. India is the home of meditation and it has been an intrinsic part of our culture and philosophy for thousands of years. Now is the time to spread the practice and adopt it pervasively. I firmly believe that rediscovering meditation and our spiritual heritage will be a key success factor for India's renaissance in the twenty-first century and also its great gift to the rest of the world.

17

Meditation (Vipassana)
The Key to Connecting with the Self

Go within every day and find the inner strength so that the world will not blow your candle out.
—Katherine Dunham,
African American choreographer,
anthropologist and social activist

I have mentioned Vipassana meditation practice as an essential part of my mindfulness journey in previous chapters. Let me now talk about it in more detail, to help you understand what it entails.

I still remember when I completed my first ten-day Vipassana meditation course, in 2016. It had been perhaps the most intense ten-day experience of my life. I had been practising meditation for over twenty-five years and followed the Art of Living (founded by Sri Sri Ravi Shankar) for the past fifteen years. However, nothing prepares you for eighty sessions and 100+ hours of meditation across a ten-day period. Each day starts in the wee hours of the morning, around 4 a.m., and ends at 10 p.m., while maintaining complete silence through the period. All mobiles, laptops, reading or writing material are taken away at the start of the course. Clearly the path of pure dharma is not for the faint-hearted!

Vipassana meditation's objective is to purify the mind and to do so by getting to the root cause of our miseries (e.g., cravings, aversions, obsessions, egocentricity). Many forms of meditation use verbalization (e.g., mantras) or visualization (e.g., some image or other focusing forms) that help you get to a meditative state quickly and feel a state of bliss and calmness. Vipassana takes the tougher but perhaps purer route of just focusing on natural breath and body sensations. Its core philosophy is that you are responsible for your own salvation and you have to do that within the framework of your body. You start by observing your breath at the tip of your nostrils. As the mind starts getting calm and more attentive, you start observing body sensations (which are always there but the mind is not tuned to observe them) and progressively their intensity and flow through their body increases.

Vipassana is the meditation technique discovered and taught by Gautama Buddha over twenty-five centuries ago in India. From India, Vipassana travelled to other parts of the world along with the Buddha's teachings. While the Buddha's teachings have largely been preserved in many parts of Asia, the Vipassana meditation technique in its pure form survived only in Myanmar (Burma). An Indian industrialist based in Myanmar, Shri S.N. Goenka learnt this technique and brought it back to its country of origin after twenty-five centuries.[1]

Key concepts of Vipassana

Over a ten-day course, every evening there was a distinct 1.5-hour video talk by S.N. Goenka where some deep lessons about the philosophy and concepts of Vipassana and the Buddha's teachings were shared. The following were five key concepts that I took away from these talks and my introspection:

1. **Focus on dharma**: The anchor of the Buddha's philosophy is dharma, which denotes behaving morally or in accordance with the universal laws of nature. The philosophy is not based on any religious dogmas, does not talk about any creator God and does not even reference or acknowledge the soul within. Its focus is dharma, which the Buddha has summarized to mean three things:
   i. not harming others,
   ii. doing wholesome actions and
   iii. purifying your mind.

2. *Sheel-samadhi-prajna*: The eightfold path of Buddha can be divided into three parts, 'sheel' or conduct, 'samadhi' or meditation and 'prajna' or wisdom. Sheel or the right conduct is the first platform on which the other two are built progressively. The right sheel enables samadhi (for e.g., discipline enforced during the course is a key enabler of meditation), and samadhi further leads to prajna or wisdom. While there is a sequential flow between the three, there is also a recursive relationship between them. Samadhi leads to better sheel, similarly prajna leads to better samadhi and sheel. Furthermore, the focus is that these aspects, especially prajna, to be not just at an intellectual level but at an experiential level.

3. **Three aspects of the ideal mind**: Through meditation sessions and discourses, Goenka ji details the ideal nature of mind. It has three aspects: a calm and quiet mind, an alert and attentive mind and a balanced and equanimous mind. These are the essential requirements of good meditation and also its outcomes.

4. **Sensations as the root to overcoming miseries**. The path's objective is to eradicate life's miseries (for e.g., cravings, aversions, obsessions, egocentricity) at their root. Buddha's great insight was that these miseries are because of our reaction or addiction to sensations. It is this link between sensations and miseries

that Vipassana seeks to sever by developing a dispassionate and accepting view towards all sensations whether good or bad.

5. **Impermanence.** Almost every meditation session over the ten days finishes with the call 'Anicca' or impermanence. This is a core belief about the nature of existence in Buddhist philosophy. It is the realization of impermanence that is the root of prajna or wisdom. It is the realization of impermanence that allows you to develop a dispassionate view towards sensations, good or bad and thus eradicate your obsessions.

After the Vipassana course, 6 March 2016, Igatpuri, India.

My personal experiences in the Vipassana course

Vipassana is a very tough course. Sitting for such long hours in meditation, maintaining silence and having no contact with the external world is a tough process. Goenka ji, in one of his first talks, mentioned that the ten-day Vipassana course is like a deep surgery. Well, it certainly felt that way and led to some deep, moving experiences.

1. **Taming of the monkey mind.** When you meditate for long hours, the mind becomes clearer and you feel lighter. It forces the discipline of living in the present moment. Personally, sitting at a stretch and that too without changing my posture was a huge test and development of my will power. There were moments most days when I questioned myself why I was putting myself through such a tough process. But I feel good that I preserved and completed the process.

2. **Overcoming cravings and obsessions.** Over the ten days, I was able to get to the root of many deep-rooted insecurities and limiting patterns. And this happened without forcing myself to do so. The most dramatic change that happened was in my craving for food. I love to eat and it is perhaps my comfort spot. Over the ten days, my diet progressively reduced to less than 1/5th of my usual intake. By the end of the ten-day period, my diet was a light breakfast at 6:30 a.m., lunch without rice at 11 a.m. and lemon water with a banana at 5 p.m. This would have been unimaginable for me earlier.

3. **From gross to subtle, there is always another level.** Almost every day, the intensity of the meditation process kept getting raised. From observing your breath, to doing so in a narrower area, to observing sensations progressively across the body, to eventually feeling a flow of vibrations across the body—you traverse quite a journey in ten days. Two powerful realizations happened in the process. First, vibrations always exist in our body, but normally we feel only the gross sensations like pain and itching. It is only when our mind gets calm and attentive that we can go from gross to subtle and observe these vibrations.

Second, the process keeps surprising you. You discover a level of subtlety in your body that wasn't discernible before.

4. **From intellectual to experiential.** I like to understand things on an intellectual plane. That can be exciting but concepts can remain abstract. The Vipassana approach allows you to experience vivid, deep and seemingly abstract concepts. One of the core concepts of Vipassana is impermanence. This came alive for me across meditation sessions. The nature and intensity of sensations you experience changes significantly across sessions and often within sessions. Initially there was a feeling of disappointment with not being able to feel subtle vibrations in a sustained manner. But it did drive home the concept of impermanence and that we should maintain equanimity across all situations.

Vipassana was a challenging process and it did not always bring the feeling of calm and bliss that one often gets from some other meditation techniques. But I really appreciated that it is a very intellectually honest process. There is little hype, no leap of faith or reliance on the divine. It is a scientific, practical and down-to-earth process. It does not promise a 'quick fix' and sets expectations clearly that the ten-day course is just the beginning of a long journey of self-observation, purification and realization.

My final thought is a sense of wonder about the progress ancient India had made in the science of human existence and the wealth of concepts and techniques they created for human advancement. Being a long-time practitioner of the Art of Living, I always felt it was such a brilliant synthesis of ancient Indian thinking and practices. Vipassana has exposed me to a different but equally powerful technique and set of concepts. Truly, spirituality and meditation are India's great gift to the world. I pray that all of us discover meditation in our daily lives, whether in this form or another. This might well be the secret weapon for not just retaining, but strengthening the human edge in the AI age.

MANTRA 4

LEARN TEAMWORK AND RESILIENCE FROM SPORTS

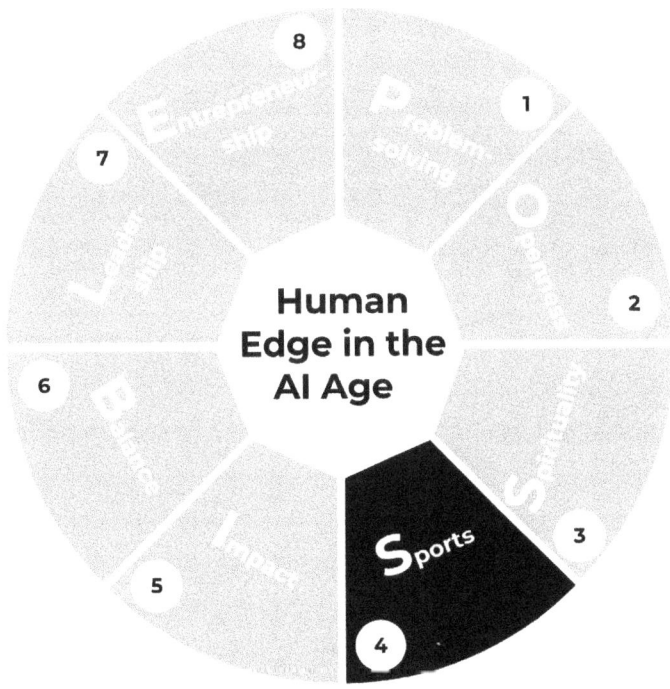

The POSSIBLE Framework

Introduction to Mantra 4
Learn Teamwork and Resilience from Sports

Training for Turbulent Times: Grit, Grace and Growth

> *Sports is a great metaphor for life. It teaches you how to handle wins, losses and everything in between.*
>
> —*Billie Jean King,*
> *Celebrated American Tennis player*

Few arenas mirror the challenges of life and leadership as vividly as sports. The highs of victory, the lows of defeat, the demand for discipline, teamwork, resilience and adaptability—all these elements make sports a powerful teacher. The lessons learnt on the field go far beyond the game itself, shaping character, leadership and the ability to navigate high-pressure situations.

The power of sports in the AI age

You might wonder—why a section on sports in a book about AI? In the fast-paced and uncertain AI age, where complexity is rising, change is constant and resilience is paramount, sports offer invaluable lessons for success.

- **Teamwork is more critical than ever:** In an interdependent world where no one can win alone, sports teach us how to build strong partnerships while maintaining a competitive edge—a vital skill in the AI era.
- **Resilience defines winners:** Disruption is the norm in the AI age. Like athletes who push through injury and adversity, professionals must learn to stay focused and bounce back in high-pressure situations.
- **Well-being fuels performance:** As technology nudges us toward more sedentary and screen-heavy lives, sports help restore mental and physical balance, providing energy, vitality and perspective.

Lessons from Sports for Life and Leadership

To bring this mantra alive, I explore four landmark moments from the world of team sports, each offering a powerful insight:

1. **Seizing the Moment:**
   India's T20 World Cup win is a masterclass in timing and bold execution. In high-stakes moments, it is the ability to act decisively that separates winners from the rest.

2. **Resilience Under Pressure:**
   India's historic Test win in Australia is a story of grit, recovery and determination. Even when everything went wrong, the team found a way to fight and win—a mindset critical for navigating the uncertainties of the AI era.

3. **Underdogs Can Win:**
   The 2018 FIFA World Cup showed how teams like Croatia—without the traditional scale or star power—rose through focus,

adaptability and relentless effort. The AI age offers similar leapfrog opportunities for those who invest smartly and move with agility and intent.

4. **The Power of 'We':**
   The 2014 World Cup revealed that even the most talented individuals cannot win alone. True success comes from collaboration—the kind that brings together diverse strengths in pursuit of a shared goal.

My Personal Journey with Sports

Sports have been a profound influence on my life. Growing up, I lacked confidence and was frequently unwell. Fortunately, my school had a good basketball programme and I decided to enrol in it, even though I was not very good at it. Over time, I got better at the sport, felt stronger overall and that boosted my self-confidence. Then, I quickly picked up football and volleyball and played all three sports through high school and college. My self-confidence surge was not just limited to sports; it rubbed into other aspects of my life such as academics and extra-curricular activities.

My character and leadership style has been deeply shaped by playing team sports. I learnt the power of a team, how to connect and inspire different personality types, how to win and equally how to bounce back from defeat. Moreover, sports built lifelong friendships, which continue to be an important anchor of my life. I strongly believe sports should be an essential part of the education process, even more so in the AI age.

Mastering the sports mindset in the AI age

As we navigate this new era, the qualities that define great athletes—resilience, adaptability, teamwork and clutch performance—are more relevant than ever. With AI reshaping industries and automating routine tasks, it is these very human skills that will distinguish leaders from the rest.

To embrace the sports mindset in work and life, consider these key principles:

- **Develop mental toughness:** Push through adversity and stay focused under pressure.
- **Build strong teams:** Collaboration and trust beat individual brilliance.
- **Seize defining moments:** Be ready to rise when it matters most
- **Embrace adaptability:** Like athletes adjusting to game conditions, professionals must evolve with changing dynamics

Sports are a great way to boost your health and energy, which itself is very important in the digital and AI age. But they are more than that, they are a microcosm of life, offering some of the most profound lessons on success, failure, leadership and teamwork. By embracing the principles of resilience, collaboration and adaptability, we can elevate not just our performance but also our ability to lead and inspire in an ever-changing world.

18

India's T20 World Cup Triumph in 2024
Seizing the Moments of Truth

Nothing is permanent in this wicked world—not even our troubles.
—*Charlie Chaplin,*
Internationally acclaimed English comic actor,
film-maker and composer

India's 2024 T20 World Cup victory was a moment of immense pride and happiness for Indians, especially after the heartbreaking loss in the ODI World Cup final in 2023. It was not about an underdog defying the odds; it was a well-deserved reward for a team that consistently performed at the highest level, however had failed to win a major international trophy for eleven years. In this tournament, they were among the favourites and they finally lived up to that reputation. Time and again, they rose to the occasion, delivering under pressure, making tactically sound decisions and ensuring they played like champions.

Their journey was marked by composure, resilience and the ability to convert key moments into lasting impact. This chapter explores the key takeaways and learnings from India's triumphant campaign, which can be applied beyond cricket—whether in business, leadership, or life itself.

1. **Perseverance is vital:**
   Setbacks do not mean the end of the journey, they are stepping stones in your path to success. Perseverance is what truly defines the winners and India's T20 World Cup win in 2024 is a testament to that. The team had put in immense effort leading up to the tournament, and despite setbacks in the ODI World Cup 2023, they did not lose heart. They continued to work hard, learn from their mistakes and ensured they were prepared to perform at the highest level. If you have worked hard for something and it hasn't worked out, do not give up. You might get the rewards later or at some other place. Keep at it!

   Perseverance is about staying committed, learning from past failures and continuing to put in effort. Success will come, even if not immediately. The key is to trust the process and remain determined.

2. **It's not over until it's over:**
   One of the critical aspects of India's victory was their ability to snatch wins from the jaws of defeat. Cricket, like life, is unpredictable, and no match is truly lost until the last ball is bowled. This was demonstrated during both the matches against Pakistan and the final against South Africa.

   During the final against South Africa, the odds were stacked heavily against India. At the 16-over mark, South Africa was cruising at 151 for 4, needing only 26 runs from 24 balls. According to the host broadcasters, India's win predictor stood at a mere 3.38 per cent.[1] Yet, in a stunning turnaround, Jasprit Bumrah and Hardik Pandya delivered clutch performances, tightening the bowling attack and shifting the game's momentum.

Similarly, against Pakistan, India defended a meagre total of 119 runs. At one point, Pakistan was in a commanding position, requiring just 40 runs with 7 wickets in hand.² But India's disciplined bowling unit triggered a collapse, turning a probable defeat into a six-run victory.

These examples prove that no situation is ever beyond redemption. Belief, resilience and the willingness to fight till the end can change the final outcome.

3. **Seize the moments of truth:**
Big victories are often built on small moments that define the outcome of a game. For India, Suryakumar Yadav's acrobatic catch in the final was one such defining moment. South Africa, with David Miller at the crease, looked set to chase down the target. As Miller launched a powerful shot towards the boundary, Suryakumar leapt at full stretch, perfectly judging his jump and executing an incredible catch to turn the game in India's favour.

This one act lifted the team's morale, shifted the psychological advantage and ultimately proved decisive. It highlights how tiny moments of execution, whether in sports or life, can make the difference between success and failure. Champions recognize these moments and seize them.

4. **Individual brilliance can make the difference:**
While teamwork is the foundation of success, individual brilliance can be the difference-maker. Throughout the tournament, Jasprit Bumrah stood out as the tournament's most impactful bowler, delivering match-winning spells in high-pressure situations. His pinpoint accuracy and ability to bowl unplayable deliveries in the death overs created panic among opponents, often single-handedly shifting momentum in India's favour.

Even in the final, when South Africa appeared to be in complete control, Bumrah's disciplined spell created pressure and eventually turned the game. His ability to consistently deliver in crunch moments was the big differentiator for India in this tournament. This underscores the importance of individual contributions within a team. While collective effort is vital, an exceptional performance by one person can change the outcome for everyone.

5. **Adapt to thrive:**
    The 2024 T20 World Cup was unique as it was played across vastly different conditions, from the unpredictable drop-in pitches in the USA to the varied surfaces of the West Indies (St. Lucia, Barbados and Guyana). Success depended not just on skills but on the ability to adapt to each new challenge quickly.

    India's batters adjusted their game plan according to the pitch conditions, playing aggressively on good batting surfaces but adopting a cautious, calculated approach on slower pitches. The bowlers too adjusted their lengths and variations to suit the demands of each surface. This flexibility proved crucial in how the Indian team navigated through tough situations and emerged victorious.

    Adaptability is the key to success in any field—whether sports, business or life. Those who are rigid in their approach struggle, while those who evolve with circumstances find ways to succeed.

India's 2024 T20 World Cup victory is a testament to excellence, resilience and execution under pressure. It was not just a triumph but a validation of their relentless journey of unwavering belief, preparation, talent and hard work. This team didn't just stumble upon glory—they earned it through perseverance, adaptability, the determination to rise when it mattered most and with the ability to seize crucial moments. Their journey serves as an inspiring blueprint for success, both on and off the field.

19

India's Magnificent Test Series Win in Australia in 2021

Bouncing back from the Brink

Victory belongs to the most persevering.

—Napoleon Bonaparte,
French military general and statesman

Cricket has always been more than just a sport in India. It's like a religion. This sport is more than just entertainment. It is woven into the cultural fabric of the nation and receives an almost divine reverence from its followers. From tier-one cities to remote villages, cricket matches bring life to a standstill, uniting people of diverse backgrounds in a shared passion. The fans that fill the cricket stadiums and those watching from the other side, on the TV screens, are united, in their celebration of victories as if they were festivals and in mourning losses as if they were the loss of a loved one. For many Indians, cricket heroes are not just athletes but demigods, their feats on the pitch inspiring awe and devotion. This deep connection to cricket is evident in how the sport significantly influences our lives.

I have been following the Indian cricket team passionately for the past forty-plus years. While there are many memorable matches that I have witnessed over the years, I would like to talk about the 2021 Test Series in Australia that left a lasting impact on me. This Test Series win in Australia was definitely one of the absolute best moments for the Indian cricket team. It was up there or even better than Wadekar's team's series wins in West Indies and England in the early 1970s, Kapil's Devils World Cup win in 1983 and Laxman and Dravid's heroics in Kolkata in 2001.

The reason why this series win was so incredibly special was because rarely in cricket, perhaps in all sports, had one team faced such a mountain of adversities and still come through to win. The series started in the worst possible fashion with a loss in Adelaide and with the team recording the lowest ever score in India's Test history, an unbelievable 36 all out! That must have been soul crushing enough but that was not all. The captain and the team's most talismanic batsman had to go back from the tour on paternity leave. Then started the most bizarre sequence of injuries where the team lost the top six bowlers and two key batsmen. How do you even put up a playing eleven in such circumstances? On top of all of that, the team faced racial abuse by the crowds, constraints of Covid lockdown and all this in a country where it has been very difficult to win at the best of times. They were facing a high-quality team thirsting for revenge (after the previous series loss), with a world-class bowling attack at their peak consistently resorting to intimidatory, near 'bodyline' bowling. Despite all that, how a young Indian team came to win against all these odds is the stuff of legends, which would be discussed for a long time to come.

I always found sports to provide the most incredible lessons in life and in leadership. Reflecting on that magnificent test series, here are the six management lessons that I would like to share with you:[1]

1. **The winning attitude: Fearlessness + high pain tolerance + bouncing back**

    The most endearing images of the series was the breathtaking and scarcely believable counterattack that Shubman Gill and Rishabh Pant launched on the last day of the Brisbane Test. They fearlessly launched a push for victory, when conventional wisdom would have suggested protection and playing defence as the prudent strategy. This fearlessness is a hallmark of the New India, the Young India. Fearlessness is a key attitude required today in the business world, where being too defensive can often be a recipe for failure in a very fast-changing environment.

    While the young Indian team exhibited amazing fearlessness, it was accompanied in equal measure by another attitude—the ability to bear pain. Hanuma Vihari and Ashwin played with severe injuries on the last day of the Sydney Test to save the match. Pujara took one body blow after another (it was sickening to even watch!) on the last day of the Brisbane match. Without these heroic efforts, without this gutting it out through extreme pain over extended periods, India would have lost the series 3-1. This is an important management lesson. Whether you are in the early stages of building a business or you are trying to turn around a business, you will face pain. Therefore, you need to develop a high tolerance for it.

    The final piece of the Indian team's winning attitude was bouncing back. I can only imagine what kind of blow 36 all out would have been for a team that had set very high standards for themselves. To bounce back from such a low, to go on to win the next Test match in Melbourne was simply remarkable. From what I've read, Coach Ravi Shastri and Captain Ajinkya Rahane did not dwell too much on the Adelaide disaster and started preparing for the next match. That is a great lesson. In the business world today, it is inevitable that you will face failures at various stages. The ability to not let that affect you and to bounce back is a necessary attitude every professional needs to have.

2. **Depth comes from process + structure**
   One of the most remarkable stories of the series and a key success factor was the seemingly infinite depth of the Indian squad. After every injury a new, young player would step up and just deliver. Young players like Shubman Gill, Mohammed Siraj and Washington Sundar, who all made their Test debuts in this series, played like experienced professionals. Even the relatively unknown and unheralded T. Natarajan, who was part of the Test squad as a nets bowler, showed a lot of composure when given the opportunity. What explains this depth?

   This foundation was not built overnight. There was a process and structure behind it working for a number of years, courtesy the Under-19 and India A, India's second-tier national team, apprenticeship structure put in place by the great Rahul Dravid. Under his guidance and mentoring, India's U-19 teams have reached a very high level of quality and professionalism. Most of the young stars were the product of that Under-19 process and structure. The depth was further nurtured by the Indian Premier League (IPL) structure, which gave opportunities to domestic players to observe and compete with world-class players.

   This is such an important management lesson. Great success is never an accident nor is it instantaneous. If you want great success in future, you have to invest in the right processes and structure and groom talent from within well in time.

3. **Leadership model: The warrior monk**
   A lot of credit for the win should go to Captain Ajinkya Rahane. He was a stand-in skipper, picking up the pieces after a debilitating defeat, facing a continual barrage of challenges and

yet he delivered a historic victory. This was not a fluke. Ajinkya displayed some very deep and remarkable leadership attributes.

He was calm, not very expressive and had a monk-like stillness about him. Instead, he let his bat do the talking, especially his innings in Melbourne. He did not get provoked by the many challenges both on and off the field. He demonstrated respect for the opposition (presenting Nathan Lyon a signed jersey for his 100th Test) despite such a hard-fought series. And celebrated the younger players consistently (inviting T. Natarajan to hold the trophy).

In him, I saw a warrior monk, very calm and anchored, yet with a fierce determination and resolve for the right action. He serves as a great example for leaders in the complex business world we operate in today.

4. **Role models**

I have mentioned the 'winning attitude' earlier. This did not happen suddenly. Indian cricket has been fortunate to have generations of captains and key players who demonstrated a winning attitude, each building on the previous one and providing an even finer example. It started with Sourav Ganguly who brought self-confidence and expression. M.S. Dhoni built on it in his own unique way, bringing calmness but also fun while having the finishers drive. Virat Kohli might seem aggressive but he is a lot more than that. In fact, he is highly intelligent and highly committed. In addition to these stellar captains, we have had the remarkable generation of Sachin Tendulkar, Rahul Dravid, V.V.S. Laxman and Anil Kumble, all of whom embodied quality, grit and commitment. And how can we forget the fearlessness and fun of Virender Sehwag?

As discussed earlier in the point on process and structure, no success is overnight. Role models have a critical role in inspiring and showing the way.

5. **Need balance: Youth + experience**
This series win was a celebration of new India, of the young stars like Rishabh Pant, Shubman Gill, Mohammad Siraj and the fearlessness and the spirit they brought. However, the series win could not have happened without the experience of veterans like Ajinkya Rahane, Cheteshwar Pujara and Ashwin. That is another important management lesson; you need to build the right balance of youth and experience in the team or organization. Diversity and inclusion, when done right can have a significant, positive impact for organizations—younger people bringing the drive for new ideas and innovation, while experienced ones know the business context, pitfalls, etc.

6. **Adversity can be an opportunity**
As I mentioned earlier, this Test series win was remarkable and unique because it was in the face of an unbelievable mountain of adversities. I believe that these adversities were also a contributing factor in the team being able to raise its performance to such amazing levels. It brought the team even closer together, emphasized the team over individual brilliance, strengthened the team's resolve, presented opportunities to newer players and forced them to apply new and more creative strategies.

This is such an important lesson both in business and in life. Obstacles are inevitable. See them as an opportunity. If used well, adversities can become your biggest growth opportunity.

In an era defined by constant disruption and accelerated change, resilience, adaptability and leadership aren't just good to have, they're essential. Sports offers us living proof that grit, courage and belief can turn even the most daunting challenges into breakthroughs. These are exactly the traits we must cultivate—in individuals and teams alike—to thrive in the AI age.

20

The 2018 Football World Cup
The Rise of the Underdogs

It always seems impossible until it's done.
—*Nelson Mandela, Anti-apartheid revolutionary and political leader*

World Cup tournaments provide a global platform for teams from various countries to compete, to prove their mettle to the world, in various types of sports. Each of these tournaments has its own unique history, traditions and impact on the sport it represents, bringing together the best athletes from around the world to compete at the highest level. It also has a lasting impact on millions of people around the world who come together virtually or live, to celebrate the spirit of competition, unity and national pride. The shared experiences of victories and defeats, the display of skill and perseverance and the emotional highs and lows echo far beyond the stadiums, influencing cultures, economies and social dynamics across the globe.

Football is the universal sport, nicknamed 'The Beautiful Game'. And the World Cup evokes passions and interest like no other event in the world. But more than anything, I find that these matches have a way of teaching us a lot about business and life. One such memorable tournament for me was the 2018 FIFA World Cup in Russia. It was a tournament unlike any other, filled with surprises, upsets and unforgettable moments. While the world watched in awe as France claimed their second World Cup title, the real story of the tournament for me was the **rise of the underdogs**. Smaller nations, often overlooked and underestimated, stepped into the spotlight, challenging football giants and earning the respect and admiration of fans worldwide.

From Croatia's heroic journey to the final to the spirited performances of teams like Japan, Russia and Morocco, the World Cup demonstrated that in the modern game, reputation counts for little and performance on the day is everything. The underdogs showcased immense determination, skill and team spirit, proving that with the right mindset and preparation, any team can defy the odds.

Below are the seven learnings I took away from this World Cup. These observations are not just about sports, they are equally relevant for management and for life.[1]

1. **The world is getting flatter, competition is intense**: There were no easy matches in this World Cup. Other than England's thrashing of Panama, almost every match was very close. The so-called minnows—Morocco, Japan, Iran, Iceland and many more—came well prepared, were well drilled defensively and gave the majors a tough fight, even if they did not win matches. This means the margin of error is low, luck plays an important part and nobody can take success for granted.

2. **Reputation means nothing, performance is everything**: On paper, Germany and Spain had the strongest squads. However, both struggled to make an impression and were knocked out early. Germany's demise was particularly remarkable. They have an incredible record in major competitions, but this time they

did not just fail to progress to the next round but finished last in their group!! And, with their confused team selection and drab performance on the pitch, this result was not undeserved. Clearly in a flatter world, reputation means nothing, performance on the day is everything.

3. **Old order changeth, again and again**: Winners of past several World Cups have often failed to progress beyond the first round of the next World Cup and this bizarre phenomenon was repeated this time with Germany. Powerhouses like Italy and Netherlands failed to even qualify for this World Cup. The 'Tiki Taka' style that made Spain so dominant not so long back, seemed like a joke this time, especially in their match against Russia. It shows that there are no permanent success formulas and you cannot afford to sit on your laurels. 'Business as usual' is the kiss of death and constant innovation is the only way to move ahead.

4. **Superstars make way for the underdogs**: The two dominant players in the world over the past ten years, Christiano Ronaldo and Lionel Messi, barely made a mark in this World Cup. Ronaldo had one great game (against Spain) and Messi one great goal. Both could not help their teams progress beyond the second round. Their heir apparent, Neymar, tried hard but will be remembered more for his theatrics. Who would have thought that Luka Modric, Eden Hazard and Griezmann would emerge the top three players of the tournament? The most influential players of this World Cup were understated, hardworking and focused on their team.

5. **Rise of the youth brigade**: This World Cup was a celebration of youth. Nineteen-year-old Kylian Mbappe dazzled with his speed and skills and emerged as one of the most influential players of the tournament. France, the winner, had one of the youngest squads with an average age of twenty-five years. Perennial

underachievers England had their best tournament for twenty years all thanks to the speed and spirit of their young team led by a young manager. This World Cup showed dominance of youthful speed over established skills, not unlike what we are seeing in the business world.

6. **Bravehearts shine**: Two teams surprised and overachieved more than anybody else—Croatia and Russia. Both were spurred by severe challenges. Croatia, a small country still suffered wounds of a tragic civil war, and Russia was constantly being lampooned by the West and under pressure to perform in their home World Cup. These challenges forged a fierce team spirit and an indomitable will to win in them. This proves once again that adversity can bring the best out of you and a strong will can move mountains.

7. **Ultimately squad depth matters**: Two teams with the strongest squads, France and Belgium, finished first and third. They were strongest both in skills and depth of squad. To last and win a long tournament, quality matters. Moreover, it is not just about the starting eleven, but the squad of twenty-three. In addition, both these teams did not achieve overnight success. Both were trained in the hard school of failures. France suffered the pain of losing Euro 2016 and the 'golden generation' of Belgium had seen multiple failures. Ultimately, quality, depth and persistence are the key ingredients of sustained success.

The 2018 World Cup in Russia showcased the extraordinary rise of underdogs, leaving us with invaluable lessons about competition, innovation and resilience. In much the same way, the AI age is set to unleash massive disruption—reshaping hierarchies and creating new pathways to success. For those willing to prepare, adapt and believe, this era offers a once-in-a-generation chance to leapfrog ahead. Success is no longer guaranteed by reputation; in a fast-changing world, true strength lies in hunger, boldness, speed and collective effort.

21

The 2014 Football World Cup

A Masterclass in Teamwork over Individual Brilliance

The strength of the team is each individual member. The strength of each member is the team.

—Phil Jackson,
American former professional
basketball player and coach

There are some valuable management lessons that can be drawn from the way individuals from diverse backgrounds and with unique skills come together to play for their country.

One such tournament that is etched in my memory, one of the greatest shows in the world, was the football World Cup in Brazil in 2014. It had been five weeks of relentless passion, skill and drama that kept so much of the world enthralled and mesmerized. When thirty-two of the world's best teams battle against each other in a fiercely competitive tournament, it produces not just riveting drama but also many useful lessons.

Here are eight management lessons from the 2014 World Cup that business leaders and organizations could benefit from:[1]

1. **Team over individual brilliance.** We are naturally drawn to individual brilliance—the mesmerizing runs of Lionel Messi, the skill of Neymar, the power of Cristiano Ronaldo. However, in the end when it was a match between the best team and the best player of the tournament, the best team won. Individual brilliance is important. Messi did play a crucial role in leading Argentina to the final but he also had a solid defence to support him. And the great Ronaldo could not carry a poor Portugal team even from the group stages. This is great learning for organizations. We often tend to focus on the charismatic leader. The leader is important but it is the team that is even more important.

2. **Youthful energy over reputations.** Spain came to the tournament as the reigning World and European Champions and their clubs had dominated the European Champions League. However, they suffered two humiliating losses and bowed out from the group stages. Their problem was resistance to change. They failed to evolve their 'tiki taka' style and went with the reputation of their aging stars, ignoring the young talent on the bench and ultimately paid the price. Unlike them, young teams like Colombia dazzled the World Cup with their youthful energy and creativity. Similarly in business, you cannot rest on past laurels and old strategies. There are always younger, more creative competitors who can surprise you.

3. **Mere emotion and good intent is not enough.** Brazil came into the tournament riding a tidal wave of national pride and expectations. The passion at display while singing their national anthem at the beginning of each match showed unmistakable intent. The emotion and spirit carried them through the group stages and early rounds, but they suffered the most humiliating defeat in the semi-finals. They were found out. They were not good enough. Emotion can give you energy, but if it is not backed by capabilities, it can fall flat. Often in the business world, leaders

go by vision and slogans, but organizations cannot succeed unless the vision is backed by clear strategy and execution.

4. **Success takes time and planning**. Most members of the victorious German team had come through their famous youth development programme. Many of them were part of the under-21 European Championship winning team in 2009. The same team had lost in the semi-finals of two previous World Cups and the last European Championship. Yet, they persisted with their coach Joachim Loew for seven years. Finally, they won the biggest prize in 2014. This clearly shows that success is not immediate. It takes time and planning. You often have to face multiple failures and need to have the strength and foresight to persist through them. This is a lesson we often forget in the business world. We often have expectations of immediate results and lose heart at the first failure. We should learn from the German team.

5. **Backline is as important as the frontline**. This World Cup was dominated by goalkeepers. Manuel Neuer of Germany, Ochoa of Mexico, Tim Howard of USA and Navas of Costa Rica emerged as the biggest stars for their teams. Moreover, in the final few matches, the defender Mascherano outshone the talismanic Messi for Argentina and Bastian Schweinsteiger was the heroic man of the match in the finals. Newspaper headlines and public imagination are captured by dazzling forwards and goal scorers. However, matches are often won or lost by the defence. There was no better example of this than Brazil's famous capitulation against Germany. Even in the business world, it is the 'frontline' staff in sales and marketing that are often the heroes. However, we need to recognize that the 'back-office' plays an equally important role in a company's success.

6. **Bench strength is crucial**. This World Cup saw more goals by substitutes than ever before. The final was won by a wonder goal

from the substitute Mario Goetze who scored from a pass by another substitute Andre Schurrle. Germany was able to shrug off the loss of the influential midfielder Sami Khedira just before the match and his replacement Christoph Kramer early in the match to still go on and dominate the midfield. On the other hand, Brazil had pinned all their hopes on Neymar and suffered a meltdown when they lost him in attack and Thiago Silva in defence. Another interesting example of leveraging the bench was the Dutch bringing on keeper Krul for the penalty shootout highlighting the importance of specialist skills. Clearly, the team that had the strongest squad, not just the starting eleven, won. Similarly, in the business world we cannot rely on a few stars. Succession planning and talent development is critical for having a pipeline of leaders who can step in at short notice.

7. **You can make the best of limited means**. The Costa Ricans were the surprise package of the tournament. A country of only 4.5 million people with few players in the top football leagues, they won their group that included three former world champions in Italy, Uruguay and England. They only lost narrowly in the quarter finals on penalties to the powerhouse Netherlands. They had a simple, focused strategy that they executed perfectly—rock-solid defence and then fast counter-attack. This shows that you can produce great results with limited means. Even in business, it is not the company with the most resources that wins. Sometimes, limited resources make you think harder about your strategy. A clear, narrowly focused strategy can work wonders when executed well.

8. **The margin of error is small**. The greatest competition in the world was won by a solitary goal in the final seven minutes of the extra time. After a flurry of goals in the group stages, most matches in the knockout rounds were won by solitary goals with 4 being decided in extra time and four going to penalties. Germany

came into the finals as the clear favourites. Yet, Argentina gave them a great fight and probably had the better chances. Clearly, the margin between a glorious win and the despair of defeat is very low. This means that you have to absolutely bring your best form and strength of character into every match. Moreover, you have to acknowledge the importance of luck. Therefore, there is no place for arrogance or hubris in sports at the highest level. This is a great lesson for all of us in business. Most industries have immense competitive pressures. No company can afford to be complacent and has to be at its very best to win in such a competitive environment.

Sports is one of the finest expressions of human endeavour and teaches us timeless lessons—about strategy, execution, resilience and, above all, teamwork. As the 2014 World Cup showed us, greatness is not just about individual brilliance, but about how people come together with purpose and trust. In the AI age, where speed and complexity are rising sharply, it is high-performing teams—not just high-performing individuals—that will define success. I hope the learnings in this chapter inspire you to strengthen collaboration and elevate your own leadership in the teams you build.

MANTRA 5

MAKE AN IMPACT

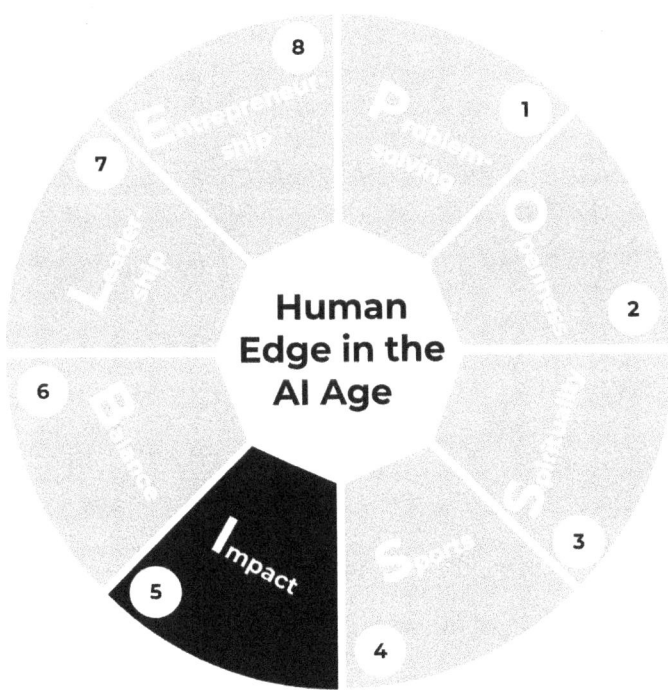

The POSSIBLE Framework

Introduction to Mantra 5
Make an Impact

Building a Life of Meaningful Impact in the AI Era

What you do makes a difference, and you have to decide what kind of difference you want to make.
—Jane Goodall, British anthropologist and zoologist

What defines a life well lived? In the end, it's not just our achievements but the impact we leave behind—on people, organizations and society. Impact is the ultimate measure of our contributions to the world. While success is often measured by individual accomplishments, true fulfilment comes from making a meaningful difference. Impact is not just about influence or scale, it is about the depth and sustainability of our contributions.

The three dimensions of impact

At its core, impact manifests in three key dimensions:

- **Personal impact:** The ability to transform oneself, develop skills- and grow into a better version of oneself. This is where impact begins—by first changing ourselves before changing the world.
- **Organizational impact:** The ability to drive change within teams, businesses and institutions. Leaders create impact by fostering cultures of innovation, growth and shared purpose.
- **Societal impact:** The broader contribution to communities and humanity at large. Those who make the biggest impact extend their influence beyond their immediate sphere to create lasting change.

Impact is a journey that starts from within and extends outwards—from personal transformation to organizational leadership and, ultimately, to shaping society.

The journey from effort to impact

Impact is a journey that starts from within and extends outward—from personal transformation to organizational leadership, and ultimately, to shaping society. This mantra explores that journey through three chapters:

1. **Finding your sweet spot:**
   The first chapter focuses on discovering the intersection of what you love, what you're good at and what the world needs. When these elements align, you find purpose and the foundation for meaningful impact.

2. **Taking the responsibility to make a difference:**
   The second chapter emphasizes personal responsibility. Impact starts small and expands as we take ownership of our actions and grow our zone of influence—from self to organization to society.

3. **Driving sustainable change:**
The final chapter puts a spotlight on sustainable development. It urges us to rethink consumption, challenge assumptions and act responsibly. I share practical steps I've taken to contribute meaningfully to this cause.

My journey with impact

Impact has been a guiding principle in the way I have approached not just leadership, business and innovation but also personal interactions. My life and career have been shaped by these three progressive dimensions of impact—first by continuously improving myself as a human being and as a leader, then driving change within organizations and ultimately striving to contribute to society through thought leadership and writing. I strongly believe that human life is a precious gift and it is our responsibility to make a positive dent in the world, to leave it a bit better than we found it. And that journey of impact outside starts with the journey inside, continuously improving ourselves to become the best versions of ourselves.

During my time at Flipkart, I witnessed first-hand how digital transformation could redefine an entire industry, making e-commerce accessible to millions in India. Later, as the CEO of Incedo, I defined our mission as making a positive long-term impact on our clients and the industries we operate in, prioritizing client impact over short-term gains. I have sought to create a culture that goes beyond business outcomes—one that enables individuals to find meaning in their work, to grow to their fullest potential and contribute to something larger than themselves. We have done that by setting up a foundation, *Digital Fundas*, that supports digital education in tier-2 and tier-3 towns in India.

Beyond the corporate world, writing *Winning in the Digital Age*, *Mastering the Data Paradox* and now this book are endeavours to share knowledge and empower professionals to navigate the complexities of modern technology and leadership. The process of articulating these insights and then sharing them has been deeply fulfilling, as it allowed me to extend my impact beyond organizational boundaries and contribute more broadly on topics that are hugely important for any professional in today's digital and AI age.

I have been deeply engaged with the National Association of Software and Service Companies (NASSCOM), the Indian association of software companies, contributing to the development of the tech ecosystem in India. One of my most memorable experiences has been to lead this industry body in Gurgaon and turn that into a civic forum for driving sustainable transportation, one of the most critical issues for a young city.

At the heart of all these experiences has been a single, unifying idea: true impact is not just about what we achieve, but about the lives we impact, the change we enable and the legacy we leave behind.

Impact in the AI age

The rise of artificial intelligence presents a paradox. It can dramatically amplify our capacity for impact, but only if guided by human intent. AI is transforming industries, displacing old roles and creating new avenues for innovation. In this new landscape, impact is not just about keeping up with change—it's about shaping that change responsibly.

The leaders of tomorrow will be those who use AI not only for efficiency but for meaningful transformation. Whether in business, healthcare, education or climate action, AI can be a powerful tool for inclusivity and sustainability. But it must be anchored in ethics and purpose.

As AI reshapes our world, we must ask: *How will we use it to amplify our impact and create a better future?*

Impact is the highest calling of both leadership and personal growth. Whether through inner transformation, building empowered organizations, or contributing to society, our legacy is defined by the difference we make. By embracing AI as a force multiplier for good, we can leave a deeper, more lasting mark on the world.

22

Finding your 'Sweet Spot'
The Powerful Purpose of Your Life

The mystery of human existence lies not in just staying alive, but in finding something to live for.
—*Fyodor Dostoyevsky, Russian novelist*

I strongly believe that every human being has abundant potential. Everybody is blessed with some unique talents, which if discovered and nurtured can lift the person and the world around them to a higher level. However, very few achieve their full potential. In fact, most of us operate from a tiny fraction of our full potential. This is perhaps one of the greatest challenges and opportunities we have as individuals and also collectively as society, and as mankind. This question of discovering and unlocking our unique potential becomes even more important in the AI age where we are facing profound questions on our human edge.

Why are we not operating at our full potential?

Life is a voyage of discovery. Nature expects us to progress from one level to the next. At each level, we discover something new and powerful about ourselves and the world around us. This moves us towards awareness of our true calling. However, progressing from one level to another is not easy. Our life situations condition us and exert a strong gravitational pull that does not allow us to break free. The laws of physics seem to apply here. Gravity keeps us rooted. To launch a rocket into orbit you need a turbo booster. Once the rocket moves into orbit, it can stay there with little additional energy. Similarly, we need a push, a trigger, to lift ourselves from our current situation and move to the next level.

This is difficult. So, how do we progress on the journey to unlocking our potential?

I believe the key is to have a **positive and sustained purpose**, a cause to which we can dedicate our lives. This purpose will be the positive force that creates focus and commitment and can inspire extraordinary effort. It is the magnet that will create means where none seem to exist and align the forces of nature in a mysterious yet powerful way. It is indeed the turbo booster that can lift us from one level to another and in the process help us realize our full potential.

History gives us abundant examples

M.K. Gandhi was a simple man, but he had a powerful purpose: to seek freedom for India through non-violence and moral truth. This lifted him to the level of a Mahatma and ended up shaking the foundations of a mighty empire. Tulsidas was a village simpleton. His love of Rama helped him create the epic *Ramcharitamanas* and made him a saint. Joan of Arc was a young and frail peasant girl with fierce conviction in her divine mission to liberate France. Her faith helped rouse a beaten people to defeat a powerful enemy. She is revered to this day as one of the patron saints of France. This clearly shows that there is incredible power even in the meekest amongst us. A powerful purpose can unlock the amazing energies within us, not just uplifting our own selves but the world around us.

So, how do we find a positive and sustained purpose?

Finding the purpose of your life

Some might be fortunate to find a guru who helps them find their path, while others might go through dramatic events that make their life purpose clear. India's freedom fighters are an illustration of the latter. The fight for the nation's freedom inspired a generation to lift themselves up and force a change that was not seen as possible. However, most of us might not be in either of the above situations and defining our purpose might call for conscious effort.

In the daily pulls and pressures of life, the question of finding our life purpose often gets lost. You float through life driven by the forces around you. You do not seem to be in control of your own destiny. The purpose of one's life seems like a difficult puzzle. It is sometimes difficult even to find the starting point from where you can begin piecing together this puzzle. However, it is necessary that we attempt to solve this puzzle of life. Having a powerful and sustained purpose in life is the key to not only achieving your full potential but also finding lasting happiness in life. It brings you the energy and focus that can unlock your potential, spark the leader within you and lift you and your world to a different level. In addition, having clarity of purpose and being able to live it brings alignment in life, which leads to lasting happiness and inner peace.

I believe our purpose lies in the **'sweet spot', or the intersection of three forces**—our passions, our unique talents and serving important and ethical needs. Finding your 'sweet spot' is a journey. Passions are the likely starting point, but they are not enough. They need to be coupled with talent. Finally, and most importantly, you need to channelize your passions into meeting some important needs or solving some important problems around you. Magic happens when you find the 'sweet spot' at the intersection of the three forces I have mentioned. You realize the powerful and sustained purpose of your life. However, there is no predictable formula for finding this 'sweet spot'. It is a voyage, a patient journey and an exciting adventure.

Finding your sweet spot gives you the purpose of your life

Here are some thoughts on finding your 'sweet spot', your powerful, sustained purpose.[1]

Start with your passions

Passions are a gift. They are a source of energy. They light up your life and bring you joy and vitality. A life devoid of passions is not a full life. Passions are also the foundation of excellence. You are likely to give your best in what interests you and brings you happiness. Passions are like a luminous compass that lights up the way to your purpose. Follow your passions and you will have begun your journey of life well.

However, we often don't follow our passions because of our fears and conditioning. As children, we have few fears. As we grow up, we keep building fears inside ourselves and it becomes progressively more difficult to overcome them. Fears stop you from connecting with your true self. They limit your enjoyment of life. Let go of your fears and take more risks. The downside is less damaging and the upside, a lot more beneficial than you imagine. So, take that initial leap of courage and go after your passions. Be like a child, live your life freely!

The other big factor stopping us from following our passions are external expectations. As we grow up, we start internalizing the expectations of family, friends and society. We often look at the world from another's lens. We are conscious of what we are expected to achieve and how we are expected to behave. Success has a narrow and rigid definition. We often end up living our lives for others or as others expect us to. This is very limiting. We need to challenge this conditioning and live our own life while being conscious of our responsibilities and duties. So, break free from your fears and conditioning and follow your passions. That is a happy and energizing way to begin the beautiful journey of life!

Seek opportunities to serve important needs

Passion is a very important ingredient in the journey to finding your purpose, but it is not sufficient. Passion will spark the initial momentum, which may not sustain in the long term. Your passions need to be aligned with serving an important need so that the sparks of inspiration become a bright and sustainable fire. Life is not to be lived in isolation. We live in an interdependent world. One of the fundamental objectives of life is to make a positive difference in the world around us. We need to translate that into our personal purpose. Moreover, this is not just about nobility of purpose. At a more practical level, any effort needs to create value for others for it to be sustainable. You create value not just by pursuing your own self-actualization but also by solving problems or serving the needs of others. Therefore, we need to figure out how our passions and/or skills (which are internal) can be made relevant for the world around us. How can our interests and talents create value or solve problems for others? You need to link the internal with the external or, to put it in more commercial terms, you need to link supply with demand.

Solving other people's problems and creating value is not easy. We are naturally wired to be self-oriented. Therefore, it is easier for us to have an understanding of our own needs, our aspirations, our strengths and our passions first. To create value, you need to have an outside-in orientation, where you have the empathy to understand the world around you. You need to go out of your cocoon and relate to others. That allows you to understand the needs of people around you. This is necessary to spark the thought process of solving problems and creating value for others.

You also have to open yourself up to different experiences. Finding out where and how you can create value is not easy. You are unlikely to uncover significant opportunities if you look at the world through a narrow lens. Therefore, exploration and allowing oneself a range of experiences is very helpful. As you do this, you discover more about yourself and the world around you. This process can help uncover where and how you can add value.

Persist to build unique skills

Once you have identified your passion or the needs you want to serve, you need to develop the required skills or competencies. They are necessary to provide depth to your purpose, taking you from the ordinary to someone who has a significant and lasting impact on the world around you. Equally, unique skills can also be a starting point to figure out opportunities for you to add value. You are likely to find opportunities more easily when you have unique skills.

However, building skills and competence is not easy. It requires hard work, patience and discipline. Even if you are blessed with natural talents, you have to practise hard and long to build distinctive competencies. There are no shortcuts. It takes time and you have to keep at it. As you build the habit of not giving up and not taking the easy course, you will discover hidden reserves of energy within you. You will find that you are able to go on for much longer. However, even upon reaching higher and higher levels, you cannot rest on your laurels. You have to keep practising; the aim at any point is to move to the next level. The fruits of your persistence will be sweet. Once you build distinctive skills, you will find that your actions become effortless and pleasurable.

There is a powerful synergy between your passions, serving important needs and your unique skills. Deep passion fuels effort and persistence, which over time helps you build distinctive skills. Once passion and skills combine, they naturally point you towards opportunities to serve important needs. And as you begin to serve those needs, your sense of purpose deepens, often intensifying your passion, creating a positive self-reinforcing cycle.

However, this flow is not necessarily sequential or linear. The three can connect with each other in different ways. What is important is that you are able to link them well. This can lead to a virtuous cycle where they can feed into each other, each becoming stronger in the process. The 'sweet spot' that emerges then will be powerful and can create magic!

My sweet spot: Building at the intersection of purpose and paradox

As I look back on my journey—from the consulting rigour of McKinsey to building businesses at Fidelity and Flipkart and now scaling Incedo—what energizes me most is working at the intersection of a bold goal, the people who will drive it and the execution required to make it real.

Over the years, I've come to realize that my sweet spot lies in building organizations and ideas that solve deeply relevant problems at scale. The world is undergoing a seismic shift—from the Digital Age to the AI age—and this disruption needs not just architects of strategy, but also builders of systems, shapers of culture and stewards of meaning.

What drives me is a commitment to mastering duality: modern technology and timeless Indian wisdom, business performance and societal good, strategic clarity and execution excellence, speed and sustainability. These are not contradictions to be resolved but creative tensions to be navigated. That's where the human edge lies.

I love to create—companies, frameworks, books—but above all, I love enabling people and institutions to evolve meaningfully in times of change. My purpose is to be a bridge—between innovation and wisdom, thought and action, individual growth and collective impact.

If you're still searching for your sweet spot, don't chase perfection. Chase **energy**. And trust that your sweet spot is not a fixed destination—it is a lifelong **discovery**, revealed as you stretch, stumble and grow into your fullest potential.

I want to leave you with three final thoughts on how to proceed on this magical journey of discovering your 'sweet spot'—the powerful purpose of your life:

1. **Ask the question**: The starting point is to question the unique purpose of your existence. Ask that question of yourself and of nature. The answers you get in life are a function of the questions you ask. As you keep asking these challenging questions, the mist of confusion clears and the answers you seek begin to emerge.

2. **Understand the flow**: Everything that happens in your life happens for a reason. All the answers you seek are within you, so reflect on your life experiences to connect the dots and find your purpose. Whatever has happened in your life has happened for a

purpose. As you piece the jigsaw puzzle of your life together, it is very likely that the purpose of your life will jump out at you.

3. **Keep faith**: Finding the powerful purpose of your life is an unpredictable journey. It is equally possible that the answer lies on the next corner or is far away. The answers may take some time coming but keep the faith that God has a special purpose for you. Seek persistently and with belief, and the answers will start to follow.

Finding the powerful purpose of life is one of the most profound quests of mankind. It is a quest that you must attempt. If you can find your 'sweet spot', it will lift you and the world around you to a higher level. Mahatma Gandhi put it beautifully when he said, 'Find purpose, the means will follow.' However, finding your purpose requires patience. It's the greatest adventure of your life. Begin it—with courage, curiosity and conviction.

23

Take Personal Responsibility and Change the World

Change will not come if we wait for some other person or some other time. We are the ones we've been waiting for. We are the change that we seek.

—Barack Obama, American politician,
44th President of the United States

One day in Gurgaon, stuck for over an hour in a traffic jam near Cyber City, I found myself railing against poor planning and failed systems. Then it hit me: I had been part of this city's growth. Why hadn't I done more to shape it?

We often cry about the 'system' and find faults in the situations and people around us. We blame the 'system' for various problems that we face on a day-to-day basis, whether it is corruption, traffic or pollution. We are perennially disappointed with the companies we work in, whether it is with their policies, their politics or them not recognizing our worth. Even in our personal lives, we have ready explanations for what other people are doing wrong and what they should do differently. However, we rarely look within to see what *we* could do differently. This is a negative cycle. You change nothing and keep living in frustration and disappointment.

Why does this happen? Why do we see others as the problem and not take responsibility for our problems ourselves?

Blame is easy. Change is hard—but possible

It is human nature to excuse or rationalize one's own shortcomings while focusing on the obvious improvement needs of others. Our ego is the big culprit, which creates a sense of separateness and also makes us defensive. It makes us stand apart from the 'system', as opposed to being part of it. Even when we recognize the problem for what it is, there is often a sense of helplessness about any one individual's ability to change the 'system'. The 'system' often appears like an unshakable giant, impossible for an individual to move. Therefore, you end up rationalizing that it is pointless to make the effort.

The other challenge is inertia and fear of the unknown, which makes it difficult to move from the status quo. We certainly crib about the status quo but often find it difficult to rouse ourselves to action to change it. Inertia makes it difficult to leave the safe harbours of our daily existence. It requires additional effort and risk-taking to break away and set sail for the open seas. Fear of uncertain storms often overpowers the excitement of opportunities.[1]

We can keep crying about the 'system'. We can keep explaining how we are in the right or how little influence we have on the 'system'. That is futile. Your frustrations and self-pity will make no difference. Any 'system' is nameless and faceless. You cannot hold it accountable. It cannot change on its own. Clearly, you cannot leave it to divine intervention. So, what choice do you have? If you are suffering, then it is in your interest to do something about the 'system'. Given that the most control you have is over your own actions, it is best to start by taking personal responsibility. Your efforts will not be wasted. Any 'system' is made up of individuals. When enough individuals change, there comes a tipping point when the 'system' also starts changing.

Responsibility builds leaders

We often feel that our influence on the 'system' is limited. The funny thing about influence is that if you act on what is in your zone of influence, that zone keeps expanding. This leads to growing confidence and broader impact. Conversely, if you keep focusing on what is not in your zone of influence, the boundaries keep pushing in, further limiting what you control. This only leads to further despair and frustration. Clearly, it is better to act and grow your zone of influence, as opposed to it continuing to push into you.

Moreover, if you aspire to develop and be recognized as a leader, you have no option but to take broader ownership. Leadership is about going beyond the self and creating a wide-reaching impact. As you take personal responsibility for the problems around you, the leader within you grows. We see numerous examples of this. Many leaders might have been spurred on their leadership journey by a personal hurt (for example, Mahatma Gandhi, George Washington and Nelson Mandela), but they gained success because they took ownership of problems on behalf of others and created a substantial impact.

Start small. Grow your zone of influence

How do we make the change? The starting point is self-awareness. We must realize that the only thing we can control is our actions and we are accountable for them. You can keep floating through life, frustrated and beaten by the system and the circumstances. On the other hand, you can stop, take personal responsibility and do something about your circumstances. If you are not completely satisfied with a situation, ask yourself, 'What can I do about it? If I can't control it, how can I positively influence it?'

It is perhaps best to start small and focus on the self and on issues most in your control. They could be as simple as not wrongly overtaking on the roads, not throwing litter in public spaces, or not bribing the traffic cop when you can. In personal life, it could be about being more empathetic and seeing issues from the other's perspective. At work, it could be giving your 100 per cent to your job, reaching out to a colleague who needs help, reaching out to the company to point out a wrong policy or two and suggesting solutions. If you see problems in your industry or local community, then you could create a forum to get people together to discuss the matter and take collective action on it. As you log in the small personal victories, your self-confidence grows, you gain more clarity on how to make broader change and eventually your zone of influence grows—from the individual level to your organization and eventually to society at large.

Evolution as a Leader

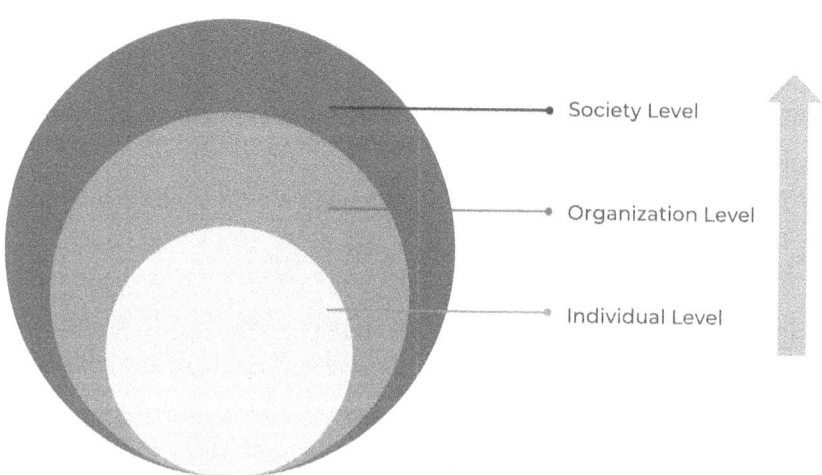

There are, of course, limits to human action and what you can influence at a given point in time. Therefore, it is important to be able to understand and discriminate between what you can change and what you cannot at any point. However, the possibilities for human action and influence are far greater than what we often realize. Moreover, as I have said earlier, when we focus on action, our zone of influence expands to include what might not have been within our control earlier.

Evolution of my consciousness and impact

I have been fortunate that I have had some incredible growth opportunities in my student and professional life. Each of them has helped me discover a next level of consciousness and grow my impact. I would like to share three sets of experiences and how they have helped me evolve—1) Self and task focus, 2) People development and focus on giving not getting and 3) Society and focus on sustainable development.[2]

Stage 1: Aravali hostel, IIT Delhi

Where it all began—learning to lead with passion and excellence

My first significant leadership experience was my hostel at IIT Delhi. The four years I spent at IIT Delhi were an incredible learning experience. I had the opportunity to be the sports secretary of my hostel in the third year and the house secretary in the fourth year. IITians are very competitive and this is not just in academics but extends to sports and co-curricular activities as well. I was ignited by that competitive spirit. I was totally driven by the ambition to help my hostel Aravali be the best in IIT and win all the championships. I set very clear goals for myself and the hostel. We built a great team that was infused with the same passion and we achieved great success together. We won the Sports Championships in impressive style in my final year dominating across sports. Moreover, we won the Best Hostel trophy in three out of my four years at Aravali.

While I built a dedicated team and a great following, at heart I was a **task leader**. My single-minded focus was victory for my hostel. That clear and energizing goal generated tremendous energy and was a life-shaping experience for many of us. However, there was a flip side to it. It made us over-competitive, which brought conflict with the other hostels. Moreover, we were not able to take everybody along even in our own hostel. Those who were not into sports or co-curricular activities perhaps saw me as being 'over the top' aggressive and arrogant.

Stage 2: McKinsey Knowledge Centre

Shifting the lens—from self-drive to people leadership

My second stage of leadership evolution began when I took on the role of leading the McKC from 2002 to 2010. But the backstory matters. After graduating from IIT and then topping the MBA programme at IIM-Lucknow, I joined McKinsey & Company—then the most coveted job for MBAs in India. I had a smooth, upward trajectory. But in 2000, I left to pursue entrepreneurship. As I mentioned earlier, my venture, ActiveKarma, turned out to be a great disaster.

In 2002, I returned to McKinsey—but instead of consulting, I joined a small back-office unit called McKC, which supported consultants with research. I saw it as a chance to learn how to build and manage a business—something I realized I hadn't mastered during my startup. It was a stark contrast to the consulting frontlines, where even junior consultants interacted with CEOs. At McKC, I found myself, at the age of thirty, leading a young team who saw me as an ex-consultant with all the answers.

Once the initial excitement wore off, doubts crept in. The work felt narrow, and the personal learning curve seemed flat. But then came a shift in perspective. I realized I was too focused on myself. Instead of asking what I was getting, I started asking what I was giving. That changed everything—from a task leader, I grew to be a **people leader** and **organization builder**.

I focused on coaching, creating opportunities and building confidence in the team. And something magical happened—people blossomed. They, in turn, transformed McKC from a small research support centre into an innovation hub. It grew from thirty to forty people to over 1000 professionals, spanning diverse disciplines. Today, McKC is a global pioneer in high-end research and analytics from India.

That growth wasn't driven by me alone. It was fuelled by a generation of empowered professionals. I had simply shifted my focus—from self to others. And in doing so, I saw not only McKC flourish, but experienced profound personal growth as a leader. This experience taught me a fundamental truth: when you stop chasing outcomes for yourself and start giving to others, what you receive in return is far greater than you could have imagined.

Stage 3: Fidelity and NASSCOM

Expanding the horizon—leading for industry and society

The third stage of my leadership journey began when I left McKinsey after twelve fulfilling years. I joined Fidelity, a global asset management firm, which became a turning point in broadening both my perspective and purpose.

At McKC, I had grown from task leader to people leader. But in hindsight, my life had been singularly focused—dedicated almost entirely to McKinsey, with little bandwidth for anything else. Fidelity offered a wider canvas. I now oversaw multiple functions and played multiple roles globally, which allowed me to step back, reflect and adopt a more holistic view.

I began to feel a growing responsibility to give back—to the industry and to society. That led me to NASSCOM, the industry body for the IT and BPO sectors in India. Through NASSCOM, I took the lead on an initiative to define a new vision for multinational firms operating in India. This helped reposition Global Capability Centres (GCCs) from transactional support units to strategic hubs of innovation and value creation.

At the same time, I became involved in shaping civic and social initiatives in Gurgaon, where Fidelity's India operations were based. Gurgaon, despite being a modern IT hub, faced serious infrastructure and sustainability challenges. Along with other industry leaders, we recognized that our businesses couldn't thrive in isolation. We needed to help improve public transport, women's safety and the employability of local youth through better education.

This phase helped me evolve from a one-dimensional corporate leader into a more multi-dimensional human being—a **society leader**. I began to understand the interdependence between business and society and the role of leadership in bridging that gap. I also met several remarkable individuals—entrepreneurs and social leaders who had walked away from successful careers to dedicate themselves to public service. Their journeys sparked deeper questions in me about the true purpose of life.

This experience reinforced a simple truth: when you are fortunate enough to have a platform, you also have a responsibility. A responsibility to look beyond self-interest, and to help shape a better, more inclusive world.

Closing thought

The world today is more complex, connected and technologically advanced than ever before. AI is transforming everything—from how we work to how we live—but it cannot replace human will, intention and responsibility. In fact, as machines become more capable, it becomes even more critical that we do not outsource our agency.

It's easy to blame systems, institutions, or even technology. But when we do that, we unknowingly give up our power to change things. Personal responsibility is the human edge—because it starts with a decision that only we can make: to act, to care and to contribute.

Taking responsibility doesn't always mean changing the world—it might mean picking up one issue, one cause, one frustration that you care about deeply and doing something about it. That small ripple can spark wider change.

As Mahatma Gandhi said, *'You must be the change you want to see in the world.'* These are not just poetic words. They're a daily discipline. If more of us embraced this spirit, we would build not only better lives for ourselves, but also a world where human potential and technology evolve together, in harmony.

In the AI age, *taking personal responsibility is not optional—it is essential.* The future doesn't just happen to us. We shape it, one action at a time.

24

Sustainable Development
Rethinking Consumption

It's time to shift from being consumers to being caretakers. We have the power to shape a sustainable world through our choices.
—Mari Copeny, African-American youth activist and philanthropist

The AI age is ushering in an era of abundance—unprecedented growth, speed and scale. But this growth comes with a hidden cost: rising consumption, inequality and ecological stress. As individuals and organizations chase more, faster and bigger, we must confront a fundamental question: **can we grow without breaking ourselves and the planet?**

Fast pace in everything we do and a relentless drive for growth is making sustainability a real question mark. Ever-increasing desires and search for growth are the cause of stress at the individual level, lack of judgement and unethical behaviour among corporations and increasing crime, pollution and a variety of disasters in our societies. Corporate leaders in today's age cannot ignore these issues; they have to step up and address them directly.

Now, for sustainable development, it is critical to rethink our current mindsets and approach to consumption. Mahatma Gandhi captured the problem beautifully when he said: '**There is enough for everyone's needs but not for everyone's greed.**' However, solving this problem is easier said than done. Our current mental and economic models at all levels—individual, corporate, societal—are driven by growth. They are about ever-increasing needs and desires and the constant race to fulfil them. The desire for growth is a source of motivation for and a driver of human endeavour. It is this desire for growth that has helped human civilization develop over many millennia. However, mankind's unending pursuit of desires and growth directly contribute to personal stress, corporate misconduct and societal decay.

This is a complex issue, and I do not have any 'silver bullet' answers. However, I would like to share with you some of my practical attempts to address this challenge in my different roles—as an individual, a corporate leader, a citizen and society leader.[1]

1. **Individual**
   The root cause of the consumption debate lies at the individual level. It is ever-increasing individual desires that eventually reflect in our collective behaviours as a society. We work hard towards meeting our desires, which, however, keep growing. As soon as we fulfil one cherished desire, a new one seizes us. It becomes very difficult to break this cycle. This leads to increasing stress and loss of peace of mind. Stress does not just mean loss of mental peace; it is also one of the key root causes of diseases like hypertension and diabetes.

   Yoga and meditation have been of great help to me in finding balance in my life. I have been following the Art of Living practices for more than twenty years now, and have been reading the ancient Indian spiritual texts, especially the Bhagavad Gita. All this has helped me understand life better and go deeper within myself. As you do all this, the feverishness of desires in you reduces and you feel content and at peace with yourself.

We live in a material world and it is not possible for most of us to withdraw and become hermits. However, it is possible and desirable to find a balance between spirituality and materialism in our daily lives. I would encourage all of you to explore spirituality and adopt some spiritual practices in your daily lives.

2. **Corporate leader**

Just as individuals are pulled by the pursuit of more, businesses often chase unbounded growth. But infinite growth on a finite planet is a paradox. Companies that maximize short-term profit without regard to long-term impact may win the quarter but lose the future. I strongly believe that the companies of the future will need to operate with a dual lens: growth with responsibility, profit with purpose.

Many economic models have been experimented with in the recent centuries, but eventually capitalism has emerged as the most effective model. The entire basis of this model is free markets and growth. If you look at how capital markets value companies, growth expectation is clearly the biggest driver of value. This focus on constant growth leads to many problems. The over-leveraging of companies, the high levels of debt in financial institutions and the resultant (and frequent) financial crises are all outcomes of this obsession with growth. At the same time, we do not have an alternate economic model yet. Despite its many ills, capitalism, with its growth focus, makes for the most tenable economic model today.

I am sure that over a period of time, our thinking will evolve and newer economic models will emerge. The question is, what can corporate leaders do *today*? We can perhaps differentiate between *good growth* and *bad growth*. The former benefits many, while the latter is self-centred and often leads to disastrous consequences.

The way many companies are trying to focus on 'good growth' is by putting the **customer above profit**. Companies that are truly customer-centered focus on identifying and serving the genuine needs of their customers. They place customer interest above their own interests. They ignore short-term profit considerations, knowing that if you do the right things for the customer, profits will follow in the long term. In my corporate experience, the customer-centric approach is the most important mantra for ensuring 'good growth' and building a high-quality business. Most successful companies (including the three that I have had the privilege of working with—McKinsey, Fidelity, Flipkart) and my own firm Incedo, have customer-centricity as their guiding mantra.

3. **Citizen and society leader**
   From 2010 to 2016, I had the opportunity to co-chair and later chair the NASSCOM Regional Council for Haryana. With over 3,00,000 IT-BPM professionals based in Gurgaon (likely ~5,00,000 in 2025), the sustainability of the city was inextricably tied to the future of our industry. As I engaged more deeply with Gurgaon's civic challenges—traffic congestion, public safety and rising pollution—it became clear how broken our urban planning had become.

   The root of the problem was clear: our cities are built for cars, not people. In Gurgaon, as in many Indian cities, cars are both status symbols and default mobility tools. Their numbers grow exponentially, while public infrastructure fails to keep pace. The result: choked roads, unsafe streets and some of the worst air pollution levels in the world.

   In contrast, cities like Amsterdam and Copenhagen have reclaimed their streets through a very different model—one that prioritizes walking, cycling and public transport. Inspired by these global examples, we began championing the idea of active commuting through NASSCOM. I referenced this story in the previous chapter, but it bears repeating here because of what it taught me about sustainability. Initially, we tried to drive change through policy engagement. But when progress stalled, we shifted gears. We focused on individual behaviour change, not getting bogged down in battles with bureaucracy.

We encouraged CEOs and industry leaders to walk, cycle and use public transport—living the change we all wanted to see. Slowly, this sparked a wider community movement. One visible outcome was *Raahgiri Day*, where roads are closed to cars and opened for people. Over time, these visible shifts led to tangible action from local authorities.

This experience reminded me of a truth we often forget: we don't need to wait for perfect conditions to act. Yes, policy matters—but people move systems. Even seemingly small actions—choosing to walk, to speak up, to organize—can create powerful ripple effects that reshape entire systems.

In an AI-driven world where systems are becoming more complex and abstract, this lesson is even more critical. It is our daily, human choices—what we consume, how we move, what we stand for—that will shape whether this new era becomes sustainable or self-destructive. Technology can scale intent, but only we define the intent.

Rethinking consumption is not a straightforward problem—it touches every aspect of how we live, work and define success. There are no easy answers, but I am heartened that this conversation is no longer confined to activists or academics—it is becoming mainstream, and urgently so.

As we navigate the AI age—a time of exponential possibility—it becomes even more essential to anchor ourselves in timeless wisdom. I leave you with three reflections that can guide us toward a more sustainable future.

At the **individual level**, we must learn to balance material growth with spiritual grounding, so that we live with greater clarity and contentment.

At the **corporate level**, we must move from short-term profit to long-term purpose, placing customers and communities at the heart of value creation.

And at the **societal level**, the path forward must be paved not just with policy, but with everyday citizen action—through conscious choices, behavioural shifts and a renewed sense of responsibility.

The AI age may optimize everything—but it is only through restraint, reflection and responsibility that we'll create a world worth living in.

MANTRA 6

FIND THE RIGHT BALANCE

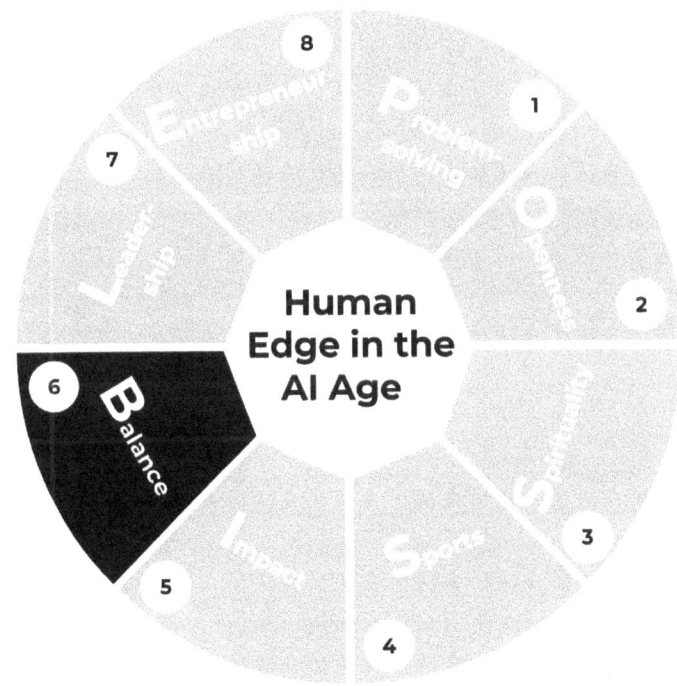

The POSSIBLE Framework

Introduction to Mantra 6

Find the Right Balance

Mastering Duality, a Key Skill for Thriving in a World of Opposites

> *The wise see knowledge and action as one; they see truly.*
> —Bhagavad Gita, Chapter 5, Verse 5

In a world of relentless change, balance or mastering duality is no longer a luxury—it is a survival skill. The AI age is accelerating contradictions at an unprecedented pace, making the ability to balance opposing forces more essential than ever. AI-driven automation is boosting efficiency, yet demanding greater human creativity. The speed of decision-making is rising, yet deep thinking and reflection remain critical. Organizations must rapidly innovate, yet must maintain stability and trust.

Technology is reshaping industries, work and leadership at breakneck speed and individuals who can navigate these dualities not by choosing one side, but by integrating both—will thrive. The future belongs to those who can execute today while strategizing for tomorrow, who can leverage AI without losing the human touch and embrace speed while making thoughtful, ethical choices.

Life is built on dualities—day and night, chaos and order, logic and emotion. Just as nature thrives on balance, so must we. But balance does not mean compromise; it means learning to integrate opposing forces into a greater whole. Those who master this art will thrive in the modern world.

Understanding and navigating dualities

This mantra explores the art of balance through three key chapters, each offering a different lens:

1. **Beyond trade-offs:**
   Learn how to harness tensions—like growth vs. profitability and strategy vs. execution—not by choosing sides, but by integrating opposites into higher-order solutions.

2. **Momentary vs momentous:**
   Reflect on the contrast between enjoying the present and building a lasting legacy, as seen through the emotional lens of a college reunion.

3. **Two-speed execution:**
   Learn how to toggle between short-term delivery and long-term vision, a duality, which is commonplace at the heart of leadership and innovation.

My journey with balance

I have always been fascinated by duality and naturally reflect on both sides of any situation. Among these, the balance between spirituality and materialism has been particularly significant for me, a theme I have explored multiple times in this book. Throughout my career, I have grappled deeply with dualities—sometimes agonizing over them.

At McKinsey, I learnt to balance external expectations as a consultant with my own entrepreneurial instincts. This tension led me to embrace both strategy and execution, ultimately making strategy-to-execution one of my defining skills. At Incedo, I constantly navigate long-term vision vs short-term execution, client expectations vs employee well-being and growth vs profitability—a delicate act that requires constant recalibration. In my personal life, I juggle professional commitments, writing and my deep attachment to family, each demanding a careful balance.

One of the most profound lessons I've learnt is that balance is not about choosing a static middle ground—it is about transcending trade-offs to see the bigger picture and align with a higher goal. True balance comes from choosing the 'and' over the 'either-or', adjusting dynamically between opposing forces. It's knowing when to push and when to pause, when to drive efficiency and when to invest in innovation, when to trust data and when to listen to intuition.

To illustrate, take the balance between customer and employee needs—often seen as opposing forces. However, with a high-quality business model, serving customers well naturally leads to a more engaged, motivated workforce. True balance is not about trade-offs, it is about finding synergies that elevate both sides.

Mastering balance in the AI age

To cultivate balance, consider these key principles:

- **Embrace duality**: Understand that conflicting forces can be complementary rather than opposing.
- **Develop range**: Build the capability to operate in both strategic and executional modes.

- **Prioritize mindfully**: Recognize when to focus on speed vs depth and stability vs disruption.
- **Pause and recalibrate**: Regular reflection helps avoid burnout and ensures alignment with long-term goals.

Mastering balance is not about choosing between extremes but about harmonizing them. The world is not black and white, it is a spectrum of possibilities. Those who learn to balance opposing forces with agility and wisdom will lead the way in the AI age.

Balance is not a destination but a mindset—one that allows us to navigate complexity with clarity and confidence.

25

Beyond Trade-offs

How to Harness Opposites in the AI Age

There is both joy and suffering on planet Earth because this beautiful world is a world of duality—a world of opposites. There is an opposite side to everything.

—Rhonda Byrne,
Australian television writer and film producer

Among the many challenges the VUCA world throws at you, there is one that is particularly significant—mastering duality. It is the need of the hour in an increasingly competitive digital and AI age to manage contradictions or seemingly conflicting objectives at the same time.

Opposite values are complementary and coexistent in nature—day/night, heat/cold and male/female—while they seem opposite but are necessary to complete each other's existence—and it is no different in business. Individuals in the AI age face many conflicting objectives, or what I like to call 'dualities'. While these dualities are very evident, they are not easy to deal with. As individuals, we tend to develop preferences, get stuck in a particular mode of working and

Mastering duality - A key skill for leaders to succeed in the Digital and AI age

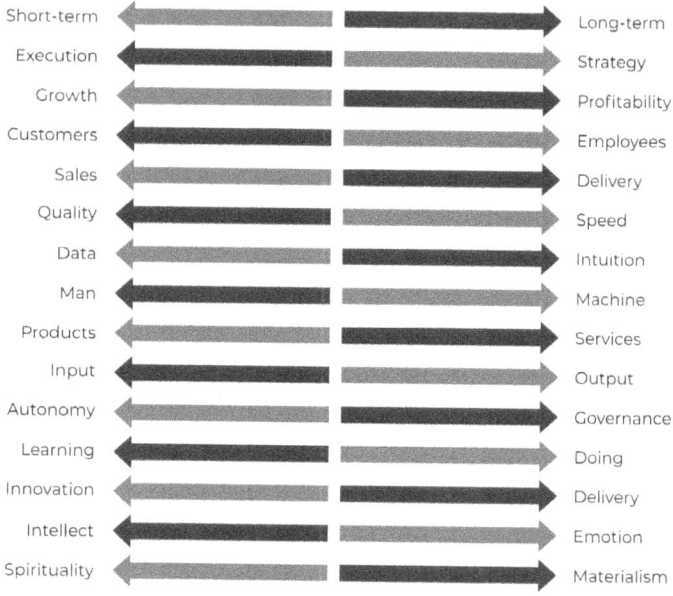

thus tend to focus on only one aspect of the complementary values. In some cases, our way of dealing with this is to make trade-offs between the opposing values. My submission is that complementary values or conflicting objectives are such an intrinsic feature of the AI age that we need to go beyond the trade-offs and master operating with duality—create win-win on both values.

Let us now explore fifteen dualities or opposites that I see commonly in business and in life. I will briefly delve into why these conflicting objectives are often difficult to balance and share some high level thoughts for finding balance across them:[1]

1. **Short-term vs long-term:** The high velocity of change and shrinking business and product cycles call for intense short-term focus. However, in parallel, if you do not invest in the long term, you will not have a future. Moreover, the short term and

long term are not parallel tracks, they need to connect with each other. Many of us get stuck in either short-term or long-term frames and find it difficult to toggle between the two.

2. **Execution vs strategy:** In my first book, *Winning in the Digital Age*, I shared that there has been a reversal in the traditional strategy-to-execution cycles in the VUCA world and there is even more focus on execution today. However, it is important to connect the dots from execution and develop clarity on strategy. Strategy to execution is no more linear but iterative, so it becomes even more important to toggle seamlessly between the two.

3. **Growth vs profitability:** This is a classic conundrum—one that is becoming even more difficult to balance in the digital age. Revenue growth and profitability are the twin pillars of enterprise-level value creation. However, it is not easy to manage both at the same time. Revenue growth typically requires investments, which hit your profitability. This becomes even more challenging when profitability is already under threat in many areas because of pricing pressures and rising costs. So, it is a great challenge to develop a distinctive and effective business model that can drive growth and profitability at the same time.

4. **Customers vs employees:** Customers are the bedrock of any business, and in the digital age, which is characterized by hypercompetition and abundant choices, customer-centricity becomes even more important. Driving for customer delight will likely require employees to go the extra mile. But if you are not careful, this might compromise your employee mission. I believe that in the digital age, it is important to be both customer-centric and employee-centric at the same time. And, if you balance the two axes (customers and employees) well, it can create a virtuous cycle for your business.

5. **Sales vs delivery:** Sales and delivery require different mindsets. Sales is often about selling a promise, while delivery is about

making it happen. Sales often tends to be aggressive and delivery conservative. If you oversell, you will falter in delivery. At the same time, if your promise is too conservative, you might not be able to sell anything.

6. **Quality vs speed:** While driving at speed, your chances of accidents increase. Similarly, in business, pushing for speed can result in compromising quality. A good example of this is in recruitment: pushing for scale-up can end up compromising both candidate quality and experience. However, speed is one of the defining features of the AI age and you have to build execution at speed as an organizational muscle. However, it is imperative to find the formula to ensure high quality while operating at speed.

7. **Data vs intuition:** We have talked at many points in the book about how data is exploding in volume, variety and velocity, a focal point of my second book *Mastering the Data Paradox*. Data explosion, coupled with the rise of data science and AI, enhances fact-based decision-making. However, the role of intuition does not go away. It becomes even more important. Intuition is a source of creativity and competitive advantage. Hence, it is important to master both these capabilities for thriving in the AI age. The key lies in developing these seemingly opposite capabilities at the same time—a structured process for working with data and a reflective process for deepening intuition.

8. **Man vs machine:** The relentless march of technology, led by artificial intelligence as its torchbearer, is leading to the redesign of many jobs and processes. The question is, how best can leaders designing the jobs and processes of tomorrow understand and incorporate the complementary capabilities of both machine (technology) and man (human capabilities)? I strongly believe it is an AND, not an OR opportunity.

9. **Products vs services:** In technology, there has been a divide between products and services. These are typically different

business models and require different mindsets and processes and are typically delivered by different types of companies. However, the boundary between products and services has been blurring. Many services companies are developing product/intellectual property capabilities, while product companies are realizing the need for client-specific customization.

10. **Input vs output:** Business leaders, especially those running public companies, are measured on the basis of their output—for example, financial results and stock market performance—and this tends to take a lot of their attention. However, if there isn't focus on the right inputs—for example, investment in capabilities, talent and culture—it will be difficult to sustain high-quality output. At the same time, if your efforts (input) are not anchored by a clear end in mind (output), you might lose your way.

11. **Autonomy vs governance:** The fast pace of the AI age means that traditional command-and-control structures cannot work. To ensure the speed of decision-making and action, you require autonomy at various levels of an organization. At the same time, the need for governance and risk management does not go away. How do you balance autonomy and governance at the same time?

12. **Learning vs doing:** The dynamic nature and high velocity of change in the AI age make continuous learning imperative. At the same time, it is critical to have a bias for action. Learning and doing can take time away from each other, but it is important to find the right balance between the two.

13. **Innovation vs delivery**: Innovation is one of the key success factors in the AI age. However, innovation by definition implies creativity, experimentation and risk-taking. On the other hand, high-quality delivery typically requires predictability and consistency. Often, innovation and delivery call for two different mindsets and metrics. It is more important than ever before to manage both at the same time.

14. **Intellect vs emotion**: The battle between head and heart is a perennial one. Most of us have a dominant style. The conflicting requirements in the AI age implies that all executives need to develop and use their IQ and EQ equally. A balance of intellect and emotion, of head and heart, is more important than ever before for a leader.

15. **Spirituality vs materialism:** We have talked about this in Mantra 3. In a highly frenzied and volatile world, being able to find peace in the midst of chaos is extremely important. When there is so much happening outside, being able to go deep within and anchor oneself becomes even more important. It is no wonder that meditation or mindfulness is moving from the personal realm and finding increasing acceptance at the workplace, even in boardrooms. While spirituality and materialism might seem at odds with each other, I strongly believe that having a strong spiritual core is increasingly important to succeed in the crazy VUCA world we live in today.

The kind of values discussed above make for a long list; these are but a sample of the conflicting objectives leaders face in the digital and AI age. Now, the question is, how can you improve your ability to handle conflicting objectives? I have five suggestions from my experience:

1. **Build awareness and understanding of the complementary values** and the realization that you have to master both. You don't need to settle for trade-offs; win-win solutions are possible.
2. **Get a range of experiences**, which broaden your worldview and give you an understanding of different aspects of reality.
3. **Bring diverse talents together in the team**. While it is desirable for an individual to master a range of complementary values, it might not be easy to do so. Bringing together talent with diverse backgrounds and experiences can help bring the complementary values together as a team.

4. **Have a sounding board.** In our personal lives, our spouse or partner complements us. They are not just a sounding board but also often hold a mirror to us, helping us see the bigger picture of life. Similarly, in our professional life, it is very important to have a trusted sounding board, whether it is a mentor or a colleague, who can help us go beyond our biases and see the bigger picture.

Five ways to address duality and handle conflicting objectives

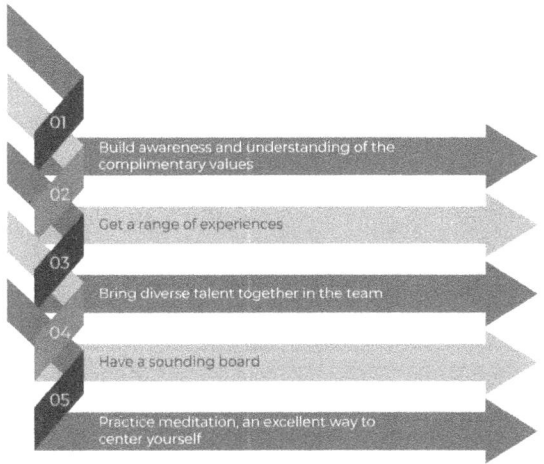

5. **Practise meditation.** This is an excellent way to centre yourself. The challenge with complementary values is that we tend to get stuck in extremes. I have seen it through my personal experience that the practice of meditation brings clarity to any complex situation and helps you get to win-win solutions.

Complexity is a defining feature of the digital and AI age, which confounds us by presenting many conflicting objectives before us. Therefore, mastering duality is a key skill for us to succeed in this era. It is a difficult task, but those who are able to master different aspects of duality will grow to a different level of maturity, both as professionals and as human beings.

26

Momentary Versus Momentous

Within this moment, the only moment that exists, the past, present and future are contained.

—Gautam Buddha,
spiritual leader and Founder of Buddhism

We live in a fast-paced, success-driven world where it is easy to get caught up in the relentless pursuit of goals and milestones. We often find ourselves so focused on the future that we forget to appreciate the present. In this chapter, I share my personal journey of understanding the delicate balance between living in the moment and striving for lasting impact. Through experiences and reflections shared with lifelong friends, I found some insights on how we can find fulfilment in both our everyday moments and our broader aspirations.

Something dawned on me during a short trip to Sikkim with my college buddies of thirty years. This was the second time we had done this boys trip, and it was proving to be a hugely enjoyable ritual. It was a great opportunity for all of us to let our hair down and feel young again. In the midst of all the fun, we also ended up having some rather profound discussions—perhaps reflecting that most of us were on the other side of fifty.

Late into the third night of our trip, we started questioning ourselves on the biggest learning in our lives over the past few years. My friend Pawan posed what all of us felt was a great question—*Is life momentary or momentous?*[1]

All six of us in the group are high-achievement, high-intensity types of guys, so this was a soul-searching question. Pawan's question brought the realization that the beauty of life is in the present moment. The present moment is real while the future is uncertain. However, in focusing on future goals, we often miss out on living the present moment fully. We often don't appreciate the beauty and joy that is around us—our families, our friends, our passions, the simple joys of a leisurely cup of morning tea, hearing the birds chirp, gazing at the night sky and much more. If we lived all the moments of life fully, it would be a life well lived. Moreover, it is a string of beautiful moments that make our life momentous. If we do the small things right, the big things have a greater chance of happening. Or as we often used to say in Fidelity, if you take care of the pennies, the pounds will take care of themselves.

At the same time, there is a counterpoint. While being happy in the present moment is important, it involves the risk that we could just float through life without making a difference. If one lives with the attitude of 'here and now', there is nothing wrong with that; however, no progress can ever be made if lived by that rule. Life is a great gift. Life is about being the best you can be and leaving a positive legacy. All of us have the opportunity to do something momentous with our lives, but that is easier said than done. It takes vision, effort and perseverance. It is not just 'going with the flow' but keeping the bigger picture in mind. It is about having the courage to dream and to shape the future. The human race has progressed over civilizations because of the momentous achievements of many. All of us have the seed of greatness and the opportunity to create lasting positive impact within us.

This dichotomy—of life being momentary or momentous—became very real as we ended up discussing how we could contribute to positive change in India. Our views on how we could make an impact were very different. Some felt that we should be like a *jugnu*, a firefly and spread light in our vicinity. In other words, lead a principled life, do the best we can and be a good example to others. There was a strong alternate view—the problems of India were, and still are, so massive that we needed significant systemic change. Just being a *jugnu* would be wasted effort. It would not make a real difference. We needed momentous change that required great thought, massive mobilization and sustained action.

With my friends after having the momentary vs momentous discussion, 15 February 2014, Sikkim, India.

My two cents

As I said in the previous chapter too, life is full of contradictions—yin and yang, good and evil, birth and death, happiness and sadness and many more. There are so many dualities in life that coexist and we have to find the golden mean—the optimal balance—across them. Similarly, life is both momentary and momentous and we have to live at both levels. We should absolutely live every moment fully as if it is our final moment. Being in the present moment makes us happy and stress-free. However, while life is about being happy, it is also about making a positive difference. Life is momentous when one believes that one is not alone but a part of the whole. This view allows one to create not merely for one's own consumption but for that of the others, for the future and for the world. This, however, requires one to expand one's consciousness, be detached from the outcome of one's labour, for sometimes, the fruits may not even be visible in one's own lifetime. We need to be *Karmayogis*, someone who performs their actions without attachment to results, seek a higher purpose, be the best we can and leave a lasting legacy.

The beauty is that momentary and momentous need not be contradictory; they can not only coexist but support each. As mentioned earlier, it is **a string of beautiful moments that make our life momentous**. Being in the present moment allows us to better spot and realize the opportunities that life offers us to move towards our higher purpose.

Going back to our earlier discussion on driving change in India, of course the country faces huge problems that need massive system change. However, the size and complexity of the problems are so daunting that they can lead to inaction. For most of us, it is natural to think that one individual cannot make any real impact and we end up not doing anything. That is where it is important to be a *jugnu*. If all of us can do the right thing and make some positive changes around us, it will start moving the needle and could lead us to the tipping point where the system starts moving. At the same time, we need to realize that this is not a deterministic equation of cause and effect, so we should not be disappointed if results are not immediate. However, we need to take positive action and to persist with it. Action, however small, is much better than inaction.

So, going for the momentous milestones should not stop us from living the moment fully. At the same time, living in the moment should not mean that we lose sight of the momentous. It is about finding the right balance. Where we draw the line is a personal decision. I hope all of us find the right balance and have the good fortune where we fully live the moments and also realize momentous impact in our lives.

27

Learn Two-Speed Execution

You can't grow long-term if you can't eat short-term. Anybody can manage short. Anybody can manage long. Balancing those two things is what management is.

—*Jack Welch, former chairman and CEO of General Electric*

The modern leader must be both a sprinter and a marathoner—often on the same day. As the co-founder and CEO of Incedo, it certainly feels like that to me! I wear many hats, each representing different aspects of my responsibilities. When formulating strategies, I focus on the big picture—building a road map for the next three to five years. At the same time, I spend a significant amount of time in operational reviews, evaluating progress across business units and key initiatives, which require a critical and analytical mindset. Another large part of my time is spent with clients, where I shift to a listening and problem-solving mode. Additionally, I dedicate focused time to writing books like this one, which demands ideation, research and deep reflection.

And when I return home, I engage with my family, who have their own expectations of me. Each role demands constant **context**

switching—shifting gears between situations, people and problems. This reality is not unique to me; in today's complex world, most of us must juggle multiple responsibilities, both at work and at home. Thriving in this environment doesn't just require hard work—it requires mastering the art of two-speed execution.

The need for agile thinking: A two-speed mindset

This constant switching of roles and objectives underscores a deeper truth: we live in a world of dualities, where managing contrasting demands is no longer a choice but a way of life. Balancing strategy and execution, or long-term and short-term demands, is no longer optional—it's essential in today's complex world. However, mastering these dualities requires distinct mindsets or speeds, as I like to call them. One is fast, urgent and reactive; the other is patient, reflective and forward-looking. The ability to transition smoothly between these speeds is a hallmark of agile leadership and human adaptability.

I first introduced this concept in *Winning in the Digital Age*[1] and expanded on it in *Mastering the Data Paradox*.[2] In those books, I framed it primarily in the context of business transformation and technology execution. But as I've reflected more deeply, I've come to realize: this is not just a business challenge—it's a life skill.

The key lies in **mental agility**—the ability to shift mindsets quickly and intentionally. This is the essence of **two-speed thinking**, which allows you to move seamlessly between:

Speed one: Immediate execution

Fast-paced tasks that demand action, focus and quick decision-making.

In business and tech, this includes:

- Responding to a client escalation
- Fixing a production issue
- Running a high-stakes daily operations review

In daily life, it might be:

- Managing a busy morning routine with your kids
- Handling an unexpected travel delay
- Navigating a packed to-do list

Speed One is about delivering now, high velocity, high precision and under pressure.

Speed two: Long-term thinking

Work and actions that require time, reflection and sustained effort.
In business, this includes:

- Crafting a multi-year strategy
- Building new capabilities in AI or digital transformation
- Mentoring the next generation of leaders

In life, it might look like:

- Investing in your physical or mental well-being
- Writing a book or building a creative practice
- Reflecting on your purpose or planning your next life chapter

Speed Two is about building what lasts—deep work, strategic thinking and long-term value.

Most people gravitate towards one speed based on personality, comfort or context. Speed One offers the thrill of urgency and the comfort of routine—tasks get ticked off, problems get solved and results are visible. Speed Two, on the other hand, offers depth, meaning and long-term impact, but it requires patience and doesn't offer instant rewards.

That's why many people get stuck in Speed One. It feels productive, even addictive. But true leadership lies in holding both—delivering results today while building the future. Speed Two is what ultimately shapes careers, organizations and lives. It's like going to the gym; progress may be slow and invisible at first, but over time, it's transformational.

In the AI age, advantage doesn't come just from moving fast—it comes from knowing **when** to move fast and when to slow down. That's what makes two-speed thinking such a critical human edge. But how easy is it really, being able to smoothly switch between these fast and slow modes? That takes some serious mental agility to nimbly shift gears mentally and that's precisely where we run into the challenge of context switching.

Let me explain more.

The challenge of context switching

While two-speed execution is essential, transitioning between these modes is far from easy. It requires more than just time management—it demands cognitive agility and emotional awareness. Here are three key challenges:

1. Natural preference for one mode

Most of us are more comfortable at one speed than the other.

- Strategists, researchers, academicians and writers tend to favour Speed Two—immersed in reflection, analysis and creation.
- Operators, project managers and sales professionals often operate in Speed One—driven by deadlines, action and responsiveness.

But success demands both. A strategy without execution is empty. Execution without reflection can become reactive and short-sighted.

2 Mental effort and fatigue

Switching between speeds isn't just a shift in task—it's a shift in mindset. This cognitive gear-shifting can be mentally taxing, especially under pressure. It leads to decision fatigue, reduced creativity and eventually, exhaustion. Imagine a student who's just wrapped up a fast-paced marketing presentation and now has to dive into a detailed economic analysis. That shift doesn't just require time—it demands mental reorientation and energy. These transitions happen constantly in modern work and life—and they rarely come with built-in recovery time.

3. The illusion of productivity

Frequent, unstructured switching between tasks can create a false sense of momentum. You feel busy—but aren't truly effective. Research shows that poor context switching can reduce productivity by up to 80 per cent, as your brain repeatedly loses focus and must reorient itself.[3]

Getting stuck in Speed One can lead to burnout and reactivity. Staying too long in Speed Two risks inaction and irrelevance. The real art lies in finding your rhythm and learning when to switch. In a world where machines can move fast, it's the human ability to choose the right pace that becomes a superpower. The next question is: how do we train ourselves to do it better?

Cultivating a two-speed mindset: The SHIFT framework

So, how do you develop the mental agility to toggle effectively between Speed One and Speed Two? Mastery doesn't come overnight—but it can be cultivated through practice, structure and self-awareness.

Here's a simple, memorable framework I use: **SHIFT**. Each letter represents a key principle to help you master two-speed execution.

S—Structure time for both speeds

Without deliberate planning, Speed Two tasks—like deep thinking, writing or strategic reflection—will always get pushed aside by urgent demands.

I intentionally block time for long-term activities. For example, I write between 11 p.m. and 1 a.m.—a protected slot in my day. Similarly, I carve out time for meditation and exercise to ensure long-term well-being. If it's not on your calendar, it probably won't happen.

H—Hone both muscles

Most of us naturally favour one speed over the other. But sustained success requires building strength in both.

Early in my career at McKinsey, I was trained in strategy, which made me comfortable in Speed Two. But when I launched my first startup, ActiveKarma, I realized execution was a different muscle. I deliberately moved into operational roles—like leading the McKC—to sharpen my Speed One skills.

Similarly, someone naturally action-oriented must learn to slow down, reflect and plan. You grow by stretching beyond your default mode.

I—Immerse fully in one mode at a time

Once you've allocated time, give yourself fully to the mode you're in.

When working on a book, I shut out distractions and immerse myself in writing and research. On the other hand, when handling urgent client issues, I focus entirely on Speed One execution—knowing that mental clutter will block deeper insight later.

Even computers don't truly multitask, they switch tasks in rapid sequence. Human brains need focused immersion to operate at their best.

F—Find pauses between modes

Switching isn't just mental—it's physical and emotional too. Without brief resets, rapid toggling can be draining.

Between meetings or major tasks, I take short walks or moments of silence to reset my mind. I also practice meditation daily, often twice a day, to clear mental clutter and sharpen focus. These pauses don't waste time, they protect your energy and help you enter the next mode with presence and clarity.

T—Train through deliberate switching

Like any skill, two-speed execution sharpens with deliberate practice. At first, the switching feels effortful—but with time, it becomes instinctive, fluid and powerful, and you move from **conscious competence** (switching with effort) to **unconscious competence** (switching with ease).

Just as athletes train their bodies, leaders must train their minds. Daily reflection, feedback loops and mindfulness practices like meditation help you build this switching capability. I meditate at least once—and often twice—a day to sharpen this mental muscle and maintain clarity.

Mastering two-speed execution is not about doing everything at once. It's about knowing what to do when, and how to show up fully in each moment. In a world that pulls us in every direction, SHIFT offers a way to lead with intention, not just reaction.

The AI future requires two-speed thinking

As the world becomes more AI-driven and relentlessly fast-paced, operating at just one speed—whether it's execution or reflection—will no longer be enough. Machines can optimize for speed. But it is our uniquely human ability to shift gears, think in dual time horizons and apply judgement in complexity that will set us apart.

Mastering two-speed thinking isn't just about productivity. It's about staying balanced, making better decisions and thriving in complexity. It enables us to deliver in the now while designing the future. It helps us stay grounded in a world of constant acceleration, and intentional in a world of endless distraction. In the AI age, this mindset will be a defining edge—for individuals, for leaders and for the institutions they shape.

MANTRA 7

UNLEASH THE LEADER WITHIN YOU

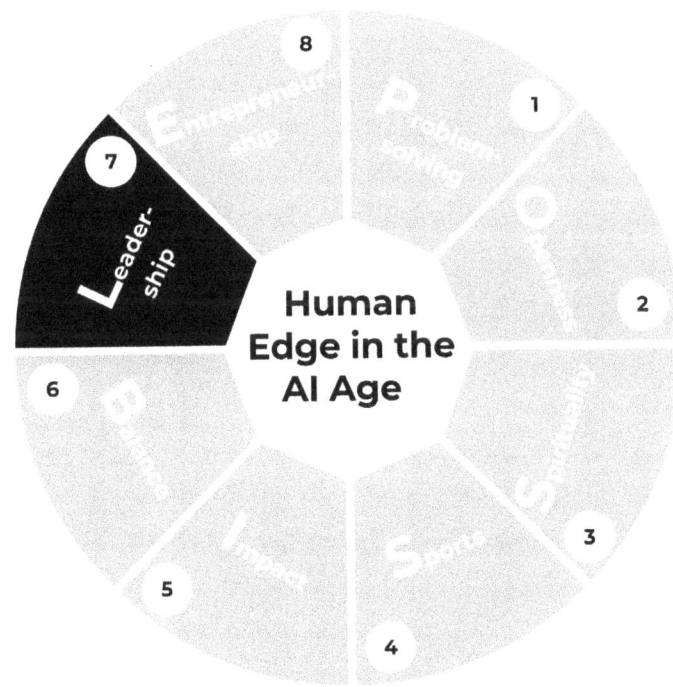

The POSSIBLE Framework

Introduction to Mantra 7
Unleash the Leader within You

Leading from Within: Courage, Clarity and Connection

Do not follow where the path may lead. Go instead where there is no path and leave a trail.
—Ralph Waldo Emerson, American essayist

We are living in a time when the very definition of leadership is being reimagined. The AI age is upending traditional hierarchies, flattening organizations and democratizing access to information. Authority is no longer derived from position alone, but from the ability to inspire, adapt and deliver impact. In this new world, leadership is not a title, it is a mindset. It is about how we show up—with courage, clarity and the ability to connect.

The AI age demands a new kind of leader. One who is self-aware, adaptable, emotionally intelligent and values driven. The future will not be led by the smartest person in the room, but by those who can mobilize people, drive change and build trust across diverse teams and environments. In fact, it perhaps marks the end of the Age of Managers—task-focused, control-oriented professionals who thrived in linear, predictable systems. What we now need are leaders who can embrace ambiguity, balance competing priorities and lead from within.

Four facets of modern leadership

This mantra explores the evolving nature of leadership through four chapters:

1. **Ten leadership fundamentals**
   Timeless principles that continue to matter—even more so—in the age of intelligent machines.

2. **The 5Cs of leadership as service**
   How great leaders inspire others by practicing care, clarity, courage, connection and conviction—creating environments where people thrive.

3. **Leading through change**
   Practical strategies for navigating transformation—arguably the most essential leadership skill in the AI age.

4. **Creating More Leaders**
   True leaders build future leaders. This chapter explores how to nurture leadership through mindset, mentorship and opportunity.

My journey with leadership

I have had the privilege of working with and learning from exceptional leaders throughout my career—from my early days at McKinsey to playing a global leadership role at Fidelity. Joining McKinsey in 1996, during its early years in India, was a transformative experience. I had the opportunity to closely observe great leaders like Anupam Puri and even Rajat Gupta, the firm's global managing partner, witnessing first-hand how leadership is not about titles but about being a role model, coaching others and enabling their growth.

Early in my career, I realized that leadership opportunities come in many forms. At IIT, I was elected sports secretary—an unexpected role for an introvert like me. But it unlocked a flood of passion and energy, which has since become a defining trait of my leadership style. Later, leading the McKC provided an incredible opportunity to develop as a leader early in my career, teaching me how to build and scale something from the ground up. My time at Flipkart and now at Incedo has further shaped my leadership journey, giving me the chance to lead in high-growth, high-impact environments.

Through these experiences, I have come to understand that leadership is not about being in charge. In fact, it is not even about you. Leadership is about contributing to a cause, taking initiative, being accountable and helping others grow. True leaders create more leaders—and that is the impact I have always aspired to make.

Principles for leading in the AI age

In an era shaped by AI and digital transformation, leadership requires new skills and mindsets. Here are some principles to cultivate strong leadership in today's world:

- **Lead with purpose**: Define a mission that goes beyond profit and inspires people to contribute to a greater cause.
- **Empower and develop talent**: The best leaders create more leaders by providing opportunities for growth and mentorship.

- **Balance adaptability with conviction**: Stay open to change while staying true to core values and principles.
- **Leverage technology wisely**: AI can enhance decision-making, but human leadership will always be essential in shaping vision and values.
- **Lead with integrity and courage**: Effective leadership requires making tough decisions, taking risks and standing by one's values even in the face of adversity.

Leadership is not about waiting for a title or position—it is about action. It is about seeing challenges as opportunities, inspiring those around you and making a difference. In the AI age, leadership will not be defined by hierarchy but by impact.

Every individual has the potential to be a leader. By embracing leadership as a mindset rather than a role, we can navigate uncertainty with confidence, drive meaningful change and unleash the leader within ourselves and those around us.

28

Effective Leadership Traits in the Digital Age

A leader is one who knows the way, goes the way, and shows the way.
—John C. Maxwell, renowned leadership expert, author and speaker

A question that I often get asked is, '*What are the traits of an effective leader in the digital age?*'

In my view, it is important to first find anchors in the fundamental principles of leadership that remain constant. In this chapter, I share my personal beliefs on the timeless principles of leadership. These are by no means the last word on leadership, but they are perspectives that are important to me and which I try to live by.[1]

1. Leadership is about **helping others realize their full potential**. Every person has unique and abundant potential. A leader helps people realize their potential by challenging and stretching them.
2. Leadership is about **making a difference**. It is about striving to create a positive and lasting impact in all aspects of your work and life. In any situation, ask not what you are getting but what you are giving.

Effective leadership traits in the Digital Age

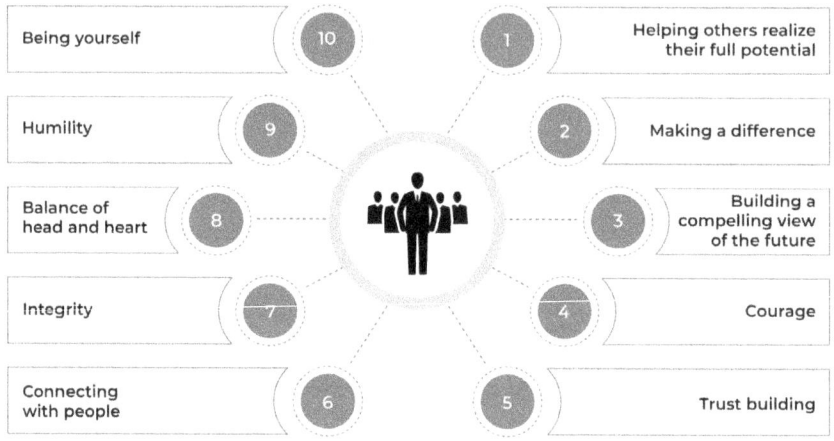

3. Leadership is about **building a compelling view of the future**. A leader must have an inspiring vision that will benefit the organization and will provide a sense of common purpose and direction to the team.

4. Leadership is about **courage**. A leader must take risks and not be afraid of treading a new path. Leadership means saying what you mean and having the spine to stand up for your beliefs.

5. Leadership is about **trust building**. Trust is a force multiplier. Building it requires suspending your own agenda, walking the talk and delivering on promises.

6. Leadership is about **connecting**, about touching both the hearts and minds of people. It is about communicating and connecting with warmth and openness at all levels. People need to see and hear you for themselves.

7. Leadership is about **integrity**, about striving to do the right thing so you have a clear conscience and can hold your head high.

8. Leadership is about the **balance of head and heart**. It is about both delivering excellent business results and being an empathetic

and caring people leader. A leader must consciously find that balance.

9. Leadership is about **humility**. About not letting success or position go to your head. It is about staying humble and grounded, which will earn you the love and respect of people. It is about listening better and avoiding making big mistakes.

10. Finally, leadership is about **being yourself**. Each one of us has unique strengths. So leadership means being authentic, digging within yourself, introspecting and defining your own leadership mantra and style.

These ten leadership fundamentals remain constant providing a stable foundation in an ever-evolving AI world. I believe it is important for any leader to stay anchored to these fundamentals that will provide helpful guidance for their leadership journeys.

29

How Great Leaders Inspire Others

The world is changed by your example, not by your opinion.
—Paulo Coelho, Brazilian lyricist and novelist

The ability to inspire others is a critical test of a leader. To achieve outstanding results in an increasingly complex world of digital and AI, you need to go beyond managing output metrics like revenue or profitability. You need to connect with people on a deeper level, inspiring them from within. Inspiration is the elixir that helps individuals go beyond their ordinary limits and achieve great results. And it is not just about results and performance. Inspiration is also the spark that helps people rise and realize their full potential. This aspect is very precious to me. I believe that helping others realize their full potential is one of the biggest contributions that any human can make. Truly, the ability to inspire is a necessary requirement for a leader to go from good to great. So, how do great leaders inspire others? There is a '**5 Cs Formula**'[1] to it.

Let's delve into the 5 Cs that I have seen great leaders use to inspire—cause, care, courage, communication and character—in detail:

1. **Cause:** Identify and champion a cause or vision that makes a real difference. A cause that goes beyond the mundane and touches an emotional chord. A cause that is meaningful today and will lead to a better tomorrow. Great leaders focus on the 'why', the purpose. Once the purpose is clear, the means follow. A powerful purpose can help bring disparate individuals together as a team and galvanize them to go beyond their ordinary limits.

   Martin Luther King Jr. galvanized a nation by championing a cause that went beyond individual interests—the fight for civil rights. His iconic 'I Have a Dream' speech was not just a call for policy change; it was a vision of a better tomorrow that inspired millions to take action.

2. **Care:** Leadership is not about the leader but about leading. It is not about your own dreams but about touching and bringing to life the silent dreams of others. Develop a genuine interest and empathy for others, understand their goals and aspirations and look to contribute to their progress. Suspend your self-interest; ask not what you are getting from any situation but what you are giving to it. As you give, you get a lot more in return. When you go beyond your self-interest and tap into what matters to others, you will build their trust and they will willingly go the extra mile for you.

   As CEO of Microsoft, Satya Nadella transformed the company's culture by emphasizing empathy and a growth mindset. His leadership was not about personal ambition but about empowering employees, fostering innovation and making Microsoft a more inclusive and people-centric organization.

3. **Courage:** You can inspire others only when you are inspired yourself. Walk the talk and have passion for the cause at hand.

Take risks and say what you mean. Any worthwhile cause will face some roadblocks. Opposition and challenges are the real tests for a leader, they are moments of truth. You need to have the spine to stand up for your beliefs and your people. You have to persevere in the face of difficulties and not give up. That is crucial for your credibility. People will observe your approach, and your personal example of courage and commitment will ignite those around you.

Nelson Mandela spent twenty-seven years in prison, never wavering from his commitment to end apartheid in South Africa. His courage to forgive, reconcile and stand firm on his values despite immense pressure made him one of the most inspiring leaders of all time.

Great leaders' 5 Cs Formula to inspire others

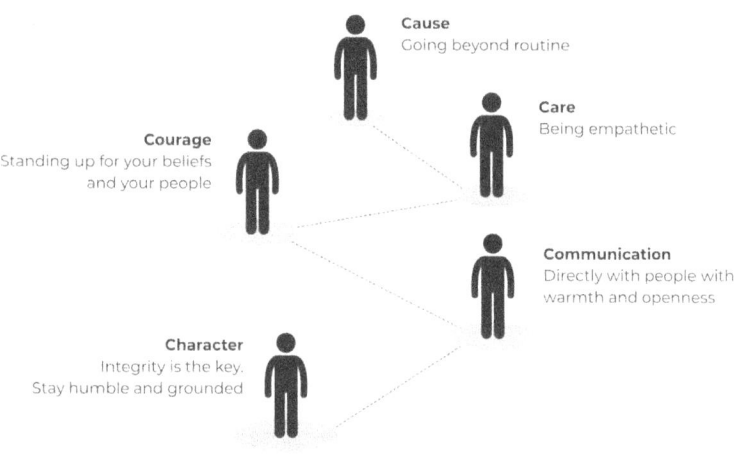

4. **Communication**: Connect directly with people and get your message across. Don't depend only on formal channels (which are often impersonal) or on others to carry your message.

People need to see and hear you for themselves. You need to touch both hearts and minds. For that to happen, it is not your polish but your authenticity and intent that matter. Communicate often and do it with warmth and openness. Moreover, do not just talk but also listen. Listening is even more critical for a leader. You will learn a lot and others will feel valued. Listen with sincerity and patience and follow up on your conversations.

> *Steve Jobs was a masterful communicator, known for his ability to captivate audiences with his vision. His legendary product launches were more than just presentations, they were storytelling masterpieces that inspired both customers and employees by connecting innovation to human aspiration.*

5. **Character**: All your great work as a leader can be undone by a single moment of indiscretion on your part. Integrity is like glass or a mirror which, once broken, can never be repaired. Always strive to do the right thing. However, recognize that as human beings, we are fallible; there is both good and bad within us. Many great leaders fall because they become arrogant, stop listening and lose touch with the people. Always stay humble and grounded. Humility will earn you love and respect from people. It will also allow you to listen better and avoid making big mistakes.

> *Mahatma Gandhi's unwavering integrity and moral leadership made him one of the most respected figures in history. He practised what he preached, leading by example through non-violence and personal sacrifice, earning the trust and devotion of millions.*

I hope these '5 Cs' will help you hone your own leadership skills and inspire those around you. While I have shared a framework with you, I want to emphasize that leadership is about finding your own personal style. There is no right or wrong way. A leader needs to be authentic and true to themselves. Each of us has unique strengths and views of the world based on our life experiences. Your formula for inspiring others could well be very different from mine. So learn from others but dig within and find your own formula. That is your best chance of success. Finally, please remember that leadership is a journey. You are not born a leader, but you realize the leader within you through your actions. Just focus on your karma as a leader, and you will find yourself continuing to grow as an inspiring one.

30

Lessons in Change Management

> *Without change, there is no innovation, creativity or incentive for improvement. Those who initiate change will have a better opportunity to manage the change that is inevitable.*
> —William Pollard, American physicist, Episcopal priest and founder of Oak Ridge Associated Universities

Change, for any organization, is inevitable. And the velocity of change in the business environment in the AI age is now higher than ever before. The global economic outlook continues to be uncertain, business cycles are becoming shorter, existing markets are declining and new ones becoming significant, customer needs are changing, technology is continuing to evolve at a dazzling pace and there is a lot of opportunity for innovation. Organizations have no option but to adapt to the many changes happening in their environment in the digital age. Those who step up and capture the opportunities can become world-beaters. Equally, those who fail to adapt can easily fade away. Despite the inevitability of change, many organizations struggle to get going with meaningful change, and even those who do, often find it difficult to implement their change management programmes and derive the desired results from them.

Clearly, change management is a story of many paradoxes. Change is inevitable, but very difficult to initiate and implement. Get it right and you become a world-class achiever; get it wrong and you can destroy a business built over many decades. It can be a source of energy for people or destroy their morale. For leaders, change can even make you a hero or a villain!

I have had the opportunity to be centrally involved in change management across multiple organizations. It started in McKinsey, where I had the opportunity to transform the McKC from a back-office research centre into a cutting-edge innovation centre. My change management journey continued at Fidelity International, then Flipkart and now at my firm Incedo. While the industry focus and the change management objectives have been different across the organizations I have been involved in, there have been some common lessons.[1]

Best practices in change management

Change management is a fascinating but complex topic. Even after my experience with change management for over twenty-five years as a manager, consultant and senior leader, I still see myself as a keen student of this topic, and I am continuing to learn.

From what I have learnt over the years, here are the seven change management best practices according to me:

1. **Focusing on the right type and amount of change**: Change is inherently difficult, so it is important to focus one's efforts and not dissipate one's energy. For example, there is often an over-reliance on changing organizational structures as a way of driving performance change. In my experience, such changes cause a lot of heartburn while rarely fulfilling their promise. In addition, it is important to recognize that any organization has only a certain capacity to absorb change. Therefore, it is critical to prioritize

and sequence change initiatives, so managers have clarity on what to focus on and equally the capacity to execute the changes. This is an area where my perspective, as a manager, has changed significantly from when I was a consultant. As a consultant, I was focused on getting all possible smart ideas on the table. As a manager, I realized that if you put too much on the table it will confuse your people. To ensure successful execution, you have to focus on a few, not many, ideas.

2. **Establishing the 'why' clearly and persistently**: The biggest challenge in change management is to move people out of their 'comfort zones' and get them to truly accept the need for change. Inertia is inherent in human beings. We like predictability and certainty. We convince ourselves that what we are doing is the right thing. Moreover, it is hard for people to achieve the objectivity needed to question and change their daily routine while they are actively immersed in it. Therefore, it is critical that you establish the need for change clearly and persistently.

It is important to go beyond the corporate logic and see the change from the perspective of the individual—why should they change, what can they do differently and what will the impact be. In doing this, you have to appeal to both the head and the heart. Moreover, you need to be persistent in establishing the need for change as people rarely accept significant change at one go. You have to keep at it. If you are persistent, you can reach a tipping point when people finally get convinced about the need for change. That is perhaps the most important milestone in your change journey.

3. **Identifying change agents**: It is critical to have a core team of committed and inspiring change agents at the centre of any transformation programme. No leader, however inspiring, can drive significant change alone. You need force multipliers—individuals who not only embrace change themselves but actively

evangelize it across the organization. These are the people who will stay committed through the ups and downs, ensuring the change gains momentum and sustains itself.

Certain types of individuals are naturally more open to change—those with high levels of positivity, personal confidence and a broad, future-oriented outlook. They are analogous to the 'early adopters' in marketing—the ones willing to take a leap before others.

For example, at the McKC, I was trying to lift its role from a support capability to an innovation hub and pioneer new services like analytics. While many senior leaders in McKinsey were sceptical—worried about disrupting existing processes— we found a champion in a small practice, risk management. A young practice leader, who had a background in data science, quickly grasped the vision and started piloting new analytics offerings with his clients. His success not only validated the new initiative but inspired other practices to follow suit, creating a ripple effect of adoption.

In my experience, change agents are often found in the second line of management rather than the first. Senior leaders can sometimes be too vested in the status quo, while mid-level leaders and high-potential employees see opportunities in change. Identifying and empowering these individuals is crucial to making transformation a reality.

4. **Focusing on some early wins**: Driving change is not just about strategy but also about tactics. You need to ensure some early wins. This will build credibility for your change agenda so that it is no longer merely conceptual but also tangible. It is not easy for people to agree to change when the status quo is disturbed. Moreover, people have an inherent distrust of words and respond much better to actions or outcomes that are concrete and visible. Early wins will work as compelling reference cases and help you gather momentum. They will help build an understanding

among the team about what you are trying to accomplish and encourage people to embrace the change

5. **Going slow to go far**: While I have talked about early wins, it is important to recognize that organizations have a lot of inertia and change, especially in mindset and behaviours, takes time. You have to be patient and persistent. Often, new managers rush to declare all that was done before them as rubbish in their frenzy to change everything. This is a recipe for failure. You have to take the time to fully understand the situation, especially the history and culture of the organization and build trust with the people. The 'Hare and Tortoise' story is very relevant in change management. You need to take not a one- or two-year view but a three-to-five-year view for achieving substantial change outcomes especially if you are looking to change the culture and the core DNA of an organization. I have experienced that progress at the two-year mark can be underwhelming, but if you are persistent, results in the three-to-five-year period can be outstanding. Therefore, you need to pace yourself and set realistic expectations. Do not lose heart. It is OK to lose or not fight a few battles. If you are persistent, results will come.

6. **Building a stakeholder coalition**: Driving meaningful change in any organization requires building a strong stakeholder coalition, understanding organizational politics, recognizing power centres and working strategically to align key players with your change objectives. One of the most important lessons in my corporate journey has been accepting the reality of organizational politics. Self-interest is an inherent aspect of human nature, so politics exists in all organizations, and rather than resisting it, you must learn to navigate it effectively.

Moreover, organizational politics is not necessarily negative—when approached with the right intent, it can be a powerful force for good. Any organization will have power centres and people take cues from influential figures. If you can understand the motivations of key stakeholders and align your change initiative with their interests, you can create momentum and accelerate adoption. If you don't, resistance from influential players can quickly derail your efforts.

For example, at Flipkart, a major restructuring effort was planned to reduce operating costs significantly. While there was initial alignment within the leadership team, many subsequently backtracked because they feared a threat to their authority and team structure. Rather than confronting them head-on, I built a stakeholder coalition by engaging with senior board members. They had strong historical relationships and played a pivotal role in reframing the restructuring as a company transformation and not just a cost-reduction exercise. By securing visible support from influential stakeholders, we were able to reduce resistance and ensure the change was implemented with speed and conviction.

Building a stakeholder coalition is not about manipulation, it is about understanding interests, aligning incentives and creating shared ownership of change. The key is to identify the right influencers, gain their trust and work through them to build momentum, ensuring that the change is not just accepted but actively championed across the organization.

7. **Communication**: Communication is absolutely critical. There are four aspects important in communication—keeping it simple, coverage of all levels, frequency and consistency and openness and honesty. You need to articulate the need for change (why), your vision (what) and the benefits of the change for the organization and its individuals in a simple manner. Often, the messages remain limited to the top levels and do not reach down the line, and if they do, they are articulated in ways that are not relevant for the majority of the staff. Moreover, you need to communicate often and be consistent in your messaging. When

you are going through change, people feel insecure and have a high need to know. Repetition helps in such cases. Finally, you need to be open and honest with your employees, even if you are relaying bad news. That works much better than trying to hide or soft-pedal any difficult messages.

I hope these best practices help you play a positive leadership role in transforming your organization in this digital and AI age. Please remember, change management is not just about the CEOs, HR or the senior management, but something that professionals at all levels can and need to play a role in.

Change needs to happen across the organization. This presents opportunities for professionals at every level of the organization to step up and make a difference. If you aspire to develop as a leader, then be proactive and take ownership of the change opportunities around you. Don't let the size of the challenge weigh you down. Just be positive and focus on your karma. You will be surprised how much power your individual actions can have.

31

How to Create Great Leaders

The task of the leader is to get people from where they are to where they have not been.
—Henry Kissinger, American diplomat and author

I strongly believe that the true mark of a great leader isn't just individual success—it's the ability to grow other leaders. The most effective leaders inspire, elevate and invest in those around them, helping others discover and unlock their leadership potential.

Over the years, I've come to realize that leadership isn't an exclusive trait—it's a capability that can be nurtured with the right mindset, guidance and opportunity. In this chapter, I want to share a few key insights and strategies that I've found valuable in building and empowering future leaders—in teams, organizations or life.[1]

Leadership can be viewed from many levels—corporate, individual, national and global. At any level, a true leader must be rooted in:

1. **Doing the right thing rather than the easy thing**: This means a leader is fearless and makes clear and courageous decisions even in ambiguous situations.

2. **Focusing on the larger goal versus personal goals**: This calls for selflessness. Leaders help their teams grow by aligning towards a common purpose and cohesively working towards the larger goal.

3. **Inspiring people to go beyond the direction set by himself**: This asks for long-term vision on the part of the leader but also trust in the team and providing them the freedom to surpass his vision.

So, how should we create leaders who are fearless, selfless and visionaries?

Five mantras to create great leaders

Here are some of the key realizations from my own transformation into a leader and nurturing hundreds of successful leaders over the past three decades:

1. **Unlock the leadership potential**

   My experience with leadership is that a 'born leader' is a myth. All of us have the seeds of leadership within us. It just needs the right trigger and context to unlock our leadership potential. This, to me, has to be the starting point for any leader. You have to believe in the vastness of human potential and constantly be on the lookout for opportunities to unlock the leadership potential in yourself and your colleagues.

   To share an example from my own life, I was an introvert growing up and only an average sportsperson in school. But things changed dramatically during my time at IIT Delhi. When I was elected as the sports secretary, it felt like a daunting responsibility at first. Yet that very responsibility became the spark that began to dissolve my fears and self-doubt. It wasn't just an opportunity, it was a platform that unlocked energy, confidence and a deep sense of purpose in me. It marked the beginning of my leadership journey, not only empowering me but inspiring others around me.

Five mantras to create great leaders

2. **Create stretch opportunities**

The tasks that challenge you to overcome your fears and inhibitions and push you beyond your comfort zone, are the ones that make you accomplish much more than you think you can. This eventually transforms you into a leader. Developing as a leader is like the process of a caterpillar becoming a butterfly. The outcome is beautiful but the process is tough. You have to break through shells, which is painful.

I've personally experienced this during my initial days at McKinsey as a young associate. One day, a senior partner asked me to join a meeting with the CEO of a reputed financial institution, where he asked me to comment on some very sensitive topics. I was initially very hesitant, but it forced me to raise my game and communicate as a peer. This was an important catalyst for accelerating my consulting journey and I still thank him for that opportunity. Over time, stretching has become my signature leadership style, to push my colleagues to go beyond what they think they can do.

3. **Giving before getting is key**
   One of the most counterintuitive yet profound lessons in leadership is that the path to personal growth often begins with a shift in focus—from self to others. Early in our careers, we are naturally preoccupied with personal milestones: roles, recognition, rewards. But true leadership is born when we begin to prioritize the development and success of those around us. It is in giving—our time, trust, attention and care—that we often unlock our own potential as leaders.

   I learnt this lesson during my journey at the McKC that I have shared in Chapter 23. The transition from consulting to an operating role was not easy and made me anxious about my growth prospects especially in a nascent business unit. However, I soon realized that my team was also looking up to me with similar concerns. It was then that I decided to consider my team's development as the priority instead of obsessing about my personal professional growth. This shift in focus from 'short term and self' to 'long term and others' led to me grooming many young colleagues in the team and their stepping up as leaders, eventually leading to the phenomenal growth of our knowledge centre. It became a hub of innovation and a source of multiple new services that revolutionized McKinsey's business model. This success also enabled me to grow into a senior leadership position, which would not have been possible otherwise.

4. **Start with yourself and be an inspiring role model**
   To inspire others, you have to be inspired yourself. Our personal values and actions are the most potent way of influencing those around us. Leadership is not something you can fake, it is who

you are. If you are in a position of influence, people are always observing you. It is important to be authentic and stay consistent with your values, even in moments of stress. How leaders handle 'moments of truth' defines their legacy.

I have been fortunate to observe some truly inspiring leaders—both in professional settings and beyond—who have deeply impacted me and shaped my own development as a leader. During my time at IIT, I saw many examples of seniors and peers who, despite their demanding academic schedules, brought tremendous passion and commitment to our intense inter-hostel competitions and created a sense of community—an early lesson in leadership that stayed with me. At McKinsey, I had the privilege of observing Anupam Puri, whose ability to balance strategic vision with deep personal engagement left a lasting impression. His ability to remain calm under pressure and bring clarity to complex problems was truly inspiring. Later, at Flipkart, I saw first-hand how Sachin Bansal and Binny Bansal built not just a company but an entire e-commerce ecosystem in India—leading with bold ambition, resilience and an unwavering belief in their mission.

Observing and learning from these leaders reinforced a fundamental truth: leadership is not about authority or position, it is about character, consistency and the ability to inspire through actions.

5. **Take responsibility to create leaders**

    While on our own journey of becoming a great leader, it is equally important—and perhaps more meaningful—to help others rise alongside us. Leadership is not meant to be a solo pursuit. True leadership multiplies. It's about creating the conditions where others are inspired, empowered and encouraged to rise.

This begins not with authority or formal position, but with a mindset shift: from being the change to enabling change in others. Too often, we get caught up in critiquing the system or waiting for someone else to act. But leadership is rarely top-down—it emerges when individuals take ownership. I saw this powerfully during the Raahgiri movement in Gurgaon, where a few committed citizens took initiative and catalyzed systemic change. The lesson is clear: when people lead with conviction, others follow—even institutions.

And just as systems respond to conviction, so do individuals. I believe we are surrounded by extraordinary potential, especially in the youth. What often holds them back is not capability, but the absence of belief, opportunity or example. That's where we, as leaders, have a responsibility—to mentor, challenge, trust and create space. Sometimes, all it takes is one person who sees something in them before they see it in themselves. When we take responsibility for building leaders around us, we don't just expand our impact—we spark a ripple effect that can reshape the future.

It is incredibly energizing to witness the passion, awareness and potential I see in today's youth. In a world being reshaped by AI, their curiosity, creativity and courage are the raw materials of leadership. All it takes is the right spark—an environment that encourages initiative, nurtures character and inspires purpose. As parents, educators, mentors and leaders, we all have a role to play in unlocking this potential. If we can channel their energy and equip them with the timeless principles of authentic leadership, I am confident we will see a wave of great leaders emerge across every field. These young leaders won't just adapt to the AI age—they will define it, proving that the human edge, powered by values and vision, remains irreplaceable.

MANTRA 8

BE AN ENTREPRENEUR

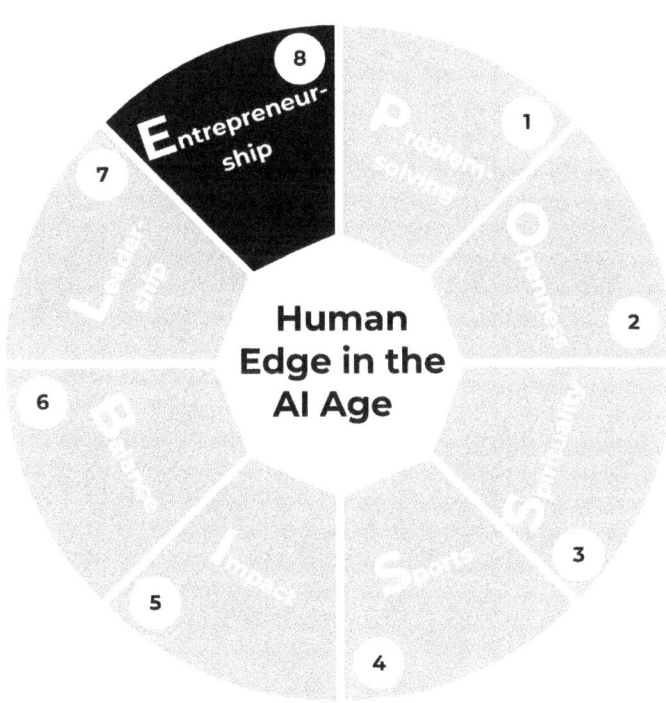

The POSSIBLE Framework

Introduction to Mantra 8
Be an Entrepreneur

Everyone Can and Should be an Entrepreneur in the AI Age

> *The future is not something we enter. The future is something we create.*
> Leonard I. Sweet, author and theologian

Entrepreneurship is one of the most powerful expressions of the Human Edge. At its core, it's about imagination, initiative and impact. It's the ability to see possibilities where others see problems, to take risks and shape new realities. As we step into the AI age, entrepreneurship is no longer just for startup founders or business elites—it is a mindset and skill set that every individual needs.

The AI age is not just disrupting jobs; it is reshaping the very idea of what a career looks like. Many traditional roles are disappearing, but in their place lies the rise of something exciting—**the Age of Entrepreneurs**. This doesn't just mean more startups. It means that, across sectors and professions, more people must think and act like entrepreneurs: spotting opportunities, solving problems and creating value.

AI is transforming industries, creating new business models and changing how value is created and captured. In this dynamic environment, the most exciting opportunities are unlikely to go solely to the biggest companies or the smartest algorithms—they will go to those with the courage to act, the imagination to dream and the tenacity to build.

This isn't just about launching startups—it's about taking ownership, driving transformation and shaping the AI age on our terms. Whether you're building a company, leading change in an organization or pursuing a passion project, thinking like a creator will be your superpower.

Key dimensions of the entrepreneurial mindset

This mantra explores four dimensions of entrepreneurial thinking drawn from personal experiences, visionary leaders and even nature:

1. **Your time is now!**
   This chapter explores why the AI age is the best time in history to become an entrepreneur. I offer ten actionable mantras drawn from my own journey to help readers take the plunge.

2. **Inventing the future**
   Inspired by the life of Steve Jobs, this chapter emphasizes how great entrepreneurs don't just improve, they reimagine. Jobs' relentless pursuit of bold, differentiated visions offers timeless lessons.

3. **Moonshot thinking is key to make the impossible possible**
   Drawing from Elon Musk's journeys with Tesla and SpaceX, this chapter extracts six core lessons about bold bets, unconventional thinking and persistence.

4. **Growing through adversity to win big**
   Reflecting on the giant sequoias—the massive, ancient trees, famously located in Sequoia National Park in California, known for their scale and towering presence, this chapter explores how enduring resilience and growth through adversity are essential to building legacies that last.

My journey with entrepreneurship

Entrepreneurship has been an integral part of my journey. Early in my career, I launched ActiveKarma, a startup focused on digital wellness. While the venture did not succeed, the lessons I learnt were invaluable—from navigating uncertainty to making tough decisions and bouncing back from failure.

Leading the McKC was like launching a startup within McKinsey. What started as a back-office research unit evolved into a global innovation hub, pioneering advanced analytics and more. The catalyst? An entrepreneurial culture where everyone thought like an owner. It taught me a lasting lesson: entrepreneurial thinking isn't just for startups—it's essential even within large organizations. Innovation, I realized, can emerge from the most unexpected places—even a back office.

Later, at Flipkart, India's marquee startup, I saw the raw power of entrepreneurship to drive industry disruption. Flipkart wasn't just a company, it was a movement that redefined e-commerce in India. It dared to take on Amazon's deep pockets and won with grit, creativity and hustle. That experience deepened my conviction that entrepreneurship isn't about playing the odds, it's about having the audacity to reshape them.

At Incedo, I have continued to embrace this mindset, fostering innovation within the organization and developing cutting-edge capabilities across digital, data and AI. Whether in a startup or a large enterprise, the core principles of entrepreneurship remain the same—vision, risk-taking, adaptability and resilience.

Principles for entrepreneurial success in the AI age

Entrepreneurship is often glamorized, but the reality is more complex and far more rewarding. In the AI age, success will come to those who can balance bold vision with grit and resilience. Here are five principles that I believe are essential:

- **Think like a builder**: Start with action. Ideas are important, but execution is everything. Learn to build fast, iterate and adapt.
- **Embrace intelligent risk**: Risk-taking doesn't mean recklessness. It means being willing to step into the unknown after thoughtful assessment.
- **Stay purpose-driven**: Don't just chase the next shiny object. Solve real problems. Create value. Stay anchored in a larger mission.
- **Build resilience**: You will fail. That's part of the journey. What matters is the ability to bounce back, learn and keep going.
- **Unlock others' creativity**: Great entrepreneurs build movements. They inspire, enable and elevate others. Entrepreneurship is not a solo act.

A call to action

The future belongs to creators. Whether you're twenty-five or fifty-five, in a startup or a large corporation, working in tech or healthcare—thinking like an entrepreneur will be your superpower in the AI age. Don't wait for the perfect plan. Don't wait for someone to give you permission.

You already have what it takes. The AI age is full of opportunity for those who dare to dream and build. The time to act is now.

32

Your Time Is Now!
Ten Mantras for Young Entrepreneurs

The entrepreneur always searches for change, responds to it, and exploits it as an opportunity.
—Peter Drucker,
*Austrian American management consultant,
educator and author*

In this chapter, I will tell you why I think the AI age is the right time for young professionals to consider entrepreneurship. I will also share with you ten mantras for success, which I have gained from my own experiences as an entrepreneur. My insights are based on four sets of experiences—starting and failing in my own startup (ActiveKarma, 2000–02); working for many years as an intrapreneur in McKinsey and Fidelity; my leadership role at Flipkart, and leading Incedo, where, as a co-founder, I am building a high-growth digital, data and AI services firm.

Why should young professionals become entrepreneurs?

I strongly believe today is a great time to be an entrepreneur and all of you should consider this path. There are at least five reasons why:

A. **Technology disruption is creating unprecedented new opportunities**: The velocity of technological change and business disruption we are witnessing is perhaps unprecedented in human history. Mobile, e-commerce, cloud and big data have changed consumer behaviours and business models dramatically, and yet these trends are barely fifteen years old. We are now into the next phase of technology, which AI is dominating. Technology change is a great equalizer. While large companies may have deep pockets and a greater capacity to invest, they often struggle to harness new technologies. Legacy systems and organizational inertia can slow them down, making it difficult to break from existing processes and fully embrace innovation.

   Smart entrepreneurs are best placed to experiment and leverage new technology. We have seen with the example of Flipkart, Paytm, MakeMyTrip and Ola in India how you can leverage new technology (e-commerce) to create huge businesses in less than ten years. And this is just the tip of the iceberg. I have explored in Chapter 4 how AI will fundamentally reshape every industry, creating tremendous opportunities for entrepreneurs.

B. **It accelerates personal growth**: If you are ambitious and want to change the world, then entrepreneurship is the path for you. Pursuing your own idea provides a great sense of ownership and independence, which is difficult to find in a job. It creates a sense of purpose and energy that helps you grow as a person and achieve impact that will be impossible in a standard job. I meet many young entrepreneurs and I am always amazed at how much they grow and mature in a short period of time. In addition to personal growth, entrepreneurship offers, of course, the opportunity for life-changing wealth creation. Jobs today pay well but it is nothing compared to the wealth you can create through a successful venture.

C. **There is availability of risk capital and an entrepreneurial ecosystem**: In the past two decades, we have witnessed exponential development in the venture capital industry and entrepreneurial ecosystem. Capital is now available for each step of the entrepreneurial journey, even for very early-stage ideas. This makes it easier for young professionals to pursue their ideas without betting on the hard-earned money of their parents. Capital also helps them scale up their ideas rapidly. Most importantly, many economies are developing an active entrepreneurial ecosystem where experienced entrepreneurs and professionals are themselves investing into ventures and are available for mentoring and support.

D. **The cost of failure is not high**: My parents' generation saw a lot of hardship and was very risk-averse. These conservative mindsets have historically permeated in our society and acted as a deterrent for taking risks. However, mindsets in most societies today are very different. The cost of failure is low. I have already mentioned the availability of risk capital. Even more importantly, there are abundant opportunities and company mindsets have changed. An individual whose startup has failed is not frowned upon. In fact, failure is increasingly seen as a positive experience. I have seen it in my own example. In fact, a lot of what I have achieved in my corporate career is because of the invaluable learnings from the failure of ActiveKarma.

E. **You can make a contribution to your country**: To illustrate, for a country like India, its biggest asset is its age pyramid. Almost half the population of 1.45 billion is below the age of twenty-five. However, this also presents the massive challenge of job creation. The government and the public sector will never be able to create the required number of jobs and massive entrepreneurial activity is needed to fill this gap. Moreover, entrepreneurs can create world-beating, successful ideas and companies and put India on the world map. The IT and BPM industry, which was driven by first-generation entrepreneurs, has done that very successfully over the past twenty years. There are opportunities for Indian entrepreneurs to rise and dominate in many more sectors.

As I have discussed extensively in Section I of this book, AI is likely to result in significant job losses and estimates suggest that it could be up to 50 per cent over the next fifteen years.[1] This is a massive number. At the same time, AI will also enable the solution of many problems that could not be solved earlier, creating many new business opportunities. This presents tremendous opportunities for entrepreneurs. Clearly, to succeed in the AI age you can't rely on a job; being an entrepreneur is a much more lucrative path. I strongly believe the AI age heralds the 'Age of Entrepreneurs', an unprecedented and exciting opportunity for value creation.

Hopefully I have convinced all of you to become entrepreneurs. Let me now share some insights based on my experiences that can help you succeed as an entrepreneur.[2]

Ten success mantras for young entrepreneurs

Exceptionally successful entrepreneurs are often mavericks; they have an X factor, which is difficult to replicate. However, I will still attempt to share ten mantras based on my experiences that should improve your chances of entrepreneurial success.

1. **Follow your passion and mission:** This has to be the starting point of your entrepreneurial journey, a core idea or purpose that really drives you. Entrepreneurship is a tough journey and there will be many moments when you might feel like giving

up. It is this passion for your idea, a sense of mission that will keep you going. Moreover, entrepreneurship is a journey into the unknown. When you are creating something new, it is difficult to be clear about your strategy and plans at every stage. Your passion and mission will give you the necessary direction in moments of uncertainty. For example, Flipkart has a clear and strong mission, 'transforming lives of a billion Indians through technology'. While the Flipkart strategy might have kept changing over the past ten years, this mission has provided a strong anchor and inspiration for the organization.

2. **Route to clients:** Customers are the lifeline of any business and this is even more critical for a startup. You might have a great concept or product, but if you can't get clients, your business will never take off. That is why you really need to think from a client perspective—what real needs you are looking to solve and will the client pay for it—versus thinking about a business idea just from your perspective. For a B2B business, your first few clients might come based on your relationships. While for a B2C business, the key consideration is customer segmentation and targeting. You will not be able to be everything to everyone, certainly not in the early stages of your business.

3. **Be audacious:** Audacity is the willingness to take bold risks. This is a core aspect of the culture I saw at Flipkart and one that inspired me a lot. To build something new, especially in a new or changing industry, you cannot be incremental. You have to think big, take bold risks and believe you can change the world. The great Steve Jobs famously said, 'Those who are crazy enough to believe they can change the world are the ones who actually do so.' This is a key success factor for successful entrepreneurs across generations. This is certainly true for this generation's superstars like Jeff Bezos, Elon Musk and Jack Ma and a key factor behind

Ten mantras for young entrepreneurs

their companies' astounding success. This is also the quality that makes companies like Flipkart and Ola dream big and take on giants like Amazon and Uber.

4. **Innovate by connecting the dots**: Innovation is the foundation of a startup. To drive innovation, having a deep understanding of the customer is key. You need to have an intimate understanding of their pain points. However, this will not happen sitting in a room. One must go out and seek a range of life experiences.

The most powerful innovation often happens by connecting the dots across different areas. This was the unique strength of the great Steve Jobs. He was able to connect the dots across his life experiences and passions to create many market defining innovations. The iPod was a celebrated example where his passion for music, technology and design all came together. The other key requirement for innovation is deep product and tech expertise. As we have discussed earlier, technology disruption is the most defining feature of the world we are living in, and it is at the heart of breakthrough opportunities for entrepreneurs. So, I encourage you to learn and build deep engineering expertise.

5. **Build an effective team:** We are in an increasingly complex environment where it is almost impossible for any individual, however talented, to have all the skills required to build a successful business on their own. Therefore, it is very important for an entrepreneur to build an effective team. While building a team, we often seek people like us (I did that when I built my venture ActiveKarma; all three of us were from IIT Delhi). While it is critical that you work with people who have similar values, it is equally important to bring together people with complementary skills. Most successful partnerships have been between leaders who had such complementary strengths. For example, Bill Gates and Paul Allen at Microsoft—Gates was the strategist and business leader, while Allen was the technology visionary. Similarly, Steve Jobs and Steve Wozniak at Apple—Jobs had an unmatched sense of design, user experience and business vision, while Wozniak was the technical genius who built the first Apple computers. Larry Page and Sergey Brin at Google combined Page's focus on ranking algorithms with Brin's expertise in AI and innovation. In India, the founding team of Infosys exemplified this principle—Narayana Murthy provided the leadership and vision, while co-founders like Nandan Nilekani, Kris Gopalakrishnan and Shibulal brought strengths in business development, technical architecture and operations. These examples underscore the fact that while shared values create alignment, it is complementary skills that drive success.

6. **Secure adequate funding:** It is critical that you secure adequate funding sooner than later for your venture. While the power of your idea and team are the most important determinants of the success of your venture, lack of funding is the factor that can take you to failure immediately and irreversibly. Many entrepreneurs try to time the market or to delay funding to maximize value. Don't delay raising funding; secure the future of your venture first. If your venture survives and thrives, you will create enough

personal value for yourself. If it gets strangled for funds and dies, your high ownership of the venture will not help. Another point of funding is that the questioning you face in the process also helps you sharpen your idea, improving your chances of success. A final point on funding is while raising too much capital can be a problem (it can lead to inefficient use of funds), make sure you raise adequate capital to scale up and tackle competition.

7. **Practise continued patience and resilience:** The entrepreneurial journey can be a roller-coaster with many ups and downs. I have not yet come across any successful startup that has not gone through a near-death experience at some point in their journey. Therefore, you need to have the patience to play for the long term and the resilience to bounce back. As mentioned in the first point, deep passion for the idea and a sense of purpose inspire you to see the long term and help you ride through short-term challenges. It helps you value and enjoy the daily journey and not be obsessed with outcomes. In addition to this, I believe it is important to have anchors in life outside of work. They give you strength, help you see the big picture of life and bounce back from disappointments. For example, my anchors are my family, spirituality (meditation + Bhagavad Gita) and sports. These anchors have made me resilient and helped me bounce back from the many challenges I have faced.

8. **Tell your story passionately, clearly and repetitively**: It is very important that you as an entrepreneur are able to tell your story passionately, clearly and repetitively. You need to do so to sell your idea to investors, to attract talent to join your team and most importantly to convince customers. And, you have to do so multiple times over because you will not succeed in any of the above three tasks the first time around. Nobody else can tell your story with the authenticity and power that you can do so yourself. You cannot delegate this to anybody else.

You will also need to become a master networker. In today's interconnected world, you will have to build a web of partnerships—with customers, suppliers, investors, advisers and mentors. For this, you have to be proactive and learn to reach out. Sometimes entrepreneurs, especially technologists, can be introverts. You have to get out of that and build both your willingness and skills to network. The future of your venture depends on it.

9. **Stay humble**: The world is changing so fast that you can never sit back on your laurels and allow hubris to settle in. Arrogance is a sure shot recipe for failure. A strong trait of a successful entrepreneur is that they approach life as a student. We meet people, we learn; we read something, we learn; we watch a movie, we learn; we have any experience, we learn. If one is not humble, one will not learn. One who does not learn will not succeed. This has never been truer.

10. **Manage opposites**: This is a philosophical point but a very important one. In the complex and fast-evolving business environment today, you need to build the ability to manage many opposites. You need to have very sharp execution focus; at the same time, you need to be strategic. You need to survive in the short term while building for the long term. You need to ensure outstanding customer experience and growth while also ensuring profitability. These opposites can become difficult to manage; however, they are inevitable. It is important that you recognize this and build your mental ability to balance these opposites. The ability to manage this duality will be one of the most important skills in the twenty-first century (I have talked extensively about this in Mantra 6 on Balance).

The above insights should inspire you to pursue your entrepreneurial journey in the AI age with even more passion and clarity. The time to start your journey is now, so go forth with hope and energy and let a thousand flowers bloom. This is the best possible journey you can take for yourself and for your country.

So, go forth and shine on, you crazy diamonds!

33

Inventing the Future

Lessons from the Incredible Life Story of Steve Jobs

We're here to put a dent in the universe. Otherwise, why else even be here?

—*Steve Jobs, American businessman, inventor and co-founder of Apple Inc*

Steve Jobs was one of the most fascinating icons of our age. He had a revolutionary impact across multiple industries—personal computers, mobile phones, music, movies and retailing. His record of innovation and transformation is unbelievable; in this respect he is perhaps the tallest amongst business leaders in recent history. I gained a deeper understanding of Steve Jobs after reading his biography by Walter Isaacson.[1] It is a detailed life story of a complex and fascinating personality. The book surprised me as Jobs came across as a lot more complex than what I earlier understood him to be. I was also rather taken aback and disappointed by the many imperfections in his personality. However, as I read on through Isaacson's book, I developed a better understanding and even deeper respect for Jobs and Apple's remarkable achievements.

Here are the eleven key lessons I have taken away from Jobs' extraordinary life story:[2]

1. **Passion**: The defining characteristic of Jobs was his sheer intensity. And that intensity came from his three primary passions—to build great products, to build Apple into an enduring company and to make a 'dent into the universe'. The most visible of his passions was for products. He prioritized products over profits and strove for perfection in his products. This passion for products clearly paid rich dividends, as Apple ended up creating a series of industry-shaping innovative products that also led to great financial success for the company. Jobs believed that life does not just happen to you but that you can shape the future. His philosophy is well captured by Apple's famous 1997 'Think Different' commercial, an immortal quote which is worth coming back to again: **'The people who are crazy enough to think they can change the world are the ones who do.'** This great passion for making a real difference was the force that led him to incredible feats.

2. **Intersection of engineering and arts:** For me, one of the most unique aspects of Steve Jobs's talents was his ability to straddle and assimilate the seemingly contrasting worlds of engineering and arts. He had a range of eclectic interests, from music to calligraphy to Hindu philosophy to Zen Buddhism. He was able to bring intuition and empathy from the world of humanities into the staid world of engineering and technology. That was perhaps the distinguishing feature of Apple that separated its products so much from other technology companies. Jobs put it nicely, 'I'm one of the few people who understands how producing technology requires intuition and creativity, and how producing something artistic takes real discipline.'[3] This concept of the intersection of disciplines has many lessons for both new-age professionals and for industries in need of transformation.

Significant innovation happens not within a box but at the intersection of different fields. This will increasingly become a formula for the future, especially so in the digital and AI age.

3. **End-to-end ownership**: Jobs' quest for perfection led to his insistence that Apple have end-to-end control of every product it made. He doggedly pursued vertical integration across design, hardware, software and content. This approach could be attributed to Steve Jobs' obsession with control. However, there is a positive basis to this approach. Steve believed that he had to take responsibility for ensuring that the customer got a superb product, and for that end-to-end ownership was necessary. Apple's ability to integrate hardware, software and content into one unified system enabled it to impose simplicity and avoid the fragmentation that an 'open architecture' approach could lead to. This 'closed loop' approach was a key secret behind Apple's success. It led to great products, helped Apple achieve high profit margins even with small market share and was the foundation for new innovative products like the iPod, iPhone and iPad. The Jobs example explains why some entrepreneurs who have a long-term orientation look to have end-to-end control over all aspects of the value chain.

4. **Simplicity**: Steve Jobs had a strong belief in simplicity and minimalism, likely influenced by his interest in Zen Buddhism. His maxim was that 'Simplicity is the ultimate sophistication.' This mantra is reflected both in his products and in his personal life. The intuitive usability of Apple products, which has been one of the keys to their success, was driven by the focus on reducing clutter and ensuring that interfaces were as simple as possible. This **simplicity was achieved not by avoiding but by mastering complexity**. It took a lot of thought and detailing to get to those simple designs that would be most intuitive for users. Jony Ive, Apple's former design chief, captures this

Inventing the future - Lessons from Steve Jobs' life

Diagram showing lessons radiating from a portrait of Steve Jobs: Passion, Intersection of Engineering and Arts, End-to-end ownership, Simplicity, Reality distortion, Perfectionism, Focus, Resilience, Connecting the dots, Nobody is perfect, Different paths are possible.

philosophy well, 'You have to deeply understand the essence of a product in order to be able to get rid of the parts that are not essential.' Simplicity is reflected in Jobs' personal life as well—in his trademark black turtleneck shirt and denim trousers or his relatively spartan home. He believed that material possessions often cluttered life rather than enriched it. Jobs' example brings out both the value of simplicity and also the depth that goes into achieving simplicity.

5. **Reality distortion**: One of the more surprising discoveries from Isaacson's book was about Jobs' 'reality distortion field', or simply put, bending reality. Jobs would envision seemingly impossible outcomes. However, he had the ability to get others to trust him and then see reality the way he wanted them to, often against their judgement. This led them to achieving outcomes that appeared impossible to them earlier. One of Jobs' friends put it well, 'If he's decided that something should happen, then he's just going

to make it happen. If you trust him, you can do things.'⁴ At some level, this seems delusional, and even manipulative. However, it does prove that extraordinary results can be achieved by having a very clear picture of the outcomes you want, a strong will and conviction to achieve them and the confidence and charisma to focus and align others on achieving that vision.

6. **Perfectionism:** Jobs was a perfectionist. He was not just a great visionary but had an incredible eye for detail. Isaacson's book has many examples of Jobs picking up mistakes that the entire product team had missed. Jobs had also imbibed the philosophy that people do judge a book by its cover. He would spend an incredible amount of time on the product packaging and its initial look and feel for the customer. However, it was not just about his products' look and feel for Jobs. He was equally obsessed about getting the internals of all his products perfect. He had learnt early in his life from his father that a good carpenter uses good wood and finish even for the insides of a cupboard. He carried this lesson throughout his life. There is a fascinating story about how he insisted that the rows in the circuit of Apple computers be lined perfectly. Jobs' perfectionism is a great lesson in 'God is in the details', especially for senior executives often obsessed with grand strategy.

7. **Focus:** Jobs was able to channelize his intensity and perfectionism through sharp focus. On his return to Apple in 1997, he saved the company from bankruptcy by reducing the number of products and focusing on single products in each of the four well-defined segments. There are many stories of how he would take charge of the whiteboard at business meetings, slashing down the many ideas presented to just three priorities. His focus extended to the choice of people he would work with. He wanted to work only with A-players and was brutal in weeding out B-players. He did not want to waste his time and dilute the organizational quality with B-players. His obsessive focus did sometimes have negative

effects, most notably in his personal life. He would filter out whatever he did not want to focus on or did not have the time for. This resulted in his indifference towards his first daughter when she was very young, and perhaps even to the delay in focusing on treating his cancer. However, on the whole, his focus helped him channelize his intensity and achieve extraordinary outcomes that might not have been possible otherwise.

8. **Resilience**: Jobs' life story is one of amazing resilience and recovery from adversity. Jobs was kicked out of Apple, a company he had founded with a lot of passion, at the age of thirty. For most people, that would have been a knockout blow. However, Jobs was able to pick himself up and keep going. He faced more failures, notably at NeXT Computers, but he persevered. And in a remarkable reversal of fortune, he came back to Apple and led it to unprecedented glory. This resilience is apparent also in his battle with cancer. He did lose his third battle with cancer, but he came back from his first two battles, each time leading Apple to major product breakthroughs. Jobs' life story is a great example of a man never giving up, a lesson that if you persevere you can achieve a better future, whatever the challenges in your present.

9. **Connecting the dots**: Jobs' impact grew exponentially over the course of his career. This was because of his ability to 'connect the dots' across his many life experiences and to learn from his mistakes. Jobs was a rebel in his youth—experimenting with drugs, dropping out of college (but learning calligraphy in the process) and making a self-exploration trip to India. This was not a standard recipe for greatness in the business world. However, Jobs was able to connect these experiences into a unique success formula. Jobs also had more than his share of failures—getting kicked out of Apple, the struggles to build a successful business at NeXT and the misplaced focus at Pixar on hardware. Again, Jobs was able to learn and grow from

these failures. This comes out clearly as you compare his two stints at Apple. Act 1 at Apple was successful, but patchy. His contribution in setting up the company was secondary to that of Steve Wozniak, the technical genius who created the personal computer. Moreover, the negative aspects of his personality began to emerge and overshadow his contributions, resulting in his unceremonious ouster from the company in 1985. In Act 2, back at Apple, he was unbelievably successful, bringing in revolutionary thought leadership and creativity to the company. The series of industry-shaping products he created—iMac, iPod, iTunes, iPhone, iPad—were unprecedented, and Apple became the most valuable company in the world.

Jobs' story illustrates the power of the learning curve. Jobs might not have started out as a technical genius, but he was able to evolve into a creative giant by connecting the dots in his life. He didn't invent many things outright, but he was a master at putting together ideas, art and technology in ways that invented the future. Jobs' life story is a great lesson in the value of having varied life experiences. Moreover, it shows that if we look within and reflect deeply on our experiences and intuitions, we will find answers to our most difficult questions.

10. **Nobody is perfect:** Jobs was a complex person with many contradictions and imperfections. I found his interpersonal style to be particularly disappointing. He was brutal with his colleagues, bullying them and publicly humiliating them. He was manipulative, not taking no for an answer. He seemed to take credit for ideas that often came from others. He also seemed to lack integrity and consistency in some of his dealings. Most sad for me was his lack of loyalty—he was mean and ungrateful to some of his close friends. Yet, despite these failings, most colleagues loved working with him and, of course, he achieved phenomenal results.

There are three important lessons in this:

a. Nobody is perfect, not even a great and highly acclaimed genius like Jobs.
b. We should not focus too much on an individual's imperfections but look at the whole.
c. We should not be too judgemental about what works and what does not—Jobs' style was not 'copybook' but achieved tremendous results.

11. **Different paths are possible**: Jobs' life and work are in great contrast with those of some other geniuses, particularly the phenomenal business leader, Bill Gates, who interestingly, was also born in 1955. Two individuals and their life and work philosophies could not be more different. Jobs was the eternal rebel, temperamental and charismatic. Gates is more the establishment type, his approach is more balanced and orthodox. The two adopted very different philosophies towards technology and product development. Jobs had a strong belief in end-to-end integration and 'closed' systems, while Gates has been one of the strongest votaries of the 'open architecture' approach. Despite their different personalities and approaches, both created tremendously successful companies and are amongst the most admired role models of our times. Their intersecting life stories prove that there is no one path to success.

Different paths are possible and can be equally successful, both at work and in life. Therefore, we should choose our own path, based on our own strengths and situation.

Reading Isaacson's biography of Steve was both an emotional and intellectual experience for me. Jobs had a fascinating life and there is so much to learn from it. His life achievements are so tremendous that he almost seems like a 'super man' who was transported from an alien planet to earth for a period of time! I am not sure if Jobs as a leader can be followed in entirety or if that's even a desirable thing to do. However, there are certainly many lessons from his incredible life that all of us could learn and take inspiration from. If we could imbibe and consistently live even a few of these lessons, they would possibly help us progress on our path towards realizing our full potential.

I want to end this note with one of Jobs' favourite comments, which he used in his famous Stanford commencement address: '**Stay hungry, stay foolish**.' This, in many ways sums up his life philosophy and is a great message to take away.

34

Elon Musk's Moonshot Mentality in the AI Era

> *If something is important, you should try, even if the probable outcome is failure.*
>
> —Elon Musk, CEO of Tesla and SpaceX

Elon Musk. He's either a genius or a madman, depending on who you ask. But one thing's for sure: he's X-ing out the competition. He has fundamentally disrupted every industry he's touched—electric vehicles, space exploration, social media—and shown us what extraordinary entrepreneurial leadership looks like. And in the AI age, that's what matters. AI is a revolution, and revolutions aren't polite. We need entrepreneurs who are willing to break things, to challenge the conventional wisdom, to forge their own path. And Musk? Love him or hate him, he embodies this spirit.

It makes you wonder—are the very traits that make Musk so polarizing—his restlessness, defiance of convention and relentless drive to disrupt—also what fuel his bold vision and breakthrough innovations? As Walter Isaacson explores in his biography, this may be the same fire that propels him forward and powers his extraordinary achievements. In this chapter, I want to explore key lessons from his life for entrepreneurial success[1] in this new AI-driven world.[2]

Bet big - Lessons from Elon Musk's life

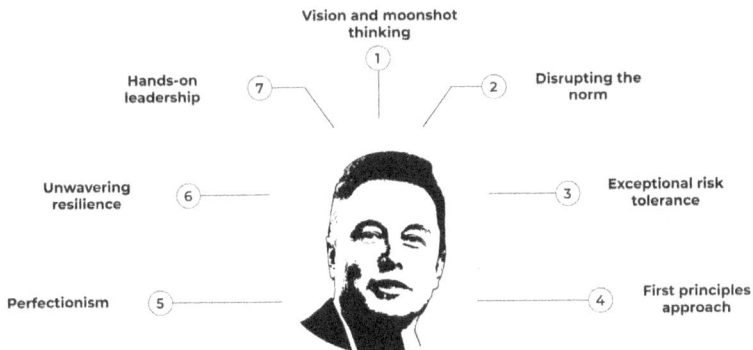

1. **The making of a maverick:** We're all shaped by our experiences, right? The things that happen to us, especially growing up, shape who we become. This truth resonates powerfully in the story of Elon Musk. His craving for drama, that almost unbelievable tolerance for risk, the sheer scale of his ambitions, that intensity—which sometimes seem almost ruthless—aren't just personality quirks; they're echoes of his past. Looking at his childhood in South Africa, you start to see the connections. Growing up in Pretoria, he was a voracious reader, often escaping into the worlds of science fiction and fantasy, perhaps a way to cope with a challenging environment. He was bullied, targeted for being socially awkward, even brutally beaten at school. He learned a tough lesson: if someone bullies you, you should hit back harder. His days at the wilderness survival camp Veldskool, practically paramilitary training, further reinforced this idea of toughness and resilience.

His relationship with his father, Errol—a volatile man prone to tirades who often told Elon he was useless and pathetic—

was deeply tumultuous. This mental torture, while damaging, also forged a certain resilience. His father instilled a belief in innovation but also immense pressure to succeed. This complex, often painful relationship, left an indelible mark. It explains the mood swings, the intense focus, the occasional plunges into what those around him called 'demon mode'. The trauma of his childhood, the constant pressure and emotional abuse clearly left a lasting impact, influencing his personality and motivations.

It's undeniable that such experiences can have profound psychological consequences, sometimes even manifesting in ways that resemble aspects of post-traumatic stress disorder (PTSD). It also explains his aversion to contentment, his need to dream big, his relentless pursuit of the extraordinary. And then you see what he's done—SpaceX, Tesla, becoming the richest person on the planet—and it's just . . . mind-blowing.

2. **Vision and moonshot thinking:** Elon Musk is known for audacious goals, not incremental improvements. He never plays small. He's obsessed with making a *dent* in the universe, a cosmic impact that resonates for generations. And I believe, in the AI age, this grand thinking is totally essential. AI presents vast opportunities, but realizing them requires entrepreneurs who think big, envision the impossible and inspire others.

   Consider SpaceX. Musk's ambition wasn't just about building a better rocket. He was (and is) aiming for Mars. Colonizing it. That kind of moonshot thinking, that refusal to accept the impossible, fuelled breakthrough innovation and propelled his teams to make the impossible happen.

   Tesla wasn't just about an electric car, it was a shot across the bow of the entire auto industry and a bid to a sustainable future. Musk's vision? Nothing less than replacing gas-powered cars entirely by building and selling electric vehicles at a scale the world had never seen. This required the complete reimagining of the business itself. Selling directly to consumers and bypassing dealerships was a direct challenge to long-standing industry norms.

Then there's Twitter (now X). Musk didn't just buy a platform. He sees it as an 'everything app', a central hub for communication, commerce and who knows what else. And he's doing it his way, bypassing traditional PR and communicating directly with users.

He makes you think, doesn't he? He's not just asking 'why not?' He's compelled by something more, a vision so grand it's almost breathtaking. In the AI age, this kind of ambition is what will define the future. It's about having the guts to redefine what's possible and build a future beyond our wildest imaginations.

3. **Relentless execution and insane risk-taking:** Musk doesn't just dream, he acts. Vision without execution is just hot air. His approach? Move fast, break things, learn faster. This 'move fast and break things' mantra, while controversial, is pure Musk.

   Rapid prototyping, constant iteration—it's how he rolls. But it's not just about speed, it's about insane risk. Musk operates on another level, repeatedly betting *everything* on his ventures. He invested his entire PayPal fortune into Tesla and SpaceX, risking near-bankruptcy. He started Neuralink long before AI-human interfaces were mainstream. He pushed AI and self-driving at Tesla when others dismissed it. He doubled down on Tesla when it struggled. He risked billions on Twitter (now X). These don't seem to be calculated risks, they're high-stakes gambles, demonstrating a willingness to bet it all for a vision he believes in.

   And here's the kicker: he doesn't always win. SpaceX rockets exploded repeatedly before a successful launch. Tesla was on the brink of bankruptcy multiple times. Even the Twitter acquisition: don't even get me started on that one! But Musk? He doesn't flinch. He dusts himself off and gets back in the ring. Setbacks are inevitable. What distinguishes successful entrepreneurs is not their ability to avoid problems, but their ability to learn from them, adapt and keep pushing forward. Musk has demonstrated time and again that success often hinges on the ability to pick yourself up and keep iterating.

This insane risk-taking, this unbreakable resilience and this relentless execution—it's the Musk trifecta. And it's exactly what you need in the AI age. AI is the wild west. You need this instinct to bet big on the future, to execute like hell and to rise from the flames—that's what separates the dreamers from the crowd.

4. **First principles and hands-on approach:** Musk's 'first principles thinking'—questioning fundamental assumptions—isn't just theoretical, it's the driving force behind his hands-on approach. He doesn't just ask 'what' but 'why', obsessively dissecting the mechanics of everything he touches. This pursuit of fundamental understanding often enables him to focus on what truly matters and solve the fundamental problem in the industry.

For example, Tesla's Gigafactory is a perfect example. He saw the potential of electric vehicles but knew battery technology was holding them back. He built the Gigafactory, and he was there on the factory floor, sleeping there even, ironing out the production issues and working directly with the engineers, until a revolutionary electric car was delivered at scale. That's not just leadership, it's obsession.

Similarly, the SpaceX manufacturing rocket was about deeply understanding the engineering challenges. Musk's on the factory floor, not in some ivory tower, pushing the boundaries of engineering. That's how SpaceX breaks through barriers.

Then there's X. Musk's takeover wasn't just about owning a social media platform, it was about owning the technology. His first act? Demanding engineers print out their work. He got deep into the code to understand every aspect of the platform.

The lesson? Get your hands dirty and be in the details. That's how you build expertise, that's how you stay ahead of the curve, that's how you fuel innovation, that's how you win. In the AI age, where algorithms, data and processing power are the new gold, this hands-on, no-holds-barred approach isn't just an advantage, it's the only way to survive.

5. **Disrupting the norm:** Elon Musk's approach is defined by a relentless questioning of assumptions. He doesn't just challenge the status quo, he interrogates it. He ignored experts who said private companies couldn't launch rockets, applying first principles to the physics and engineering challenges and finding a different path. He broke auto industry rules by selling cars directly to consumers, bypassing dealerships and challenging the established model.

    He even replaced PR teams with direct communication on X, applying a first-principles lens to how companies should communicate in the modern age. This relentless questioning, this refusal to accept 'that's just how it's done', is the engine of his disruption.

    AI is inherently disruptive, and this mindset is crucial for entrepreneurs looking to transform industries. It means questioning conventional wisdom and finding novel solutions to existing problems.

6. **Building high-performing teams:** The talent war is fierce. Musk's focus on hiring smart and firing fast, while controversial, highlights the importance of building a strong team. Musk's zero tolerance for mediocrity is well-documented. He's got a Steve Jobs' level, relentless pursuit for perfection. Why? Because he's chasing impossible goals. He's not building ordinary companies, he's building rockets, electric cars and 'everything apps'. He needs extraordinary talent to achieve these extraordinary feats.

He's fired CEOs at Tesla and PayPal for underperformance. He removed Twitter's entire executive team upon acquisition. Tesla engineers know Musk personally evaluates performance and subpar performance isn't tolerated. These actions, while sometimes seen as ruthless, illustrate a commitment to excellence essential for driving innovation and achieving ambitious goals. And it's this same relentless pursuit of excellence, coupled with his massive, almost God-like visions, that has cultivated cult-like followings for Tesla, SpaceX and even for himself. Talent may fear him, but they also *respect* him, and they want to be part of something *bigger* than themselves.

In today's rapidly evolving technological landscape, where talent is the key differentiator, building a high-performing team is paramount.

The AI age demands a new breed of entrepreneur—one who embraces the maverick spirit, thinks in moonshots, executes relentlessly and isn't afraid to challenge conventional wisdom. If Steve Jobs was a maverick, Elon is on a completely different level. Perhaps fitting for the crazy AI age we are in. His journey, with all its triumphs and tribulations, offers a powerful road map. It's a reminder that true innovation requires not just vision, but unwavering resilience, hands-on involvement and a willingness to bet big on the future.

In the face of unprecedented change and opportunity, it's these qualities—the Musk mindset—that is a powerful example for entrepreneurs who will shape the AI-powered world.

35

Lessons in Longevity and Greatness from the Giant Sequoias

The creation of a thousand forests is in one acorn.
—Ralph Waldo Emerson, American essayist

The giant sequoias at the Sequoia National Park in California are a remarkable sight. They are like gentle giants as they are not just the largest trees in the world, but also amongst the oldest living organisms on earth. On average, they are 200–300 feet tall, with the oldest growing up to 3000 years. The largest tree in the world, General Sherman, has a height of 275 feet (equivalent to a twenty-six storeyed building) and is nearly 2500 years old.

Phew! That is simply awe-inspiring. Spending time amongst the giant sequoias a few years back was a deeply moving experience for me. As was my time spent with their cousins, the Coastal Redwoods, in Muir Woods outside San Francisco. They were really special experiences. Besides being awestruck and humbled by the sheer size of these giants, I had a bit of a meditative experience in their presence. These 'immortals' have a tranquil presence that touches your core. You feel that within them lie the secrets of all creation and eternity.

Below are some key lessons for entrepreneurs based on my experience of visiting these gentle giants.[1]

Lesson 1: The smallest of seeds can produce the tallest of trees
The giant sequoia comes from a tiny cone. The sequoia cone is the size of a chicken egg with seeds smaller than oat flakes. This is such a powerful reminder of the infinite potential of life. Within the smallest of us lies the potential for greatness. This is a great lesson in hope, respect and humility. Hope and respect that amazing potential lies in every being. And humility to not dismiss any person or situation lightly, because great depth and potential might lie within them, which we might not see today.

Seven life lessons from the Giant Sequoias

With friends and family, 01 September, 2017, California, United States, Author's personal collection

Lesson 2: Believe in the power of positioning and luck
The giant sequoias grow in a fairly small region. There are only sixty-five groves found in an area of a mere 144 sq. km in the Sierra Nevada ranges in California. The trees need a humid climate, characterized by dry summers and snowy winters, and

granitic-based residual and alluvial soils, which this region has. Even within a grove, not all sequoias end up being giants. Their positioning in the grove, access to sunlight, surroundings and other factors play a key role in the eventual size they will attain. This is a powerful life lesson—many might have the same intrinsic potential but being at the right place at the right time can make all the difference in eventual success.

Lesson 3: Keep growing bigger and taller with age
The hardiness, age and size of the giant sequoias are all connected. They keep growing in size and strength as they get older and therefore are even more difficult to be blown over by winds. They seem to have conquered diseases and natural death and die only by accident, from falling down. The older sequoias are therefore even more magnificent. That is a powerful inspiration for us humans in so many ways. The big lesson for me was to never stop growing and that our best days are ahead of us. Moreover, understanding the value of longevity is crucial. If you can stay the course, you can achieve great impact.

Lesson 4: Build your strength through community
Giant sequoias have surprisingly small roots, only six feet to twenty feet deep. Yet, these shallow roots support the giants for thousands of years. The answer lies in the fact that sequoias grow close to each other and their roots are intertwined. It is this matting of their roots, the network effect, that gives sequoias the incredible strength and stability they have. It is a powerful reminder of the strength of the community and that no individual can stand tall without the support of many.

Lesson 5: Leave a legacy behind
When a mother sequoia tree falls, it doesn't mark the end of its life entirely. Beneath the surface, its extensive root system

remains alive, becoming a vital source of nutrients and stability for the younger sequoias growing nearby. The baby sequoias tap into the mother tree's robust taproot, to thrive and grow. This remarkable underground support system is the legacy of the mother tree, as she continues to nurture the next generation long after her towering presence has fallen.

Similarly, it is our duty to create something that will help the next generations build their futures. I believe it is every individual's responsibility to leave this world a slightly better place than we found it. This means helping people around us grow to their full potential, encouraging them to lead healthier, wiser and fuller lives.

Lesson 6: Know that fire is important for growth

Perhaps the biggest secret of the giant sequoias' longevity is how they survive fires. The Sierra Nevada region, the habitat of the giant sequoias, is dry and prone to lightning. This is a deadly combination that results in many fires, resulting in a big survival challenge for the sequoias. We found many sequoias in the park with large fire scars. However, sequoias have a great mechanism in their bark to overcome fires. Their bark is very thick (~3 feet) and has tannin, which protects it from fire. Giant sequoias are able to not just survive fire but also use it for regeneration and growth. Fire clears the undergrowth and opens their cones, allowing the seeds to germinate. Moreover, fire removes the competing thin-barked species around, promoting growth of these ancient giants. In fact, fires are typically followed by a growth spurt in the giant sequoias.

Their mastery of fire is such a powerful lesson for us. Life throws many challenges our way. The way we tackle them determines how we grow in life. We need to develop our own unique coping mechanisms (thick bark and tannin for the giant sequoias). The most successful are able to not just survive the challenges but use it as an opportunity for fuelling further growth. That is such a beautiful and powerful life lesson. This lesson has been so true during the Covid-19 pandemic, where high-quality resilient companies have outperformed during these difficult times.

Lesson 7: Even the mightiest can fall
The mighty sequoias are unique with their fire-resistant bark. The tannin protects them from fire. However, even the mightiest have their vulnerabilities. In case of a giant sequoia, lightning-sparked wildfires or high-intensity fires, difficult to contain in time, can pierce through their fire-resistant exteriors. Once the fire gets past the bark, there's nothing to stop it. In such situations, while the flames disappear, the embers remain smouldering. Such trees continue to slowly burn, as the inside of the tree provides an oxygen-rich environment and shelter for the fire. While the embers don't burn up the tree immediately, they slowly burn it from the inside out. Such trees are known to have continued to smoulder for up to two years from past wildfires.

The key lesson here is that even if we are very strong, we are fallible. We can be brought down not only by external fires but also internal weaknesses that might not be very visible. For example, harbouring negative feelings and emotions like anger, hatred, wrongdoing, self-doubt etc. for too long, can ignite a slow-burning fire within us. Continuing to hold on to those feelings can consume us gradually from the inside, causing harm and destruction. It's important to address and let go of these feelings to prevent them from affecting our well-being.

These life lessons of hope, courage, excellence, resilience and longevity are inspiring for me, and I hope they inspire you to strive for greatness and become the source of strength during tough times. However, mere words cannot do justice to these magnificent, immortal giants. I strongly encourage you to go and see the sequoias and absorb for yourself the mystery and wonder of these incomparable giants. They have stood the test of time well and are worthy inspirations for us to navigate the many changes in the AI age.

Conclusion

Timeless Wisdom for Daily Living in the AI Age

You have the right to action, but not to its fruits. Perform your duty with equanimity.

—*Bhagavad Gita, Chapter 2, Verse 47*

As we reach the end of this book, we find ourselves at the same inflection point where many individuals, organizations and societies now stand—a moment of reckoning. Understanding the incredible promise and disruption of the AI age—and the critical importance of revitalizing the human edge as our method for success—has been a deeply personal journey. Writing this book has been my way of making sense of the turbulent tides ahead.

Through this shared journey, I hope you've found your own sense of clarity—perhaps even a spark of resolve. Because this moment of reckoning isn't about succumbing to fear, it's about recognizing the weight of the present, acknowledging the challenges and preparing ourselves to actively shape the future we want to see.

The AI age is here, and with it comes a fundamental shift in how we live, work and find meaning. We are witnessing the end of the era of jobs—as we've known them for decades, some perhaps for centuries—and the dawn of something altogether new: the era of entrepreneurs. Not just startup founders, but individuals in every domain who must now think like creators, builders, innovators and self-driven problem-solvers.

But such a dramatic shift is not just about changing roles—it forces us to confront deeper tensions within ourselves and our world.

The AI age is bringing with it a deep and disorienting duality. The fear of job losses and the thrill of entrepreneurial opportunities may be the most visible, but they are far from the only ones. We are grappling with the tension between stability and reinvention, structure and freedom, comfort and courage, intelligence and wisdom. Between personalization and privacy, autonomy and control, human empathy and machine precision. Between the security of the known and the pull of the possible. Between accelerating technological progress and the enduring search for spiritual grounding. On the one hand, we can stay with the tried-and-tested path that has served us well in the past, even though the world around us is changing dramatically in the AI age. On the other, we can embrace the uncertainty of a future that feels inevitable, yet deeply unfamiliar. A future that challenges the very identity and purpose we've built our lives around. And whenever we're caught between such dualities, decision-making becomes harder not because we lack options, but because we must choose between two paths—both challenging in their own ways.

This transition is both daunting and exciting. For many, it evokes confusion, fear and inertia—very much like Arjuna on the battlefield of Kurukshetra in the epic Mahabharata where he was supposed to fight against his own kin. Arjuna faced a profound inner conflict: retreat from the battle, avoid the pain and cling to the familiar ties that defined his identity or step into the chaos, embrace his duty and move forward into an uncertain future that challenged everything he believed in. Faced with a choice that shattered his sense of identity and moral clarity, Arjuna laid down his bow. He questioned not just the battle, but the purpose of action itself.

In many ways, that is where we find ourselves today. The familiar paths—college degrees, steady jobs, management structures—are all being upended. In their place lies a new battlefield: fast-changing, AI-infused and unpredictable. The questions we now face are eerily similar to Arjuna's dilemma:

- What is my role in this future?
- Can I stay relevant in a world where machines learn faster than I do?
- What if my skills—or even my sense of self—becomes obsolete?

In that moment of crisis, Krishna shared with Arjuna the amazing wisdom of the Bhagavad Gita, which is not just a philosophical exhortation but a powerful and timeless framework to act—and to do so with clarity, courage and inner alignment. That's precisely why I turn to the Bhagavad Gita in closing this book.[1]

Why the Gita?

The Gita is not a religious text in the narrow sense. It is a manual for navigating chaos, a leadership handbook for moments of profound disruption. Over 2000 years old, it remains astonishingly relevant because it is not just concerned with what to do—but how to think, act and evolve.

In writing this book, I have drawn equally from modern experience and ancient wisdom—from boardrooms and battlefields, from algorithms and awareness. The Gita, for me, represents the timeless bridge between these worlds.

The POSSIBLE framework through the lens of the Gita

In the second section of this book, I presented eight timeless mantras for thriving in the AI age, captured in the **POSSIBLE** framework. While framed in a modern context, these ideas are deeply aligned with the teachings[2] of the Gita.[3]

Let's reimagine them through Krishna's guidance to Arjuna:

POSSIBLE Mantra	Gita Parallel	Essence
P—Problem-Solving	Viveka (Discernment)	See reality clearly. Ask better questions. Seek root causes, not noise.
O—Openness to Change	Shraddha (Faith and Receptivity)	Be willing to learn, unlearn and grow with trust and humility.
S—Spirituality	Yoga (Union of action, thought and self)	Anchor in self-awareness. Connect action with deeper meaning.
S—Sports/Resilience	Karma Yoga (Detached, disciplined effort)	Play fully. Persevere. Let go of results, not effort.
I—Impact	Seva and Dharma (Selfless service)	Act for the world, not just the self. Align action with higher purpose.
B—Balance	Samatvam (Equanimity in success and failure)	Stay centred amidst volatility. Balance ambition with surrender.
L—Leadership	Lokasangraha (Uplifting society through action)	Inspire through service. Lead not by control but by example.
E—Entrepreneurship	Swadharma (Own unique path or calling)	Create from within. Solve problems only you are meant to solve.

Towards the entrepreneurial sage

One thing is clear: in this era of AI, standing still is not an option. To not just survive but thrive, we must sharpen our human edge—that deep reservoir of uniquely human instincts, values and capabilities. Our edge won't come from chasing what machines can do—but from rediscovering what only we can be. It's not about chasing something outside of us. It's about rediscovering who we truly are.

As Viktor Frankl said, 'Between stimulus and response there is a space. In that space is our power to choose our response. In our response lies our growth and our freedom.' In a world increasingly driven by algorithms, that space—our human edge—has never been more essential.

AI may be the most powerful external force reshaping the world, but the most important transformation must happen within us.

As machines get faster, humans must get deeper.

As algorithms scale intelligence, we must scale consciousness.

As jobs vanish, we must reimagine ourselves as **entrepreneurial sages**—those who build not just apps, but awareness; not just companies, but contribution.

This is not the time to cling to what was. It is the time to evolve—in mind, spirit and action.

A final call

Like Arjuna, you may feel unsure. That's natural. But also like Arjuna, you have within you the strength to act—with clarity, purpose and possibility.

The world needs you, not as a cog in the machine, but as a conscious creator of what comes next.

So, I leave you with the same invitation Krishna gave:

Stand up. Pick up your bow. And act with awareness, positivity and decisiveness.

The future is not fixed.

The future is not artificial.

The future is POSSIBLE.

Let's go forth and make it *limitless*.

Writing this book has been a journey of introspection, learning and hope. I invite you to embark on your own journey and rediscover the edge that makes us human.

Carpe Diem!

Acknowledgements

'We do not inherit the Earth from our ancestors, we borrow it from our children.'

—*Native American Proverb*

After my first two books, which focused on digital and data respectively, it was obvious that my next book would be on AI—completing the magnificent trifecta of digital–data–AI that is reshaping every aspect of work and life today. However, this book is different. While the first two explored the intersection of business and technology and were written primarily for technology practitioners and enthusiasts, this one takes a human lens. It is meant for a broader audience—including young adults and teenagers.

The inspiration for this broader perspective came from my dear wife Arpna, who encouraged me to distil my life learnings into a book that would speak to our children, who are now between the ages of eighteen and twenty-five. That guidance shaped the approach I have taken—simplifying complex ideas, making them accessible and grounding them in personal experience, not just external research. In many ways, this book is a legacy for them and their generation—a way to share the values, principles and reflections I have gathered over a lifetime. As we stand on the threshold of the AI age, with so many big questions to answer and unprecedented opportunities to shape the future, my hope is that this book equips them to navigate this era with confidence, character and clarity.

A core theme of this book is how we can navigate the extraordinarily dynamic and ever-changing AI age by leaning on timeless principles. This inspiration comes from my deep grounding in Indian spiritual wisdom and practices, which I was fortunate to be exposed to from a young age. For this, I owe special gratitude to my maternal uncle, Mr B.M. Khanna. Some of my most cherished childhood memories are of walks with him, where he would pose fundamental questions and encourage me to meditate alongside him. A senior technocrat and former chairman of India's national telecom operator, he was a role model to me—proof that one could succeed in the modern world of business and technology while being deeply rooted in spiritual principles. This integration of the timeless and the contemporary has become a north star for my life and is deeply woven through the fabric of this book.

Writing this book has been a personal and reflective journey. The POSSIBLE framework, which sits at its core, is drawn from my lived experiences and insights. At the same time, like my previous books, it rests on rigorous research—particularly in understanding the implications of the AI age for jobs, industries and humanity's future. I would like to acknowledge the outstanding work of the research team at the Incedo Insight Institute—Rahul Kumar, Surbhi Mehta, Ida Nair Sharma, Rajul Misra and Shweta Modgil. Your dedication to deep, grounded research across every theme in this book has been invaluable.

I am also deeply grateful to my colleagues at Incedo, and to my former colleagues at McKinsey, Fidelity, Flipkart and ActiveKarma. Each of you has played a pivotal role in shaping my understanding of digital transformation and AI. Our shared experiences have underscored the enduring power of human values in an increasingly automated world, and that belief forms the heart of this book.

This book would not have been possible without the trust placed in us by our clients at Incedo. Partnering with you on your data and AI transformation journeys has offered rich, first-hand insights that have shaped my views on the megatrend of AI and its long-term implications.

My heartfelt thanks to my editors—Radhika Marwah, Saba Nehal and Sakshi Sharma—at Penguin Random House India. Your continued partnership and discerning editorial insights have been instrumental in chiselling this manuscript into a compelling and coherent exploration of the human edge in the AI age.

And finally, I am equally grateful to my international publishing partners at Bloomsbury— Jacquie Flynn, Rahul Shrivastava, Leo Stanley, Julie Kirsch, Tricia Currie-Knight, Mikayla Lindsay, Peter Perez, and Veronica Dove. Your commitment, collaboration, and speed in preparing this book for readers around the world have been truly inspiring.

Notes

Preface

1. Job loss 50% by 2040- Helen Russell, 'In the future, you'll share your work with robots... unless you're a woman,' BBC Science Focus Magazine (20 September 2023), accessed on 11 June 2024, and viewable at: https://www.sciencefocus.com/future-technology/will-we-work-in-the-future; Job loss 35% by 2040- Jan Hatzius, Joseph Briggs, Devesh Kodnani, Giovanni Pierdomenico, The Potentially Large Effects of Artificial Intelligence on Economic Growth, Goldman Sachs (26 March 2023), accessed on 11 June 2024, and viewable at: https://www.key4biz.it/wp-content/uploads/2023/03/Global-Economics-Analyst_-The-Potentially-Large-Effects-of-Artificial-Intelligence-on-Economic-Growth-Briggs_Kodnani.pdf.

Introduction

1. Dan Muse, 'Dreamforce 2024: Latest news and insights', CIO (20 September 2024), accessed on 19 December 2024, and viewable at: https://www.cio.com/article/3516181/dreamforce-2024-latest-news-and-insights.html.

Chapter 1: The Irresistible March of the AI Age

1. Nitin Seth, *Mastering the Data Paradox: Key to Winning in the AI Age* (18 March 2024), accessed on 11 June 2024, and viewable at: https://masteringthedataparadox.com/.

2   Keith D. Foote, 'A Brief History of Natural Language Processing', Dataversity (6 July 2023), accessed on 11 June 2024, and viewable at: https://www.dataversity.net/a-brief-history-of-natural-language-processing-nlp/.
3   Ben Tarnoff, 'Weizenbaum's nightmares: how the inventor of the first chatbot turned against AI', *Guardian* (25 July 2023), accessed on 11 June 2024, and viewable at: https://www.theguardian.com/technology/2023/jul/25/joseph-weizenbaum-inventor-eliza-chatbot-turned-against-artificial-intelligence-ai.
4   Will Douglas Heaven, 'Google just launched Bard, its answer to ChatGPT—and it wants you to make it better', *MIT Technology Review* (21 March 2023), accessed on 11 June 2024, and viewable at: https://www.technologyreview.com/2023/03/21/1070111/google-bard-chatgpt-openai-microsoft-bing-search/.
5   Karl Montevirgen, 'OpenAI American artificial intelligence (AI) research organization', *Britannica Money* (26 February 2025), accessed on 11 June 2024, and viewable at: https://www.britannica.com/money/OpenAI.
6   Sarah O'Neill, 'The History of OpenAI', LXA (2 May 2023), accessed on 11 June 2024, and viewable at: https://www.lxahub.com/stories/the-history-of-openai.
7   Irene Solaiman, et al., 'Release Strategies and the Social Impacts of Language Models', OpenAI (1 August 2023), accessed on 11 June 2024, and viewable at: https://cdn.openai.com/GPT_2_August_Report.pdf.
8   Abhijeet Kumar, 'OpenAI launches enhanced GPT-4 turbo for ChatGPT plus users and developers', *Business Standard* (11 April 2024), accessed on 11 June 2024, and viewable at: https://www.business-standard.com/technology/tech-news/openai-launches-enhanced-gpt-4-turbo-for-chatgpt-plus-users-and-developers-124041100491_1.html.
9   Nitin Seth, *Mastering the Data Paradox: Key to Winning in the AI Age* (18 March 2024), accessed on 11 June 2024, and viewable at: https://masteringthedataparadox.com/.
10 Nitin Seth, *Mastering the Data Paradox: Key to Winning in the AI Age* (18 March 2024), accessed on 11 June 2024, and viewable at: https://masteringthedataparadox.com/.
11 'IoT devices 'to generate nearly 80 zettabytes of data' by 2025', ARO Tech (13 April 2023), accessed on 11 June 2024, and viewable at: https://aro.tech/insights/blog/iot-devices-to-generate-nearly-80-zettabytes-of-data-by-2025/.

12 Brian Eastwood, 'What is synthetic data — and how can it help you competitively?', MIT Sloan (1 January 2023), accessed on 11 June 2024, and viewable at: https://mitsloan.mit.edu/ideas-made-to-matter/what-synthetic-data-and-how-can-it-help-you-competitively.
13 David Reinsel, John Gantz and John Rydning, 'The Digitization of the World From Edge to Core', Seagate (1 May 2020), accessed on 11 June 2024, and viewable at: https://www.seagate.com/files/www-content/our-story/trends/files/dataage-idc-report-final.pdf.
14 Ibid.
15 Unstructured Data, Mongo DB, 2025, accessed on 11 June 2024, and viewable at: https://www.mongodb.com/resources/basics/unstructured-data#:~:text=From%2080%25%20to%2090%25%20of,used%20to%20guide%20business%20decisions.
16 'Congruity 360, The Future of Data: Unstructured Data Statistics You Should Know', MIT Sloan (25 September 2023), accessed on 11 June 2024, and viewable at: https://www.congruity360.com/blog/the-future-of-data-unstructured-data-statistics-you-should-know/#:~:text=Unstructured%20Data%20is%20Growing%2055,expanding%20realm%20of%20unstructured%20data.
17 'Matillion and IDG Survey: Data Growth is Real, and 3 Other Key Findings', Matillion (26 January 2022), accessed on 11 June 2024 and viewable at: https://www.matillion.com/blog/matillion-and-idg-survey-data-growth-is-real-and-3-other-key-findings#..
18 Open Data Inventory (ODIN), Open Data Watch (9 August 2023), accessed on 11 June 2024, and viewable at: https://odin.opendatawatch.com/; ODIN Biennial Report (1 July 2023), accessed on 11 June 2024, and viewable at: https://odin.opendatawatch.com/Report/biennialReport2022
19 ODIN Biennial Report (1 July 2023), accessed on 11 June 2024, and viewable at: https://odin.opendatawatch.com/Report/biennialReport2022
20 Jermey Kahn, 'OpenAI launches long-awaited GPT-4.5—but 'Orion's' capabilities already lag competitors', *Fortune* (28 February 2025), accessed on 7 March 2025, and viewable at: https://fortune.com/2025/02/27/openai-gpt-4-5-orion-launch-sam-altman-benchmarks/.
21 Gadi Singer, 'Fundamental Choices Impacting Integration and Deployment at Scale of GenAI into Businesses', Intel (10 February, 2024), accessed on 25 August 2024, and viewable at: https://community.intel.com/t5/Blogs/Tech-Innovation/Artificial-Intelligence-AI/The-AI-Developer-s-Dilemma-Proprietary-AI-vs-Open-Source/post/1634729.

22 Restack, 'Resnet50 Number Of Parameters', Restack (26 February 2025), accessed on 26 February 2025, and viewable at: https://www.restack.io/p/resnet50-answer-number-of-parameters-cat-ai.

23 Petru Potrimba, 'What is ResNet-50?', Roboflow (13 March 2024), accessed on 26 June 2024, and viewable at: https://blog.roboflow.com/what-is-resnet-50/.

24 Agam Shah, 'Generative AI to Account for 1.5 per cent of World's Power Consumption by 2029', HPC Wire, (8 July 2024), accessed on 19 September 2024, and viewable at: https://www.hpcwire.com/2024/07/08/generative-ai-to-account-for-1-5-of-worlds-power-consumption-by-2029/.

25 'Sustainable AI, microML.IN', Medium, (18 September 2024), accessed on 7 October 2024, and viewable at: https://medium.com/@microml.in/sustainable-ai-a2bcc09da1dc.

26 'Electricity Consumption by Country 2024', World Population Review, (2022), accessed on 11 June 2024, and viewable at: https://worldpopulationreview.com/country-rankings/electricity-consumption-by-country.

27 Bloomberg Professional Services, 'Introducing BloombergGPT, Bloomberg's 50-billion parameter large language model, purpose-built from scratch for finance' (30 March 2023), accessed on 11 October 2024, and viewable at: https://www.bloomberg.com/company/press/bloomberggpt-50-billion-parameter-llm-tuned-finance/.

28 Antoine Boudet, 'Med-PaLM 2: Google's AI that can answer medical questions like an expert', Medium (13 August 2023), accessed on 11 June 2024, and viewable at: https://medium.com/@antoinestory/med-palm-2-googles-ai-that-can-answer-medical-questions-like-an-expert-70964f1f6b93.

29 Misha Bilenko, 'Introducing Phi-3: Redefining what's possible with SLMs', Microsoft Azure (23 April 2024), accessed on 11 June 2024, and viewable at: https://azure.microsoft.com/en-us/blog/introducing-phi-3-redefining-whats-possible-with-slms/.

30 Arun Chandrasekaran, '3 Bold and Actionable Predictions for the Future of GenAI', Gartner, (12 April 2024), accessed on 11 June 2024, and viewable at: https://www.gartner.com/en/articles/3-bold-and-actionable-predictions-for-the-future-of-genai.

31 'Charles Babbage: His life and contributions', Stanford (1998-99), accessed on 11 June 2024, and viewable at: https://cs.stanford.edu/people/eroberts/courses/soco/projects/1998-99/babbage/bio.htm#.

32 Carla Tardi, 'What Is Moore's Law and Is It Still True?', Investopedia (2 April 2024), accessed on 11 June 2024, and viewable at: https://www.investopedia.com/terms/m/mooreslaw.asp#.
33 Jaime Sevilla Molina, et al., 'Compute Trends Across Three Eras of Machine Learning', ResearchGate (1 February 2022), accessed on 11 June 2024, and viewable at: https://www.researchgate.net/publication/358603924_Compute_Trends_Across_Three_Eras_of_Machine_Learning.
34 Ibid.
35 Rick Merritt, 'Why GPUs Are Great for AI', Nvidia, (04 December 2023), accessed on 11 June 2024, and viewable at: https://blogs.nvidia.com/blog/why-gpus-are-great-for-ai/
36 Marius Hobbhahn and Tamay Besiroglu, 'Trends in GPU price-performance', AI Alignment Forum (1 July 2022), accessed on 11 June 2024, and viewable at: https://www.alignmentforum.org/posts/c6KFvQcZggQKZzxr9/trends-in-gpu-price-performance.
37 Rob Wile, 'Why everyone is suddenly talking about Nvidia, the nearly $3 trillion-dollar company fueling the AI revolution', NBC News (24 February 2024), accessed on 11 June 2024, and viewable at: https://www.nbcnews.com/business/business-news/what-is-nvidia-what-do-they-make-ai-artificial-intelligence-rcna140171.
38 Anthony Gregerson, 'Implementing Fast MRI Gridding on GPUs via CUDA', Nvidia (2008), accessed on 11 June 2024, and viewable at: https://www.nvidia.com/docs/IO/47905/ECE757_Project_Report_Gregerson.pdf.
39 Hassan Mujtaba, 'World's First GPU With HBM2 and 10.6 TFLOPs of Compute On A Single Chip', WCCFTech (5 April 2016), accessed on 11 June 2024, and viewable at: https://wccftech.com/nvidia-pascal-tesla-p100-gp100-gpu/#.
40 Rob Williams, 'Nvidia Turing & Ampere CUDA & OptiX Rendering Performance', TechGage (29 December 2020), accessed on 11 June 2024, and viewable at: https://techgage.com/article/nvidia-turing-ampere-cuda-optix-rendering-performance/.
41 'Nvidia Blackwell B100, B200 GPU Specs and Availability', DataCrunch (24 June 2024), accessed on 19 August 2024, and viewable at: https://datacrunch.io/blog/nvidia-blackwell-b100-b200-gpu.
42 Scott Daly, 'Nvidia Confirms Blackwell Ultra and Vera Rubin GPUs Launch Schedule', 9meters (28 March 2025), accessed on 2 June 2025, and viewable at: https://9meters.com/technology/graphics/nvidia-

confirms-blackwell-ultra-and-vera-rubin-gpus-on-track-for-2025-and-2026#:~:text=Current%3A%20Blackwell%20B200%20series,Ultra%20 (according%20to%20Nvidia's%20roadmap)

43 'Nvidia Market Cap 2010-2024 | NVDA, Macrotrends (2025)', accessed on 10 February 2025, and viewable at: https://www.macrotrends.net/stocks/charts/NVDA/nvidia/market-cap#google_vignette.

Chapter 2: AI Is Surpassing Human Capabilities

1. Oliver Lange and Luis Perez, 'Traffic prediction with advanced Graph Neural Networks', Google, (3 September 2020), accessed on 11 June 2024, and viewable at: https://deepmind.google/discover/blog/traffic-prediction-with-advanced-graph-neural-networks/.
2. Ibid.
3. Nicole Kobie, 'DeepMind's new AI can spot breast cancer just as well as your doctor', *Wired*, (1 January 2020), accessed on 11 June 2024, and viewable at: https://www.wired.com/story/deepmind-google-ai-breast-cancer/.
4. Ibid.
5. Ibid.
6. Ibid.
7. Tanya Petersen, 'AI's new power of persuasion: it can change your mind', EPFL, (15 April 2024), accessed on 17 October 2024, and viewable at: https://actu.epfl.ch/news/ai-s-new-power-of-persuasion-it-can-change-your-mi/.
8. Francesco Salvi, et al., 'On the Conversational Persuasiveness of Large Language Models: A Randomized Controlled Trial', Arxiv.org, (21 March 2024), accessed on 17 Oct 2024, and viewable at: https://arxiv.org/pdf/2403.14380.
9. Ibid.
10. 'How Meta Movie Gen could usher in a new AI-enabled era for content creators', Meta, (04 October 2024), accessed on 17 Nov 2024, and viewable at:https://ai.meta.com/blog/movie-gen-media-foundation-models-generative-ai-video/.
11. William R. Small, et al., 'Large Language Model–Based Responses to Patients' In-Basket Messages', Jama Network, (16 July 2024), accessed on 17 Oct 2024, and viewable at: https://jamanetwork.com/journals/jamanetworkopen/fullarticle/2821167.

12 'AI tool successfully responds to patient questions in electronic health record', NYU Langone Health / NYU Grossman School of Medicine, (16 July 2024), accessed on 17 Oct 2024, and viewable at: https://www.sciencedaily.com/releases/2024/07/240716122707.htm.
13 'The LLM Will See You Now AMIE, a chatbot that outperforms doctors in diagnostic conversations', The Batch, (12 June 2024), accessed on 17 Oct 2024, and viewable at: https://www.deeplearning.ai/the-batch/amie-a-chatbot-that-outperforms-doctors-in-diagnostic-conversations/.
14 'AMIE 2024: Unleashing a New Era of AI Excellence in Medical Diagnosis', HyScaler, (18 January 2024), accessed on 1 July 2024, and viewable at: https://hyscaler.com/insights/how-amie-unleashing-ai-in-medical-diagnosis/.

Chapter 3: The Human Quotient Is Facing Its Toughest Trial

1 Editorial Team, 'Replika AI: Unlocking 30 Million Users', Artificial Intelligence + (6 January 2025), accessed on 21 February 2025, and viewable at: https://www.aiplusinfo.com/blog/replika-ai-unlocking-30-million-users/.
2 'Emotion AI Market Size, Share, Competitive Landscape and Trend Analysis Report, by Component, by Enterprise Size, by Application: Global Opportunity Analysis and Industry Forecast, 2023-2032', Allied Market Research (1 September 2023), accessed on 11 June 2024, and viewable at: https://www.alliedmarketresearch.com/emotion-ai-market-A231628#:~:text=Emotion%20AI%20Market%20Statistics%2C%202032,22.7%25%20from%202023%20to%202032.
3 Charles Johnston, 'The Yoga sutras of Patanjali, 'The book of the spiritual man'; an interpretation', Rarebook Society of India (1912), accessed on 11 June 2024, and viewable at: https://www.rarebooksocietyofindia.org/book_archive/196174216674_10152640362806675.pdf.
4 Nitin Seth, *Mastering the Data Paradox: Key to Winning in the AI Age* (18 March 2024), accessed on 11 June 2024, and viewable at: https://masteringthedataparadox.com/.

Chapter 4: AI Will Fundamentally Reshape Every Industry

1 Nitin Seth, *Mastering the Data Paradox: Key to Winning in the AI Age* (18 March 2024), accessed on 11 June 2024, and viewable at: https://masteringthedataparadox.com/.

2   Baradari, Dünya, et al., 'NeuroChat: A Neuroadaptive AI Chatbot for Customizing Learning Experiences', MIT Media Lab (10 March 2025), accessed on 11 April 2025, and viewable at: https://www.media.mit.edu/publications/neurochat-a-neuroadaptive-ai-chatbot-for-customizing-learning-experiences/.

3   'Diabetes impacts you in more ways than you can imagine', Twin Health (2025), accessed on 11 April 2025, and viewable at: https://ind.twinhealth.com/twin-diabetes-consultation-lp/.

4   Nicoletta Boldrini, 'Agentic AI: The Dawn of Cognitive Autonomy', Tech4Future (27 January 2025), accessed on 11 April 2025, and viewable at: https://tech4future.info/en/agentic-ai-cognitive-autonomy/.

5   Auto GPT (2025), accessed on 11 April 2025, and viewable at: https://agpt.co/.

6   Yogendra Sisodia, 'Open Devin: Making an autonomous AI engineer for exploratory data analysis', Medium (31 March 2024), accessed on 11 April 2025, and viewable at: https://medium.com/@scholarly360/open-devin-making-an-autonomous-ai-engineer-for-exploratory-data-analysis-0082fe5127dc.

7   Sichu Zhangi, 'How much faster can coding assistants really make software delivery?', Thoughtworks (18 February 2025), accessed on 11 April 2025, and viewable at: https://www.thoughtworks.com/en-in/insights/blog/generative-ai/how-faster-coding-assistants-software-delivery.

8   Ben Wiseman, 'What Can Copilot's Earliest Users Teach Us About Generative AI at Work?', Microsoft (15 November 2023), accessed on 11 April 2025, and viewable at: https://www.microsoft.com/en-us/worklab/work-trend-index/copilots-earliest-users-teach-us-about-generative-ai-at-work.

9   'What is Robotic Process Automation (RPA)?', Bakertilly (1 November 2024), accessed on 11 April 2025, and viewable at: https://www.bakertilly.com/insights/what-is-robotic-process-automation-rpa.

10 Sakana.AI, 'The AI Scientist: Towards Fully Automated Open-Ended Scientific Discovery', Sakana.AI (13 August 2024), accessed on 11 April 2025, and viewable at: https://sakana.ai/ai-scientist/.

11 Anne Trafton, 'Using AI, scientists find a drug that could combat drug-resistant infections', MIT News (25 May 2023), accessed on 11 April 2025, and viewable at: https://news.mit.edu/2023/using-ai-scientists-combat-drug-resistant-infections-0525.

12 Zaina Haider, 'Hypernetworks in Generative AI', Medium (20 February 2025), accessed on 11 April 2025, and viewable at: https://blog.gopenai.com/hypernetworks-in-generative-ai-29d8fe51c0fd
13 'Airbnb Unveils AI Concierge, Revolutionizing Travel Planning', The Silicon Review (2 April 2025), accessed on 11 April 2025, and viewable at: https://thesiliconreview.com/2025/04/airbnb-ai-concierge-launch.
14 Pranav Dixit, 'Female influencer creates AI-powered "virtual girlfriend" that could earn Rs 41 crore a month', Business Today (13 May 2023), accessed on 11 April 2025, and viewable at: https://www.businesstoday.in/technology/news/story/female-influencer-creates-ai-powered-virtual-girlfriend-that-could-earn-rs-41-crore-a-month-381005-2023-05-12.
15 'Perfect Parties Start Here', PartyPlease (2025), accessed on 11 April 2025, and viewable at: https://partyplease.co/.
16 Jaitashri Bhoir, 'Why D2C is the Future of Retail: Key Strategies for Success', gupshup (16 April 2025), accessed on 11 April 2025, and viewable at: https://www.gupshup.io/resources/blog/future-of-retail-with-d2c-marketing.
17 Tamara Kostova, 'GenAI Vs. Robo-Advisors: Considerations for The Financial Industry', Forbes Business Council (15 August 2024), accessed on 11 April 2025, and viewable at: https://www.forbes.com/councils/forbesbusinesscouncil/2024/08/15/genai-vs-robo-advisors-considerations-for-the-financial-industry/.
18 Sambhavi Gopalakrishnan, '21 Ways AI in Education Is Reshaping the Industry', Vlink (7 January 2025), accessed on 11 April 2025, and viewable at: https://vlinkinfo.com/blog/ai-in-education-industry/.
19 Uttam Kumaran, 'How Amazon Uses Big Data', Brainforge (2025) accessed on 11 April 2025, and viewable at: https://www.brainforge.ai/blog/how-amazon-uses-big-data.
20 Mary Ann Azevedo, 'Stripe says AI startups are growing faster than SaaS ever did, and calling them wrappers 'misses the point', TechCrunch(27 February 2025), accessed on 11 April 2025, and viewable at: https://techcrunch.com/2025/02/27/stripe-ceo-says-ai-startups-are-growing-faster-than-saas-ever-did-and-calling-them-wrappers-misses-the-point/.
21 Benedikt Gieger, Dominik Metzger, 'Harnessing AI technology to build autonomous supply chains', WEF (3 March 2025), accessed on 16 April 2025, and viewable at: https://www.weforum.org/stories/2025/03/harnessing-ai-technology-to-build-autonomous-supply-chains/.

22 Leandro DalleMule, 'How AI is Changing Insurance', Insurance Thought Leadership, Inc, (3 September 2024), accessed on 16 April 2025, and viewable at: https://www.insurancethoughtleadership.com/ai-machine-learning/how-ai-changing-insurance.
23 ''How machine learning works for payment fraud detection and prevention', Stripe (27 June 2023), accessed on 16 April 2025, and viewable at: https://stripe.com/in/resources/more/how-machine-learning-works-for-payment-fraud-detection-and-prevention.
24 'About CUDA', Nvidia (2025), accessed on 11 April 2025, and viewable at: https://developer.nvidia.com/about-cuda.
25 'Financial infrastructure to grow your revenue', Stripe (2025), accessed on 11 April 2025, and viewable at: https://stripe.com/in.
26 'Bring your ideas to life for Rs.20/month', Shopify (2025), accessed on 11 April 2025, and viewable at: https://www.shopify.com/in/free-trial.
27 Snowflake (2025), accessed on 11 April 2025, and viewable at: https://www.snowflake.com/en/.
28 Databricks (2025), accessed on 11 April 2025, and viewable at:https://www.databricks.com/.
29 Anthropic (2025), accessed on 11 April 2025, and viewable at:https://www.anthropic.com/.
30 Jennifer Dublino, 'What Is Dynamic Pricing and How Does It Affect E-Commerce?', Business.com (10 February 2025), accessed on 11 April 2025, and viewable at: https://www.business.com/articles/what-is-dynamic-pricing-and-how-does-it-affect-ecommerce/.
31 Geri Mileva, 'Top 10 AI Influencers Making Waves on Instagram', Influencer Marketing Hub (21 March 2025), accessed on 11 April 2025, and viewable at: https://influencermarketinghub.com/ai-influencers-instagram/.
32 Melissa Reeve, 'How autonomous AI pipelines will transform marketing campaigns', Martech (13 November 2024), accessed on 16 April 2025, and viewable at: https://martech.org/how-autonomous-ai-pipelines-will-transform-marketing-campaigns/.
33 Tamara Kostova, 'GenAI Vs. Robo-Advisors: Considerations For The Financial Industry', Forbes Business Council (15 August 2024), accessed on 11 April 2025, and viewable at: https://www.forbes.com/councils/forbesbusinesscouncil/2024/08/15/genai-vs-robo-advisors-considerations-for-the-financial-industry/.
34 Sameera Devuruwan, 'The Impact Of Artificial Intelligence On Decentralized Finance', Forbes Business Council (28 August 2024),

accessed on 11 April 2025, and viewable at: https://www.forbes.com/councils/forbesbusinesscouncil/2024/08/28/the-impact-of-artificial-intelligence-on-decentralized-finance/.

35 Mohamed Khalifa, Mona Albadawy, Usman Iqbal, 'Advancing clinical decision support: The role of artificial intelligence across six domains', ScienceDirect (17 February 2024), accessed on 11 April 2025, and viewable at: https://www.sciencedirect.com/science/article/pii/S2666990024000090.

36 Kinza Yasar, '6 AI nurse robots that are changing healthcare', TechTarget (18 March 2025), accessed on 11 April 2025, and viewable at: https://www.techtarget.com/whatis/feature/AI-nurse-robots-that-are-changing-healthcare.

37 Stephanie Neil,' Laying the Groundwork for a Self-Optimizing Plant', AutomationWorld (20 October 2020), accessed on 11 April 2025, and viewable at: https://www.automationworld.com/control/article/21199010/laying-the-groundwork-for-a-self-optimizing-plant.

38 'Four times better: AI tutors will soon outperform private tutors, predicts 'Godfather of AI' Geoffrey Hinton', Business Today (8 April 2025), accessed on 19 April 2025, and viewable at: https://www.businesstoday.in/latest/trends/story/four-times-better-ai-tutors-will-soon-outperform-private-tutors-threaten-traditional-universities-says-geoffrey-hinton-471277-2025-04-08.

39 Paul Pokotylo, 'AI in Agriculture: Revolutionizing Crop Management and Yield Prediction', Keymakr.com (4 December 2024), accessed on 10 April 2025, and viewable at: https://keymakr.com/blog/ai-in-agriculture-revolutionizing-crop-management-and-yield-prediction/.

40 'Precision Agriculture: Benefits and Challenges for Technology Adoption and Use', U.S. Government Accountability Office (31 January 2024), accessed on 10 April 2025, and viewable at: https://www.gao.gov/products/gao-24-105962.

41 Kayleigh Bateman, '3 ways autonomous farming is driving a new era of agriculture', WEF (20 January 2022), accessed on 10 April 2025, and viewable at: https://www.weforum.org/stories/2022/01/autonomous-farming-tractors-agriculture/.

42 'Citizen Service AI Market to Reach USD 81.3 Billion by 2030, Expanding at a 36.7% CAGR', Persistence Market Research (16 April 2025), accessed on 20 April 2025, and viewable at: https://www.openpr.com/news/3973358/citizen-service-ai-market-to-reach-usd-81-3-billion-by-2030.

43 'Estonia is the e-governance leader in Europe', e-Estonia.com (11 May 2022), accessed on 10 April 2025, and viewable at: https://e-estonia.com/estonia-is-the-e-governance-leader-in-europe/.

44 'AI technology boosts efficiency of government services in China', People's Daily (4 March 2022), accessed on 10 April 2025, and viewable at: https://www.prnewswire.com/news-releases/ai-technology-boosts-efficiency-of-government-services-in-china-302392456.html.

45 'Autonomous Construction Equipment Market to Reach USD 27.61 Billion by 2032 Owing to Technological Advancements and Labor Shortages', SNS Insider (Globe Newswire) (21 February 2025), accessed on 10 April 2025, and viewable at: https://www.globenewswire.com/news-release/2025/02/21/3030527/0/en/Autonomous-Construction-Equipment-Market-to-Reach-USD-27-61-Billion-by-2032-Owing-to-Technological-Advancements-and-Labor-Shortages-Report-by-SNS-Insider.html.

46 Anthony Witherspoon, '10 top micro SaaS examples: Building profitable apps for success', Saas Alliance (3 June 2024), accessed on 12 April 2025, and viewable at: https://www.saasalliance.io/10-top-micro-saas-examples-building-profitable-apps-for-success/.

47 'Generative AI could raise global GDP by 7%', Goldman Sachs (5 April 2023), accessed on 11 September 2024, and viewable at: https://www.goldmansachs.com/insights/articles/generative-ai-could-raise-global-gdp-by-7-percent.

48 Michael Chui, et al., 'The economic potential of generative AI', McKinsey (14 June 2023), accessed on 11 June 2024, and viewable at: the-economic-potential-of-generative-ai-the-next-productivity-frontier.pdf.

49 Miguel Carreon, Michael De La Cruz (mdelacruz), 'IDC FutureScape: The AI Pivot Towards Becoming an AI-Fueled Business', IDC (21 October 2024), accessed on 11 June 2024, and viewable at: https://www.idc.com/getdoc.jsp?containerId=prAP52668124.

50 Ellyn Shook and Paul Daugherty, 'Work, workforce, workers - Reinvented in the age of generative AI', Accenture (18 January 2024), accessed on 11 June 2024, and viewable at: https://www.accenture.com/content/dam/accenture/final/accenture-com/document-2/Accenture-Work-Can-Become-Era-Generative-AI.pdf.

Chapter 5: All Jobs Will Change in the AI Age

1 Benny Traub, et al., 'Modeling the AI-Driven Age of Abundance: Applying the Human-to-AI Leverage Ratio (HAILR) to Knowledge

NOTES 441

      Work', SSRN (9 January 2024), accessed on 11 June 2024, and viewable at: https://papers.ssrn.com/sol3/papers.cfm?abstract_id=4663704.
2. Ibid.
3. Ibid.
4. Susan Lund, Richard N. Cooper, Peter Gumbel, 'What can history teach us about technology and jobs?', McKinsey (16 February 2018), accessed on 11 June 2024, and viewable at: https://www.mckinsey.com/featured-insights/future-of-work/what-can-history-teach-us-about-technology-and-jobs.
5. The percentage projections in this section are based on current estimates of the global workforce, assuming approximately three and a half billion people are employed today. This baseline is considered constant over the next ten to fifteen years for the purpose of analysis. Jobs impacted would mean roles that are eliminated or significantly altered or reimagined requiring individuals to transition to new roles, acquire new skills or adapt to changing workplace dynamics. Job loss denotes a situation where an individual becomes unemployed.
6. Job impacted - 40% by 2026 - 'How Gen AI could reshape the work?,' Morgan Stanley Research, (8 November 2023), accessed on 11 June 2024, and viewable at: https://www.morganstanley.com/ideas/generative-ai-future-of-work; Job impacted - 11-22% by 2025-James Manyika, Susan Lund, Michael Chui, Jacques Bughin, Lola Woetzel, Parul Batra, Ryan Ko, and Saurabh Sanghvi,' Jobs lost, jobs gained: What the future of work will mean for jobs, skills, and wages,' McKinsey & Company (28 November 2017), accessed on 11 September 2024, and viewable at: https://www.mckinsey.com/featured-insights/future-of-work/jobs-lost-jobs-gained-what-the-future-of-work-will-mean-for-jobs-skills-and-wages; Jobs impacted-47% jobs in US and 27% globally by 2025- 'What happened to jobs at high risk of automation?,' OECD (19 January 2021), accessed on 11 September 2024, and viewable at: https://www.oecd.org/content/dam/oecd/en/publications/reports/2021/01/what-happened-to-jobs-at-high-risk-of-automation_ffdb138f/10bc97f4-en.pdf; Jobs impacted-66%in US by 2030-Gregory Daco, 'How GenAI will impact the labor market,' EY (15 April 2024), accessed on 11 September 2024, and viewable at: https://www.ey.com/en_gl/insights/ai/how-gen-ai-will-impact-the-labor-market ; Jobs lost-2-3% by 2030-Kristalina Georgieva, 'AI Will Transform the Global Economy. Let's Make Sure It Benefits Humanity,' IMF (14 January 2024), accessed on 11 September 2024,

and viewable at: https://www.imf.org/en/Blogs/Articles/2024/01/14/ai-will-transform-the-global-economy-lets-make-sure-it-benefits-humanity; Jobs impacted-44-46% work hours by 2035-Ellyn Shook, Paul Daugherty, 'Work, workforce, workers - Reinvented in the age of generative AI', Accenture (18 January 2024), accessed on 11 June 2024, and viewable at: https://www.accenture.com/content/dam/accenture/final/accenture-com/document-2/Accenture-Work-Can-Become-Era-Generative-AI.pdf; Jobs impacted-92% globally by 2040-Francisca Domínguez Zubicoa, '92% of IT jobs will be transformed by AI', CIO (12 August 2024), accessed on 11 June 2024, and viewable at: https://www.cio.com/article/3485322/92-of-it-jobs-will-be-transformed-by-ai.html; Jobs lost-2-3% by 2035-'The Future of Jobs Report 2023', WEF, (30 April 2023), accessed on 11 June 2024, and viewable at: https://www3.weforum.org/docs/WEF_Future_of_Jobs_2023.pdf; Jobs lost-50% by 2040-Michael Chui, Kweilin Ellingrud, and Asutosh Padhi, 'Will generative AI be good for US workers?', McKinsey & Company (9 August 2023), accessed on 11 June 2024, and viewable at: https://www.mckinsey.com/mgi/overview/in-the-news/will-generative-ai-be-good-for-us-workers; Jobs lost-5% in Latin America by 2035-Juana Casas, 'AI could eliminate up to 5% of jobs in Latin America, study finds', Reuters (1 August 2024), accessed on 11 June 2024, and viewable at: https://www.reuters.com/technology/artificial-intelligence/ai-could-eliminate-up-5-jobs-latin-america-study-finds-2024-07-31/; Jobs lost-15-35% by 2035- Jan Hatzius, Joseph Briggs, Devesh Kodnani, Giovanni Pierdomenico, 'The Potentially Large Effects of Artificial Intelligence on Economic Growth', Goldman Sachs (26 March 2023), accessed on 11 June 2024, and viewable at: https://www.key4biz.it/wp-content/uploads/2023/03/Global-Economics-Analyst_-The-Potentially-Large-Effects-of-Artificial-Intelligence-on-Economic-Growth-Briggs_Kodnani.pdf; Jobs lost-50% by 2040-Helen Russell, 'In the future, you'll share your work with robots... unless you're a woman', BBC Science Focus Magazine (20 September 2023), accessed on 11 June 2024, and viewable at: https://www.sciencefocus.com/future-technology/will-we-work-in-the-future; Jobs lost-30% by 2040-John Hawksworth, Richard Berriman, Euan Cameron, 'Will robots really steal our jobs?', PwC (8 February 2018), accessed on 11 June 2024, and viewable at: https://www.pwc.com/hu/hu/kiadvanyok/assets/pdf/impact_of_automation_on_jobs.pdf

7   James Manyika, Susan Lund, Michael Chui, Jacques Bughin, Lola Woetzel, Parul Batra, Ryan Ko, and Saurabh Sanghvi, 'Jobs lost, jobs gained: What the future of work will mean for jobs, skills, and wages', McKinsey & Company (28 November 2017), accessed on 11 September 2024, and viewable at: https://www.mckinsey.com/featured-insights/future-of-work/jobs-lost-jobs-gained-what-the-future-of-work-will-mean-for-jobs-skills-and-wages
8   'The Future of Jobs Report 2023', WEF, (30 April 2023), accessed on 11 June 2024, and viewable at: https://www3.weforum.org/docs/WEF_Future_of_Jobs_2023.pdf
9   Marius Hobbhahn and Tamay Besiroglu, 'Trends in GPU Price-Performance', Epoch AI (27 June 2022), accessed on 1 March 2024, and viewable at: https://epoch.ai/blog/trends-in-gpu-price-performance.
10 Sam Altman, 'Three Observations', Sam Altman Blogs (10 February 2025), accessed on 1 March 2025, and viewable at: https://blog.samaltman.com/three-observations.
11 'Will the $1 trillion of generative AI investment pay off?', Goldman Sachs Insights (5 August 2024), accessed on 11 December 2024, and viewable at: https://www.goldmansachs.com/insights/articles/will-the-1-trillion-of-generative-ai-investment-pay-off.
12 Michael Shirer, 'IDC: Artificial Intelligence Will Contribute $19.9 Trillion to the Global Economy through 2030 and Drive 3.5% of Global GDP in 2030', IDC (17 September 2024), accessed on 1 March 2025 and viewable at: https://www.idc.com/getdoc.jsp?containerId=prUS52600524.
13 'What happened to jobs at high risk of automation?', OECD (19 January 2021), accessed on 11 September 2024, and viewable at: https://www.oecd.org/content/dam/oecd/en/publications/reports/2021/01/what-happened-to-jobs-at-high-risk-of-automation_ffdb138f/10bc97f4-en.pdf.
14 Jan Hatzius, Joseph Briggs, Devesh Kodnani, Giovanni Pierdomenico, 'The Potentially Large Effects of Artificial Intelligence on Economic Growth', Goldman Sachs (26 March 2023), accessed on 11 June 2024, and viewable at: https://www.key4biz.it/wp-content/uploads/2023/03/Global-Economics-Analyst_-The-Potentially-Large-Effects-of-Artificial-Intelligence-on-Economic-Growth-Briggs_Kodnani.pdf.
15 Youssef Saba, 'Elon Musk: 10 billion humanoid robots by 2040 at $20K-$25K each', Reuters (29 October 2024), accessed on 1 March 2025, and viewable at: https://www.reuters.com/technology/elon-musk-10-billion-humanoid-robots-by-2040-20k-25k-each-2024-10-29/.

16. Francisca Domínguez Zubicoa, '92% of IT jobs will be transformed by AI', CIO (12 August 2024), accessed on 11 June 2024, and viewable at: https://www.cio.com/article/3485322/92-of-it-jobs-will-be-transformed-by-ai.html.

17. Job loss 50% by 2040- Helen Russell, 'In the future, you'll share your work with robots… unless you're a woman', BBC Science Focus Magazine (20 September 2023), accessed on 11 June 2024, and viewable at: https://www.sciencefocus.com/future-technology/will-we-work-in-the-future; Job loss 35% by 2040- Jan Hatzius, Joseph Briggs, Devesh Kodnani, Giovanni Pierdomenico, 'The Potentially Large Effects of Artificial Intelligence on Economic Growth', Goldman Sachs (26 March 2023), accessed on 11 June 2024, and viewable at: https://www.key4biz.it/wp-content/uploads/2023/03/Global-Economics-Analyst_-The-Potentially-Large-Effects-of-Artificial-Intelligence-on-Economic-Growth-Briggs_Kodnani.pdf.

18. James Manyika, Susan Lund, Michael Chui, Jacques Bughin, Lola Woetzel, Parul Batra, Ryan Ko and Saurabh Sanghvi, 'Jobs lost, jobs gained: What the future of work will mean for jobs, skills, and wages', McKinsey & Company (28 November 2017), accessed on 11 September 2024, and viewable at: https://www.mckinsey.com/featured-insights/future-of-work/jobs-lost-jobs-gained-what-the-future-of-work-will-mean-for-jobs-skills-and-wages.

19. Francisca Domínguez Zubicoa, '92% of IT jobs will be transformed by AI', CIO (12 August 2024), accessed on 11 June 2024, and viewable at: https://www.cio.com/article/3485322/92-of-it-jobs-will-be-transformed-by-ai.html.

20. Benny Traub, et al., 'Modeling the AI-Driven Age of Abundance: Applying the Human-to-AI Leverage Ratio (HAILR) to Knowledge Work', SSRN (9 January 2024), accessed on 11 June 2024, and viewable at: https://papers.ssrn.com/sol3/papers.cfm?abstract_id=4663704.

21. James Manyika, Susan Lund, Michael Chui, Jacques Bughin, Lola Woetzel, Parul Batra, Ryan Ko, and Saurabh Sanghvi, 'Jobs lost, jobs gained: What the future of work will mean for jobs, skills, and wages', McKinsey & Company (28 November 2017), accessed on 11 September 2024, and viewable at: https://www.mckinsey.com/featured-insights/future-of-work/jobs-lost-jobs-gained-what-the-future-of-work-will-mean-for-jobs-skills-and-wages.

22. Oskar Mortensen, 'How Many People Work at OpenAI? Statistics & Facts (2025)', SEO.AI (2 December 2024), accessed on 1 March 2025 and viewable at: https://seo.ai/blog/how-many-people-work-at-openai.

23 Daniel Højris Bæk, 'How Many Employees Does Deepseek AI Have?', SEO.AI (28 January 2025), accessed on 1 March 2025 and viewable at: https://seo.ai/blog/how-many-employees-does-deepseek-ai-have.
24 Oskar Mortensen, 'How Many People Work at Microsoft? Statistics & Facts (2025)', SEO.AI (8 December 2024), accessed on 1 March 2025 and viewable at: https://seo.ai/blog/how-many-people-work-at-microsoft.
25 The percentage projections in this section are based on current estimates of the global workforce, assuming approximately three and a half billion people are employed today. This baseline is considered constant over the next ten to fifteen years for the purpose of analysis. Jobs impacted would mean roles that are eliminated or significantly altered or reimagined requiring individuals to transition to new roles, acquire new skills or adapt to changing workplace dynamics. Job loss denotes a situation where an individual becomes unemployed.
26 Joaquin Fernandez, 'The leading generative AI companies', IOT Analytics (4 March 2025), accessed on 11 March 2025 and viewable at: https://iot-analytics.com/leading-generative-ai-companies/#:~:text=1.
27 'Nvidia Corporation (NVDA), Nvidia Employees (2025)', Stock Analysis (7 April 2025), accessed on 7 April 2025, and viewable at: https://stockanalysis.com/stocks/nvda/employees/.
28 'Snowflake: Number of Employees 2020-2025 | SNOW', Macrotrends (2025), accessed on 7 March 2025 and viewable at: https://www.macrotrends.net/stocks/charts/SNOW/snowflake/number-of-employees; Company Press Release, 'Databricks Deepens San Francisco Investment with New Office and Multi-Year Data and AI Summit Commitment', Databricks (6 March 2025), accessed on 15 March 2025 and viewable at: https://www.databricks.com/company/newsroom/press-releases/databricks-deepens-san-francisco-investment-new-office-and-multi.
29 Michael Shirer, 'IDC: Artificial Intelligence Will Contribute $19.9 Trillion to the Global Economy through 2030 and Drive 3.5% of Global GDP in 2030', IDC (17 September 2024), accessed on 11 October 2024 and viewable at: https://www.idc.com/getdoc.jsp?containerId=prUS52600524.
30 'Employment Impact Assessments (EmpIA) Analysing the employment impacts of investments in infrastructure', International Labour Organization (2021), accessed on 11 January 2025, and viewable at: https://www.ilo.org/sites/default/files/wcmsp5/groups/public/@ed_emp/documents/publication/wcms_774061.pdf

31 Company website, Intelli Referee, (2025), accessed on 11 March 2025 and viewable at: https://intellireferee.ai/.

Chapter 6: The Human Advantage

1. 'Are We Becoming More Risk-Averse?', NC State University (2 June 2013), accessed on 11 June 2024, and viewable at: https://erm.ncsu.edu/resource-center/society-risk-aversion/.
2. 'Digital Overload and Its Impact on Cognitive Function', Indian Counselling Services (2 December 2024), accessed on 11 June 2024, and viewable at: https://www.indiancounsellingservices.com/digital-overload-and-its-impact-on-cognitive-function/.
3. 'Social isolation and loneliness', AIHW (30 April 2024), accessed on 11 June 2024, and viewable at: https://www.aihw.gov.au/mental-health/topic-areas/social-isolation-and-loneliness.
4. 'Elon Musk's 'New World' mission: How Mars could become humanity's next frontier', *Economic Times* (27 December 2024), accessed on 11 January 2025, and viewable at: https://economictimes.indiatimes.com/news/international/global-trends/elon-musks-new-world-mission-how-mars-could-become-humanitys-next-frontier/articleshow/116707274.cms?from=mdr.
5. 'Will it be possible? Elon Musk says he will ensure over a million people live on Mars in 30 years', *Economic Times* (16 October 2024), accessed on 11 January 2025, and viewable at: https://economictimes.indiatimes.com/news/international/us/will-it-be-possible-elon-musk-says-he-will-ensure-over-a-million-people-live-on-mars-in-30-years/articleshow/114262220.cms
6. Mike Wall, 'NASA delays Artemis 2 moon mission to 2026, Artemis 3 astronaut landing to mid-2027', Space (6 December 2024), accessed on 28 April 2025, and viewable at: https://www.space.com/space-exploration/artemis/nasa-delays-artemis-2-moon-mission-to-april-2026-artemis-3-lunar-landing-to-mid-2027
7. Dr Ramesh Bijlani, 'Sri Aurobindo's Philosophy: Supramental Consciousness', Pragyata (27 July 2018), accessed on 11 June 2024, and viewable at:https://pragyata.com/sri-aurobindos-philosophy-supramental-consciousness/.
8. Matthijs Cornelissen, 'Sri Aurobindo's evolutionary ontology of consciousness', Indian Psychology Institute, accessed on 11 June 2024,

and viewable at: https://ipi.org.in/texts/matthijs/mc-consciousness-mit.php.

Chapter 7: Seven Steps to Structured Problem-Solving

1. Charles Conn, Hugo Sarrazin and Simon London, 'How to master the seven-step problem-solving process', McKinsey (13 September 2019), accessed on 28 July 2025, and viewable at: https://www.mckinsey.com/capabilities/strategy-and-corporate-finance/our-insights/how-to-masterthe-seven-step-problem-solving-process.
2. Nitin Seth, *Mastering the Data Paradox: Key to Winning in the AI Age* (18 March 2024), accessed on 11 June 2024, and viewable at: https://masteringthedataparadox.com/.

Chapter 8: Identifying the Core Problem: Lessons from 'The Goal'

1. Eliyahu M. Goldratt, The Goal, North River Press (1984), accessed on 11 June 2024, and viewable at: https://northriverpress.com/wp-content/uploads/2014/07/The-Goal-FSB-Interviews.pdf.

Chapter 9: Things I Wish I Learnt in Business School: Ten Key Problem-Solving Frameworks

1. Nitin Seth, '9 things I wish I knew in Business School', Blogspot (9 August 2014), accessed on 11 June 2024, and viewable at:https://nseth71.blogspot.com/2014/08/9-things-i-wish-i-knew-in-business.html.
2. 'What is the Trust Equation?', Tick HR solutions, accessed on 11 June 2024, and viewable at:https://www.tickhr.com/what-is-the-trust-equation/.

Chapter 10: Role of Wisdom in the AI Age

1. Ellen Lloyd, 'Nanna: Mesopotamian Moon God, Lord Of Wisdom And Father Of The Gods', Ancient Pages (1 April 2017), accessed on 11 June 2024, and viewable at: https://www.ancientpages.com/2017/04/01/nanna-mesopotamian-moon-god-lord-wisdom-father-gods/
2. Nitin Seth, *Mastering the Data Paradox: Key to Winning in the AI Age* (18 March 2024), accessed on 11 June 2024, and viewable at: https://masteringthedataparadox.com/.

3   Judith Glück, 'The Wisdom Researchers and the Elephant: An Integrative Model of Wise Behavior', Sage (02 June 2022), accessed on 11 October 2024, viewable at: https://journals.sagepub.com/doi/10.1177/10888683221094650.
4   'What does Silicon Valley Bank's collapse mean for the financial system?', Livemint (11 March 2023), accessed on 11 October 2023, and viewable at: https://www.livemint.com/market/what-does-silicon-valley-bankscollapse-mean-for-the-financial-system-11678512462626.html.
5   R.L. Ackoff, 'From data to wisdom presidential address to ISGSR, june 1988', Journal of Applied Systems Analysis 16, (July 1989): 3–9, accessed on 11 June 2024, and viewable at: https://jglobal.jst.go.jp/en/detail?JGLOBAL_ID=200902025826559076.
6   T.S. Elliot, 'The Rock', Wisdom Portal, accessed on 11 October 2023, and viewable at: https://www.wisdomportal.com/Technology/TSEliotTheRock.html.
7   Daniel Kahneman, *Thinking Fast And Slow*, Farrar, Straus and Giroux Amazon (25 October 2011), accessed on 11 October 2023 and viewable at: https://dn790002.ca.archive.org/0/items/DanielKahnemanThinkingFastAndSlow/Daniel%20Kahneman-Thinking%2C%20Fast%20and%20Slow%20%20.pdf.

Chapter 11: Cultivating Openness to Change

1   Spencer Johnson, *Who Moved My Cheese?*, Vermilion London (7 September 1998), accessed on 11 June 2024, and viewable at: https://www.google.co.in/books/edition/Who_Moved_My_Cheese/toxlBwAAQBAJ?hl=en&gbpv=1&pg=PA12&printsec=frontcover.

Chapter 12: The Need for Redefining Learning Approaches

1   Albert Christopher, 'The Future of Data Science Jobs: Will 2030 Mark Their End?', Medium (20 September 2024), accessed on 11 December 2024, and viewable at: https://medium.com/dataseries/the-future-of-data-science-jobs-will-2030-mark-their-end-d01b1a52ce4a#:~:text=According%20to%a%20report%20by,a%20total%20elimination%20of%20roles.
2   Mahalia Mayne, 'Two thirds of employers value soft skills more than educational qualifications when hiring, research finds', People Management CIPD (16 August, 2024), accessed on 12 January, 2025,

and viewable at: https://www.peoplemanagement.co.uk/article/1885308/two-thirds-employers-value-soft-skills-educational-qualifications-when-hiring-research-finds.

Chapter 13: The Art of Learning to Learn

1. Clare Pain, 'Curiosity puts brain in state to learn', ABC Science (3 October 2014), accessed on 11 June 2024, and viewable at: https://www.abc.net.au/science/articles/2014/10/03/4099204.htm
2. Sandrijn van Schaik, MD, PhD, *Deliberate Practice* - UCSF Medical Education, University of California, San Francisco, accessed on 11 June 2024, and viewable at: https://meded.ucsf.edu/sites/meded.ucsf.edu/files/inline-files/pearls-deliberate-practice.pdf.

Chapter 14: Spiritual Balance: A Necessity in Today's AI Age

1. Nitin Seth, 'Spiritual Balance – a necessity in today's material world', Blogspot (26 August 2013), accessed on 11 June 2024, and viewable at:https://nseth71.blogspot.com/2013/08/spiritual-balance-necessity-in-todays.html.

Chapter 15: Eleven Laws of Spirituality

1. Nitin Seth, 'My Success Beliefs - 11 Laws of Spirituality', Blogspot (17 May 2017), accessed on 11 June 2024, and viewable at:https://nseth71.blogspot.com/2017/05/my-success-beliefs-11-laws-of.html.

Chapter 16: My Mindfulness Journey

1. Nitin Seth, 'My Mindfulness Journey and Learnings', Blogspot (28 September 2017), accessed on 11 June 2024, and viewable at: https://nseth71.blogspot.com/2017/09/my-mindfulness-journey-and-learnings.html.

Chapter 17: Meditation (Vipassana)—The Key to Connecting with the Self

1. Nitin Seth, 'My first Vipassana Meditation course', Blogspot (9 March 2016), accessed on 11 June 2024, and viewable at: https://nseth71.blogspot.com/2016/03/my-first-vipassana-meditation-course.html.

Chapter 18: India's T20 World Cup Triumph in 2024: Seizing the Moments of Truth

1. 'IND vs SA, T20 WC Final: Win Predictor At 3.3% Shows How Team India Snatched Victory From Jaws Of Defeat', The Free Press Journal (1 July 2024), accessed on 11 February 2025, and viewable at: https://www.freepressjournal.in/sports/ind-vs-sa-t20-wc-final-win-predictor-at-33-shows-how-team-india-snatched-victory-from-jaws-of-defeat.
2. Alagappan Muthu, 'IND vs SA, Bumrah spearheads India's defence of 119; Pakistan on brink of elimination', ESPN Cric Info (9 June 2024), accessed on 11 February 2025, and viewable at: https://www.espncricinfo.com/series/icc-men-s-t20-world-cup-2024-1411166/india-vs-pakistan-19th-match-group-a-1415719/match-report.

Chapter 19: India's Magnificent Test Series Win in Australia in 2021: Bouncing Back from the Brink

1. Nitin Seth, '6 Management Lessons from India's magnificent test series win in Australia', Blogspot (27 January 2021), accessed on 11 June 2024, and viewable at: https://nseth71.blogspot.com/2021/01/6-management-lessons-from-indias.html.

Chapter 20: The 2018 Football World Cup: The Rise of the Underdogs

1. Nitin Seth, 'Reflections on the 2018 World Cup - Rise of the Underdogs', Blogspot (16 July 2018), accessed on 11 June 2024, and viewable at: https://nseth71.blogspot.com/2018/07/reflections-of-2018-world-cup-rise-of.html.

Chapter 21: The 2014 Football World Cup: A Masterclass in Teamwork over Individual Brilliance

1. Nitin Seth, 'Management Lessons from the 2014 Football World Cup', Blogspot (16 July 2014), accessed on 11 June 2024, and viewable at: https://nseth71.blogspot.com/2014/07/management-lessons-from-world-cup.html.

Chapter 22: Finding your 'Sweet Spot': The Powerful Purpose of Your Life

1. Nitin Seth, 'Finding your "Sweet Spot" – the powerful purpose of your life!!', Blogspot (13 February 2012), accessed on 11 June 2024, and viewable at: https://nseth71.blogspot.com/2012/02/finding-your-sweet-spot-powerful.html.

Chapter 23: Take Personal Responsibility and Change the World

1. Nitin Seth, 'Take personal responsibility and change the world!!', Blogspot (27 January 2012), accessed on 11 June 2024, and viewable at: https://nseth71.blogspot.com/2012/01/i-am-ok-you-are-not-ok.html.
2. Nitin Seth, 'Evolution of leadership – "Leadership by Consciousness"', Blogspot (15 December 2013), accessed on 11 June 2024, and viewable at: Evolution of leadership – "Leadership by Consciousness" | Nitin's Fundas.

Chapter 24: Sustainable Development: Rethinking Consumption

1. Nitin Seth, 'Sustainable Development – Rethinking Consumption', Blogspot (26 January 2015), accessed on 11 June 2024, and viewable at: http://nseth71.blogspot.com/2015/01/sustainable-development-rethinking.html.

Chapter 25: Beyond Trade-Offs: How to Harness Opposites in the AI Age

1. Nitin Seth, *Winning in the Digital Age* (25 February 2021), accessed on 11 June 2024, and viewable at: https://www.winninginthedigitalage.com/.

Chapter 26: Momentary versus Momentous

1. Nitin Seth, 'Is life momentary or momentous?', Blogspot (23 February 2014), accessed on 11 June 2024, and viewable at: https://nseth71.blogspot.com/2014/02/is-life-momentary-or-momentous.html.

Chapter 27: Learn Two-Speed Execution

1. Nitin Seth, *Winning in the Digital Age* (25 February 2021), accessed on 11 June 2024, and viewable at: https://www.winninginthedigitalage.com/.
2. Nitin Seth, *Mastering the Data Paradox: Key to Winning in the AI Age* (18 March 2024), accessed on 11 June 2024, viewable at: https://masteringthedataparadox.com/.
3. Duda Bardavid, 'Drag's Context Switching Survey: Here's How to Stop it Once and For All', Drag (10 February 2025), accessed on 11 February 2025, and viewable at: https://www.dragapp.com/blog/context-switching-productivity/#:~:text=While%20the%20computer%20scientist%20and,losing%2080%25%20of%20your%20productivity.

Chapter 28: Effective Leadership Traits in the Digital Age

1. Nitin Seth, 'My Leadership Beliefs', Blogspot (6 February 2011), accessed on 11 June 2024, and viewable at: https://nseth71.blogspot.com/2011/02/my-leadership-beliefs.html.

Chapter 29: How Great Leaders Inspire Others

1. Nitin Seth, 'How Great Leaders Inspire Others – The "5 Cs" Formula!!', Blogspot (21 November 2011), accessed on 11 June 2024, and viewable at: https://nseth71.blogspot.com/2011/11/how-great-leaders-inspire-others-5-cs.html.

Chapter 30: Lessons in Change Management

1. Nitin Seth, Winning in the Digital Age (25 February 2021), accessed on 11 June 2024, and viewable at: https://www.winninginthedigitalage.com/.

Chapter 31: How to Create Great Leaders

1. Nitin Seth, 'How to Create Great Leaders', Blogspot (12 October 2018), accessed on 11 June 2024, and viewable at: https://nseth71.blogspot.com/2018/10/how-to-create-leaders.html.

Chapter 32: Your Time Is Now!: Ten Mantras for Young Entrepreneurs

1. Helen Russell, 'In the future, you'll share your work with robots... unless you're a woman', BBC Science Focus (20 September 2023), accessed on 11 June 2024, and viewable at: https://www.sciencefocus.com/future-technology/will-we-work-in-the-future.
2. Nitin Seth, 'Your time is now!! - 8 mantras for young entrepreneurs', Blogspot (12 May 2017), accessed on 11 June 2024, and viewable at: https://nseth71.blogspot.com/2017/05/your-time-is-now-8-mantras-for-young.html.

Chapter 33: Inventing the Future: Lessons from the Incredible Life Story of Steve Jobs

1. Walter Isaacson, 'Steve Jobs by Walter Isaacson', Hachette Digital (2011), accessed on 11 June 2024, and viewable at: https://www.google.co.in/books/edition/Steve_Jobs/26ev_abfrU8C?hl=en&gbpv=0.
2. Nitin Seth, 'Lessons from Steve Jobs incredible life story', Blogspot (09 June 2013), accessed on 11 June 2024, and viewable at: https://nseth71.blogspot.com/2013/06/lessons-from-steve-jobs-life-story.html.
3. Walter Isaacson, *Steve Jobs*, Hachette Digital (2011), accessed on 11 June 2024, and viewable at: https://www.google.co.in/books/edition/Steve_Jobs/26ev_abfrU8C?hl=en&gbpv=0.
4. Ibid.

Chapter 34: Elon Musk's Moonshot Mentality in the AI Era

1. Walter Isaacson, *Elon Musk*, Simon & Schuster UK (12 September 2023), accessed on 11 June 2024, and viewable at: https://www.google.co.in/books/edition/Elon_Musk/HjyvEAAAQBAJ?hl=en&gbpv=0.
2. Ashlee Vance, *Elon Musk : How the Billionaire CEO of SpaceX and Tesla is Shaping our Future*, Virgin Books (May 2016), accessed on 11 June 2024, and viewable at: https://www.penguinrandomhouse.co.za/book/elon-musk-how-billionaire-ceo-spacex-and-tesla-shaping-our-future/9780753555644.

Chapter 35: Lessons in Longevity and Greatness from the Giant Sequoias

1   Nitin Seth, '5 life lessons from The Giant Sequoias', Blogspot (30 August 2017), accessed on 11 June 2024, and viewable at: https://nseth71.blogspot.com/2011/11/how-great-leaders-inspire-others-5-cs.htm.

Conclusion: Timeless Wisdom for Daily Living in the AI Age

1   Nitin Seth, 'Central messages of Bhagavad Gita', Blogspot, (31 August 2014), accessed on 11 June 2024, and viewable at: https://nseth71.blogspot.com/2014/08/central-messages-of-bhagwad-gita.html.
2   Eknath Easwaran, *The Bhagavad Gita*, Google E-books (1985), accessed on 11 June 2024, and viewable at: https://books.google.co.in/books?id=bcnJAAAAQBAJ&printsec=frontcover&source=gbs_ge_summary_r&cad=0#v=onepage&q&f=false.
3   Nitin Seth, 'Timeless Lessons from Bhagavad Gita for Business Leaders – Part 1', Blogspot (18 August 2020), accessed on 11 June 2024, and viewable at: https://nseth71.blogspot.com/2014/08/central-messages-of-bhagwad-gita.html.